RELIGION AND CRIMINAL JUSTICE

Revised First Edition

Edited by William J. Cook, Jr.
Westfield State University

Bassim Hamadeh, CEO and Publisher
Michael Simpson, Vice President of Acquisitions
Jamie Giganti, Senior Managing Editor
Miguel Macias, Graphic Designer
John Remington, Senior Field Acquisitions Editor
Natalie Lakosil, Licensing Manager
Kaela Martin, Interior Designer

First published in the United States of America in 2016 by Cognella, Inc.

Cover image copyright © Depositphotos/londondeposit

Printed in the United States of America

ISBN: 978-1-63487-538-7 (pbk) / 978-1-63487-539-4 (br)

www.cognella.com   800-200-3908

Contents

Part II

Part III

Appendix: Case Studies

Dedicated to the Memories of:

John Walsh, S.J.

Edith F. Preuss, B.D.

Wade Benjamin, D. Min.

Each a friend and mentor.

Zeus: *"Look you now how ready mortals are to blame*

the gods. It is from us, they say, that evils come,

but they even of themselves, through their own blind folly,

have sorrows beyond that which was ordained."

Homer's The Odyssey, I. 32-34,

Translation by A.T. Murray

(Harvard University Press, 1938)

Preface

This book began with a desire to help the homeless—especially homeless veterans—who in some areas may number as many as one-quarter of all who live on the streets. Additionally, it seemed appropriate to dedicate this book to those who have a desire to study the discipline of criminal justice and to work to make our world safer and more just.

Most of the proceeds from the sale of this book—since it is a book about religion—will be donated to an ecumenical program named "Cathedral in the Night," which serves the spiritual and physical needs of the homeless citizens (a fair number of whom are veterans) of the streets of Northampton, Massachusetts. The balance will be donated to a scholarship fund for criminal justice students at Westfield State.

The editor wishes to acknowledge the contributions of others who have added in some way to this book:

The authors, who so generously contributed their work to this project;

Ms. Jamie Giganti, Senior Managing Editor, for her clear and kind guidance in overseeing revisions to the first edition;

Ms. Monika Dziamka, editor, who continued with the project when other responsibilities beckoned;

Ms. Rachel Singer, Associate Production Editor, who pleasantly and efficiently coordinated changes to this new edition;

Ms. Ali Papakyrikos, Westfield State criminal justice student, who was an able and exemplary research assistant;

Ms. Susan Cook, who assisted with the administrative details and was a cheerful supporter of the project;

Westfield State University for granting the editor a sabbatical to complete this book;

Mr. Jack Doxey, chairperson, Homeless Veterans Working Group (VFP, San Diego, California), who helped the editor understand the grave situations faced by many homeless veterans;

and last, but in no measure least, Jacques, our canine, whose tail-wagging good humor helps keep everything in perspective.

Introduction

Y ou may be wondering why anyone would study the topic of religion and criminal justice. After all, what does *religion* have to do with the justice system? This is a fair question because, in America, religion is usually practiced as something that is part of the private area of a person's life. But the answer to the question may surprise you. Consider the following:

+ Much violence such as terrorism and hate crime is done in the name of religion.
+ There are criminal statutes that are meant to restrict some religious practices like snake handling or parents' refusal to seek medical care for a seriously ill child.
+ Positive changes in our society have resulted from the efforts of religious leaders: for example, in the 1700s, the Quakers worked to make prisons more humane, and in the 1900s, ministers such as Martin Luther King Jr. were instrumental in bringing about reforms to protect the rights of persons of color.
+ Many concepts in our justice system are derived from religious traditions such as Judaism or Christianity.

The reality is that religion has much to do with criminal justice. This is not only historically true, but it is true today as well. First, let's take a historical example. In ancient Rome, not practicing the official state religion was a capital crime. So, if a Roman citizen was denounced as a practitioner of another faith such as Christianity, then that person would face the death penalty if he or she did not renounce the prohibited religion.

In modern times, we might think of the separation of church and state that is so much a cornerstone of government in the United States. Yet, as one looks at the development of the criminal justice system, one sees the many influences of religion. For example, many of our criminal statutes have roots in the laws of the Puritans of the Massachusetts Bay Colony, and, as noted earlier, Quakers and Calvinists attempted to make punishment in prisons more humane. Religious leaders were also involved in the reform of policing at the turn of the last century.

Today, religious beliefs may be found underlying discussions related to the death penalty, child abuse, polygamy, immigration laws, and the use of hallucinogenic drugs, just to name a few issues. As one looks around the world, one sees that there are various views of what constitutes justice that are rooted in differing religious beliefs.

For criminal justice practitioners operating in a world that grows ever smaller, it is very important to understand not only about different religions, but to be able to discern the difference between what might be called "healthy" religious practice and fanatical observances. Ignorance about religion could lead to tragic—or, at the very least, embarrassing—consequences, as in the recent case of an official counterterrorism briefer who was reported by the news media to have told his audience that Roman Catholics and Baptists, two very large and mainstream Christian denominations in the United States, were terrorists.[1] (The briefer's superiors later retracted the briefer's comments because they did not reflect official policy and attributed the error to inexperience.)

Thus, to really understand some important current issues and facets of the criminal justice system, one must have a basic knowledge about world religions and religious practices. Yet, many people today are functionally illiterate about religion. For example, informal research conducted by Professor Stephen Prothero, who gave students in a class at a major university a quiz on basic information about major world religions, revealed that almost all flunked the quiz; this author has repeated the experiment in classes at a state university with similar results. Also reported by Prothero in his book, *Religious Literacy*,[2] was that other researchers had found that only half of American adults could name even one of the four Christian Gospels; most Americans did not know that Jonah was a book in the Bible; and ten percent of Americans thought that Joan of Arc was Noah's wife. (Want to try the quiz? Here is a link: http://www.pewforum.org/files/2007/12/protheroquiz.pdf).

The purpose of this text is to help you to become religiously literate, especially as it relates to criminal justice and to understand the influence of religion on the development of our nation and its justice system, so that you will have a better comprehension of its significance and impact even to this day.

We'll begin by defining several important terms such as religion, spirituality, and fundamentalism. Then, we'll present an overview of the structure of this book.

RELIGION

Religion is thought to be derived from a Latin word, *religio*, which means awe, supernatural feeling, or even ritual. Some think that another Latin word, *religo*, is the root; this word means to bind fast or to moor.[3] For the ancient Romans, however, religion—that is, *religio*—had little to do with beliefs and more to do with ritual practices such as making offerings to their gods. Today, the word religion refers to both rituals and beliefs.

Drawing upon the meanings of these two Latin words, we see that religion has to do with supernatural feelings or awe (such as one might feel looking at a beautiful sunset). It may also have to do with ritual practices such as daily prayers or votive offerings like gifts or money given to a deity or deities. But there is also the sense of "mooring," which is when someone anchors a boat; thus, religion can provide a way for people to feel "anchored" in the world; that is, to give meaning to their experience.

Glenn Holland, a contemporary scholar of religious studies, offers this perspective in discussing the meaning of religion in the ancient world:

> *... we might want to think about religion in terms of*
> *what all the activity associated with it seems to be aimed at,*
> *what people are trying to do through the activities that we*
> *identify as "religious." One possible answer is that they are*
> *establishing and maintaining a relationship with a god or gods*
> *by worshipping them and doing what the gods command. So,*
> *we might say that religion is activities aimed at pleasing a*
> *god or gods.*[4]

So, religion in the ancient world involved efforts to control the forces of the environment; the ancient peoples believed that sufficient rainfall, rich harvests, and good fortune all depended on pleasing the deity or deities. At that time, what someone believed was not as important, perhaps not even significant; rather, right practice, known as **orthopraxy**, was what counted. This would mean, for example, offering the proper sacrifices at the correct times to the god or gods, lest misfortune or punishments occur.

As humankind evolved in its religious experience over the millennia, there was an increasing turn toward a more personal, internalized relationship to the divine. One classic definition which reflects this change was proposed about a hundred years ago by the American philosopher and psychologist William James (1842–1910), who said that religion is:

> *The feelings, acts, and experiences of individual men in their*
> *solitude, so far as they apprehend themselves to stand in*
> *relation to whatever they consider the divine. Since the*

*relation may be moral, physical, or ritual, it is evident that
out of religion in the sense that we take it, theologies,
philosophies, and ecclesiastical organizations may secondarily
grow.*[5]

In James's definition of religion, we see an emphasis on the psychological features of religion. Thus, there is a focus on interior experiences such as feelings that one might have in relation to what a person believes is a divinity or, as James describes it, the "divine."

James's definition is valuable, but it is not definitive because it does not clearly address cases in which the idea of the "divine" would not apply; as it happens, belief in a god may not always be present in a given religion. Therefore, one can find it difficult to develop a good working definition of religion because, in some cases, "it may not even be concerned with god or gods ... (but) spirits of some sort, and some religions, like Buddhism, have no gods of any sort."[6] Consequently, some scholars have rejected using any set definition of religion.

However, for the sake of clarity in our study of religion—that is to say, to specify what we will be studying—let's consider this definition from the *New Oxford American Dictionary*, which says that the word **religion** is used to describe:

1. The belief in or worship of a superhuman controlling power, especially a personal god or gods;
2. A particular system of faith and worship;
3. A pursuit or interest to which someone ascribes supreme importance.[7]

Thus, when we study religion, we are examining what Herling describes as "one mode of constructing worlds of meaning, worlds in which men find themselves, and in which they choose to dwell."[8] Another way of describing this is, as Huston Smith maintains: "Religion is not primarily a matter of facts; it is a matter of meanings."[9] In a later chapter, we will explore this topic more thoroughly.

SPIRITUALITY

Perhaps you have heard someone say, "I am spiritual, but not religious." Usually, what someone means by such a statement is that he or she is interested in a relationship to the divine, but does not want to be involved in a more formal religious practice such as going to church or temple regularly. As it happens, many people have left mainstream churches, but they still feel a need for some experience of the transcendent.

So, what is meant by spirituality? It is a difficult term to define because it can be used differently by different people. Sometimes, people will use both religion and spirituality to mean the same thing. However, spirituality is often something "improvised and individual."[10] This means that a person has created it, to some degree, for her- or himself. Spirituality can concern higher entities, experiencing the sacred, finding meaning in life, or feeling connected to others or to nature. Spirituality often involves self-help, as well as a search for inner healing and the mystical. In later chapters, we'll explore this topic more.

FUNDAMENTALISM

Fundamentalism is a word that has evolved in its meaning, especially over the past 20 years; it now is used for much wider applications. So, in a sense, it has lost a degree of its original meaning and acquired new nuances.

Originally, it referred to a movement within American Protestantism that occurred about a hundred years ago with the publication of a set of pamphlets called "The Fundamentals." Essentially, this movement argued that the Bible was *inerrant*; soon, those who subscribed to this view were referred to as "fundamentalists."

Today, the term is applied to some Christians, but it can also be used for some Jews, Muslims, Sikhs, and Hindus. It can even be applied sometimes in nonreligious circumstances; for example, it has been used about economists! Obviously, then, the word fundamentalism could not have its original connotations. Instead, in current times, it could be said that a fundamentalist is a person who has "a religious way of being that manifests itself in a strategy by which beleaguered believers attempt to preserve their identities as individuals or groups in the face of modernity and secularization."[11]

To understand what is happening, one must keep in mind the rapid spread of globalization. Suddenly, many people are confronted with very different cultures, some of which can be threatening to a person's worldview; religion is part of a person's worldview. Hence, fundamentalism, in the modern sense, is a reaction against what has been called "religion shock."[12] A person reacting to that shock or tension can fall into extremism, sectarianism, or an overemphasis on ideological purity. However, what is important to keep in mind, especially for someone who studies criminal justice, is that one should not make a simple equation between modern fundamentalism and violence; it is usually not the case that such a fundamentalist is violent. However, under certain circumstances, the fundamentalist views can be associated with violence. We'll return to this in later chapters.

STRUCTURE OF THE BOOK

This book has three sections. In the first section, we'll look at the relationship between religion and criminal justice from many different angles. In Part Two, we'll discuss major religious traditions in America. Then, in Part Three, there is a variety of essays covering different issues related to religion and criminal justice that should be very useful for class discussions. Finally, in the Appendix, there are six case studies for students to practice examining situations where religion has somehow "gone off the rails."

Part One

Chapter One describes the history of the influence of religion on the development of the criminal justice system. In Chapter Two, modern issues related to religion as it affects policing, the courts, and corrections will be reviewed. Chapter Three is an introduction to the discipline of religious studies so that a criminal justice student will have a basic knowledge about that field. Chapter Four continues the introduction to religious studies by reviewing work from the 20th century. Chapter Five looks at findings from the social sciences concerning religious behavior and religious persons.

Part Two

In Chapter Six, the Rev. Timothy Oslovich, a Lutheran minister and college instructor, presents the basics about Christianity. In Chapter Seven, Dr. Steven Blackburn, an expert on Arabic and Semitic scriptures, introduces the reader to Islam. Chapter Eight is an introduction to Judaism. Chapter Nine covers the history, beliefs, and practices of Hinduism. Chapter Ten explains fundamental concepts about Buddhism. And Chapter Eleven is a discussion of New Age spirituality and neo-paganism.

Part Three

In Chapter Twelve, the Rev. Gordon S. Bates, former executive director of the Connecticut Prison Association (later the Community Partners in Action), explains how religion influenced the development of the correctional policies of retribution and rehabilitation. Chapter Thirteen, written by scripture scholar Dr. Wayne Rollins, looks at how a myth can foster prejudice and hatred, but forgiveness by the victim can help transform the attitudes of an offender. An approach toward justice that could produce the kind of personal transformation described in Chapter Thirteen is explained by Dr. Thomas Roscoe, a retired chief probation officer and professor, who discusses restorative justice, which has developed from values promulgated by the Judeo-Christian tradition. Chapter Fifteen examines the problem of religious violence and its causes. In Chapter Sixteen, Fr. James Keenan, a moral theologian and professor, looks back on the life of his father, a New York City police officer, and traces the influences of faith and virtue in his father's life and work. Dr. Andrew Skotnicki, a religious studies scholar, examines in Chapter Seventeen how religion has played a part in the development and dynamics of prisons. In Chapter Eighteen, Allison Drude Cook, a yoga teacher, introduces the reader to effective techniques for controlling stress and developing spirituality through yoga practice. The Book of Revelation is discussed in Chapter Nineteen, and a few different methods of interpreting this apocalyptic scripture are examined. Finally, in Chapter Twenty, three important topics—prejudice, ignorance, and spirituality—that are related to the development of an effective understanding of religion's influence on inter-personal dynamics, as well as personal growth, are discussed.

The editor hopes that this book will add to a most necessary and beneficial conversation about religion in our society among those who study criminal justice.

END NOTES

1. Markay, Lachlan. "Department of Defense Classifies Catholics, Evangelicals as Extremists." *Washington Free Beacon*, April 5, 2013, http://www.washingtontimes.com/news/2013/apr/5/dod-presentation-classifies-catholics-evangelicals/#ixzz2Q1EA7JQX

2. Prothero, Stephen. *Religious Literacy: What Every American Needs to Know—And Doesn't* (New York: HarperCollins, 2007), 38–39.

3. Moorwood, James, ed. *The Oxford Latin Minidictionary* (New York: Oxford University Press, 1995), 223.

4. Holland, Glenn S. *Gods in the Desert: Religions of the Ancient Near East* (Lanham: Rowman & Littlefield Publishers, Inc., 2010), xxiii.

5. James, William. *The Varieties of Religious Experience: A Study in Human Nature* (New York: Seven Treasures Publications, 2009), 27.

6. Holland, xxiii.

7. "religion, *n.*" *Oxford Dictionaries.com*, http://www.oxforddictionaries.com/us/definition/american_english/religion

8. Herling, Bradley l. *A Beginner's Guide to the Study of Religion* (New York: Continuum International Publishing Group, 2007), 19.

9. Smith, Huston. *The World's Religions* (New York: HarperCollins Publishers, 1991), 10.

10. Ammerman, Nancy T. "Spiritual but Not Religious? Beyond Binary Choices in the Study of Religion." *Journal for the Scientific Study of Religion* (2013) 52(2): 259.

11. Ruthven, Malise. *Fundamentalism: A Very Short Introduction.* (New York: Oxford University Press, 2007), 5–6.

12. Ruthven, 30.

Part I

1. A Historical Perspective on Religion and the Development of Criminal Justice

By William J. Cook Jr.

THE ANCIENT WORLD

The development of criminal justice was heavily influenced by religious belief and practices. Many aspects of our modern legal and judicial practices are rooted in the customs and laws of ancient peoples. To begin, we'll need to consider the ways of the ancient Babylonians, Israelites, Greeks, and Romans.

In the world of ages past, life was especially precarious, so people were very concerned with controlling their environment: securing rain for crops, preventing pestilence or disease, and protection from attacks by adversaries. But because this was the era before the development of the scientific mind-set, the common assumption was that powerful, generally invisible entities such as spirits, gods, or goddesses were responsible for happenings in the human world. Therefore, humans tried to influence these powerful beings with incantations, offerings, and other activities meant to please or appease these spirits, gods, or goddesses.

Many people believed in destiny, which means that the pattern and events of their lives had been decided for them by these deities. In ancient Greece, it was believed that three goddesses, Clotho, Lachesis, and Atropos, were the ones who spun, measured out, and snipped the threads of a person's life. The Romans also believed in the three fates, whom they called the *Parcae*.[1] So, it is essential to keep in mind that there was a fundamental belief in the societies of

Figure 1.1: *Ten Commandments* **by Rembrandt is an image that depicts the artist's view of Moses holding the two tablets with the Ten Commandments.**

the ancient world that a god, or gods and goddesses, were actively controlling everyday events; laws and justice developed at that time must be understood in relation to this understanding that deities were so involved in human affairs.

The earliest known set of written laws was instituted in Babylon and is known as the **Code of Hammurabi.** Dated to about 1750 BCE, the laws were engraved into a stone stela (i.e., a black basalt column engraved with thousands of lines of writing) on which was displayed an image of Hammurabi receiving the authority to write the law book from the Sun God and God of Justice, who was named Shamash. It was situated in the marketplace so all could see it and be thankful to Hammurabi for the law. One key principle of the Code of Hammurabi was the *Lex Talionis* (Law of Retribution), which is the familiar "An eye for an eye, a tooth for a tooth." Though this may seem harsh by modern standards, it was an innovation in the ancient world, as it prevented an endless cycle of feuding.[2] The writing on the stela also indicates that "the king set up the law with the aim of protecting the weak against the strong, procuring justice for the orphan and widow, and establishing equity in the land."[3]

We see then that Hammurabi was a king, but he was also a religious leader; this gave his code of laws a special significance. Because he was also a religious leader, he shared in the power of the divine. Panzarella and Vona describe the situation in this way: "(w)hatever earthly power the king had derived from the belief that the king was the visible representative of the deity, perhaps even the deity himself."[4] Essential to the Code of Hammurabi was the requirement of swearing of oaths to the gods—who were believed to control all things that happened—to prove the truthfulness of one's allegations or perhaps assertions of innocence. Panzarella and Vona note that the "code assumed that the conduct of individuals would be guided by the necessity to keep oaths sworn to the deities."[5]

The influence of the Code of Hammurabi would be found in the laws of other people born many generations later in other parts of the world.

The law in ancient Israel was based on the **Mosaic Code**, a code of laws believed to have been given to the Jewish prophet, Moses, by God on Mount Sinai; the heart of this set of laws is popularly known as the **Ten Commandments**; more formally they are known as the **Decalogue**. The story of the Mosaic Code was told in the Bible in the book of Exodus (20:1–17) and Deuteronomy (5:6–21). The background to the story of the Israelites being given these laws is that they were freed from bondage in Egypt when they were led away by Moses, who had received a call to do this from the God of the Israelites. In the book of Exodus, it is recounted that after the Israelites were saved in this way, God had formed a **Covenant** with them. In its religious meaning, this Covenant is an agreement between God and the Israelites to be in a relationship; thus, God would be *their* God, and they would be God's people.

These are the Ten Commandments given to Moses on Mount Sinai, which are listed in Chapter 20 of the book of Exodus in the Bible:

And God spoke all these words:

[2] *"I am the Lord your God, who brought you out of Egypt, out of the land of slavery.*

[3] *"You shall have no other gods before me.*

[4] *"You shall not make for yourself an image in the form of anything in heaven above or on the earth beneath or in the waters below.* [5] *You shall not bow down to them or worship them; for I, the Lord your God, am a jealous God, punishing the children for the sin of the parents to the third and fourth generation of those who hate me,* [6] *but showing love to a thousand generations of those who love me and keep my commandments.*

[7] *"You shall not misuse the name of the Lord your God, for the Lord will not hold anyone guiltless who misuses his name.*

[8] *"Remember the Sabbath day by keeping it holy.* [9] *Six days you shall labor and do all your work,* [10] *but the seventh day is a sabbath to the Lord your God. On it you shall not do any work, neither you, nor your son or daughter, nor your male or female servant, nor your animals, nor any foreigner residing in your towns.* [11] *For in six days the Lord made the heavens and the earth, the sea, and all that is in them, but he rested on the seventh day. Therefore the Lord blessed the Sabbath day and made it holy.*

[12] *"Honor your father and your mother, so that you may live long in the land the Lord your God is giving you.*

[13] *"You shall not murder.*

[14] *"You shall not commit adultery.*

[15] *"You shall not steal.*

[16] *"You shall not give false testimony against your neighbor.*

[17] *"You shall not covet your neighbor's house. You shall not covet your neighbor's wife, or his male or female servant, his ox or donkey, or anything that belongs to your neighbor."*

To fulfill their part of the Covenant, the Israelites would obey God's law, which was given to Moses.

The Ten Commandments are the "only legal text in Hebrew Scripture expressed as God's direct address to Israel."[6] Because it was expressed in this way, that is to say, that the Ten Commandments were the express will of God for the people, then the laws were given a primacy and power over the people who were to hear them. The Ten Commandments, which have a patriarchal point of view, appear to be addressed to wealthy males, but that is common among the laws of that period and region of the world. However, what makes the Decalogue (i.e., the Ten Commandments) different from other legal codes dating from that era is that it contains only the "absolute laws—which spell out neither the circumstances nor the penalties for an offense."[7] Similar codes of other ancient peoples were typically written more in the style of case law, which means that they described what should be done in a specific instance. The penalties—in most cases, death—for violating the Ten Commandments are to be found in other places in the Bible.

One other notable feature of the Ten Commandments is that they can be organized into two categories. The first category are the laws that defined the Israelites' obligations to God; secondly, there is another grouping of laws that describe their obligations to other people. As both sets of obligations are presented side-by-side, Burnette-Bletsch observes that "the combination of religious and social obligations in the Ten Commandments ... suggests that Israel considered one's duties toward God and neighbor inseparable and mutually reinforcing."[8]

A second collection of laws found in the Book of Exodus is referred to as the **Covenant Code.** This section (Exodus 20:22–23:19) makes the application of the Ten Commandments more specific. Offenses such as violence, stealing, bestiality, paganism (i.e., worship of another god than that of the Israelites), abuse, kidnapping, slander, perjury, bribery, are listed along with the penalties prescribed for them. In the case of "striking a person mortally" (i.e., killing), there must be consideration given to whether or not the act was premeditated. This shows that there was a concern with a person's *intentions*. This approach was not typical in the ancient world, as intentions were generally not considered.

It is in the Covenant Code that one finds a situation in which the *Lex Talionis* (Law of Retribution) is applied: if two fighting men unintentionally injure a pregnant woman and she is harmed, then it is written that "you shall give life for life, eye for eye, tooth for tooth, hand for hand, foot for foot, burn for burn, wound for wound, stripe for stripe."[9] The *Lex Talionis* applied here derives from the Code of Hammurabi, but has this distinction: it does not specify that the victim must be of "high social stature" as the Babylonian law did; another difference between the Mosaic Code and the Code of Hammurabi is that, under the Laws of Moses, the death penalty is prescribed less frequently. Finally, the Mosaic Code is different in that it reflects concern for social outcasts or socially weak persons such as slaves, the poor, or sojourners and aliens from other lands.[10] The effect of the Israelites' own experience of being slaves in Egypt appears to be reflected in these protections.

In ancient Greece, religion was very important; it can be argued that the significance of the gods to the Greeks is reflected in the execution of Socrates, the renowned philosopher, after he was convicted of (among other offenses) not acknowledging—that

Figure 1.2: The Ordeal of Fire was a medieval test of innocence—if the accused's hand burned, he was considered guilty.

is, respecting—the official, traditional gods and of creating new gods.[11] The first written set of laws among the ancient Greeks were those of **Draco**, who lived around 600 BCE, followed later by the Code of Solon. Solon, who lived about a century later, was a chief magistrate in Athens and a lawgiver who brought reform and undid many of Draco's laws. Among the Greeks, it was not held that these laws had been given to them by the gods, but the laws were seen "as essential to keep from offending the deities."[12] Not offending the gods was of grave concern to them because the gods were believed to be capricious, easily offended, and often given to meddling in the affairs of mankind. Stability in one's life and community depended on obeying the laws. As Panzarella and Vona, two criminal justice scholars, observe:

> *Even the government of Athens, where reason was*
> *so important, was considered a reflection of the wills of*
> *the deities. People who were accused of committing crimes*
> *but claimed to be innocent had to swear oaths of innocence,*
> *believing that false oaths would be punished severely by the*
> *deities.*[13]

Thus, unlike the Israelites, the Greeks did not believe that their laws had been given to them by a divine being, but nevertheless, obeying these laws that men developed through their use of reason was necessary for a person to be safe from divine retribution or punishment. Also important to note is that because of this viewpoint, the use of oaths in criminal trials could be considered effective.

The Romans were famous for their laws—in fact, their legal traditions are one of the significant legacies of Roman civilization. Similar to the Greeks, the Romans did not believe that their laws had been given to them by the deities; but this did not mean that the laws did not have a religious context. Among the Romans, "the authority of the deities as well as punishment by the authorities were the forces behind the laws."[14] In Rome, one was expected to practice the state religion, which would usually include recognizing the divinity of the emperor (Caesar was the first emperor believed to be descended from the god, Mars) and doing incantations, as well as offering sacrifices and pouring libations (e.g., wine) to the gods, who were then expected to act favorably toward the *communitas*, or community. Those who did not comply with these requirements were considered to have committed treason, and, as in the case of some early Christians who refused to do such practices, would be sentenced to death. Thus, among the Romans, we see that they viewed their laws as the work of humans, but that the authority of the leader (i.e., the emperor) who enforced these laws was derived from his own divinity as the descendant of a god.

MIDDLE AGES

In the Middle Ages, the period extending from the fifth to the 15th centuries, one sees the impact of religious belief in the efforts to bring about justice through the practice of the **Ordeal**. By this time, in the Western world, the dominant religious practice was Christian; hence, that is the tradition that influenced both law and justice in the Middle Ages; the Roman Catholic Church eventually took the place of the Roman Empire and therefore was involved in the administration of justice. It was a time when there was no separation between church and state. Similarly, there was a blurring between the concepts of crime and sin. **Crime**, of course, is said to be a violation of a code of law which is secular and thus was created by humans for the ordering of life in a community—that is, to keep people safe and to protect their interests. **Sin** is defined as an offense against God's laws and is a religious concept.

What was the Ordeal? Essentially, it was believed that if a person accused of a crime were subjected to a painful and harmful procedure, then, if she or he were innocent, God would protect her or him. Trial by water usually involved dunking a person to see if he drowned; if he didn't, then he must be innocent, as he enjoyed God's protection. There was trial by fire in which a person's hand might be forced into burning coals and then checked later to see if he had sustained a burn, which indicated guilt. A variation of this might be to have a person walk across red-hot surfaces such as plowshares—as was claimed to have happened in the case of the empress of the Holy Roman Empire, Cunigunde (975–1040), who was accused of adultery, but who remained unharmed by the intense and burning heat of the surfaces upon which she was made to walk during her ordeal.

A clergyman generally would be present during the ordeal, praying and officiating at the event, as is depicted in the illustration from a liturgical book known as the *Rituale Romanum* (i.e., Roman Ritual) used in the Middle Ages. Jones and Johnstone have described a different version of the Ordeal that took place during the religious service known as the Mass, or Communion Service, when the accused person, after hearing a prayer that warned of the danger of what was to follow, was required to receive the consecrated host:

> … it being widely believed that if one guilty of crime
> or perjury took consecrated bread into his mouth he would
> choke or die. … The practice of taking the "Sacred Morsel"
> or Corsned (not a host but a meal of cheese and barley
> bread) … was seen in the case of Godwin, Earl of Essex,
> who died in 1053 while eating the sacred morsel, having
> denied playing any part in the death of the king's brother.[15]

Eventually, the acceptance of church involvement in such rituals changed, however, and it was discontinued in the time of Pope Innocent III (1198–1216) with a decree, or formal order, by the Fourth Lateran Council (a council is a meeting of all of the bishops of the Roman Catholic Church, which decides issues of doctrine and policy). Once the church had prohibited clergy from participating in ceremonies related to an Ordeal, the practice of subjecting accused persons to such torments rapidly fell into disuse.[16]

The influence of the Church on matters related to criminal justice can also been seen in what was known as the **Benefit of Clergy**. Clergy such as priests or deacons, as seen in the eyes of the Church in the Middle Ages, had a higher status than laypeople (i.e., ordinary persons), and therefore should not be judged by them. This was a task for the ecclesiastical courts, which had jurisdiction in sacred matters, and clergy ultimately came under the authority of the pope, who was the head of the Church and acted as the Supreme Judge, with bishops as lawgivers and judges in their own dioceses.[17] The exemption for clergy, or Benefit of Clergy, was also extended to monks and nuns and persons who wore habits (i.e., special clothing worn by religious orders) and allowed them to be tried for criminal offenses in ecclesiastical courts rather than in secular courts. The Benefit of Clergy (the test for which was the ability to read, since it was mostly only clergy who could read at that time) was eventually extended to other persons who could read, such as secular clerks and the nobility.[18] Later, the privilege was then used by some people—even common people—to avoid the death penalty, since that penalty would not be imposed by an ecclesiastical court; the privilege was finally ended in 1823.[19]

PURITAN NEW ENGLAND

Our focus will now shift to North America in the 17th century. In 1630, the group of English religious reformers known as the Puritans were sailing aboard the ship *Arabella* to the New World when their leader, a lawyer named John Winthrop (1588–1649) (who would one day serve as governor of the Massachusetts Bay Colony) spoke about their "errand," or mission. Using images drawn from the Bible, he noted that, just as God had formed a covenant with Moses, so, too, was there such a covenant with the Puritans; further, Winthrop cautioned them that God would be vengeful if they did not fulfill their covenantal duties. They were going to build a utopia, a "city on a hill" that would serve as a "beacon" to mankind about how life should be lived by god-fearing Christians that someday, according to one modern historian, also would be "the road leading from the Anglican establishment to a renovated England."[20] That same historian refers to the Puritans' enterprise in the New World as an "infant theocracy" (**theocracy** literally means "rule by God"), which the Puritans conceived in this way:

> But, from the start they sounded a different note. Theirs was
> a peculiar mission, they explained, for they were a "peculiar"
> people," a company of Christians not only called but chosen,
> and chosen not only for heaven but as instruments of a sacred
> historical design. Their church-state was to be at once a model
> for the world of Reformed Christianity and a prefiguration of
> New Jerusalem to come.[21]

Theirs was a severe world in which Puritans saw themselves as having a great responsibility, for they thought that the "destiny of Christ's people in America was the destiny of humankind ... (and) the holy men and institutions of times past, though inscribed in Scripture (i.e., the Bible) ... served now to illustrate the settler's place."[22] The Puritan settlers also believed that God was vengeful and would punish them for their failures, but the punishments would be to bring corrections or discipline, not destruction. It is this worldview, so steeped in Biblical imagery and the expectation of the end times (i.e., the apocalypse), as well as their sense of great responsibility, that forms the backdrop for the code of laws that was developed for the Massachusetts Bay Colony.

Government in the Massachusetts Bay Colony was heavily colored by religion. According to Clyde A. Holbrook, a professor of religious studies, the Puritan leader John Winthrop envisioned a "partnership of religion and civil government within a political unit." This meant that there would be virtually no separation between church and state, so there could only be one religion practiced in the colony. Holbrook explains that "it was reckoned that toleration of more than one religion within a state could only lead to social disorder. One

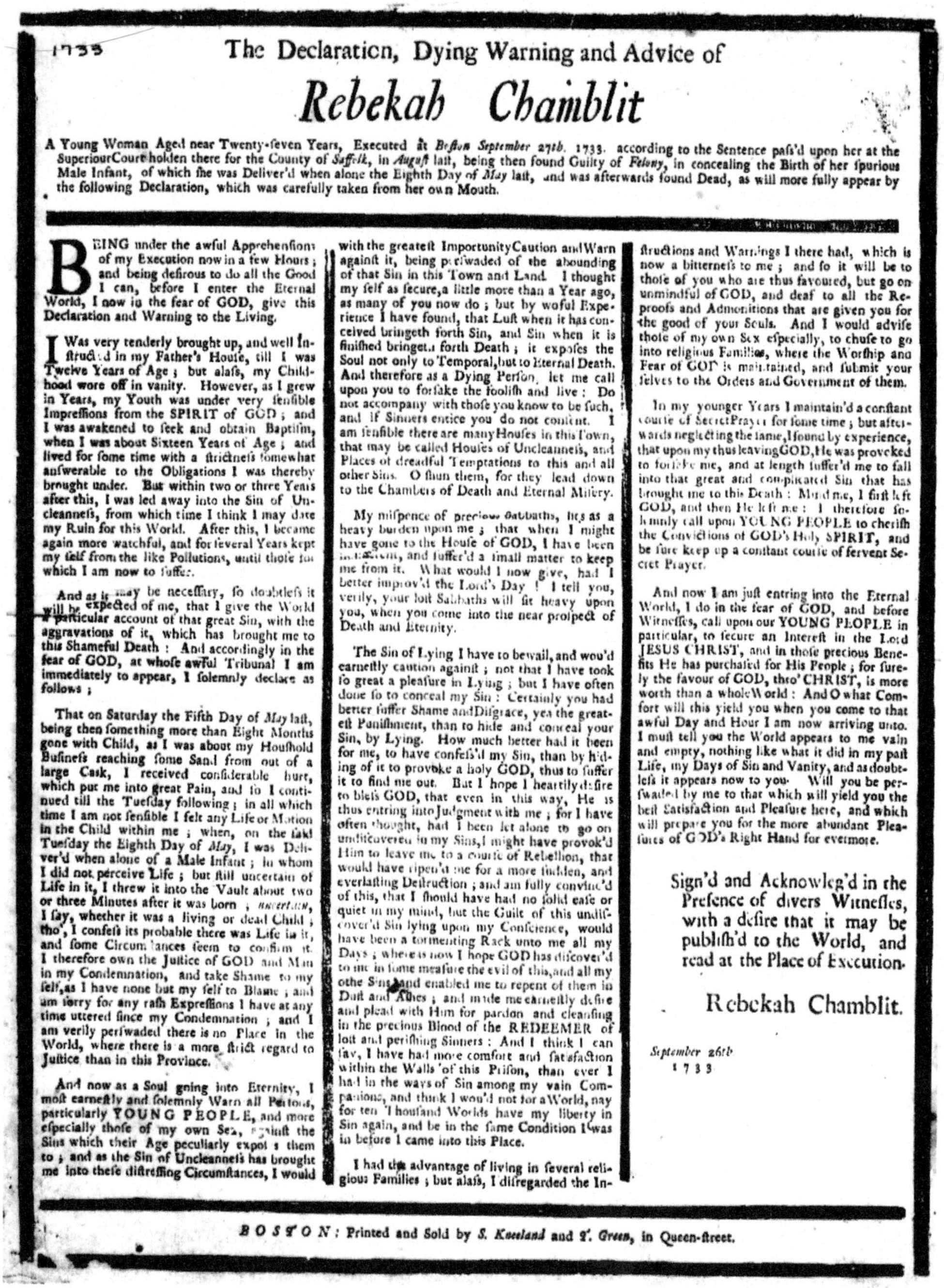

Figure 1.3: The Declaration of Rebekah Chamblit is a statement of repentance of a young 18th century woman accused of infanticide.

established religion was necessary to uphold good government and the security of the entire society."[23] Anyone who practiced another form of Christianity from the Puritans, for example, the Quakers, was expelled from the Massachusetts Bay Colony.

Behavior that was considered sinful was punished by the Church by admonishing the person or by excommunicating an errant member (i.e., throwing him out of the congregation). But among the Puritans, there was a blurring of the line to some degree between the concepts of crime and sin; they were often seen as one and the same. In the Massachusetts Bay Colony, according to James MacLear, "(c)rime could not simply be identified with an act forbidden by the law of a sovereign state when the church had a hand in deciding that sin was a crime and the state treated crime as a sin.[24] The result was that something relatively innocuous—but sinful and criminal to the Puritan, such as criticizing a minister (behavior we simply ignore today)—would also become a concern of the government and subject to its authority to correct or punish. The reason for this is that "sins treated as crime lay in the jurisdiction of the state."[25]

The model for the laws which would be instituted in the Massachusetts Bay Colony was found in those given by God to Moses because, according to James MacLear, the Puritans "turned in fascination to the Old Testament accounts of Jewish law and government. In ancient Israel they found the only example of God's perfect rule among his chosen people." John Cotton (1585–1652), a Puritan scholar and minister, was appointed to a committee by the General Court to develop a code of law for the colony in 1636. MacLear notes that when Cotton wrote the draft of a new code of law, he "relied heavily on scripture for constitutional and criminal law," but Cotton's version was never adapted because "while sharing Cotton's general outlook, Massachusetts magistrates were not so tied to Biblical warrant or so scrupulous in framing positive law."[26] Simply put, Cotton's proposed laws were too strict; thus, soon after rejecting Cotton's proposed laws, there was a different Code of Laws adopted by the General Court in 1641 written by another minister, John Ward; this set of laws was referred to as "The Liberties of the Massachusetts Colonie in New England."

The "Liberties" were laws that were designed to protect the "inviolability of a man's life and honor."[27] The code stipulated that a person could not be arrested, banished, or harmed physically unless there was a publicly known law that justified the action taken against him; further, it required that every person should be treated equally before the law.

In 1648, the "Liberties" would be revised, with more laws added; this code would serve the colonists for over one hundred years. In the **Code of Laws of 1648**, known formally as "**The Book of the General Lawes and Libertyes Concerning the Inhabitants of the Massachusetts**," there are two general trends in the laws that were promulgated: some laws reflect a direct religious influence, while others are more secular. So, there are the "Capital Crimes," which are taken essentially from the Ten Commandments and the Mosaic Code; the other offenses named in the laws are less serious. This second grouping of laws that were implemented was intended to restrict behavior that would be disruptive in the life of the community, but these laws do not have a biblical underpinning.

The heading of the capital crimes included these offenses for which the death penalty was prescribed: (1) worship of another God; (2) being a witch; (3) blasphemy, speaking disrespectfully or the cursing of God or the "Holy Religion"; (4) murder (premeditated); (5) slaying a person in anger or "cruelty of passion"; (6) slaying another by poison; (7) lying (i.e., having sex) with a beast (the animal would be killed, too); (8) a man lying with another man; (9) adultery; (10) stealing a man or "man-kinde" (i.e., kidnapping); (11) bearing false witness (i.e., to lie) so another loses his life as a result; (12) conspiring to insurrection or rebellion against the government; (13) any child, age 16 or older, with "sufficient understanding," who smites (strikes a heavy blow) or curses his or her father or mother (unless the child was treated negligently or cruelly by parents); (14) a rebellious son, aged 16 and having "sufficient understanding" who does not obey the voice of his father or mother; (15) any man "ravishing" a maid or single woman who is above ten years of age (i.e., rape); however, there is also the possibility of the judge imposing "some other grievous punishment" instead of death for this crime.

With the exception of the last offense (rape), each of the capital crimes was referenced by citing the appropriate verses from the Bible. So, for example, the crime of "stealing a man", which is what modern law calls kidnapping, is based on verse (16) of Chapter 21 of the Book of Exodus, which states (in modern translation): "Whoever kidnaps a person, whether that person has been sold or is still held in possession, shall be put to death." Or, in the case of the rebellious son, the reference is verses (21–22) of Chapter 21 in the Book of Deuteronomy, which says: "If someone has a stubborn and rebellious son … They shall say to the Elders of his town, 'This son of ours is stubborn and rebellious …' Then all the men of the town shall stone him to death."

A partial list of the other crimes or offenses and the attached penalties that were specified in the Code of Laws of 1648 includes: burglary and theft; fornication; gaming (i.e., shuttleboard); idleness; drunkenness; lying; and tobacco use. The penalty for burglary was to be branded with the letter B on the forehead; if the man was convicted of burglary for a third time, he would be put to death "as being incorrigible." Interestingly, if the burglary were committed on a Sunday (the Lord's Day), he would be branded and have one ear cut off. The penalty for "gaming" was a fine of five shillings. Drunkenness was fined at the rate of ten shillings, while "tippling at an unreasonable time" was penalized by a fine of five shillings. If a person could not pay the fine, he would be sentenced to placement in the stocks for one hour or longer (the stocks, or pillory, was a wooden frame which bound a person's head and hands while he was displayed for public ridicule). For lying, if a person were found to "wittingly and knowingly" deceive others with "false news or reports," then he could be fined ten shillings or placed in the stocks; a second offense of lying would bring a fine of 20 shillings or whipped up to ten lashes.

The Code of Laws of 1648 is notable in that it requires that a person accused of a crime such as lying or being stubborn also to have been capable of knowingly committing it; the Puritans saw the "age of discretion" as 14 years old. There is also a prohibition of torture. The law specified that "no man shall be forced by torture to confess any crime against himself or any other." (However, after a person had been convicted, limited torture could be used to get the identities of coconspirators or confederates.)

One fascinating page in the story of the Puritans' influence on criminal justice can be seen in the crime literature they developed to discuss public executions, which were generally done by hanging the convicted person. It has been reported that few occasions elicited as much interest among the colonists in New England; there were crowds numbering in the thousands who came to see these public executions.[28]

Clergymen were highly visible when executions occurred. Usually, according to Daniel A. Cohen, a scholar who has studied these events, there were sermons delivered by prominent ministers on the Sunday preceding the execution or on the actual day it occurred.[29] The accused would frequently be brought into the church to sit among the congregants when the sermon was delivered, and that person would also be castigated, or publically shamed, for his or her capital crime. These were opportunities for the clergy to strengthen the morality of the community by using the example of the convicted criminal, who was now a fallen sinner. The convicted person would be reminded of the torments of hell that would be his destiny for having committed the crime and would be encouraged during the sermon to repent and seek eternal life while there was still time before execution.

After the execution, written copies of these sermons were published and read widely by all social classes, as they were very inexpensive, costing only a couple of pennies. In these tracts, the minister showed how "the condemned criminals had been undone by their fatal wickedness, warned others against the same kind of misconduct and justified capital punishment."[30] They catalogued the kinds of sins (which were also frequently considered crimes in Puritan society) that would lead someone to a state of human degradation: "drunkenness, Sabbath-breaking, disobedience to parents, sexual indulgences, wicked company, swearing and cursing, stealing, and lying" were among the offenses they identified.[31]

Sometimes, the convicted person's declaration of guilt was also published. These were written under the supervision of a minister. An example of this can be seen in the "Declaration, Dying Warning and Advice of Rebekah Chamblit" published in 1733. Rebekah Chamblit (1706–1733) was a 26-year-old unmarried woman who became pregnant and gave birth to a child who apparently was born dead. She was convicted of infanticide "in concealing the birth of her spurious male infant which she delivered when alone ... and was afterwards found dead ..." There is little doubt that she attempted to conceal what happened because there was such great societal rejection reserved for an unwed mother—she would be brought before a court and "warned out of town," meaning banishment, a fearsome penalty in a time when life lived away from society was precarious. Sharon M. Harris, who has studied Chamblit's declaration and others like it, says that initially, Chamblit maintained she was innocent, but later in the declaration, she recounts "her wayward life and pleas for God's forgiveness," leading Harris to conclude that "it is impossible to know whether the texts attributed to the accused women represent their own words … their true beliefs and feelings."[32]

Though Puritan ways may seem harsh by our standards (obviously, some practices were indeed harsh), there is much to be said to their credit. Two especially important contributions are the concept of protecting individual rights, which was embodied in the "Liberties" (for example, that all persons be treated equally before the law) and the view that human nature—when fallen into sinfulness or criminality—could be reformed. Implicit in accepting the idea of the possibility of a wayward person reforming or changing for the better is a socially sanctioned forgiveness that is not typical of modern society.

There were some in this period of time who disagreed with the prevailing views of the Puritans in Massachusetts; one such person was Roger Williams (1603–1683), a Puritan minister and theologian. Williams rejected the theocracy in Massachusetts. According to the authors Panzarella and Vona, Roger Williams "considered it a debasement of religion that the colony of Massachusetts was ruled as a theocracy by a committee of ten religious leaders. He wanted absolute separation of religion from government and politics."[33]

Williams had a charter to start a new colony where there would be no state or official religion; this colony was in the area we know today as Rhode Island. The charter for the new colony authorized persons of all faiths, even unbelievers, to live there and be treated as equals. In the words of Panzarella and Vona: "Roger Williams is credited as the inventor of tolerance. His colony was the first place in the world to give equality to all faiths … . Williams thought that a person could be a true believer and still live peacefully in society with other people who had different beliefs."[34]

By the time of the Revolutionary War, religion had lost much of its political power, as the people no longer saw themselves as a "special, divinely chosen community."[35] There are two factors that might explain how this happened. First, after 1684, religious tolerance was now the rule. Secondly, many people had stopped attending church.

In summary, we have seen that the religion of the Puritans was very influential in the development of criminal law in our country; their views established an early baseline for which behaviors would be prohibited and punished by the law. And though our modern criminal codes seem a far cry from those of the Puritans, their shadow extends over criminal law to this very day. Clyde A. Holbrook describes the Puritans' influence in this way:

The statutes of the Code of 1648 in other forms survive in our laws against sodomy, rape, stealing, treason, homicide and perjury. Nor have we ever surrendered attempts to enforce an externalized righteousness by legal and judicial means. The state, for example, still interferes with the free practice of religion when, as in the case of child neglect arising from religious belief, it steps in to protect the welfare of minors. The courts may not recognize sins as a legal category, but they punish acts that some people count to be sins.[36]

AGE OF ENLIGHTENMENT

Occurring mostly during the 18th century (i.e., the 1700s), the Age of Enlightenment was a time in which scholars in Europe, especially in England and France, questioned religious and political authority and asserted the efficacy of science in explaining many things that touched upon human life. Of course, these ideas spread to the Americas.

Two criminal justice scholars, Panzarella and Vona, point out that during the Age of Enlightenment, philosophers like the Englishman Thomas Hobbes and the French Jean-Jacques Rousseau said "that society and government were the results of natural causes, not divinely ordained." Continuing, they argue that as a result of this change in perspective, "it became a new faith that governments derived their power from the people, not from a deity." In our own country, they note that "the Constitution of the United States, a product of the Enlightenment, was conspicuous for making no mention at all of a deity … in theory, at least, for the moment, the state was separated from religion."[37]

RELIGIOUS REVIVALS AND SOCIAL REFORMS

During the 1800s, the power of religion reasserted itself during religious revivals in America. Known as the "Second Great Awakening" and the "Third Great Awakening," these were periods of renewal occurring among groups of Protestant Christians of different denominations led by such famous individuals as Charles L. Finney (1792–1875) and later Dwight L. Moody (1837–1899), William Booth (1828–1912), and Catherine Booth (1829–1890) (the Booths were the founders of the Salvation Army), among others. The influence of these revivals of religious fervor encouraged abolitionism (working to end slavery) and greatly impacted how the country approached criminal justice. It has been said that "religious convictions and religious organizations played supporting roles, and sometimes leading roles in lawmaking, court decisions, correctional institutions and correctional philosophies … (and) led the way in developing humane penitentiaries and modern probation policies."[38]

In the early 1800s, there were significant reforms in corrections that were the result of efforts by religious leaders. The changes actually started in 1786, when Quakers (a Christian religious denomination) were able to change the law in Pennsylvania to stop physical punishments such as whipping or bodily mutilation and utilize prison confinement instead; the first institution to be established for this purpose was the Walnut Street Prison in Philadelphia.

Under this new system, the convicted individual who was placed in prison would not be allowed to work, but instead was expected to remain in isolation. The purpose of this was to encourage him to examine his life and reform it. It happened that the change was a move in the right direction, but it had certain flaws such as the debilitating effects of silence and isolation upon prisoners' mental health. Much more about this topic will be discussed in a later chapter that appears in Section 3 of this book.

In the 1890s, one of the first leaders in the reform of policing was the **Rev. Dr. Charles H. Parkhurst**. Dr. Parkhurst opposed the corruption that was rampant in New York City's police department at that time. On Valentine's Day in 1892, he preached a sermon that accused New York City government, known as "Tammany Hall," as well as police officials of being "a lying, perjured, rum-soaked and libidinous lot" that allowed "brothels, gambling parlors, and opium lairs to flourish openly in Manhattan."[39]

The sermon caused a sensation and led to Dr. Parkhurst's summons before a grand jury to testify about what he knew about specific instances of corruption. He was unable to offer specific information—such as events, names, places, and dates—that would serve as evidence of his charges, so he exited the grand jury room as an embarrassed man. Undeterred, in the company of a member of his church and a private detective, he ventured forth into an exploration of New York City's criminal underworld. When he emerged from his odyssey after touring houses of prostitution, gambling dens, drug parlors, and illegal taverns, Parkhurst not only had specific information about what was happening, but he had the identities of the police officers (i.e., their badge numbers) whom he observed in these places.

When Parkhurst's information was revealed, it brought about the election of a new reform-minded government that limited the direct control politicians had over police and changed how police officers were hired and promoted. Teddy Roosevelt, later to become president of the United States, was appointed to be the new police commissioner in New York City and proved himself to be a virtuous leader of the freshly scrubbed department. Thus, it is the Rev. Dr. Parkhurst who is recognized as the first reformer of urban policing in our nation.

SUMMARY

In this chapter, we have traced the history of the influence of religion upon criminal justice in ancient times, in the Middle Ages, and up through the first two centuries after the founding of our country after the Revolutionary War. We have seen that in the ancient world, in some societies, there was a belief that laws were God-given; in other societies, that was not so, but in either case, there was a prevailing fear that violating the law would bring about retribution or punishment by the god or gods.

As society developed in Europe and America, there were some very positive influences that religion had upon the development of the administration of justice. The concept that someone must *intend* to commit an offense before being punished, that there should be equal justice before the law, and that a person might be reformed are just some of the religiously influenced ideas that have had an effect on how the modern practice of criminal justice is envisioned.

KEY TERMS

+ Age of Enlightenment
+ Benefit of Clergy
+ Code of Hammurabi
+ Code of Laws of 1648
+ Covenant
+ Crime
+ Decalogue
+ Lex Talionis
+ Mosaic Code
+ Ordeal
+ Sin
+ Theocracy

REVIEW QUESTIONS

1. What is the Code of Hammurabi? Why is it significant?
2. What was the Roman view of religion and law?
3. What is the Decalogue? Why is it significant?
4. How did criminal laws develop in America?
5. How was religion a factor in the administration of justice in the 19th and 20th centuries?

END NOTES

1. "Fates." *Ancient Greece and Rome: An Encyclopedia for Students*, ed. Carroll Moulton, vol. 2 (New York: Charles Scribner's Sons, 1998), 63–64. *Gale Virtual Reference Library*. Web. Sept. 2, 2014.

2. Calvo, Sherri Chasin. "Ancient Writings Shed Light on Past Civilizations." *Science and Its Times*, ed. Neil Schlager and Josh Lauer, vol. 6: 1900 to 1949 (Detroit: Gale, 2000. 6–9. *Gale Virtual Reference Library*). Web. Sept. 2, 2014.

3. Kippenberg, H. G. "Codes and Codification." *Encyclopedia of Religion*, ed. Lindsay Jones, 2nd ed., vol. 3 (Detroit: Macmillan Reference USA, 2005), 1842–1847. *Gale Virtual Reference Library*. Web. Sept. 2, 2014.

4. Panzarella, Robert, and Daniel Vona. *Criminal Justice Masterworks: A History of Ideas About Crime, Law, Police and Corrections* (Durham: Carolina Academic Press, 2006), xvii–xviii.

5. Panzarella and Vona, xviii.

6. Burnette-Bletsch, Rhonda. *Studying the Old Testament: A Companion*, 74.

7. Burnette-Bletsch, 74.

8. Burnette-Bletsch, 74.

9. New Revised Standard Version Bible, Exodus 21:23–25.

10. Burnette-Bletsch, 77–78.

11. "Religion, Greek." *Ancient Greece and Rome: An Encyclopedia for Students*, ed. Carroll Moulton, vol. 3 (New York: Charles Scribner's Sons, 1998), 170–173. *Gale Virtual Reference Library*. Web. Sept. 2, 2014.

12. Panzarella and Vona, xviii.

13. Panzarella and Vona, xviii.

14. Panzarella and Vona, xviii.

15. Jones, Mark, and Peter Johnstone. *History of Criminal Justice* (Waltham: Anderson Publishing, 2012), 47.

16. Jones and Johnstone, 50.

17. Ojetti, Benedetto. "Ecclesiastical Courts." *The Catholic Encyclopedia*, vol. 4 (New York: Robert Appleton Company, 1908). 4 Sept. 2014 http://www.newadvent.org/cathen/04447a.htm

18. Burtsell, Richard. "Benefit of Clergy." *The Catholic Encyclopedia*, vol. 2 (New York: Robert Appleton Company, 1907). 4 Sept. 2014 http://www.newadvent.org/cathen/02476a.htm

19. Jones and Johnstone, 50.

20. Bercovitch, Sacvan. *The American Jeremiad* (Madison: The University of Wisconsin Press, 1978), 5.

21. Bercovitch, 7–8.

22. Bercovitch, Sacvan. *The Puritan Origins of the American Self* (New Haven: Yale University Press, 1975), 62.

23. Holbrook, Clyde A. "Crime and Sin in Puritan Massachusetts." *Crime, Values, and Religion*, ed. James M. Day and William S. Laufer (Norwood: Ablex Publishing Corporation, 1987), 5.

24. MacLear, James F. "New England and the Fifth Monarchy: The Quest for the Millennium in Early American Puritanism." *Puritan New England: Essays on Religion, Society and Culture*, ed. Alden T. Vaughn and Francis J. Bremer (New York: St. Martin's Press, 1977), 68, 73.

25. MacLear, 14.

26. MacLear, 68, 73.

27. MacLear, 9.

28. Cohen, Daniel A. *Pillars of Salt, Monuments of Grace: New England Crime Literature and the Origins of American Popular Culture, 1674–1860* (New York: Oxford University Press, 1993), 3.

29. Cohen, 3.

30. Cohen, 6.

31. Cohen, 49.

32. Harris, Sharon M. "Feminist Theories and Early American Studies." *Early American Literature*, vol. 34, no. 1 (1999), 90–91.

33. Panzarella and Vona, xxix–xxx.

34. Panzarella and Vona, xxx.

35. Breen, Timothy H., and Stephen Foster. "The Puritans' Greatest Achievement: A Social Study of Social Cohesion in Seventeenth-Century Massachusetts." *Puritan New England: Essays on Religion, Society and Culture*, ed. Alden T. Vaughn and Francis J. Bremer (New York: St. Martin's Press, 1977), 120.

36. MacLear, 20.

37. Panzarella and Vona, xxvi.

38. Panzarella and Vona, xxxi.

39. Raab, Selwyn. "Taking on Tammany, 100 Years Ago," In the *New York Times*. http://www.nytimes.com/1992/02/14/nyregion/taking-on-tammany-100-years-ago.html

2. Religion and Criminal Justice

The Modern Era

By William J. Cook Jr.

OVERVIEW

In this chapter, we will examine some of the ways in which religion continues to influence the criminal justice system. The chapter will be divided into two sections. In the first section, we will examine religious issues that have an impact on the three divisions of criminal justice: policing, the courts, and corrections. Then, our focus will turn to the presentation of a listing and discussion of crimes that can be seen to involve religion, either as a cause or facilitating factor.

During the 20th century, some significant changes happened in society. One of the most notable changes, from the perspective of our interest in criminal justice, is the waning influence of institutional religion in society. The days when someone like Parkhurst or later, Dr. Martin Luther King Jr., could create such a wave of change after delivering a fiery sermon have waned noticeably. By the late 1960s, there was even much talk about the "death of God"—in fact, it was even a cover story in *Time* magazine in 1966. Nevertheless, most people report religion as still important in some way to their lives. (Note: There are some dramatic differences in attitudes about religion among the millennial generation, which we'll explore in the next chapter.) In the next section, we'll look at how religion is a factor that affects the police in the work that they do, as well as in their being employees of the state.

POLICING

There are two areas we will examine to understand more about the relationship between religion and policing. The first one concerns the police as employees. The second will relate to how the police understand and interact with less conventional religious groups.

Religion and Employment Issues

As America has become more diverse, so have its police forces. For about the first 100 years of formal policing in the United States, most of the officers, if they were religious, were members of either the Protestant or Catholic churches; this is to say that they were Christians of one stripe or another. Since coworkers and supervisors shared somewhat similar cultural backgrounds, then friction that might arise over religious differences was limited, but could be a factor sometimes as the religion one practiced was really related to one's ethnicity, a frequent source of tension. This was true of larger society as well. The point is that they may not have always liked or tolerated one another, but they did basically understand each other.

In modern society, there is quite a variety of religious traditions being practiced: today, one can find Buddhist, Muslim, Rastafarian, and Mormon police officers, among others. Because of the different requirements in observing other religious traditions, this can create tension in the workplace, too. What if an officer wants to wear dreadlocks as part of a religious observance? Or a beard? What if she wants to wear a religious symbol pinned to her uniform? What if an officer does not want to work on her Sabbath? These are all religiously tinged issues that relate to the employment of police officers.

There are special obligations that inhere to being a police officer—there are expectations for officers which do not apply to people employed in ordinary occupations. Nevertheless, police officers still have First Amendment Rights with regard to the practice of religion. Also, **Title VII of the Civil Rights Act of 1964** prohibits discrimination in the hiring or firing or conditions of employment of a person on the basis of religion. This law applies to police officers as well. Additionally, employers are expected to make reasonable accommodations to prevent an employee's suffering discrimination at work because of religion.

Some interesting cases involving religion and police as employees have been described by Richard G. Schott. One case that Schott describes, for example, took place in Texas, where there was a Christian police officer who had become accustomed to wearing a gold cross on his jacket's lapel when he worked in plain clothes. A problem occurred when he was reassigned to work in uniform; he now placed the cross pin on his uniform shirt. The police department had a regulation that prohibited an officer from doing such a thing without the chief's authorization, which he was not given; instead, he was offered other accommodations such as being able to wear a religious bracelet or to continue wearing the cross, but in such a way that it was covered under his shirt or collar or returning to plainclothes duty, for which there was no restriction on wearing a cross. The officer refused to accept the accommodations and was fired. An appeals court upheld the firing and asserted that the prohibition of wearing the religious symbol on a uniform was not a violation of the officer's First Amendment rights.[1]

In New Jersey, two Muslim police officers objected to a department's regulation against employees wearing beards for religious reasons as being an unfair restriction. The department did, however, allow officers who presented a medical excuse to wear beards. The court held that the officers did have a right to wear beards for religious reasons, as there was already an exception to the prohibition of beards that was allowed for medical reasons. The case might have had a different outcome if it had happened that there had been no exceptions allowed by the police department to the prohibition of beards, especially if the blanket prohibition was justified by a specific requirement such as the need to have cleanly shaven faces to safely use protective gear such as a gas mask.[2]

What if a police officer were to object to an assignment for religious reasons? What if the assigned duty was perceived by the officer to conflict with his or her religious precepts or the morality of his faith tradition? Would that be acceptable? A police officer in Indiana refused to report for duty at a casino, as he claimed that it would violate his religious beliefs since the assignment would have him indirectly supporting gambling, which was prohibited by his religion. He was fired for insubordination; his dismissal was upheld by the court, as it was held that police officers had to "leave their religious (and other) views behind," for they had a duty to protect all citizens and could not favor some persons over others for reasons of religious practice.[3]

In another case, a sheriff's deputy refused to work on the Sabbath. The need of the department was that all employees had to work on rotating shifts, so no one could be excused from assignments because of having been scheduled to work on his or her Sabbath. However, the department did offer the deputy some accommodations such as being allowed to arrange swaps with other employees to get the day off or being permitted to take a personal or vacation day off when work had been assigned for a Sabbath. The employee did not accept the accommodations, actually left work when not authorized to do so, and due to other disciplinary charges, too, was fired. An appeals court held that the firing was justified because the employer had offered accommodations, but that such cases needed to be decided on a "case by case" basis.[4]

Religion and Policing

In the 1980s and 1990s, America's attention was sometimes focused on news stories about violence occurring in reality or as a possibility among some groups of persons who were members of religious sects. Of course, that there could be a connection between crime and religion (especially in aberrant forms) was nothing new. In our own country, the Ku Klux Klan, with roots extending back more than 100 years, had a long history of using religious symbols (e.g., burning crosses). But the difference in modern times is that, beginning in the 1960s and 1970s, there was a tidal wave of new religious groups. Some of these new groups were characterized by holding beliefs and following practices that were very different from those of most persons who had been familiar with or raised in some Judeo-Christian tradition (in other words, people mostly knew others who were Jewish, Protestant, or Catholic). Compounding the difficulty in the changing situation was that some of these new groups claimed to be "Christian," but they held beliefs that were atypical of mainline Christian churches; for example, the idea that Jesus Christ was blond-haired and blue-eyed and not Jewish. By the late 1970s, an event shocked people worldwide and drew the question about what was happening with religion into sharp focus. This was the mass suicide and murder of over 900 people at Jonestown, Guyana—a settlement of Americans belonging to a religious group known as the Peoples Temple and led by Jim Jones.

But though the law enforcement community has long since adopted the tools of modern science and social science—familiar today as forensic science and forensic psychology—there has been little effort to utilize the body of knowledge available among scholars of religious studies. As we noted earlier, religion is a way for people to give meaning to their lives; hence, religious studies scholars can shed light on some of the different meanings that religious people bring to life-and-death situations and ordinary events as well.

A significant problem is that, as we discussed in the last chapter, there is much ignorance about religions and religious behavior; since it can be hard to understand, some have been ready to dismiss religious behavior as reflecting a lack of education, or in worst cases, a person's craziness. Some in law enforcement have been suspicious of religion as being a cover for criminal behavior.

So, the challenge for law enforcement today is to make sense of the many new kinds of religious practices that are evident in society. How does one tell what might be "healthy" religious behavior from what is "toxic?" How does one know, as one religious scholar has asked, when religion has become "evil?"[5] And how does one know who is an expert about religions so as to evaluate his or her advice?

The first important case that gives an example of how these questions could be answered occurred in the early 1990s, when a group of religious separatists, the Montana Freemen, who believed that they were living in the end times, were interpreting events through a biblical lens. This group wanted to replace the federal government, which they considered to be evil, with an association of sovereign states. The group finally ended up in an armed standoff with police and federal agents.

Federal agents did seek advice so they could better understand the Montana Freemen, who would not recognize the authority of agents of the Federal

Bureau of Investigation (FBI) as negotiators. One of the advisers was a political scientist and three were religious studies scholars, one of whom was Catherine Wessinger. Later, when she wrote about her experience in attempting to assist law enforcement at the standoff, she mentioned that, during the standoff, one of her colleagues, Phillip Arnold, another religious studies scholar, "protested the agents' tendency to discount religion as *only* a cover for illegal activities, or *only* a product of psychological pathology."[6] Wessinger also reported that, after the incident (which was resolved successfully), the "head of the FBI's Crisis Response Group verbally told Phillip Arnold [another of the Religious Studies Scholars who was an advisor there] that 'your method works' ... (b)ut subsequently, FBI negotiators made statements to the effect that they found the religious studies advice to be irrelevant to resolving the Freeman standoff."[7]

Later, in 1993, there was a siege at Waco, Texas, involving a religious group known as the Branch Davidians that resulted in many persons being wounded and others killed, including four federal agents and 76 civilians. The Branch Davidians believed they were in the middle of the unfolding of the end times as described in the Book of Revelation in the Bible; thus, they were primed to see current events through the template of apocalyptic writings that had predicted conflict. After the event, Nancy Ammerman, a sociologist of religion, was asked to analyze what factors contributed to the tragedy at Waco and report to the Justice and Treasury departments. According to Wessinger, Ammerman found that "an important factor contributing to the branch Davidian tragedy was the nature and quality of expert advice utilized by the ATF and FBI," who had listened to "self-styled 'cult experts'" during the siege and were influenced by their perspective.[8] In other words, they were given ineffective advice because they did not apparently know how to evaluate the credentials of the supposed experts to whom they listened.

In the days since 9/11, of course, religion as a causative factor in terrorism has received much attention. In order to try to prevent terrorist attacks in America, police have begun to conduct surveillance of individuals belonging to some religions and to monitor the activities of some religious groups, even attending services. While an important function of policing is to observe the activities of persons in society to prevent crime, there are issues related to First Amendment rights.

A key issue today for law enforcement is related to the practice of **profiling**, which focuses police attention on persons of a particular religion, ethnicity, race, or nationality for no other reason than that characteristic. There has been much outcry among members of communities who have felt unfairly targeted. For example, Muslim groups have sued the New York City Police Department for "surveillance programs that mapped Muslim neighborhoods, photographed their businesses, and built files on where they eat, shop, and pray."[9] There have been reports of profiling by federal agents, too. But, the Justice Department announced recently that it would "prohibit federal agents from considering religion, national origin, gender, and sexual orientation in their investigations."[10]

For law enforcement to be effective in preventing religiously motivated terrorism, officers need to understand the culture and religious views of the community; of course, familiarity with religious studies can facilitate such understanding. In this way, contacts can be cultivated that will elicit the kinds of information needed to keep everyone safe, yet also to avoid treating innocent individuals unfairly. David Harris, in writing about the damaging effects of profiling, argues that "without strong, positive relationships of respect with the community [which] law enforcement serves, the police—whether involved in investigations of garden-variety crime, or of terrorism—cannot expect a steady flow of crucial information from the community." He notes that it was such an approach that led to the discovery and eventual conviction of individuals in Lackawanna, New York, who were supporting the goals of Al Qaeda; it was people—"not wiretaps or fancy technology"—that is to say, persons who belonged to the Arab and Muslim community there, who reported the suspicious individuals to the authorities.[11]

COURTS

Our judicial system is rooted in the expectation, based on the **Religion Clauses** of the First Amendment, that there must be a separation between church and state. Thus, you might assume that religion would hardly be evident in a court-room for, after all, the Establishment Clause prohibits legal decisions from being made on religious grounds. Yet, the reality is that religion is a factor that must be considered when one examines the functioning of our criminal courts.

Criminal justice researchers have identified the influence of religion on the different stages of judicial proceedings. The reality is that many lawyers believe that religion is an important factor in how people form their opinions and make decisions. So, for example, during voir dire (the preliminary examination of persons who may be selected as jurors), a lawyer may ask potential jurors about their religious preferences. During a trial, religious evidence might be presented by lawyers, or during closing arguments, they might refer to religious precepts such as the biblical injunction, "an eye for an eye." When sentencing defendants, judges have used religion to facilitate a convicted individual's sentence, as when a Kentucky judge gave some offenders the option of attending worship services instead of going to jail.[12]

So, though one's expectation might reasonably be that religion should be kept out of the courtroom, the reality is that it is not. Making the situation even murkier is that there is disagreement among the different states and the federal government about what is acceptable and what is not when religion is introduced into the courtroom. Finally, the effects of religion on court proceedings is an area of academic study which is relatively new and not extensively explored; thus, what can be discussed about it is limited.

In this section of the chapter, we'll look at five points in the judicial process at which religion can become a factor possibly influencing the outcome of the trial. The five points, as identified by Monica Miller, are these: (1) selecting the jury; (2) during the trial; (3) presenting closing arguments; (4) deliberating by the jury; and (5) judicial sentencing.

JURY SELECTION

Attorneys attempt to select persons for jury service who they believe will be favorable to the side they represent. Potential jurors can be rejected in two ways: one is a challenge for cause (for example, a juror might be related to the defendant in some way and can be assumed to be unable to render a fair judgment), and the other is known as a **peremptory challenge**, which allows a lawyer to reject a certain number of jurors without having to give a reason. Potential jurors cannot be rejected for reasons related to race or gender, but they can be rejected because of religion. So, potential jurors have been passed up because of their religious beliefs or membership in a particular denomination, church, or religious group. For example, Monica Miller reports the story of one prosecutor who claimed that he had made an effort to keep Jewish people from being selected for a jury because he believed that "they were less likely to vote for the death penalty."[13]

The occasions when lawyers attempt to exclude potential jurors on the basis of religion appear to be happening more frequently. Prosecutors have challenged persons because of: (a) strong belief in Christianity; (b) service as a missionary; (c) membership in denominations such as Roman Catholicism, Jehovah's Witnesses, or Pentecostalism; or (d) being a Muslim.[14] Matthews argues that rejecting potential jurors because of religion may actually be an indirect way of excluding African Americans, as they tend to be more religious than whites.[15]

The Supreme Court has not ruled on whether or not a peremptory challenge for religion is legal, so this has created a situation in which the rules about the acceptability of the practice are different among the various states. For example, Minnesota allows challenges of potential jurors on the basis of religion, while Indiana and New Jersey do not allow exclusion on the basis of religious membership alone.[16] Courts in some jurisdictions allow challenges based on an individual's religious beliefs or if he or she has religiously related employment.

Interestingly, there does not appear to be clear-cut evidence which would prove either the efficacy or the futility of this practice; however, there are some studies which suggest that religion can influence someone's decision making. Nevertheless, the overall picture is that studies of the influence of religion upon jurors or mock jurors have produced mixed results.

Some studies demonstrate that religion can have an effect on decision making: for example, in one study, it was found that Jewish jurors were more punitive toward Jewish defendants. But another study found that both Catholic and Jewish mock jurors were more lenient with members of their own religion, with Jewish persons being more lenient than Catholics. Another study found that one's religious affiliation did not predict his or her attitude toward the death penalty. Some researchers found that those who were affiliated with fundamentalist traditions tended to be more punitive, but that finding was not replicated in similar studies by others.[17]

Religion Used during the Trial

Religion, religious belief, or religious practice can appear at a trial in several ways. First, a defendant can claim that his or her religious belief is either a mitigating factor—or even a defense—for the alleged crime. Secondly, a defendant can assert that a religious delusion (a false belief) caused his criminal behavior. Finally, a defendant can appear in court wearing religious articles such as jewelry, clothing, or head coverings, as these tend to suggest to an observer that the individual is pious.

Courts have allowed religious evidence to be admitted as proof of a defendant's character. One example might be in the case of an individual who claims to have had a religious conversion to a religion such as Christianity since he or she was initially apprehended and has now amended his life (i.e., changed for the better). Miller notes that this strategy was used in the case of Terry Nichols, one of the perpetrators of the bombing of the federal building in Oklahoma City in 1995. Jurors disagreed over Nichols receiving the death penalty instead of life imprisonment, as some thought that because of his religious conversion, he "might do some good" in prison. Ultimately, he was spared and received a life sentence.[18]

In other cases, religion can also be used as a defense or a mitigating factor. There have been circumstances under which parents refuse medical care for their children because it conflicts with a religious belief that they hold, but that action could and has sometimes led to the death of the child. For example, some parents might not allow a child to have a blood transfusion since it conflicts with a religious precept that they hold, while others may even deny any medical care to their child because they believe that the healing must be accomplished through prayer. Another instance when this might occur would be when a mother refuses, for religious reasons, surgery (i.e., a cesarean operation) to deliver a child. In all of these cases, there is an interest that the state has in protecting the life of a child which must be weighed against the parents' rights to the free practice of their religion.

Some courts have accepted the arguments excusing such parental decisions, essentially acknowledging a primacy of the parents' religious rights. In other cases, courts have rejected this view and held that the child's right to life or to not be endangered must outweigh any interest of the parents.[19] It is reported that about a dozen children die each year because they were denied medical care for religious reasons. In a recent case decided in Pennsylvania, a mother and father, members of a Pentecostal Church, who believed in faith-healing and defied a court order to get medical care for their sick child, were sentenced to 20 or more years in prison following the death of their second child from treatable pneumonia. In this second case, the judge admonished them, saying: "You've killed two of your children ... Not God. Not your church. Not religious devotion—you." The mother made this statement to the judge: "My religious beliefs are that you should pray and not have to use medicine ... whatever sentence you give me, I accept." She also added that her beliefs had now changed.[20]

A defendant may claim that he or she was suffering from a mental illness at the time a crime was committed and thus assert an insanity defense. Successful use of this defense, which attributes the criminal behavior to a "mental disease or defect" that often results in an inability to know right from wrong, means that a person would not be considered responsible for the crime. According to Miller, there is a "unique legal challenge" that occurs when an accused acknowledges what he did was wrong, but believes that he was commanded by God to do it—this is referred to as a **deific decree**. In such a case, a defendant can still be found to be insane because, even though he knew the act was wrong, because of a mental disease or defect, he still believed that "God had ordained the act."

Defendants may wear religious jewelry (e.g., a cross or other religious symbol like a star), distinctive clothing, or a head covering (for example, a *takia*, worn by some Muslims or a *yarmulke*, worn by some Jewish persons) in court to try to influence perceptions about them (especially among jurors), and hence perhaps influence the outcome of the trial; others who have appeared in religious garb or with religious symbols such as rosary beads include lawyers and witnesses. Thus, the problem is that when someone sees an accused person or someone else in court wearing a religious symbol, he or she may begin to assume that person has certain positive characteristics or values such as sincerity or honesty, which may or may not be true of the person wearing the symbol. Levine, in an article examining religious symbols in the courtroom, has noted that some courts have looked at whether a particular symbol is unusual or not before prohibiting its presence; if it is a common symbol, then there does not appear to be a problem.[21] Yet, courts are divided about allowing religious symbols in the courtroom, with some courts prohibiting them as prejudicial.

Religion Used during Closing Arguments

Lawyers—both prosecutors and defense attorneys—may utilize religious appeals to support their arguments.

Prosecutors have used biblical verses in attempts to encourage jurors to vote for a death penalty, especially if there is concern about some of the jurors wavering in their resolve to apply capital punishment. Miller reports that in one case, *Greene v. State*, the prosecutor said to the jury: "Let's get down to what this trial and the laws are all about … This is retribution.'An eye for an eye and a tooth for a tooth.' Right there in the Bible …" The lawyer's goal was to get the defendant sentenced to death.[22]

Defense attorneys can also attempt to use a religious argument to try to prevent a jury from handing down a death sentence. Here, a lawyer would tend to quote passages from the New Testament of the Bible that emphasize mercy or forgiveness. For example, the attorney could quote from the Gospel of Matthew (5:38–39), which says: "You have heard it said, 'An eye for an eye, and a tooth for a tooth', but I say to you do not resist evil, if anyone strikes you on the right cheek, then offer him the other, too."[23]

Generally speaking, religious appeals to the jury, although they can be prejudicial, frequently have been allowed by trial and appeal courts; such practices, when allowed, have been construed to be **harmless error**. When such appeals have been rejected by the courts, it is for such reasons as an interference with jurors' discretion or encouraging them to rely on emotion or the Bible, rather than the applicable law, or as a violation of the 8th Amendment prohibition of cruel and unusual punishment. Nevertheless, Miller reports that research tends to show that such appeals are not effective.[24]

Use of Religion during Deliberation

If jurors use a Bible for guidance during their deliberations, then they have introduced the influence of religion into their decision making. In one case in Colorado, jurors brought a Bible into the deliberation room and referred to it as they made their decision to sentence the defendant to death. An appeals court, however, overturned the sentence because the "jurors had improperly relied on biblical passages."[25]

That jurors may not use a Bible for guidance during their deliberations does not mean that they cannot use their religious precepts in deciding a death penalty case. For example, in Georgia, a court noted that though it would be improper to use a Bible during deliberations, it did not mean "that jurors cannot rely on their personal faith and deeply held beliefs" when considering the imposition of the death penalty.[26]

Judicial Sentencing

Judges have relied on religion in making their decisions. As noted in the beginning of this chapter, a judge in Kentucky offered defendants convicted in drug cases a choice when being sentenced: they had the options of either going to jail or attending worship services. Another judge, based in Louisiana, did the same thing. Then, there was a judge in Michigan who suspended a spouse-abuser's sentence, invoking the guidance of Moses. In a case in which a man was accused of pushing his wife (who had conceived a child with his brother) against a wall, he said, "I don't believe I have the authority to punish this man ... In the eyes of Moses, the crime was not committed by her husband."[27]

Of course, judges are limited in their use of religion in the courtroom. They are not permitted to violate the **Establishment Clause** of the First Amendment. Additionally, the American Bar Association (ABA) Code of Conduct states that judges must "perform judicial duties without prejudice."[28]

There is an expectation that judges will not be biased; consequently, when they allow religion to influence the work of a court, there is obviously a question arising about whether there will be fairness in the courtroom. Some appeals courts have determined that judges who relied upon religious beliefs or tests had violated the due process rights of defendants. Nevertheless, if a judge does not allow either religious belief or strictures to be overly influential—and therefore to have formed the basis of a decision—this may be acceptable. Thus, a judge's ruling can be upheld upon review if the religion is seen as only one factor among many used in making the decision. Religion, then, can be a factor in a judge's decision; it just cannot be the *critical* factor.[29]

CORRECTIONS

Religion and Employment Issues

Essentially, the same issues that were discussed for policing are applicable to corrections. Correctional officers have First Amendment rights regarding the practice of religion, as well as the protections against discrimination of Title VII, which were both discussed in relation to policing.

Religion and Corrections

It will be recalled that religious reformers have had a profound influence on the development of corrections in the United States. For the past 20 years or so, there has been much discussion about the function of religion in the penal system. For example, following President George W. Bush's initiatives, there was a growth of what were known as **faith-based** prisons or prison units "around the country in Alaska, Iowa, Louisiana, New Mexico, Texas, Florida, Ohio, Kansas, (and) the Federal Bureau of Prisons."[30] O'Connor, Duncan, and Quillard observe that there appear to be several factors in addition to the "faith- based initiatives" that have encouraged the growth of interest in religion in the prisons. These factors include: (a) the appeal of Native American, Christian, Islamic, and Buddhist practices to prisoners; (b) the restorative justice movement; and (c) the Religious Land Use and Institutionalized Persons Act (RLUIPA), which protects the rights of prisoners to practice religion.[31]

The idea behind faith-based programs was that religious groups would begin to provide more social services around the country. However, this has been a controversial idea because of concerns about keeping in place the separation between church and state. Following a speech in 2002 by President George W. Bush that extolled faith-based initiatives, the White House created a special office that "provided large grants for projects favored by the Christian right, like Charles Colson's Prison Fellowship Ministries and Teen Challenge, a drug rehabilitation program that openly pushed religious conversion."[32]

Soon, there were reports that prisoners in the special programs often had enhanced privileges and better quarters. There were other reports of government monies being used to support evangelization or indoctrination by specific religious groups, as well as hostility toward prisoners who did not belong to the denomination running the faith-based program. Yet, others have argued that these programs had been essential for the rehabilitation of inmates, and that the abuses were infrequent.[33] Programs have continued under the Obama administration, but have had stronger restrictions on how the government funds given to faith-based groups might be used in order to limit abuse.

O'Connor, Duncan, and Quillard identify three significant concerns that should be kept in mind when corrections officials incorporate faith-based programs. First, clergy members or spiritual leaders and their followers who come to correctional facilities to offer these programs generally know nothing about prisoners or corrections, and may not understand the necessary separation between church and state. Secondly, these groups cannot be expected to (and probably do not) know how to assist in the growth of persons who belong to other denominations or religions; but they are capable of creating a support network for those whom they do serve. Finally, the volunteers who come to provide the services must be trained and supported by paid, professional correctional chaplains who know how the system functions and what methods will best serve the offenders in the institution.[34]

There are also questions about the effectiveness of using religion in the attempt to rehabilitate prisoners—what effects should properly be expected? There is evidence that religious practice has beneficial effects for prisoners. It has been found that religious practice in prison "helps people deal with guilt, find a new way of life, cope with the many losses (freedom, family, sexuality) that accompany incarceration, find a safe place ... gain access to outsiders," and also facilitates better relationships with other inmates.[35]

As a result, there is much that can be said about the influence of religion on the development and current functioning of prisons. In Section 3 of this book, there will be a more thorough examination of some of these issues relating to corrections that lie at the intersection between the studies of religion and criminal justice.

TYPES OF RELIGIOUS CRIME

In this last part of the chapter, we'll examine some of the types of crime that can be associated with religion so that we'll have a rudimentary typology of religious crime. A typology is a very useful way of categorizing various types of criminal behavior and will likely already be familiar to the reader. For example, one typology might look at the different types of property crime, violent crime, and so forth.

A simple typology of crimes that can be associated with religion might look at only two factors: (1) for some crimes, what is essential is a motivation derived from religious belief such as in the case of the commission of a hate crime; or (2) in other crimes, one finds just ordinary criminality with one significant difference, which is that a religious practice or religious affiliation has been used to facilitate that ordinary crime—for example, to commit a fraud. So, the first grouping of crimes are those committed because they are actions that are consistent with someone's religious beliefs. And the second grouping consists of crimes that are actually motivated by ordinary criminal desires (for instance, greed or lust), but involve the use of religion in some way to accomplish the criminal's goals.

A second way of developing a typology of religious crime would to be to draw upon a different set of categories. There are three categories that we'll examine: (a) property crimes; (b) crimes against persons; and (c) miscellaneous offenses. Thus, the following typology is a basic, but not exhaustive, listing and discussion of the types of crimes which can involve religion as a significant factor.

PROPERTY CRIMES

Fraud: A fraud occurs when a person deliberately deceives another in order to gain some advantage, usually property of some kind, to which he or she has no right. Religion can be seen as a factor in facilitating fraud when it happens that an unscrupulous person solicits funds from those within his or her own religious group, with the understanding that the monies will be used to support a church or religious society or charity, but it is not. Perpetrators of this kind of crime can be clergy members or lay officials. An example of this would be the case of the television evangelist and minister, Jim Bakker. In 1989, Bakker was convicted of 24 counts of fraud and conspiracy in federal court. He was accused of swindling "followers of his PTL Ministry out of $158 million" and "diverting $3.7 million to support an opulent lifestyle." Bakker had promised his followers that there would be lifetime vacations for them, vacations that he knew he could not provide. Rather, he spent money on a fleet of Mercedes and Rolls-Royces and other extravagances like an air-conditioned doghouse.[36]

A variation on this type of crime is known as "affinity fraud," which occurs when a criminal uses a connection such as membership in a religious denomination to gain others' trust and victimize them through fraud. A married couple who were based in California and Maryland developed relationships with ministers and faith-based groups and introduced themselves as philanthropists; they really were running a Ponzi scheme, which is a criminal scheme to get someone to invest money for which he will never get a return. The couple offered funding to their victims, but to qualify, the victims had to first give the couple "advance banking fees," which would be used to get the monies from an overseas bank account. The husband and wife collected about $3.7 million in "advance banking fees," but never gave any financing to those who had paid the fees. Instead, the couple bought a Bentley and other expensive cars, homes in California and Maryland, as well as traveled on private jets.[37]

<u>Embezzlement:</u> Embezzlement occurs when a person in a trusted position takes money or other property that has been placed in his or her care, but to which he does not have a right. For example, how often does one hear stories about entertainers, who are stars, who discover that they are nearly penniless because a manager or accountant they trusted was actually stealing from them all the while?

Characteristically, this crime happens in a religious context when a clergyperson or church worker such as a bookkeeper siphons off money from donations given to the congregation for the upkeep of buildings, for charity, or for the financing of other programs such as Sunday school or adult education. The embezzler steals money—typically cash and difficult to trace—and attempts to conceal the illicit activity by not recording the actual amount of contributions or by altering official records.

An example of this kind of crime was reported in the *Chicago Tribune*, when a Greek Orthodox priest was charged with felony theft after taking over $110,000 from a church trust fund over a four-year period. He used the money to pay for personal expenses such as shopping, decorating his home, and dining out at expensive restaurants. The trust fund did allow the pastor to draw up to $5,000 for specified expenses, plus an automobile and property, but the rest of the fund was to be used for building and maintaining a cultural center.[38] In another case, a laywoman who was an active church member and employed as an "accounts payable" clerk for the Archdiocese of New York was indicted for stealing over a million dollars. She did this by writing checks in small amounts (i.e., under $2500), which would not cause scrutiny by a supervisor and which were payable to one of her sons; however, no payments should have been issued to her son, as he was not a vendor. Then, to conceal the illicit checks, she would change the office's records to indicate that the payments had been made to legitimate vendors. The clerk did not live lavishly, but used the money to buy expensive dolls for a collection she had, as well as clothing and furniture. Before she was hired by the church, she had had a previous history of convictions for theft, but this was not discovered, as there had been no preemployment background check.[39]

CRIMES AGAINST PERSONS

Hate Crimes: These are crimes, often violent offenses, which are committed against another because he or she is seen to be different in some respect; characteristics that are targeted include race, sexual orientation, nationality, or religious preference. Thus, religion can be a factor in explaining how some persons commit hate crimes. Quite simply, sometimes persons have been attacked for the sole reason of being a member of a religion disliked by a majority. In our country's history, especially in the late 1800s and early 1900s, this has happened sometimes to immigrants who were Jewish or Catholic.

However, there are some persons whose religious beliefs may lead them to identify another group as an enemy, and then the possibility of violence is very real. If one looks at a group given to racism or antagonism to immigrants such as the Ku Klux Klan or Christian Identity supporters, or even neo-Nazis, one will find that some members developed a theology that supported their views about the supremacy of whites and of their own particular "brand" of the Christian religion. Followers of one of these groups, those espousing "Christian Identity" principles, deny that Jesus Christ was Jewish because they see Jews as children of Satan and assert that he was white because dark-skinned persons are beasts. So, though such a group of persons has identified themselves as "Christian"—a religion devoted to peace and love of others—one sees that the targets of their verbal attacks can be fellow Christians from other denominations (such as mainline Protestants or Catholics) or races (such as African American). An example of Christian Identity being a factor in violence occurred in Pennsylvania in 1995, when two teenage brothers were charged with killing their parents and other brother; it was reported that the boys' mother had opposed their beliefs.[40] Obviously, some aberration had developed in the theological thinking of those who could promote such hateful speech, which has led some to commit hate crimes; we'll explore more about such religious aberrations in the next chapter.

In the days since the attacks on 9/11, there has been a number of hate crimes, especially physical attacks, against Muslims; these persons are assaulted simply because of their faith in Islam. Those who would commit such attacks are likely to be ignorant of the reality that there were innocent Muslim victims who died in the 9/11 attacks, too. But, the reason for the attack is the victim's religion. Incidentally, hate crimes are increasing against persons who are Sikhs. Sikhism is a religion that began in India about 500 years ago; male Sikhs are recognizable for their distinctive head gear, or turbans. Sikhs are being assaulted because their attackers believe that their victims are Muslims.[41]

One last issue related to hate crime with religious roots that has been getting attention recently would be what could be called "intra-group" attacks (i.e., assaulting a member of one's own religion). Can such attacks be considered hate crimes? In Ohio, such a situation occurred among the Amish, who are generally a pacifistic people and are the descendants of European Anabaptists (i.e., Christians who do not baptize infants) who fled persecution by coming to America in the 1700s. An Amish leader and his followers were convicted of hate crimes after they cut off the beards and hair of fellow Amish members with whom they disagreed in order to humiliate them. Recently, a federal appeals court overturned their convictions on charges of hate crimes because, according to one of the appellate judges, who said that "for the attacks to be a hate crime, the religion of the victim must be the predominant motivating factor, and ... the evidence did not support that conclusion." Rather, the attacks seemed to be motivated by interpersonal and interfamilial disagreements. However, one of the judges on the appeals panel did not agree and said that these were, in fact, hate crimes, as they happened "because of the victims' religious beliefs."[42]

Sexual Abuse: When an adult has an illicit and predatory sexual relationship with another person, then that activity can be termed sexual abuse. The term is most often applied when children are the victims, but adults can be victimized as well. In the case of a victimized child, such a crime is especially repugnant, as it is a violation of a child's innocence.

The harm done by such abuse is compounded when the abuser is a trusted person such as a religious leader or clergy member. There is an implicit expectation that such persons will be role models of virtuous behavior in the community, and they are expected to be people in whom great trust can be placed.

In recent years, a great deal of attention in the media has been given to a sex abuse scandal involving the Catholic Church. In 2002, the *Boston Globe* published an exposé of sexual abuse committed by priests in the Boston area. The picture that emerged from the news reports was of a church hierarchy that seemed more interested in protecting the institution rather than addressing the needs of the victims. There were stories about priests who were pedophiles, who were quietly transferred to another area when a scandal occurred; then, when settled in a new place, they continued their activities. Victims were generally silenced. Kathryn Dale and Judith Alpert, psychologists who conducted research related to this issue, wrote that "some children were abused twice, the first time by the molesting priest and the second by the shielding of the molesting priests."[43]

In 2004, John Jay College of Criminal Justice published the results of a comprehensive study of sexual abuse by priests and deacons over the period ranging from 1950–2002; prior to this study, very little research had been done on clergy as sexual offenders. The John Jay study revealed that only a small fraction of all of the priests and deacons (about four percent of the total) during that 50-year period were accused of sexual abuse. The average age of onset of the behavior was about 39 years old, and more than half of those who offended only did so once, so few were persistent offenders.[44] On the other hand, nearly eight percent of those who did offend accounted for about 36 percent of all offenses, which indicates that "a small number of individuals are responsible for a large percentage of offenses."[45]

It is important to recognize that even though the media focused on priests who had been sexual abusers, there are cases involving ministers such as the cofounder of a large neo-Calvinist movement; and, here, too, church officials "failed to report the abuse to law enforcement, encouraged parents to refrain from reporting the assaults to law enforcement," and they appear to have attempted to deceive the police by creating the impression that the parents had actually forgiven the offenders who had abused their children.[46] There have been accusations against Jewish clergy and religious teachers that were presented in a documentary film, *Standing Silent*, which was released in 2011; again, one sees that these crimes of sexual abuse don't get reported to the authorities.[47]

Finally, such abuse can even target adults, as when a clergyman uses his position of authority to take advantage of a person who is vulnerable and seeking spiritual counseling. It can also be committed by laypersons who hold positions of authority within a religious organization. For example, a California real estate developer, who also served as chairman of a board of directors for a religious shrine, was accused of sexually harassing a woman whom he helped get a job as an administrative assistant at the shrine.[48]

Child Neglect: When a parent or responsible guardian does not provide adequate care for a child, this is referred to as neglect. In most cases, the typical problem is that a child is not provided with the basic necessities of food, adequate clothing, and a nurturing home.

In child neglect cases involving religion, the situation invariably involves a parent refusing to seek medical care for a sick child—not because they don't care about or love the child, but because such an action conflicts with their religious beliefs. It is estimated that about 25 children die each year in such cases. In some cases, courts have intervened and ordered parents to seek treatment for the sick child. If the child dies after not being given the opportunity to receive professional medical care, then the parents can be charged with manslaughter.

Miscellaneous Crimes and Socially Disapproved Behaviors: Some religious behaviors which have been deemed to violate social norms and have been criminalized do not fit neatly into the categories we just explored. A complicating factor is that some of these behaviors may be against the law in only some jurisdictions or in particular circumstances. Additionally, there are some religious behaviors that may not be illegal, but which may still be reprehensible.

Snake Handling: The first of the offenses that we'll examine is something that is known as snake handling. To understand this practice—which literally involves handling poisonous snakes (e.g., rattlesnakes, copperheads, and cottonmouths) during religious services—it is important to keep in mind that among some Christians, there is a belief that the words of the Bible are literally true; thus, someone who holds this view does not see any of the images used in scripture as being metaphorical. In the New Testament, in the Gospel of Luke (10:19), there is a promise that the followers of Jesus could "walk on snakes and scorpions" and "nothing will hurt you." It has been estimated that there are about 125 churches that practice snake handling; it is most popular in Appalachia, but all states in that area except West Virginia have outlawed it. Practitioners of snake handling such as Andrew Hamblin, a 22-year-old pastor and reality TV personality who was criminally charged for keeping dozens of snakes, argue that it is a matter of religious liberty.[49] Later, a grand jury exonerated him.[50] Another pastor, Jamie Coots, who has also been arrested for possessing snakes, argues that this is a matter of religious freedom, and even though his religious practice is risky, it is no different from what is done by followers of Christian Science who, by not utilizing medical practitioners when they are ill, also engage in behavior that endangers their lives.[51]

Illegal Drug Use: Some religious groups use drugs, especially hallucinogens, to facilitate their religious experience. This is permitted for traditional worship services involving indigenous peoples; thus, persons or groups seeking to abuse drugs under the pretense of religious services would not qualify. An example of a legitimate use of proscribed drugs in a religious context can be seen in the case of Native Americans. In the Native American Church, members are allowed by law to use mescaline and peyote as part of their religious services. The use is carefully controlled, following purification rituals, and is not allowed to be used capriciously; some Native Americans have been healed of alcohol addiction through these services.[52]

In 2006, the Supreme Court ruled in favor of a small religious group, Uniao Do Vegetal (UDV), or Union of the Plants, which was using the illegal drug hoasca (a tea containing the hallucinogen known as DMT, or diemethyltryptamine). Uniao Do Vegetal is a religious group that mixes Christianity and indigenous Brazilian beliefs; they believe that drinking hoasca "is sacred and connects members to God." It has been acknowledged by prosecutors that UDV's use of hoasca was a "sincere religious practice." In 1999, federal agents in New Mexico seized a shipment of Brazilian hoasca for use by UDV. Later, UDV sued the federal government and eventually the case worked its way up to the Supreme Court. The group argued that the 1993 Religious Freedom Restoration Act (RFRA) would exempt them from any laws proscribing their use of hoasca because RFRA protects persons from laws that "substantially burden a person's exercise of religion" unless the government has a compelling interest. The Supreme Court opinion compared the use of hoasca to the peyote that has been used for years by Native American tribes in their religious ceremonies and stated that the government had not shown a compelling interest in preventing the use of hoasca in religious services.[53]

Female Genital Mutilation: The genitals of both male and female children have been surgically altered sometimes in accordance with a religious tradition, but also for cultural reasons. In the case of males, this is called circumcision, and although it has roots in ancient Judaic religious practice and later in Muslim tradition, it is widely done today in Western society; it is generally accepted as hygienic and beneficial for the child. However, there was recently a controversy in Germany about circumcision because of a court ruling that held that it was a violation of a child's rights because he had no say in the decision to perform a circumcision. Eventually, after much national discussion, legislators in Germany passed a law permitting circumcision of infants, but added some restrictions for the sake of the child's safety.[54]

Female circumcision, now popularly referred to as genital mutilation, has been strongly rejected in many parts of the world. There are some who argue that the practice has religious underpinnings—for example, it has been claimed that the biblical figure Sarah took revenge on her husband's concubine, Hagar, in this way (there is no real basis for this explanation); others assert that it reflects beliefs about the bisexuality of the gods characteristic of primitive religions. Archaeologists confirm that the practice was done in ancient Egypt. Today, it is widely found in parts of Africa that are Muslim, but is also done among Christians and other religious groups in Africa. However, female genital mutilation has begun to decline—and even has been stopped in some countries—as there have been international efforts to bring an end to the practice.[55] In the United States, in the early part of the 20th century, clitoridectomies were performed by physicians as a medical treatment for excessive masturbation, frigidity, and to treat prostitutes, but that ended long ago. More recently, genital mutilation has resurfaced with an influx of immigrants from countries such as Sudan. Only some states (such as California, Illinois, New York, and Texas) have enacted laws against genital mutilation, but there is a federal criminal statute against female genital mutilation that was enacted in 1996.[56]

Spiritual Abuse: One form of spousal or intimate partner abuse can involve attacking the victim's religious beliefs and practices or spirituality. A common form of this abuse happens when the aggressor interferes with the victim's ability to practice a religion; it is an attempt to control the victim. Ways of doing this can range from simple ridicule to violating important religious rules or holidays so as to upset the victim, to physically preventing a person from attending worship services. A husband may tell his wife that "he has to punish her because she is a sinner."[57] Another version of the maltreatment occurs when the abuser uses some aspect of the victim's religion to justify the abuse—for instance, by punishing a woman because she is not subservient to her husband when some religious texts may call for such docility.

While spiritual abuse does not leave the marks, scars, or physical injuries that physical abuse can, it is still a serious concern. Such spiritual abuse is not a crime, but it is highly dysfunctional and can facilitate intimate partner violence, which is proscribed by criminal law. Recent neurological research suggests that emotional pain can be as significant as physical pain. So, since a person may find meaning and gain emotional support from a religious practice, then to prevent someone from meeting this spiritual need will potentially cause deep psychic pain and can undermine that individual. Cares and Cusick, who have researched such abuse against women, note that: "the victims of these perpetrators … are more fearful, more likely to experience serious abuse, experience abuse more frequently, sustain injury, and manifest symptoms of post-traumatic stress disorder."[58]

Religious Delusions and Criminal Behavior: It happens that sometimes an emotionally disturbed person commits a crime because he or she believes that God has ordered her or him to do so. In such a case, the person is suffering from a symptom of mental illness known as a delusion, or a false belief. To the person experiencing such a delusion, the command seems very real and may be irresistible.

Thus, a person who suffers such a delusion may be able to assert an insanity defense for crimes committed while under the influence of the delusion. Two cases involving religious mothers who killed their children are examples of persons whose defense was insanity because of a religious delusion; the outcome for each case was different, however. Andrea Yates drowned all five of her children in 2001 because she believed that Satan had ordered her to do so. Psychiatrists who testified in her case disagreed about whether she was sane or not, but one who was prominent, Dr. Park Dietz, said that he believed she knew what she did was wrong, especially as she tried to cover up the murders afterward. Yates was convicted and given a life sentence. The other mother was Deanna Laney, who had killed two of her children in 2003 by hitting them in the head with rocks because she believed that God ordered her to do so and that God would never order her to do something wrong. In the Old Testament of the Bible, stoning is portrayed as an accepted punishment for serious wrongdoers. Park Dietz testified in her case, too, but thought that Laney was not able to tell right from wrong, a standard test for Insanity in the state where she was tried. The jury later acquitted her by reason of insanity.[59]

SUMMARY

In this chapter, we first discussed some of the ways that religion or religious beliefs can influence the functioning of the modern criminal justice system. We saw that, for each of the major components of the criminal justice system—policing, the courts, and corrections—there are factors such as employee rights and employer obligations, separation of church and state, and impartiality that come into play. Then, we introduced a very basic taxonomy of crime that is either motivated by or facilitated by religion. There were three general categories discussed: property crimes, crimes against persons, and miscellaneous crimes such as snake handling.

KEY TERMS

+ Deific decree
+ Establishment Clause
+ Faith-based
+ Harmless error
+ Hate crime
+ Peremptory challenge
+ Profiling
+ Religion Clauses
+ Title VII of the Civil Rights Act of 1964
+ Voir dire

REVIEW QUESTIONS

1. What are some of the religious issues involving policing?
2. What are some of the religious issues involving the courts?
3. What are some of the religious issues involving corrections?
4. What are some of the property crimes related to religion?
5. What are some of the crimes against persons and miscellaneous crimes related to religion?

END NOTES

1. Schott, Richard G. "Religion in the Public Workplace." *FBI Law Enforcement Bulletin*, Jun. 2007, vol. 76, issue 6, 23.

2. Schott, 25.

3. Schott, 29.

4. Schott, 30.

5. Kimball, Charles. *When Religion Becomes Evil* (New York: HarperCollins Publishers, 2002)

6. Wessinger, Catherine. "Religious Studies Scholars, FBI Agents, and the Montana Freemen Standoff." *Nova Religio*, 2009, 13 (2), 39–40.

7. Wessinger, 41.

8. Wessinger, 42.

9. Appuzzo, Matt. "U.S. Move Seen to Add Limits Over Profiling." *New York Times*, Jan. 16, 2013, A14.

10. Appuzzo, A1.

11. Harris, David A. "U.S. Experiences with Racial and Ethnic Profiling: History, Current Issues, and the Future." *Critical Criminology*, 2006, 14, 235–236.

12. Miller, Monica K. *Religion in Criminal Justice* (El Paso: LFB Scholarly Publishing, LLC, 2008), 2.

13. Miller, 12.

14. Miller, 12.

15. Matthews, Christie Stancil. "Missing Faith in Batson: Continued Discrimination Against African Americans Through Religion-Based Peremptory Challenges" (2013). Available at SSRN: http://ssrn.com/abstract=2431652 or http://dx.doi.org/10.2139/ssrn.2431652

16. Miller, Monica K., Julie A. Singer, and Alayna Jehle. "Identification of Circumstances Under Which Religion Affects Each Stage of the Trial Process." *Applied Psychology in Criminal Justice*, 2008, 4(1), 140.

17. Miller, Singer, and Jehle, 141.

18. Miller, Singer, and Jehle, 147.

19. Miller, Singer, and Jehle, 148.

20. Dale, Maryclaire. "Pa. Couple Sent to Prison For 2nd Prayer Death." AP, Feb. 19, 2014, retrieved from http://bigstory.ap.org/article/pa-couple-face-prison-after-sons-prayer-deaths

21. Levine, Samuel J. *Religious Symbols and Religious Garb in the Courtroom: Personal Values and Public Judgments*, 66 Fordham L. Rev. 1505 (1998). Available at: http://ir.lawnet.fordham.edu/flr/vol66/iss4/35

22. Miller, 1.

23. Author's translation.

24. Miller, Singer, and Jehle, 154–155.

25. Miller, 22.

26. Miller, Singer, and Jehle, 159.

27. Barringer, David. "Higher Authorities." *ABA Journal*. Dec. 96, Vol. 82, Issue 12, 68–71.

28. Barringer, "Higher Authorities," 69.

29. Miller, Singer, and Jehle, 161.

30. O'Connor, Thomas P., Jeff Duncan, and Frank Quillard. "Criminology and Religion: The Shape of an Authentic Dialogue." *Criminology and Public Policy*, Aug. 2006, vol. 5, issue 3, 560.

31. O'Connor, Duncan, and Quillard, 559–560.

32. Jacoby, Susan. "Keeping the Faith, Ignoring History." *New York Times*, Feb. 28, 2009, available at: http://www.nytimes.com/2009/03/01/opinion/01jacoby.html?pagewanted=all&module=Search&mabReward=relbias%3Aw%2C%7B%221%22%3A%22RI%3A8%22%7D

33. Henriques, Diana B., and Andrew Lehren. "Religion for Captive Audiences, With Taxpayers Footing the Bill." *New York Times*, Dec. 10, 2006. Available at: http://www.nytimes.com/2006/12/10/business/10faith.html?pagewanted=all&module=Search&mabReward=relbias%3Aw%2C%7B%221%22%3A%22RI%3A8%22%7D

34. O'Connor, Duncan, and Quillard, 564.

35. O'Connor, Duncan, and Quillard, 563.

36. Applebome, Peter A. "Bakker Is Convicted on All Counts; First Felon Among T.V. Evangelists." *New York Times*, Oct. 06, 1989. Available at http://www.nytimes.com/1989/10/06/us/bakker-is-convicted-on-all-counts-first-felon-among-tv-evangelists.html

37. Singletary, Michelle. "Where Money Meets Faith, Bring Skepticism." *Washington Post*, Aug. 12, 2012. National Newspapers Premier. Web. Sept. 22, 2014.

38. Chachkevitch, Alexandra, and Lisa Black. "Priest Will Face Theft Charge: Wisconsin Officials Say Glenview Pastor Stole From Trust Fund." *Chicago Tribune*, Jun. 20, 2014. National Newspapers Premier; ProQuest Newsstand. Web. 22 Sep. 2014.

39. Otterman, Sharon, and Russ Buettner. "In a Million-Dollar Theft Case, Church Worker with a Secret Past." *New York Times*, Jan. 30, 2012. Available at: http://www.nytimes.com/2012/01/31/nyregion/new-york-archdiocese-bookkeeper-charged-with-stealing-1-million.html

40. Schneider, Keith. "Triple Murder Causes Alarm About Hate Group's Growth." *New York Times*, March 6, 1995. Available at: http://www.nytimes.com/1995/03/06/us/triple-murder-causes-alarm-about-hate-groups-growth.html

41. Brown, Matthew. "Fatal Shootings Raises Awareness of Crimes, Misunderstandings Against Sikh Religion." *Deseret News*, Aug. 6, 2012. Available at http: //search.proquest.com/docview/1034393913

42. Eckholm, Erik. "Convictions of Amish Sect Leader and Followers Overturned in Hair Cutting Attacks." *New York Times*, Aug. 27, 2014 Available at: http://www.nytimes.com/2014/08/28/us/amish-sect-leaders-conviction-is-overturned-in-hair-cutting-attacks.html

43. Dale, Kathryn A., and Judith L. Alpert. "Hiding Behind the Cloth: Child Sexual Abuse and the Catholic Church." *Journal of Child Sexual Abuse*, vol. 16 (3) 2007, 63.

44. Terry, Karen J., and Alissa Ackerman. "Child Sexual Abuse in the Catholic Church: How Situational Crime Prevention Strategies Can Help Create Safe Environments." *Criminal Justice and Behavior*, vol. 35 (5) May 2008, 648–649.

45. Piquero, Alex R., et al. "Uncollaring the Criminal: Understanding Criminal Careers of Criminal Clerics." *Criminal Justice and Behavior*, vol. 35 (5) May 2008, 595.

46. Boorstein, Michelle. "Suit Accuses Sovereign Grace Ministries of Covering Up Alleged Child Sexual Abuse: More Accusers and More Accused in a Complaint Filed Against Sovereign Grace Ministries." *Washington Post*, Jan. 15, 2003. National Newspapers Premier. Web. Sep. 22, 2014.

47. Wax, Emily. "No Longer Standing Silent." *Washington Post*, Mar. 20, 2012. National Newspapers Premier. Web. Sept. 22, 2014.

48. Agha, Laith. "Lawsuit Accuses Marin County Man of Forced Sex, Spanking Against SF Catholic Church Aide." *Oakland Tribune*, Feb. 10, 2014. National Newspapers Premier. Web. Sept. 22, 2014.

49. Blinder, Alan. "Asserting a God-Given Right to Snakes." *New York Times*, Nov. 16 2013. National Newspapers Premier. Web. Sept. 22, 2014.

50. Associated Press. "Tennessee: Pastor Is Cleared in Snake Handling Case." *New York Times*, Jan. 9, 2014, A14.

51. Coots, Jamie. "The Constitution Protects My Snake-Handling." *Wall Street Journal*, Oct. 04, 2013. National Newspapers Premier. Web. Sept. 22, 2014.

52. Korsmeyer, Pamela, and Henry R. Kranzler, Ed. "Cults and Drug Use." *Encyclopedia of Drugs, Alcohol & Addictive Behavior*, 3rd ed., vol. 1 (Detroit: Macmillan Reference USA, 2009), 452–455. *Gale Virtual Reference Library*. Web. Sept. 24, 2014.

53. Pew Research. "Supreme Court Rules That Religious Group Can Use Illegal Drug in Their Worship Services." *Religion and Public Life Project*. Feb. 21, 2006. Available at http://www.pewforum.

org/2006/02/21/supreme-court-rules-that-religious-group-can-use-illegal-drug-in-their-worship-services/

54. Eddy, Melissa. "German Lawmakers Vote to Protect Right to Circumcision." *New York Times*, Dec. 12, 2012. Available at: http://www.nytimes.com/2012/12/13/world/europe/german-lawmakers-vote-to-protect-right-to-circumcision.html

55. Greenbaum, Ellen. "Female Genital Mutilation." *Encyclopedia of Sex and Gender*, ed. Fedwa Malti-Douglas, vol. 2 (Detroit: Macmillan Reference USA, 2007), 529–531. *Gale Virtual Reference Library*. Web. Sept. 24, 2014.

56. White, Allen E. "Female Genital Mutilation in America: The Federal Dilemma." *Texas Journal of Women & the Law* 10.2 (2001): 129. *Criminal Justice Abstracts with Full Text*. Web. Sept. 25, 2014.

57. Spohn, Julie. "West Mifflin Students Hear About Abuse." *Pittsburgh Post-Gazette*, May 05, 2004. National Newspapers Premier. Web. Sept. 22, 2014.

58. Cares, Allison, and Gretchen Cusick. "Risks and Opportunities of Faith and Culture: The Case of Abused Jewish Women." *Journal of Family Violence* 27.5 (2012): 427–435, *Criminal Justice Abstracts with Full Text*. Web. Sept. 25, 2014.

59. Falkenberg, Lisa. "Experts: Psychiatrists Were Key In Child Murder Trials Testimony Made Difference In Opposing Verdicts of Two Very Similar Cases." *South Florida Sun-Sentinel*, Apr. 06, 2004. National Newspapers Premier. Web. Sept. 22, 2014.

3. Religious Studies

By William J. Cook Jr.

OVERVIEW

In this chapter, we'll look at the secular discipline of religious studies. Criminal justice is an eclectic discipline, in that it draws from other scholarly branches of knowledge such as biology, economics, legal studies, neuroscience, political science, psychology, and sociology. Given that religion continues to be a significant factor in understanding human behavior in the modern world, then it is now obviously important that those who would master the subject of criminal justice should also be familiar with basic concepts and perspectives drawn from the work of scholars in the field of religious studies.

In the legal decision rendered in *Abington School District v. Schempp*, 374 U.S. 203(1963), Supreme Court justice Tom Clark noted in the majority opinion that: "(i)t might well be said that one's education is not complete without a study of comparative religion or the history of religion and its relationship to the advancement of civilization." In this case, in which the Court held that public schools should be religion-free (i.e., religion should not be imposed on students), Justice Clark still emphasizes the importance of studying *about* religion.[1]

RELIGION

To begin, let's review what is meant by the term **religion**. Then, we'll address this question: What is religious studies? As you will perhaps recall from the introduction to this book, we said that religion is: (1) a belief in or worship of a superhuman controlling power, especially a personal god or gods; or (2) a particular system of faith and worship; or (3) a pursuit or interest to which someone ascribes supreme importance.[2] And most importantly, as Huston Smith notes, "Religion is not primarily a matter of facts; it is a matter of meanings."[3]

William Cantwell Smith once observed that "the study of religion is the study of persons … and indeed of human lives at their most intimate, most profound, most primary, most transcendent."[4] In our "most intimate, most profound, most primary, most transcendent" moments, people ask certain fundamental questions that religion answers. Hecht and Biondo list some of these questions: What happens when we die? Why are we here? Where do we come from? Why do good people suffer? Finally, who are we?[5]

Religion can be discussed as being either "ordinary" or "extraordinary." Catherine L. Albanese, a religious studies professor, defines ordinary religion as "religion that is more or less synonymous with culture … [it] shows people how to live well within boundaries."

What do we mean by boundaries? These are the limits or the borders of our lives. We have boundaries in time: stages in our lives—birth, adolescence, adulthood, and death, for example. There are the seasons of the year. There is the inner boundary, which is revealed when one asks himself this question: Who am I? There are boundaries in physical space, too. For example, there are sacred spaces or places into which we ordinarily do not cross. Jonathan Z. Smith describes a **sacred space** as "a place of clarification (a focusing lens) where men and gods are held to be transparent to one another."[6] An example of such a place can be found in the Paleolithic caves in southern France, where one travels through dark and dangerous passages to an inner cavern where, in the darkness, primitive drawings of animals on the walls "which astonish with their power and beauty" are found. One author, Bede Griffiths, says that "the pictures on the wall were the sacred images by means of which it was believed that human beings could enter into communion with divine powers."[7]

In the modern world, "ordinary" religion can be seen in ethnic customs such as dress, dietary restrictions, and observance of holidays. For example, many people give Christmas presents because that is customary on December 25th in our country, but the actual religious celebration of Christmas may not be of interest to them. Extraordinary religion "helps people transcend or move beyond their everyday culture or concerns … in the West, extraordinary religion helps connect people with god." One example of extraordinary religion might be attending a religious revival meeting or participating in a Sunday morning church service such as a Catholic Mass. Albanese gives an example of extraordinary religion in Judaism as the Sabbath meal, a "weekly family observance that joins a formal framework of prayer and blessings to ordinary conversation and enjoyment around the dinner table."[8] It can be difficult, sometimes, to separate ordinary religion from extraordinary religion, as they frequently blend together.

Another method of defining religion is to shift to a concept of **religious systems**. The concept of a "system" is familiar to students of criminal justice, since it is common to envision policing, courts, and corrections functioning as a system. Thus, in utilizing this concept, we look at the components of the system and consider how they function in relation to one another and how they all come together as a unit. Albanese has identified the four parts of religious systems as these four C's: **creed, code, cultus, and community**.[9]

Creeds: (from the Latin *credo*, I believe) are the "explanations about the meaning of human life." Sometimes creeds can be very formal such as the Nicene Creed used by many Christians; it is a basic statement of the theological principles of the Christian religion. Other religious creeds are informal and rooted in the oral traditions of a group of people.

Codes: (from the Latin *codex*, book) are the rules that the religious community follows. These rules can involve customs such as what foods to eat or clothing to wear. But, codes are also the ethical principles, or morals, that the community follows. In the Judeo-Christian tradition, one could see the Ten Commandments as an example of a code.

Cultus: (from the Latin word *cultus*, meaning worship or reverence) refers to the ways in which a community worships its god or gods. So, cultus is the term for the rituals that a religious group uses to express what they believe in the creed and hold to in the code they follow. For example, in the Christian tradition, one very important part of the cultus is known as the Eucharist, a religious service in which bread and wine (or grape juice, in some cases) are consecrated, or made holy, by a presiding priest or minister, and then shared among those who are present.

Community: (from Latin, *communitas*, partnership or fellowship) is the term for the group of people who gather together and share a common creed, code, and cultus. Sometimes, what is essential to the nature of such a group is a shared ethnic background; according to Albanese, this is particularly true in ordinary religion, as "such communities tend to be ethnic or cultural (South Asian Indians, African Americans, Polish people) uniting those who share a common land, history and language." At other times, it is that they share a formalized system of beliefs that they have learned. These communities are commonly referred to as churches, denominations, or sects. Albanese says that in extraordinary religion, "such communities, especially in the West, tend to be identified with formal institutions (Catholic, Methodist, Adventist)."[10]

Thus, religion can be seen as a system of parts that function as a whole to give a person meaning—to help the individual understand his or her place among others and in relation to a divinity or supernatural power or powers. Albanese concludes with this definition of religion: it is a "system of symbols (creed, code, cultus) by means of which a people (community) locate themselves in the world with reference to both ordinary and extraordinary powers, meanings and values."[11]

USEFUL CONCEPTS AND TERMS

As we begin to discuss the study of religions, there will be some terms with which you may be only slightly familiar, but which will be necessary for you to master in order to really understand the theories we will examine. Let's look at some of those terms:

Myth: From the Greek, *mythos*, a talk, tale, or story. In our current usage, a myth refers to a story; it is important to recognize that a myth is not necessarily untrue. While a myth may not be *literally* true, it does communicate a greater truth in religious traditions—what might be called the wisdom of the generations. Usually, myths are symbolic stories "about the origins and destiny of human beings in the world; myth relates human beings to whatever powers they believe ultimately govern their destiny and explains to them what the powers expect of them."[12]

Ritual: In speaking about religion, authors frequently refer to rituals. A religious ritual has been defined by Esposito, et al., as "*careful acts* that, in their own right, *tie and bind* people to each other and to cosmic meaning," as well as, "offering , for instance, precious gifts to supernatural beings, making pilgrimages to sacred places or engaging in meditation or other disciplines of spiritual practice."[13]

Orthopraxy: From the Greek, *orthos*, straight, and *praxis*, deed or practice. This term refers to acting in the way that one is supposed to act. Concern with orthopraxy is more typical of primitive religions, but it is still present in modern religions. Orthopraxy includes offering sacrifices, observing purity rituals, and following certain morals. So, as discussed in a previous chapter, for an ancient Roman pagan, what one believed was not so important; offering ritual sacrifices was.

Orthodoxy: Greek, *orthos*, straight, and *doxa*, notion or opinion. Orthodoxy refers to believing the right doctrine or teachings. These correct beliefs can be found in sacred texts and are explained by religious scholars. Orthodoxy is important in the traditions of Christianity and is seen in the emphasis on creeds (statements of belief) that were developed in the early Church.

Morality: Derives from Latin, *moralis*, morals. This word refers to behaving in the right way. Esposito, et al., observe that in most religious traditions, morality is tied to rituals. They note that "'(r)ight' is often defined by 'rite'—ritual patterns of behavior that keep life sacred." Morality is an essential part of religious practice because "religion is not only about sacred powers, it also describes a way of life the powers require and make possible."[14]

Symbolic Language: A symbol is something that represents something else; religious texts and language often express ideas using symbols. Therefore, it is important to recognize that one cannot take symbolic language literally—this will cause misunderstanding of the symbol's true meaning. For example, in the Book of Revelation in the Christian Bible, one sees reference to a rider on a black horse who is carrying scales; this use of symbolic language has been interpreted by scholars to refer to famine and injustice among those colonized by ancient Rome.

RELIGIOUS STUDIES

Perhaps you are familiar with the term *theology*, which is formed from two words: *theos*, which means God, and *logos*, which can be translated as the study of something; thus, the word refers to the discipline that involves the study of the nature of God and of humankind's relation to that God. Actually, this is a term that is generally used only in the Christian tradition, and theologians study philosophy, ethics, and history, as well as ancient languages and scriptures, including texts (which they translate into modern languages) that have been recovered from archaeological sites; they also examine applications of religious principles to daily life. The goal of their scholarship is to make Christianity more understandable to Christians. But as John Hinnells, a religious studies scholar, notes: "... there is comparable activity in most religions, certainly in Islam, Judaism and Zoroastrianism." He even mentions that another scholar talks about "Buddhology."[16] The key idea here is that theology looks at just one religious tradition—the tradition which that theologian or scholar practices.

Religious studies is different: it aims to study the various religions so as to understand more about the nature of religion generally and also to examine the different religious traditions individually. Friedrich Max Müller (1823–1900) was a German scholar of Sanskrit and comparative religion, who once famously observed that: "He who knows one, knows none."[17] Thus, if a person studies only one religion, then she will not understand what is unique about her own religious practice and is not studying *religion*; so, to understand what *religion* is all about, a person must study various religions. Hinnells explains that it "is only through some element of comparison that we appreciate just what is, and is not, characteristic of religions generally and what is specific to that religion."[18]

How did religious studies develop? Though it has roots in some disciplines that are ancient, it can be seen to have begun its emergence in the Age of Enlightenment. Prior to that period, however, some critical changes had occurred in the West that should also be noted. In the 1500s, the Protestant

Reformation developed, when a schism (a split) occurred in Christianity and religious leaders such as the German Martin Luther (1483–1546), the Swiss Huldrych Zwingli (1484–1531), and the Frenchman Jean Calvin (1509–1564) sought the reform of the Catholic Church and questioned its authority in some critical areas. The effect was to encourage many to realize that their religion (Roman Catholicism) was not such a monolithic reality. Additionally, beginning in the 1400s, before the Reformation, but continuing through the 1600s, was the Age of Discovery, when there were many seafaring explorers who found new places with native religions in other parts of the world. Prior to these discoveries, Europeans had studied about the ancient religions such as those of the Babylonians, Romans, and Greeks and the three contemporary religions of Judaism, Islam, and Christianity. But now they saw that other cultures had different religions with which they were not familiar—for example, religions such as Confucianism, Buddhism, or Hinduism—which they tried to understand; they found that these religions could not be easily dismissed.

ENLIGHTENMENT THOUGHT

It will be recalled that, during the Age of Enlightenment, the trend was to encourage people to use their reason and to think for themselves; that is to say, that one should not accept something simply because an authority like the Church declared it was so. As they examined religion, some Enlightenment philosophers known as rationalists believed that God could be known through reason and that reason could be used to examine critically the Bible, which, before that time, was seen as solely the revealed Word of God and not subject to human evaluation. Thus, there was a view held among some Enlightenment thinkers that religion was actually rational—this is to say they thought it made sense ethically and socially to follow the religious principles like the Ten Commandments. Religion was identified with morals.

But during the Age of Enlightenment, there was another group of thinkers known as the Romanticists, who rejected this view of the rationalists. One German scholar who applied this perspective to religion was Friedrich Schleiermacher (1768–1834). He instead held that feeling was "the source and essence of religion." In other words, Schleiermacher asserts that religion "stems from an experience that links the individual with the infinite (God) in a feeling of unification." This feeling can be described as "expansive, overwhelming and … oceanic."[19] Hence, for Schleiermacher, the source of religion is feeling, not reason.

This feeling described by Schleiermacher is the kind of thing one might experience after climbing a mountain and seeing the vista or when someone is by the sea on a clear night and sees the breathtaking canopy of stars in the heavens. Though it is not easy to describe such a feeling, it can lead persons to feel dependent on something which is infinitely beyond themselves. Beethoven, in the choral ode of his Ninth Symphony, popularly known as "Ode to Joy," incorporates a poem by Friedrich Schiller (1759–1805), which has the following lines that describe the oceanic feeling: "Brothers, over the star-tented sky must dwell a loving Father. Do you fall down before Him? Oh, World, do you sense the Creator? Seek Him above the star-tented sky! Above the stars must He dwell!"[20]

A sea change in views about religion followed with the writings of Ludwig Feuerbach (1804–1872). He was a philosopher, who as a young man told his father he wanted to study theology with Schleiermacher, but then was eventually drawn in another direction. He achieved much notoriety after he wrote a book, *Essence of Christianity* (1841), in which he argues that "religion is an alienated form of human self-consciousness insofar as it involves the relation of human beings to their own essence as though to a being distinct from themselves."[21] Feuerbach thought that religion starts with the conception of the infinite (i.e., god) which "takes on a life of its own (and) … we allow ourselves to forget that *we* are the ones who conceived it."[22]

Feuerbach, then, is saying that people create this god and project their own qualities onto the god; he also rejects Schleiermacher's emphasis on the significance of feelings. Although raised as a Christian, he rejects religion because "man's God is nothing other than the deified essence of man" and "(t)herefore, we ought to cast aside the superstitious attitudes toward God that interfere with the full development of humanity."[23] The impact of Feuerbach's radical approach will be seen in the work of later thinkers such as Karl Marx.

STUDY OF RELIGION

In the following sections, we will present quite a variety of perspectives on how to study religion. As you read through the descriptions of the key ideas of these different scholars, just try to get the big picture, which is that there are various ways of looking at and understanding the complex phenomena of religion. And if the work of a particular scholar interests you, then, it would be good to read some of that person's own writings.

The study of religion developed along two streams of thought. Some scholars focused on religion itself; sometimes they are known as "religionists." The other group has examined religion using the lens of the social sciences. In this section, we'll begin with the work of Max Müller, a religionist who envisioned the development of an all-encompassing "science of religion" and encouraged the comparison of different religions. Max Müller (1823–1900) was a German philologist (i.e., someone who studies historical linguistics) who translated the *Vedas*, Hindu scriptures, in the mid-19th century, when Europeans became fascinated by the world of the Indian subcontinent. He was interested in explaining polytheism (which comes from two Greek words, *polus*, many, and *theoi*, gods) which is found in the Hindu writings. Müller thought that it was people's experience of the infinite that resulted from their familiarity with nature, especially the sun. He hypothesizes that the names for these aspects of nature, things like the sun, came to be considered godlike through an error, or what he calls a "disease of language." Müller is remembered for creating the term the "science of religion," but his approach fell in to disuse.[24]

Rudolf Otto (1869–1937), another German scholar, built upon Schleiermacher's work, writing a book entitled, *The Holy*. Otto asserted that religious experience, or encountering "the Holy," is unique and can be explained by other things; it is an experience of the *numinous* (Latin, *numen*, divine presence or deity), which means an experience with a strongly religious or spiritual quality. The "Holy" or "Sacred" means that "which is separate from the empirical world," which, when it is described by persons "is always framed in power which attracts and repels us, so we are frightened and also curious about the sacred."[25] Otto uses a Latin expression to describe the irrational experience of the numinous: it is a *mysterium tremendum et fascinans*—it is a mystery that is both frightening and fascinating.

Otto thought that the experience of the numinous, while irrational, could induce persons to create what he called schemas, rational religious ideas that arise from these experiences. Herling gives an illustration of a schema developing when the experience of "the fearful nature of a god's holiness takes shape as a belief in god's power, righteousness and goodness; and the feeling of nouminous fascination transforms into divine 'love, mercy, pity, comfort.'" Herling also notes that Otto wanted people to "*learn about* religion by having a religious experience ... (f)or contemporary scholars, this motivation appears unabashedly *theological*."[26] Thus, he is saying that, while Otto has identified the religious experience as the way to learn about religion, modern students of religion would not be expected to take such an experiential approach, but rather, a more objective one.

Anthropology

Another perspective about how to conduct the study of religion follows from the work of those scholars who utilized the tools of the social sciences to examine it. We'll begin by looking at the work of a scholar who would be among the founders of the discipline of anthropology, Edward Burnett Tylor (1832–1917). Tylor was an Englishman who traveled to Mexico for reasons of health and did fieldwork there in the 19th century. He is known for his use of the concept of *animism*, which relates to the belief that the souls of individuals are able to continue existing after death; animism also refers to the belief in the existence of "other spirits" such as deities that control events in the material world and the afterlife. An important contribution of Tylor is that he "hypothesized in 1871 that people all over the world, regardless of their cultural traditions, require a procedure for handling the remains of a deceased family member."[27] Such a procedure is a rite, almost invariably a religious ritual. Later, Arnold van Gennep (1873–1957) would develop this theme with his concept of "rites of passage," which he uses "to describe these universal human experiences, for which all religious traditions provide procedural guidelines and networks of meaning."[28]

The rites of passage described by van Gennep are the rituals that mark the transition from one social role to another; in moving to another social role, such as when one reaches puberty, becomes a parent, or dies, a person crosses a "threshold," or *limen* (Latin for threshold). There are three consecutive stages in a rite of passage: (1) Pre-liminal Stage: here, there is a ritual involving separation from normal life and its role, being purified, and prepared; (2) Liminal Stage: rites for this stage mark the transition such as wearing special clothing, cutting one's hair, or getting tattooed, all of which signify movement to a new role or status; (3) Post-liminal Stage: reincorporates or returns the person to the community with a new status, and social celebrations mark the completion of the transition.

In evaluating the impact of the work of Tylor and van Gennep on ritual and rites of passage, the religious studies scholars Hecht and Biondo have concluded that the "major life-cycle rituals studied by E. B. Tylor and Arnold van Gennep motivated theologians, sociologists, and historians to attempt to formulate universal definitions of religion."[29] In other words, their work encouraged scholars to try to learn more about religion generally.

Psychology and Sociology

At the turn of the 20th century, a physician, philosopher, and psychologist from Harvard named William James (1842–1910) published his book, *The Varieties of Religious Experience*, which was destined to become a classic in the psychology of religion. James believed that belief in god came from an individual's experience, not from the rational proofs of theology. So, he focuses on individual experiences, for he said that there is "a state of mind, known to religious men, but to no others, in which the will to assert ourselves and hold our own is displaced by a willingness to close our mouths and be as nothing in the floods and waterspouts of God."[30] Thus, James's view of the study of religion is that "individual, interior, non-rational experience is more profound than general, objective, or intellectual conceptions … so if we wish to understand the power of something like the Bible, then we must discern the experiences that generated it."[31]

Emile Durkheim (1858–1917) was a French sociologist who is familiar to students of criminal justice because of his work in relation to anomie. However, though an atheist, he also studied religion and published a book in 1912, *The Elementary Forms of Religious Life*, in which he argues that religion is a "social phenomenon" and that "it operated to maintain social stability through the devotion of its adherents."[32] Durkheim studied primitive cultures and concluded that religion arose because of human (i.e., not divine) action and "was essential to society, whether traditional or modern ... therefore, (he) did not see it as something that could ever be outgrown by mankind or something that could be fully separated from society."[33] Judith Fox, a religious studies scholar, also observes that society needs religion "in order to maintain social cohesion and to strengthen collective feelings and ideas." As a result, religion serves the need of society. Further, she notes that Durkheim believed that religion would change in response to the development of a society, as science would challenge archaic religious views, "(b)ut new religious forms, more in keeping with the times, would inevitably arise to take their place."[34]

Durkheim is remembered for his explication of the concepts of the **sacred** and the **profane**. He says that the "division of the world into two domains, the one containing all that is sacred, the other all that is profane, is the distinctive trait of religious thought." What is the sacred? It can be beliefs, myths, or legends, but also gods or spirits, or "a rock, a tree, a spring, a pebble, a piece of wood, a house, in a word anything can be sacred. A rite can have this character."[35] The sacred must be separate from the profane, and it can be either good or evil (as can the profane). Herling observes that the sacred, a realm "which can infuse any worldly object, must be protected because it is somehow special and worthy; the other (i.e., the profane) is associated with the everyday, the mundane, or even the unpleasant."[36]

In examining primitive religions, Durkheim focuses on a concept known as totemism. By this concept, he "described how a symbol, or collective representation, can contain a sacred power able to unite a community."[37] A totem is: (1) a "plant, animal, or natural object that serves as a symbol of a clan or family among certain peoples; or, (2) a representation of this."[38] So, there are two aspects to the meaning of totem: in the first, it "symbolizes in visible and outward form the totemic principle, *mana*, that is god." And in the second meaning, it "marks off one clan from another; it is the 'flag of the clan.'"[39]

In tribal cultures, a totem such as an animal like a lion or bear becomes the symbol of belonging to the clan, and therefore, becomes sacred; the totem "possesses power ... (this) refers to the impersonal force that stands behind the totem."[40] Tribal members believe that a totem's power would protect the clan, and it joins them together as each member shares in the power brought by the totem, but none possesses it. There will be myths and rituals that incorporate the totem and "its representation appears everywhere: on the objects possessed by members, on their clothing, and even inscribed on their bodies."[41] Thus, it can be said that totems are "mystically charged emblems of group loyalties and that ritual expressed and strengthened the social organism."[42] These rituals practiced by tribal peoples brought about "feelings of dependence on society and of possession by society."[43] To understand this concept as it might apply to the modern nation, Durkheim suggests that one think of a flag and what it can mean to people, as well as how it can motivate people to make great sacrifices.

In summary, though Durkheim studied primitive religion, he believed that, in discovering the origin—or basic causes—of religion, one could apply these same principles to understand contemporary religions. As Herling explains: "The origin is always present *wherever* and *whenever* religion persists because it is a response to—it is caused by—a universal human need."[44]

The German scholar Max Weber (1864–1920) studied jurisprudence and economics was another of the founders of sociology and who also examined religion. His name is likely to be familiar to criminal justice students who have studied research methods and come across his term, *verstehen* (German for to understand), which encourages a researcher to strive to take the point of view of the group that he or she is studying—to walk in their shoes, so to speak.

Weber is well known for his work studying the effects of religion as a motivating force in a society. In his book, *The Protestant Ethic and the Spirit of Capitalism*, which was first published in Germany in 1904, he explains how capitalism was so well developed in Protestant countries, as opposed to countries where another religious perspective such as Catholicism was dominant. Weber argues that Calvinism, with its belief in predestination (i.e., that God foreordains that only some people, who are "the Chosen," go to heaven), created deep anxiety among its adherents over whether they had been chosen for salvation. So, for example, the Puritans, believing that being prosperous was a sign of being among the "Elect" or "Chosen" of God and of having been given salvation, "turned to work 'in their callings' as though their souls depended on it."[45] Thus, Weber shows that "religion, standing as ideology and as conceptual system, supplies motivation within a society … the prevailing conception of deity within a society influences individual and collective actions."[46]

In 1922, he published another book in German, *Religionssoziologie*, which would appear some 40 years later, in English, as *The Sociology of Religion*. Here, in contrast to Durkheim, Weber argues that religion serves the needs of the individual, rather than society. Anne Swidler notes that Weber begins his book by asking the reader to consider how it is that, with material needs so pressing—people need to eat, clothe themselves, and provide shelter—nevertheless "that religious meanings come to matter to human beings?" The answer, for primitive people, is that they sought the help of magicians and others who claimed to be especially powerful, to ensure that they would do well in life. Hence, Swidler observes that for Weber, "magic is the elementary form of religion."[47] Thus, the needs served by this magic in primitive society are for the basic necessities of life. However, in the more developed forms of religion that appear in more sophisticated societies, the needs of the people will be for meaning in life—that is, answers to existential questions.

The magicians in these early religious societies claimed that their special powers, called *charisma* by Weber, were derived from "spirits or other beings are 'concealed behind' and responsible for the activity of the charismatically endowed natural objects, artifacts, animals, or persons."[48] But, eventually, when there "emerges a stable clientele of worshipers—a congregation or cult—(then) do full-time religious officials or priests come into being."

When the magicians are replaced, what also occurs is that a comprehensive explanation of the world, known as metaphysics, develops in place of the "mere techniques" of magicians, and then ethics also develop in place of using coercive force. Robert A. Segal, a religious studies scholar, points out that "the combination of metaphysics and ethics makes religion 'rational'" and is the next stage after magic. Then, after a cult (i.e., a community that shares the religious beliefs) develops "does the concept of a fixed god (singular, powerful, personal, and involved) emerge in place of the magical concept of multiple, weak, nameless, impersonal, and uninvolved fleeting gods." Thus, with the development of a rational religion, one sees a "comprehensive explanation of the world, a prescribed means of securing long-term rewards, and a universal god permanently involved in human affairs."[49] This later stage in the development of religion, with the shift to a focus on "salvation," was "formulated by intellectuals and *virtuosi* ([who]) defined religion as a separable sphere of interests."[50] And in order to preserve the insights and teachings of the virtuosi (this term refers to charismatic religious leaders or prophets) for later generations, an institution arises to do so involving "bureaucracy, routines, meetings, money, etc."[51]

Weber argues that a new problem occurs with the rationalization of religion (this happens when people order religious ideas into a system); so, "people could rationalize magical practices, rituals, techniques of meditation, as well as images of the divine." For example, if people believe that an all-powerful god controls the world, then why is there suffering?[52] If magic fails, the answer is that the magic was not done the right way. But with rationalization and the ordering and consistency of beliefs that follow it, a discrepancy occurs when people believe that the gods want them to behave in a particular way (i.e., following their ethics), which they do—but they still suffer.

Segal explains that Weber thought that "rational religion must explain the failure of gods to respond to the behavior they themselves have dictated ... so the explanation sought is a theodicy."[53] A **theodicy** (from Greek, *theos*, or god, and *dikē*, or justice) is an attempt to argue that god, who is said to be all-powerful, must still probably exist, despite the presence of evil and suffering of good people in the world because the suffering that exists can be explained in some way. Thus, according to Herling, Weber thought that religions were "laying out a 'stand' against a world that often seems to be senseless: the religious 'demand' is that the world order in its totality is, could, and should somehow be a meaningful 'cosmos.'"[54] Nevertheless, Weber thinks that rationalization "would lead to progressive 'disenchantment', and ultimately to a world in which religion would disappear altogether."[55]

At the end of the 19th century, we find one more writer whose thought was influential on the study of religion: Karl Marx; of course, the works of Marx have also been significant in the development of criminological theory.

THEODICY

Human beings have always wondered about this question: Why do bad things happen to good people? And if the divine is good and just, how can this be?

+ This is the problem of theodicy.
+ Theodicy: "the vindication of divine goodness and providence in view of the existence of evil."
+ Ancient Greek roots of theodicy: theos/θεός (God), and dikē/δίκη (justice). The word was first used by Leibniz in the 1700s.

Karl Marx (1818–1883) was a German who was originally interested in philosophy, but later theorized about politics and economics. He accepted Feuerbach's view that God is created in the image of man, but disagreed about the cause of humankind's alienation. Feuerbach thought it was religion that caused alienation, but "Marx's explanation is that religion is a response to alienation in material life, and therefore cannot be removed until human material life is emancipated, at which point religion will wither away."[56] Marx thus thought that the real problem had to do with the inequality in society that capitalism produced, and it was the inequality which caused the alienation that people suffered; religion, however, facilitates the existence of inequality as it "blinds the exploited laborer, so it can only serve the interests of those in charge."[57] Marx once wrote that "religion is the opium of the people," and he was contrasting how the poor needed religion to assuage their "physical and psychological" pains because they could not afford the remedy of the rich, who had *laudanum*, a medication that really was made of the narcotic opium to soothe their pains.[58]

For Marx, religion was harmful to the poor because it "distorts the understanding of the true nature of social relations … by creating the illusion of a transcendental power of perfection that demands submission to the *status quo*," with the result that it "prevents social actors from collectively establishing a social order that would allow them to realize their full potential as social and creative human beings."[59] So, what Marx is saying is that the masses of people are exploited by the rich and that religion prevents the poor from seeing this as a problem; as a consequence of being blinded by religion, they are unable to change the situation for the better.

Marx's view of the solution is for people to change the system. Riesebrodt and Korieczny observe that Marx believes that "in order to overcome alienation, it is not sufficient to criticize religion"; but rather, "one has to overturn the class structure of capitalism and change the mode of production." Further, they say that Marx thought that "(o)nce this happened, religion would disappear and people would be able to understand and control society as rationally as they do nature and they would be free to realize their natures as social and creative beings."[60] It is interesting to note that, in the Soviet Union, where Marx's ideas were part of the underpinning for the government, religion did not disappear as he had predicted, but still flourished underground.

SUMMARY

In this chapter, we have looked at some of the key terms and concepts in the study of religion. Many theoretical perspectives on religion were examined—ranging from those of the late Enlightenment years to current views. There are the views of the religionists, who argue that religion should be studied in its own terms; others use the lenses of different social sciences to understand and explain religion. Some theorists such as Weber argued that eventually religion would eventually pass into history as an artifact of an earlier time in human development. However, that has not happened; religion is still a factor in the lives and experiences of many people around the world. Today, with the increasingly small world that is connected through rapid modes of travel and sophisticated communications technology, religion has become a most important factor in understanding other peoples and their cultures.

KEY TERMS

- Codes
- Creed
- Cultus
- Morality
- Myth
- Orthodoxy
- Orthopraxy
- Religion
- Theodicy
- Theology

REVIEW QUESTIONS

1. What is meant by religious studies?
2. How do Schleiermacher, Müller, and Otto approach the study of religion?
3. What are the contributions of the anthropologists Tylor and van Gennep?
4. What is a theodicy?
5. What do Durkheim, James, and Marx each say about religion?

END NOTES

1. McGuigan, Patrick B., and Randall R. Rader. *A Blueprint for Judicial Reform* (Washington, DC: Free Congress Research and Educational Foundation, Inc., 1981), 341.
2. "religion, *n.*" *Oxford Dictionaries.com,* http://www.oxforddictionaries.com/us/definition/american_english/religion
3. Smith, Huston. *The World's Religions* (New York: HarperCollins Publishers, 1991), 10.
4. 4 Smith, William Cantwell. "*Towards a World Theology: Faith and the Comparative History of Religion*" (New York: Orbis Books, 1989), 48.
5. Hecht, Richard D., and Vincent F. Biondo, eds. "General Introduction: Religion in the Practice of Everyday Life." In *Religion & Everyday Life and Culture,* vol. 1 (Santa Barbara, CA: ABC-CLIO, LLC, 2010), xi.
6. Smith, Jonathan Z. *Imagining Religion: From Babylon to Jonestown* (Chicago: University of Chicago Press, 1982), 54.
7. Matus, Thomas, ed. *Bede Griffiths: Essential Writings* (Maryknoll: Orbis Books, 2004), 31–32.
8. Albanese, Catherine L. *America: Religions and Religion* (Boston: Wadsworth, 2007), 5–6.
9. Albanese, 7.
10. Albanese, 7.
11. Albanese, 9.
12. Esposito, John L., Darrell J. Fasching, and Todd Lewis. *World Religions Today* (New York: Oxford University Press, 2006), 7.
13. Esposito et al., 9.
14. Esposito et al., 11.
15. Hinnells, John R. "Why Study Religion?" In *The Routledge Companion to the Study of Religion,* ed. John Hinnells (New York, Routledge, 2010), 13.
16. Hinnells, 13.
17. Swatos Jr., William H., ed. "Müller, (Friedrich) Max." *The Encyclopedia of Religion and Knowledge* (Walnut Creek, CA: Altamira Press, 1998), 315.
18. Hinnells, 14.
19. Herling, Bradley L. *A Beginner's Guide to the Study of Religion.* (New York: Continuum International Publishing Group, 2007), 51.
20. Author's translation of "Brüder, über'm Sternenzelt Muß ein lieber Vater wohnen. Ihr stürzt nieder, Millionen? Ahnest du den Schöpfer, Welt? Such'ihn über'm Sternenzelt!"
21. Gooch, Todd. "Ludwig Andreas Feuerbach," *The Stanford Encyclopedia of Philosophy* (winter 2013 edition), Edward N. Zalta, Ed. URL = http://plato.stanford.edu/archives/win2013/entries/ludwig-feuerbach/
22. Herling, 75.
23. Placher, William C. *A History of Christian Theology: An Introduction* (Louisville: John Knox Press, 1983), 278.
24. Glazier, Steven D. "Anthropological Study of Religion." In *World Religions: Continuities and Transformations,* ed. Peter Clarke and Peter Beyer (New York: Routledge, 2009), 29.

25. Hecht, Richard D., and Vincent F. Biondo, eds. "General Introduction: Religion in the Practice of Everyday Life." In *Religion & Everyday Life and Culture*, vol. 1, x.

26. Herling, 52–53.

27. Hecht and Biondo, x.

28. Hecht and Biondo, x.

29. Hecht and Biondo, x.

30. James, William. *The Varieties of Religious Experience: A Study in Human Nature* (Rockville, MD: Arc Manor, 2008), 42.

31. Herling, 53–54.

32. "Religion." *International Encyclopedia of the Social Sciences*. Ed. William A. Darity Jr., 2nd ed., vol. 7. (Detroit: Macmillan Reference USA, 2008), 159–162. *Gale Virtual Reference Library*. Web. 30 Sept. 2014.

33. Fox, Judith. "Secularization." In *The Routledge Companion to the Study of Religion*, 308.

34. Fox, 309.

35. Durkheim, Emile. *The Elementary Forms of Religious Life*, trans. Joseph Ward Swain (New York: Dover Publications, 2008), 37.

36. Herling, 55.

37. Hecht and Biondo, xi.

38. *The American Heritage Dictionary*, 2nd College Edition, s.v. "totem."

39. Pickering, W. S. F. *Durkheim's Sociology of Religion: Themes and Categories* (Cambridge: James Clarke & Co., 2009), 237.

40. Herling, 57.

41. Herling, 57.

42. Hackett, Rosalind I. J. "Anthropology of Religion." In *The Routledge Companion to the Study of Religion*, 166.

43. Segal, Robert A. "Myth and Ritual." In *The Routledge Companion to the Study of Religion*, 387.

44. Herling, 56.

45. Davis, Winston. "Sociology: Sociology of Religion [First Edition]." *Encyclopedia of Religion*, ed. Lindsay Jones, 2nd ed., vol. 12 (Detroit: MacMillan Reference, 2005), 8490–8497. *Gale Virtual Reference Library*. Web. Oct. 2, 2014.

46. Capps, Walter H. "Society and Religion [First Edition]." *Encyclopedia of Religion*, ed. Lindsay Jones, 2nd ed., vol. 12 (Detroit: MacMillan Reference, 2005), 8461–8470. *Gale Virtual Reference Library*. Web. Oct. 2, 2014.

47. Swidler, Anne. "Foreword." In *The Sociology of Religion* (Boston, Beacon Press, 1993), x.

48. Swidler, xi.

49. Segal, Robert A. "Sociology: Sociology and Religion [Further Considerations]." *Encyclopedia of Religion*. Ed. Lindsay Jones, 2nd ed., vol. 12 (Detroit: MacMillan Reference, 2005), 8487–8490. *Gale Virtual Reference Library*. Web. Oct. 2, 2014.

50. Riesebrodt, Martin, and Mary Ellen Korieczny. "Sociology of Religion." In *The Routledge Companion to the Study of Religion*, 148.

51. Herling, 61.

52. Swidler, xiv.

53. Segal, 8487–8490.

54. Herling, 62.

55. Fox, 387.

56. Wolff, Jonathan. "Karl Marx." *The Stanford Encyclopedia of Philosophy* (summer 2011 edition), Edward N. Zalta, ed. URL = http://plato.stanford.edu/archives/sum2011/entries/marx/

57. Herling, 77.

58. Christiano, Kevin J., William H. Swatos, and Peter Kivisto. *Sociology of Religion: Contemporary Developments* (Lanham: Rowman & Littlefield Publishers, 2008), 6.

59. Riesebrodt and Korieczny, 146.

60. Riesebrodt and Korieczny, 147.

4. The Study of Religion in the Modern World

By William J. Cook Jr.

RELIGIOUS STUDIES IN THE 20TH CENTURY

In this chapter, we'll look at the work of modern scholars of religious studies. At the turn of the 20th century, two psychologists appear whose thought has been influential on the study of religion: Freud and Jung. The work of Freud has also been significant in the development of criminological theory. We'll begin by looking at the work of each of these men.

Then, we'll examine the work of scholars who wrote during the last half of the 20th century. First, we will look at Mircea Eliade, who focused on what is known as the "phenomenology" of religion, then at some of the ideas of Ninian Smart, as well as on the work of two anthropologists, Geertz and Turner, who examine myth and ritual. Finally, we'll review the work of two scholars, Kimball and Gritsch, who explore some of the possible reasons explaining what happens when religion becomes "evil."

EARLY 20TH-CENTURY SCHOLARS

Sigmund Freud (1856–1939) was an Austrian physician who founded the psychoanalytic school of psychotherapy. He formulated a hydraulic model of the mind, which he divided into conscious and unconscious parts; the unconscious part of the mind is the repository of instinctual impulses and has the capability of not only

Figure 4.1: This archetypal image of a mandala, created by a patient of C.G. Jung, is a symbol of healing produced by one's unconsciousness.

influencing, but even controlling, behavior. In Freud's model, the mind develops as a child grows, and it has three parts: the *id* (instincts); the *ego* (the "I," which is conscious and controls behavior); and the *superego* (conscience). Freud once remarked that people knew they had spirits, but that he had to show them that they also had instincts.[1]

Fundamental to Freud's view of religion is that it "originates in the helplessness and anxiety of childhood and early manhood."[2] Further, he thought that religion was an illusion because "there are no referents for religious beliefs about transcendent entities such as God, the dao, and so forth … belief in God, for him, is simply a projection of the father image."[3] Thus, Freud hypothesized that a person's infantile fantasies and hopes are the source of religion; this is because, in the words of Dan Merkur, Freud thought that "a personal God is, psychologically, nothing other than an exalted father."[4] This is saying that human beings are terrified by forces of nature and by death, so, as Herling explains, people want comfort and reassurance and "need BIG parents: we call out to divine presences for help and conceive them to care for us, but they can also be quite fearsome."[5] Consequently, religion brings comfort in the face of cosmic anxieties.

Thus, though he saw religion as a "mass delusion," still Freud suggests that it is useful for society. Religion can socialize people. Civilization requires the control of our instincts—that is, to keep in check impulsive behavior that would be disruptive to society or harmful to others; Merkur observes that "religious ideals promote civilization through their internalization in the Superego … because the Superego turns aggression against the self in the form of guilt (and) that makes civilization possible."

Probing the parental images of God that Freud discussed, research finds that some people have an image of god that is consistent with the sexuality of the preferred parent; so, if the preferred parent is the mother, then God is imaged as maternal, and if the preferred parent is the father, then God is seen as paternal. Also, it has been found that "cultures that favor accepting, loving, and nurturing parenting styles tend to favor benevolent deities, while rejecting parental styles are associated with malevolent deities." Additionally, studies show that "Catholics tend to find God more maternal than Protestants do."[6]

Carl Gustav Jung (1875–1961) was a Swiss physician who was initially Freud's student, but eventually, after rejecting parts of his mentor's approach, developed the school of analytic psychology. He also has a more positive view of religion.

Jung accepts Freud's model of the unconscious, but he postulates that the unconscious has two parts. First, there is the personal unconscious, which stores our personal experiences and memories, but secondly, he identifies a part he calls the *collective unconscious*, which is the location of a kind of universal genetic memory of humankind. As one experiences his or her unconscious, the person can be overwhelmed by its power and misidentify the source of that power as a god. Herling notes that Jung believes that humans project these images onto the world, too, and says, "for example, the sun becomes a god because it is emblematic of basic human experiences of life and death (sunrise and sunset)." Thus, in a way, Jung's perspective is reminiscent of Feuerbach's view: that persons project their own image onto god.

Symbols are important in Jungian theory. He sees a symbol as "a term, a name, even a picture ... that possesses specific connotations in addition to its conventional and obvious meaning."[7] Jung also states that "we constantly use symbolic terms to represent concepts we cannot define or fully comprehend."[8] Symbols appear in dreams, and they serve as vehicles for the expression of emotion. Most significantly, according to Herling, symbols also "transmitted a universal wisdom that eluded the conscious mind."[9] An essential type of symbol would be what Jung refers to as an **archetype**. The archetypes are located in the collective unconscious and become manifest through images in dreams or art, for example. Archetypes can be said to be the ways in which the wisdom of humanity has been preserved for all generations.

There are three major archetypes: "the *anima* which represents the feminine; the *animus* which represents the masculine; the *shadow* that represents all that is rejected as evil and projected onto the other."[10] Additionally, Jung identifies other archetypes as the self (which is the union of the conscious and unconscious), the father, the mother, the child, the sage, the hero, and the trickster. Merkur observes that Jung thought that "both dreams and religious experiences are instances of direct and unmediated manifestations of archetypal images."[11] By entering therapy, a person can gain distance from archetypal images—that is, to experience them "without being compelled to act on their basis." Merkur also mentions that Jung concludes that "(o)rganized religion is semi-therapeutic ... people are effectively defended and shielded against immediate religious experience," which would involve breaking through an archetype in such a way as to be disruptive for a person's life and possibly mental health.[12]

According to Jung, the problem today is that the "modern man has lost all the metaphysical certainties of his mediaeval brother, and set up in their place the ideals of material security, general welfare, and humanness."[13] He also said:

"(h)ealing may be a religious problem."[14] Merkur argues that "Jung considered God and the Self to be archetypes ... (and) he acknowledges that the two were indistinguishable," so this is significant because Jung's "concept of Self was adapted from the Hindu *atman*, which is one with God (*Brahman*) and equivalent to the mind and substance that are the cosmos."[15] And, according to Herling, Jung's view of therapy is "the creation of a personal myth, one in which the patient could get in touch with powerful symbols and become a hero or heroine—a savior to oneself ... what else is 'linking-back' to archetypes but the essence of *religion?*"[16]

LATE-20TH-CENTURY SCHOLARS

Originally from Romania, Mircea Eliade (1907–1986) became one of the most influential scholars in the study of religion during the 20th century. He was a phenomenologist (phenomenology is the attempt to study something as it appears, rather than through the lens of a perspective such as psychology). Eliade rejected "approaches that sought to explain religion in terms of something that was not religious, such as society or the human psyche."[17] Eliade developed what he called the "morphology of the sacred" (from the Greek, *morphe*, form, and *logos*, the study of), which indicates that "he wanted to identify the basic forms through which the sacred manifested itself in human consciousness."[18] Therefore, he examined myths about origins (known as cosmogonies) and the rituals that expressed these myths. For Eliade, by reenacting the story told in a myth about the origins of the world and of a people, the participants were trying to get back to that original time and experience the sacred.

Eliade speaks about the "two modes of being in the world"—the **sacred** and the **profane**. He argues, according to Douglas Allen, that "religion always entails the attempt of religious beings to transcend the relative, historical, temporal, 'profane' world by experiencing a 'superhuman' sacred world of transcendent values."[19] So, when people listen to myths, and especially when they act out the stories of the myths, they "magically return to the time of the myth ... it is when the world is fresh that gods, the creators of myth, are believed to be closest at hand." Robert A. Segal concludes that "the return to this 'primordial time' reverses the subsequent separation from the gods, a separation that is equivalent to the fall, and is regenerative spiritually."[20]

Eliade believes that myth is not simply found among primitive peoples, but is "panhuman" and found in the present world, too; myths are something that people in all times create. Thus, Segal observes that Eliade would cite "modern plays, novels and movies with the mythic theme of yearning to escape from the everyday world into another, earlier one."[21]

Figure 4.2: Blake's *Canterbury Pilgrims* is an image of persons on a religious quest traveling to a religious site.

Another term Eliade uses is hierophany (from Greek, *hieros*, holy, and *phaino*, to appear) to describe objects or forms that could contain sacred power. Examples of hierophanies could be places, trees, eating, one's country, personal gods, or cosmic gods. Eliade speaks of modalities of the sacred (modality signifies a way that the sacred appears or is known), which William E. Paden lists as: (a) sacred space; (b) sacred time; and (c) sacredness of nature. **Sacred space** refers to the way that religions "endow special places as gateways or connectors to the world of the sacred ... it can be natural ... like rivers or mountains or they be human constructions like shrines and temples." **Sacred time**, or mythic time, comprises "ritual or festival occasions when believers step into the revered 'great time' of the founders and gods ... (it) can be accessed periodically through ritual 'openings.' ... (i)n this way the world is renewed and empowered." **Sacredness (sacrality) of nature** means that the sacred can be understood by looking at nature. There are the "infinity and transcendence of the sky, fecundity of the earth, ... the solubility and creativity of water ... these 'systems of symbolism' form connections with various religious motifs." Paden gives these examples of the connections of nature to myths: creator gods are connected with the sky, goddesses with the Earth, and water with baptismal rebirth.[22]

Ninian Smart (1927–2001), who was born in England to Scottish parents, also thought that focusing on **phenomenology** (i.e., the description of experience without explanation) would be the best way to study religion. He "emphasized suspension of one's own value judgments ... regarding religious truth claims and the need for phenomenological empathy in understanding and describing religious phenomena of others" because "religion expresses many dimensions of human experience."[23]

When studying religion, Smart identifies seven dimensions that constitute religion. These are: doctrinal, mythological, ethical, ritual, experiential, institutional, and material. So, for example, as one studies a particular religion, he or she should examine what its doctrines have to say, what the "myths" are that it espouses, as well as its ethics, its rituals, and so forth to understand that religion. For Ninian Smart, when one studies religion, she will find that the "study of religion is properly the study of worldviews."[24]

The anthropologist Victor W. Turner (1920–1983) is remembered for his work adapting van Gennep's rites of passage and also for his work examining rituals; here, we'll look at one such ritual, the pilgrimage.

Some members of religious groups are drawn to make what are known as "pilgrimages"; these are long journeys, usually to a sacred place. A pilgrimage can be considered a type of rite of passage. Turner suggests that such a journey could create what he calls *communitas*, which is a feeling of intense comradeship and equality among those experiencing the rite of passage. The reason for this is that, during the ritual, a person leaves behind his or her identity and status, becomes submissive to religious leaders during the ritual, and consequently tends to feel a bonding to others going through the same experience, since they have left the usual structures behind. They all enter a "liminal space" (recall that *limen* in Latin means threshold) during the pilgrimage; it is here that a person can experience the deeper realities in life. According to Herling, Turner's work "provides us with a theory that attempts to explain where *the sacred core* of religious life comes from: from ritual … and in particular, from rituals that mix up our everyday experience and existence."[25]

The American anthropologist Clifford Geertz (1926–2006) attempts to shift the emphasis away from looking for causal explanations to an approach that seeks to understand the meaning of symbols. One of his concepts influential in the study of religion is what he calls **thick descriptions**, which involve "identifying local knowledge and 'reading' culture as a text, as well as his accounts of religion as a cultural system."[26]

According to religious studies scholar Bradley L. Herling, Geertz sees religion as a system of symbols (symbols are things that represent ideas such as a ring representing unending love) and that "religious traditions provide a comprehensive map of the world and how to live in it." Herling says that in Geertz's view, "as a system of symbols," then religion "provides both a model of the world we inhabit (it describes it) and a *model* for our activity in the world (it recommends how to shape it)." Herling continues by observing that Geertz believes religion helps people find meaning in a world of suffering;[27] for, as Gregory Alles notes, Geertz thought that "humans need existential meaningfulness: they need to explain, endure, or justify their experiences."[28] The answers are found in religion, and it cultivates belief in these answers through ritual. For it is in ritual that "the symbols, the 'models of the world' and the 'models for life', the 'moods and motivations' are evoked, and a sense of order and meaning is cultivated."[29]

"TOXIC" AND "EVIL" RELIGION

In this section, we turn away from the work of social scientists and examine two modern paradigms of unhealthy religion that were developed by theologians; two theologians identify signs of "evil" or "toxic" religion—that is, religion that can bring suffering, violence, or strife in its wake. Though somewhat newly developed, these paradigms may serve as guides for later research about destructive religion.

In his book, *When Religion Becomes Evil* (2002), Charles Kimball, a professor of religion, argues that all religious traditions have done much good in many different ways, but all are vulnerable to becoming corrupt in any of five different ways, which he calls "Warning Signs"; when such corruption happens, the result can easily be violence. Kimball explains that the reason for this happening is that today, we live in a world of religious diversity, global interdependence, political and economic instability, and changing values, which, when combined "with narrow religious worldviews, and the violent patterns of behavior too often manifest in history … you have a volatile mix."[30]

This is a list of the "Warning Signs" that a religion is becoming corrupt:

1. Absolute Truth Claims;
2. Blind Obedience;
3. Establishing the Ideal Time;
4. The End Justifies Any Means;
5. Declaring Holy War.

1. Absolute Truth Claims

Every religion has truth claims that form the basis on which the beliefs structure rests. But religious truth claims about God or the nature of reality rely on language, and language must be interpreted. Authentic truth claims are never as inflexible and exclusive as zealous adherents may insist; thus, when the symbolic nature of language about God is forgotten, religion is easily corrupted.

Rigid truth claims, especially in times of conflict, are often the basis for dehumanizing and demonizing those who differ. Sometimes, people defending Absolute Truth claims about a sacred text will justify behavior that contradicts the principles of the sacred text. For example, Nichiren, founder of a Japanese Buddhist school, thought that the Lotus Sutra was essential and that any of his followers who killed someone who disagreed about the importance of the Lotus Sutra would not suffer the karmic consequences of the action of murder. This contradicts Buddhist precepts.

Thus, the solution to this problem of Absolute Truth Claims is to hold a view of truth that is dynamic and relational; this allows religious people to embrace and affirm foundational truths without necessarily making the religious texts into static and absolute statements.

2. Blind Obedience:

Religious movements that seek to limit the intellectual freedom and integrity of its adherents set the conditions for blind obedience. This happens when individual believers abdicate their personal responsibility and yield to the authority of a charismatic teacher or leader and become enslaved to particular ideas or teachings. This can then set the stage for violence.

An example of how this kind of blind obedience might be demanded is seen in the case of the Japanese religious group, Aum Shinrikyo. Members who questioned the leader of Aum Shinrikyo, a man named Shoko Asahara, were isolated and punished (really, tortured)—thus, others learned to simply obey. Eventually, they followed their leader in his plan to attack the Tokyo subway system with poisonous gas.

Thus, one must be wary of religious movements that seek to limit the intellectual freedom of their members. The likelihood of a religion becoming "evil" is greatly diminished when there is freedom for individual thought and when honest inquiry is encouraged.

3. Establishing the Ideal Time:

It is natural and good for people to have a desire for a more hopeful future, and it happens that religious traditions identify paths toward both short-term and ultimate goals. A problem occurs when the hoped-for ideal time is linked to a specific religious worldview, and the proponents of that worldview come to believe that they know what God wants for them and everyone else. In other words, they feel authorized to impress their model of the way life should be on everyone else—including those who disagree.

An example of this happened with the Taliban in Afghanistan. The Taliban imposed its interpretation of a very strict sharia law, using very harsh punishments. They gained a reputation for being especially oppressive of women, forbidding them from attending school, for example, and also became notorious for public executions. Their restrictions included not allowing televisions and other modern conveniences. The goal of the Taliban was to impose an antimodern ideology on others.

The reality is that none of us is living in an ideal time; of course, that does not mean there is no hope of making things better. Religious traditions can often help improve human circumstances, but care must be taken to ensure that, whatever changes are about to be implemented, these changes are also needed and wanted by those who will experience them.

4. The End Justifies Any Means:

A common way that religion is corrupted—and can become a force for evil—is when the proponents believe that the "end justifies any means," or in other words, that they can do whatever they want to achieve their goals.

According to Kimball, one sees in "healthy" religion that the *end* and the *means to that end* are always connected. Sometimes, however, people focus on just one component of a religion and *it becomes an end in itself*; further, some religious people will become consumed with achieving that end. The sign that this has happened is when compassion for others is lost. An example of this phenomenon would be when one comes to believe that a sacred space must be protected at any cost; another instance would be when the goal is maintaining or reinforcing group identity or protecting the institution or its teachings. An example of "the end justifies any means" happened when, during the clergy sex scandal, members of the Church's hierarchy silenced victims through threats in order to protect the institution from embarrassment.

Kimball notes that in all the major religious traditions, there is an emphasis on treating others with respect and love. The way to prevent the use of the-end-justifies-any-means strategies is to examine the purposes for this behavior in light of religious precepts about respecting and loving others. Thus, when a situation arises in which people are dehumanized or treated as objects, then the intended goals to be achieved by treating people in such a way should be questioned immediately.

5. Declaring Holy War:

Kimball states that declaring a Holy War is a definite sign of a corrupt religion. He argues that authentic religions have at the base of their teachings a promise of peace, both an inner peace for the person who is practicing that religion, but also as a goal for the religion's adherents to attempt to seek peace with others.

In speaking of Holy War, Kimball is really focusing on both Christianity and Islam. He argues that in both traditions, though there are scriptures that can be used to advocate violence, there are other scriptures advocating peace. And, when each of the traditions has waged Holy War, the results have not been beneficial; working for peace brings many benefits to all involved. Thus, Kimball argues that healthy religion speaks not of war, but of the promise of peace with justice.

In summary, Kimball has developed a useful model for looking at religion that has, as he says, become "evil." One may realistically question whether his five warning signs fit all religions equally well; but his approach is an excellent beginning in the attempt to develop a set of diagnostic criteria for identifying unhealthy religious practices.

Next, we'll consider the work of Eric W. Gritsch (1931–2012), who, though born in Austria, was later a theologian in America. In his book, *Toxic Spirituality*

(2009), he looks at "four enduring temptations" to Christianity, the largest religion in the world; in other words, he argues that, when Christians lost their way and wandered into distinctly unchristian behavior, there were four main "toxic Christian traditions" that led them to "ignore, indeed reject the biblical view of Christian life as shaped by the sin of idolatry."[31] Gritsch was in a position to speak authoritatively about this topic as he had grown up during the Nazi years in Europe, a time when mainstream Christianity was eclipsed in both Germany and Austria.

The first toxic tradition is **anti-Semitism**, which Gritsch defines as "the toxic, enduring attitude of 'hostility or prejudice against the Jews.'... (which can be) a theological anti-Judaism and a racist anti-Semitism." Theological anti-Semitism promulgates the view that Christians replaced the Jews as God's chosen people because they had not accepted Jesus Christ as the Messiah. Attempts to convert Jews to Christianity sometimes led to persecutions. Gritsch observes that a "racist anti-Semitism ... secularized the Christian ideology, advocating a myth of a super-race called Aryans destined to rid the world of inferior people best embodied by 'Semites' identified as Jews."[32] Sadly, this caused the Holocaust in Germany.

The second toxic tradition is **fundamentalism**, which Gritsch defines as "the toxic enduring attitude toward scripture and tradition ... that upholds belief in the strictest literal interpretation of the Bible, including its narrative, doctrines, prophecies and moral laws."[33] The essential difficulty that he saw with this viewpoint is that it is based on the assumption that all divine truth is passed along only by tradition and that human reason is unable to arrive at it. The problem with this approach is that it can become very rigid and authoritarian—that is, it can render a person unable to contemplate other viewpoints, such as happened when some of Galileo's scientific discoveries were suppressed by the Church because they contradicted the Bible.

The solution to this problem is to bear in mind that something can be "true," but not necessarily literally so. To understand how there can be different levels of truth, think of the stories we tell children such as "Little Red Riding Hood" or "Jack and the Beanstalk." Though not literally true, each of these stories can communicate a larger truth about how to live one's life.

The third toxic influence is **triumphalism**, defined by Gritsch as "the toxic enduring attitude of an 'excessive exultation over one's success or achievements (used especially in a political context)' [and involves] the issue of the relationship between spiritual and secular power."[34] Gritsch believes that triumphalism can occur when there is a fusion of spiritual and secular power, which can give rise to a theocracy or when there is such a separation of the spiritual from the secular that it leads to a disengagement from the world.

The last toxic influence is **moralism**, which Gritsch defines as "the toxic, enduring attitude in ethics, 'the practice of moralizing, especially the showing a tendency to make judgments about others' morality.' ... at stake is the issue of absolute moral control, be it by rational or physical means; the medieval Inquisition used both." Here, "the spiritual poison" is that one believes he or she alone knows what "the Divine moral mandates" are and "how they are to be obeyed."[35] It is an approach that sows fear of punishment by God in order to enforce uniformity among persons; this is done so that the religious leaders can dominate them.

Gritsch concludes his critique of the "spiritual toxins" by suggesting that the way to bring healing when any of the four toxins or poisons has emerged is to identify and expose it so it can be "neutralized like some poisons in a household."

USEFUL CONCEPT FOR STUDYING RELIGION

Finally, we conclude with a suggestion about how you might organize your thoughts as you approach your own study of the various religions. In his book, *God Is Not One*, the religious studies scholar Stephen Prothero suggests a four-part guide—a kind of template—that can be used to understand any given religion you might be studying. The template has these four parts:

1. A *problem*;
2. A *solution* to this problem, which also serves as a religious goal;
3. A *technique* (or techniques) for moving from this problem to this solution;
4. An *exemplar* (or exemplars) who charts this path from problem to solution.

So, if you were studying Christianity, the religion that most Americans practice, then the application of Prothero's four-part guide might look like this:

1. The problem is sin;
2. The solution or goal is salvation;
3. The technique for achieving salvation is some combination of faith and good works; and
4. The exemplars who chart this path are the saints in Roman Catholicism and orthodoxy and ordinary people of faith in Protestantism.[36]

In concluding this chapter, there is one more thing to mention. Some years ago, a scholar named Robert N. Bellah argued that we actually also have what he called a "civil religion" in the United States (in fact, the discussion of civil religion in America started long before Bellah). For example, there is the belief that America is a chosen nation, that we have had a "manifest destiny." Next time you are at a baseball game, see if you detect any of the evidence of our civil religion in the rituals that are followed.

SUMMARY

In this chapter, we have looked at some of the key terms and concepts in the study of religion. Different theoretical perspectives on religion were examined, ranging from those of anthropologists to psychologists. During the twentieth century, psychologists such as Freud and Jung examined religion, sometimes reaching very different conclusions about its value. Freud argued that it was essentially a neurotic behavior, while Jung saw much therapeutic value in religious symbols and practices. A different perspective on function of religion was taken by Eliade who explored the significance of the sacred and the profane as well as myths in human experience.

Turner, who was an anthropologist, saw religion as part of the way that humans make transitions into different life stages and focused on "rites of passage." Geertz, another anthropologist, explored the function of symbols in religious behavior and the usefulness of religion as a cultural system. Finally, Kimball and Gritsch, drawing on backgrounds in religious studies and theology, respond to a question about religion which is so troubling to twenty-first century persons all over the world: why does religion become evil or toxic? Each has developed a different set of symptomatic behaviors or views which tend to create the conditions under which religion becomes problematic.

KEY TERMS

- **Archetypes**
- **Anti-Semitism**
- *Communitas*
- **Phenomenology**
- **Profane**
- **Rites of passage**
- **Sacred**
- **Sacred space**
- **Sacred time**
- **Sacredness of nature**
- **Thick descriptions**

REVIEW QUESTIONS

1. How did Freud understand the function of religion in human psychology?
2. What were Jung's views on archetypes in relation to religion?
3. Explain the difference between the sacred and the profane.

4. How were symbols important in understanding religion, according to Geertz?
5. What make a religion "evil?" What makes it "toxic?"

END NOTES

1. Merkur, Dan. "Psychology of Religion." In *The Routledge Companion to the Study of Religion*, ed. John Hinnells (New York, Routledge, 2010), 188.

2. Merkur, 188.

3. Meister, Chad. "Philosophy of Religion." In *The Routledge Companion to the Study of Religion*, ed. John Hinnells (New York, Routledge, 2010), 112.

4. Merkur, 188.

5. Herling, Bradley l. *A Beginner's Guide to the Study of Religion* (New York: Continuum International Publishing Group, 2007), 80.

6. Merkur, 199.

7. Jung, Carl G., ed. *Man and His Symbols* (New York: Dell Publishing, 1968), 3.

8. Jung, 4.

9. Herling, 84.

10. Merkur, 196.

11. Merkur, 196.

12. Merkur, 197.

13. Jung, C. G. *Modern Man in Search of a Soul*, trans. W. S. Dell and Cary F. Baynes (New York: Harcourt, Inc., 1933), 204.

14. Jung, *Modern Man in Search of a Soul*, 237.

15. Merkur, 197.

16. Herling, 84.

17. Alles, Gregory. "The Study of Religions: The Last Fifty Years." In." In *The Routledge Companion to the Study of Religion*, ed. John Hinnells (New York, Routledge, 2010), , 42.

18. Alles, 42.

19. Allen, Douglas. "Phenomenology of Religion." In *The Routledge Companion to the Study of Religion*, 213.

20. Segal, Robert A. "Myth and Ritual" ." In *The Routledge Companion to the Study of Religion*, ed. John Hinnells (New York, Routledge, 2010), 380.

21. Segal, 380.

22. Paden, William E. "Comparative Religion." In *The Routledge Companion to the Study of Religion*, 231–232.

23. Allen, 214.

24. Alles, 43.

25. Herling, 66.

26. Alles, 44.

27. Herling, 68.

28. Alles, 79.

29. Herling, 69.

30. Kimball, Charles. *When Religion Becomes Evil* (New York: HarperCollins Publishers, Inc., 2002).

31. Gritsch, Eric W. *Toxic Spirituality: Four Enduring Temptations of Christian Faith* (Minneapolis: Fortress Press, 2009), 4.

32. Gritsch, 4.

33. Gritsch, 4.

34. Gritsch, 5.

35. Gritsch, 5.

36. Prothero, Stephen. *God Is Not One: The Eight Rival Religions That Run The World* (New York: HarperOne, 2010), 14.

5. Psychological, Sociological, and Neurological Research Findings About Religious Persons

By William J. Cook Jr.

SOCIAL SCIENCE RESEARCH

Religious Persons

Psychologists and sociologists have been conducting research about different aspects of the lives and beliefs of religious persons for more than a century. In this chapter, we'll look at some of their findings.

It has been found that religious beliefs are typically passed down through the family, as well as through more formal instruction, as happens in the case of Sunday school. Thus, the religious beliefs of children closely resemble that of their parents. In fact, the similarity between the religious beliefs of parents and their children is stronger than for "political, sporting, or other areas of behavior."[1] Some religious groups have a stronger desire than others that their children keep the same faith; it has been found that this value is most prominent among fundamentalist Protestants and Catholics, who tend to "demand more obedience in religious matters and use coercion and corporal punishment to enforce it."[2] Hence, children learn their basic religious beliefs through two types of social learning: modeling by the parents (i.e., showing their children by performing specific religious behaviors) and by parents rewarding children for their participation in religious activities.[3]

The psychologist Gordon Allport (1950) developed a model of religious orientation that proposes a twin-poled model of religiosity

Figure 5.1: *Augustine in Ecstasy* by de Gaspar depicts the 4th century theologian Augustine of Hippo, an intrinsically religious person.

or subjective religion; the key to the model is what can be found in a person's motivation for being religious. The first type of religious person is said to be "intrinsically" motivated, which means that such an individual is someone who really does believe in the tenets of his or her faith and takes it seriously, or as Allport and Ross state, *lives* his religion, because such persons "find their master motive in religion" and consider their other needs "strong as they may be of less ultimate significance" and are "brought into harmony with the religious beliefs and prescriptions." The intrinsically motivated person will embrace a creed or the basic beliefs of his or her religion, and then "endeavors to internalize it and follow it fully."[4]

The "extrinsically" motivated person, on the other hand, "*uses* his religion" and employs it "to provide security and solace, sociability and distraction, status and self-justification." The extrinsically motivated religious person is not concerned about his denomination's creed, which "is lightly held or else selectively shaped to fit more primary needs … . the extrinsic type turns to God, but without turning away from self."[5] Allport and Ross note it would be rare to find a "pure" case of either type.

Other characteristics of religious persons that have been studied are the negative traits of authoritarianism and dogmatism. **Authoritarianism** refers to a person's tendency to be submissive to authority, as well as to being conventional and rejecting outsiders. Adorno et al. (1950) "found that church members, especially Catholics … were more authoritarian than those with no religion and that like other authoritarians were more likely to be racially prejudiced."[6] Recent studies have focused on fundamentalists and authoritarianism. Argyle notes that Altemeyer and Hunsberger (1992) found a correlation of .68 between authoritarianism and fundamentalism, and that this is also characteristic of "Hindus, Moslems, Jews, as well as Christian fundamentalists."[7] He hypothesizes that the reason this correlation between fundamentalism and authoritarianism may exist is that "fundamentalists encourage obedience to authority, conventionalism, self-righteousness, and superiority—all aspects of authoritarianism." Other studies have looked at right-wing authoritarianism (RWA) and conclude that fundamentalists given to authoritarianism become spurred on by a threat to their beliefs. For example, in a study of authoritarianism and religion by Shaffer and Hastings, it was found that their results were "consistent with the literature indicating that threat galvanizes authoritarian tendencies at the individual level."[8]

Milton Rokeach prefers the concept of **dogmatism** to authoritarianism because of limitations that he found with the application of the latter term; dogmatism can be defined as "closed-minded." Rokeach (1955) specifies that dogmatism is: "(a) a relatively closed cognitive organization of beliefs and disbeliefs about reality, (b) organized around

Figure 5.2: *Authoritarian God* by Blake is an image of God as one who metes out punishment for those who have done wrong.

a central set of beliefs about absolute authority which, in turn, (c) provides a framework for patterns of intolerance and qualified tolerance toward others."[9] According to Argyle, dogmatic persons are "rigid in their thinking, intolerant of ambiguity, and unable to deal with new information," and when religious groups were tested on dogmatism, both American Baptists and Catholics "had the highest scores," with nonbelievers scoring the lowest on a dogmatism scale.[10] Additionally, Argyle notes that research conducted by Rokeach (1960) on dogmatism among religious persons suggests that "members of all churches tend to reject members of other churches, and rejected them more if their beliefs were very dissimilar to their own."[11]

There has also been research conducted on the positive effects of religiosity. Religious persons tend to have a lessened fear of death and actually have a slightly higher level of achievement and worldly success.[12] For example, the relationship between religiosity and its prosocial benefits for society, as well as benefits for the individual, have been investigated. Religious persons were found to be more inclined toward charity, cooperation, and volunteerism. Also, religiosity appears to discourage moral laxity and behaviors such as cheating.[13] However, other research has investigated the impact of "in-group" versus "out-group" membership on prosocial behaviors such as generosity among religious persons. It seems that the prosociality of religious persons becomes less prominent when the situation involves "outgroup" members.[14]

Other studies show that generally there appear to be beneficial health effects for the religious person. Ferraro and Albrecht-Jensen (2014) report that, while members of more conservative religious groups manifested poorer health than those belonging to more liberal denominations, "higher levels of religious practice were positively associated with better health, regardless of age …. (and) religion may have both positive and negative effects on health, although in this research the positive effect was stronger."[15] Being religious can make people more emotionally resilient, allowing them to overcome trauma, and typically appears to be beneficial for their mental health. Seybold and Hill (2001) report that a review of studies on the relationship between religiosity and mental health indicates a protective benefit.[16]

Conversions and Deconversions

Generally speaking, adolescence is a turbulent time for most young people; it is a time when new roles are tested and old ones discarded. This phenomenon can be seen in religious behavior as well, as there will be "shifts toward greater or lesser religiosity,"[17] both conversions to religion and deconversions from it. It is among adolescents that conversions most frequently occur. Hood et al. (1996) found that, in the United States and other places, the average age of conversion is about 15 or 16 years old; this trend has remained consistent for more than 40 years.[18] Other research exploring conversion to Islam that was done in England reports that conversions occurred most frequently at the age of 30.[19]

Sudden conversions can occur after individuals attend public religious meetings that are "particularly persuasive or noisy" or when the "soon-to-be" converted person has come to know and been accepted by the new religious group. Argyle notes that even the age of 15 can be explained as "the time when identity formation is taking place very actively."[20] Those who tend to convert frequently have been found to share these characteristics: a weaker relationship with their fathers (as compared to matched unconverted persons) and more socially isolated; a study by Kilpatrick and Shaver (1990) relates that "forty-four percent of individuals who were insecurely attached to their parents were likely to have experienced sudden conversions," and that sudden conversions among older persons (i.e., those over the age of 30) were precipitated by a divorce or other marital problems. It appears that God has become a substitute parent or spouse for some persons in these circumstances.[21]

Other characteristics of persons who have sudden conversions are feelings of guilt, shame, self-doubt, low self-esteem, and depression. It also happens that such a conversion can follow in the wake of a crisis; this was first noted by the psychologist William James about 100 years ago. In the case of converts to **New Religious Movements** (known also as NRMs, these are usually new sects that are not associated with mainstream religious denominations), it has been found that they show "stronger differences in personality than converts to mainstream churches"; according to Argyle, many such converts have problems of anxiety and depression, and "a high proportion are seriously disturbed."[22]

After conversion, those who previously had experienced depression or other dysphoric feelings tend to feel much better. A study by Paloutzian (1981) found that converts tend to have a stronger sense of meaning and purpose in life.[23] In another study (1999), Paloutzian reports that converts did not experience a change in temperament, but did have life-transforming changes in goals, feelings, attitudes, behaviors, and life-meaning.[24]

An example of the kind of life-transforming change that can occur for a convert is seen with drug addicts who desist from drug abuse after converting to an NRM. Argyle notes that many who have joined NRMs have been drug users, but these religious groups "have been successful in making their new members abandon drugs … . a considerable achievement since it is so difficult to cure addictions."[25] Three factors seem to account for the effectiveness of these religious groups in weaning new members from drugs: they offer strong social support in a closed community that is subject to authoritarian discipline.

It also happens that those who convert may later abandon their new religion, a process that has been referred to as **deconversion**. It is common among those who convert to NRMs, and it occurs often within the first two years after conversion. The process of deconversion is described as having five stages by Barbour: (1) loss of specific religious experiences; (2) intellectual doubt, denial, or disagreement with specific beliefs of the religious group; (3) moral criticism, which means rejection of the way of life of a religious group; (4) emotional suffering will include loneliness and grief; (5) disaffiliation from the [religious] community.[26] Janet L. Jacobs (1989) studied 40 individuals who had experienced deconversion from various groups (i.e., Christian, Buddhist, and Hindu) and found that the process involved "breaking ties with the leader and the group" after becoming disillusioned with the leader or the social life of the group. Some of the reasons they were disillusioned with the leader include physical or psychological abuse, emotional rejection, or spiritual betrayal; some of the reasons for disillusionment with the social life of the group include the person's status or position in the group, or even that there were prescribed sex roles.[27]

Religious Experiences

What do religious people experience? One approach is to recognize that there are two types of **religious experience** (sometimes abbreviated as an RE) that people commonly have. The first type is described by Argyle as "the experience of contact with a transcendent being or the presence of the holy other, what Otto (1917) called the *nouminous* experience." The second type is more unitive, and can be "the experience of the immanent unity of all things, sometimes called the 'mystical' experience."[28]

A study by Hay (1982), which was described by Argyle, found that 62 percent of religious experiences happened while a person was alone, with 9 percent in a public place and 7 percent occurring in a communal setting.[29] Greeley (1975) found that religious experiences brought happiness, but occult experiences did not, and instead made the person unhappy. While there are many triggers for religious experiences, distress or depression can be a factor. A common trigger is music, but prayer can be, too, as well as sex, or even having a baby.[30] Argyle reports that religious experiences can be found among children as early as six years old, but tend to increase in frequency with age. Women tend to report having more religious experiences than men; additionally, upper-middle-class people seem to have more religious experiences than unskilled workers, as do college-educated persons report more such experiences than those who drop out of high school.[31]

It happens that only about one-third of persons appear to have one or more religious experiences; the strongest predictor is that the person comes from a religious background. Discussing a study done by Hay and Heald (1987), Argyle notes that about 56 percent of those who attended church had a religious experience, as compared to 26 percent of those who do not; in addition, he observes that those who have religious experiences are "higher in measures of 'cognitive openness', that is that they are open to unusual, unconscious, or illogical aspects of experience."[32] Hay and Heald also found that more women (41 percent) than men (31 percent) reported having had a religious experience, with about one-third of people aged 16–24 reporting a religious experience, as compared to one-half of those over age 65.[33]

In a recently published study, Hay (2002) notes some dramatic changes in the reporting of religious experiences in Britain. In this study, Hay found that, among subjects surveyed in Britain, "over 75% of the sample claimed that were personally aware of a spiritual dimension in their experience." In 1987, in a Gallup poll, the response rate was 48 percent, so this means that the "number of people admitting a spiritual experience ... has increased by 60%." But there is an interesting parallel phenomenon occurring as well: fewer people are going to church; thus, more people are reporting religious experiences, while the very institutions that support those experiences are in significant decline.

According to Hay, the most common experience (55 percent) that people report has to do with meaning: "the recognition of a patterning of events in a person's life that convinces them in some way those events, whether happy or sad ... are part of an unfolding transcendent meaning that is not of their making." A large number of people state they felt the presence of God (38 percent)—an experience that is frequently related to having a serious illness, facing one's own mortality, or grieving a loved one's death. About 37 percent felt that they received help through prayer during times of great distress. For nearly one-third of the people (29 percent), their religious experience was an awareness of a sacred presence in nature, while about one-quarter (25 percent) believed they had been in touch with someone who had died; and about a quarter of the people (25 percent) felt they had been aware of an evil presence (this is a rise of over 100 percent since 1987).

Hay observes that, when people talk about spirituality, "they assume that spirituality has to do with religion—indeed some say that the words are identical in meaning." The question then remains: in a time when fewer people go to church, why is there such a dramatic increase in the number of people reporting religious experiences? Though he does not have a definite answer, Hay does hypothesize that the higher number of persons reporting spiritual experiences does not indicate more people are having these experiences; rather, it probably reflects a greater willingness of people to speak about it today because of a weakening of the taboo in our culture against speaking about religion. Hay notes that this taboo arises from two fears: (1) that those who speak of religious experiences will be targeted by others who want to evangelize them about a more formal or institutional religion; and (2) that they will be laughed at for sharing their spiritual or religious experiences.[34]

Religious experiences are reflective of the culture of the person who has them; different cultures encourage distinctive religious experiences. For example, in Hinduism, there is a "quest for transcendence and union with God through contemplation of God and spiritual disciplines like yoga." In Buddhism, there is a "mystical search for nirvana through loss of self and emptiness." For those practicing Judaism, "the observation of the complex rules and rituals is a source of religious experiences, but there are also mystical traditions such as ascending the ladder through the heavens to the throne of Glory."[35]

What are the effects of religious experiences? One significant effect is a positive mood and happiness; people also feel better about themselves, with less low self-esteem. Another is that persons who have had religious experiences tend to become more altruistic and have more positive attitudes toward other people. Quite often, a religious experience leads to an enhanced religious life.[36]

One question remains: what about religious experiences and mental illness? Less serious mental illness is classified as neurosis; a neurotic is someone who has a disorder that is not caused by a physical disease, but often involves anxiety or depression and results in impaired functioning, but not a break with reality. Pfeifer and Waelty (1999) report the findings of a study of neurotic patients who were religious, which indicate that "the primary factor in explaining neurotic functioning is not their personal religious commitment, but their underlying psychopathology."[37] Thus, the patients' neuroses are a function of psychological dysfunction, not religious commitment. Nevertheless, there are situations when religious beliefs may exacerbate neurotic symptoms; for example, in the case of someone who has neurotic guilt or anxiety and who is overly scrupulous about confessing his sins.

In the case of those with a more serious mental illness known as psychosis, patients have delusions or hallucinations and may attribute such experiences to God or the devil. However, it appears that even they can discriminate between the ideas of religion and illness; it has been reported that such patients who were studied "simultaneously held beliefs about having an illness called schizophrenia. These beliefs were not experienced as incompatible." An example given was that of a woman "who believed that she had an illness called schizophrenia because she sinned." The religious explanation was used to make sense of her circumstances.[38] Quite often, religious imagery appears in the delusions or hallucinations of the mentally ill, and this "can be explained by its [i.e., religion's] central cultural role."[39]

Though most psychiatrists are less religious than their patients, there is a trend today among doctors treating the mentally ill to take a "spiritual history" in addition to the traditional information collected about a patient, as this helps in "understanding an individual's coping strategies."[40] Further, there is a need for those who treat mental illness to cultivate a deeper understanding about spiritual needs and religion. This is especially important in cases involving persons who come from other religious cultures (e.g., a Latin American who believes in the "evil eye," or *mal de ojo*) than our own because of possible misunderstanding. Gupta (2010) mentions a case reported by another psychiatrist, M. Rashed, involving a British man of West African descent who had an intense experience of God that led him to social isolation, fasting, and giving away his property. His experience was diagnosed as an "acute psychotic episode… [and that] transformed a positive existential moment into one of shame and sickness."[41] In another time and place, perhaps this man would have been considered a spiritual seeker rather than mentally ill.

It has been shown that those with theological training are adept at distinguishing "mystical religious experience from psychotic episodes." DeHoff (2013) conducted interviews with pastors and pastoral counselors and reported that they used scripture, creedal beliefs, and awareness of cultural differences to distinguish experiences such as hearing God's voice or seeing visions from mental illness.[42] As Argyle concludes, "in any case, schizophrenia is far rarer than religious experiences, so it could not explain many cases."[43]

Ideas About God

It is important to recognize that while about nine out of ten persons claim to believe in God, different people report having various images of God. Gorsuch (1968) describes the following images of God that persons hold: a stern, loving father; an "omni-concept" of God (e.g., omniscient or all-knowing, omnipotent or all-powerful, etc.); the impersonal God; the kindly father; and the Supreme Ruler.[44] More recently, a study conducted at Baylor University by two sociologists, Paul Froese and Christopher Bader and described in their book, *America's Four Gods: What We Say About God—and What That Says About Us* (2010), identify four images of God. The study involved telephone surveys of a total of nearly 3400 adults, as well as 200 in-depth interviews. Interestingly, the authors also find links between one's image of God and her or his political views.

The first image of God is called the **Authoritative God** and is shared by approximately 28 percent of Americans. Such a God is "engaged in history and meting out punishment to those who do not follow him. Those who follow an Authoritarian God tend to "divide the world into good and evil people" and "appeal to people who are worried, concerned and scared."

The second image is called the **Benevolent God** and is an image shared by approximately 22 percent of the population. The Benevolent God image represents God as "engaged in our world, and loves and supports us in caring for others." For people who are drawn to a Benevolent God, "their God is a force for good who cares for all people, weeps at all conflicts and will comfort all."[45]

The third image is the **Critical God**. This is an image held by approximately 21 percent of the population. The Critical God image is a God who "keeps an eye on this world, but delivers justice in the next." This is an image that is attractive to the poor, powerless, and exploited in this world, as their expectation is that "they'll get theirs" later.

The last image is the **Distant God**; approximately 24 percent of the population share this belief. The Distant God "booted up the universe, then left humanity alone." The study shows that people who hold this view can still be religious; for example, this perspective was common among Jews, Buddhists, and Hindus. This image of God may lead to a greater sense of personal responsibility for events in the world. It may also appeal to those who "identify more with the spiritual and speak of the unknowable God behind the creation of rainbows, mountains, or elegant mathematical theorems." [46]

How these different perspectives affect people's perceptions can be seen by looking at explanations of a natural disaster such as Hurricane Katrina, the storm that savaged New Orleans or an event like the terrorist attack on September 11th, 2001. When asked about such an event, a person holding an Authoritative God image was inclined to "think God had a hand, directly punishing us for society's ways." The individual whose image is that of a Benevolent God tended to "focus on the fireman who escaped, or the people who rebuild homes, or the divine providence of someone missing a flight that crashed on 9/11." For the person who believes in a Distant God, such events as Hurricane Katrina are "just storms," and the terrorist attack was "a sign of man's inhumanity to man, not God's action or judgment." Finally, those adhering to a Critical God simply observe that "God will have the last word."[47]

These views of God can have an influence on a person's political views as well. About 87.2 percent of those believing in a Distant God think that the federal government should protect the environment better, as compared to

75.9 percent of those adhering to an Authoritarian God. But about 62.7 percent of the persons holding an Authoritarian God image want more spending on the military, while only 33.8 percent of those adhering to a Distant God image agree with that view. About 38 percent of people whose image of God is benevolent believe that "'good people' should actively seek social and economic justice." Finally, a larger proportion of the people with a Distant God Image (about 27.3 percent) support abolishing capital punishment than among those who have an Authoritarian God image (about 12.1% percent).[48]

Another perspective on the significance of the Four Images of God is revealed in the work of a neuroscientist, Andrew Newberg, in the book, *How God Changes Your Brain* (2010). Using brain scan studies, Newberg explored how different parts of the brain are related to various types of religious experience, including the image that a person has of God. The studies found correlations between subjective experiences and the neural activity in different parts of the brain. Here are some examples of the kind of experiences that are associated with various areas in the brain:

- *Occipital parietal circuit*: functions in identifying God as an object that exists in the world; young children see God as a face because of the immaturity of their brains.
- *Parietal frontal circuit*: establishes a relationship between the two objects "you" and "God" and places God in space, allowing a person to experience God's presence. When people meditate or pray intensely, it decreases activity in the parietal lobe, which results in a perception that the boundaries between "you" and "God" disappear. So, when this happens, a person experiences a sense of unity with an object of contemplation and one's spiritual beliefs.
- *Frontal lobe*: creates and integrates all of a person's ideas about God—both the positive and negative—including the logic one uses to evaluate her or his religious beliefs. This part of the brain is used to attempt to answer all the why, what, and where questions raised by spiritual issues.
- *Thalamus*: gives emotional meaning to one's concepts of God; it also gives a person a holistic sense of the world. It appears to be the part of the brain that makes God feel objectively real.
- *Amygdala*: when overly stimulated, this part of the brain creates the impression of a frightening, authoritative, and punitive God. Also, when it is overstimulated, the amygdala suppresses the frontal lobe's ability to think logically about God.
- *Striatum*: inhibits the activity of the amygdala. It allows one to feel safe in the presence of God, or whatever concept or object that one is contemplating.
- *Anterior cingulate*: allows a person to experience God as loving and compassionate. It decreases religious anxiety, guilt, fear, and anger by suppress-

Lobes of the brain

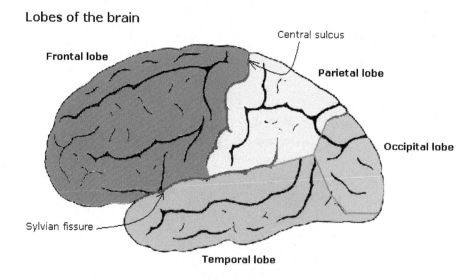

Figure 5.3: Lobes of the brain. The frontal lobe is associated with the creation of a person's ideas about God.

ing activity of the amygdala. Contemplative practices (such as meditation on God's love or on love) stimulate activity in this part of the brain, which helps an individual to become more sensitive to the feelings of others.

Hence, the activity in different parts of the brain can be associated with various subjective experiences of the religious person. When a part of the brain such as the frontal lobes or the limbic system malfunctions, then a person may experience unusual thoughts and perceptions. For example, some people with neural damage become obsessed with God, yet others can lose all interest. A person with an overactive limbic system can begin to ruminate on sin, or a person with overstimulated frontal lobes may become preoccupied with a mathematical proof of God. The occipital cortex helps someone envision an anthropomorphic (e.g., like a human being) God; the temporal lobes serve to help someone "hear" God's voice. If either of these areas is damaged or injured, then a person can see or hear phenomena that he or she may interpret as religious, mystical, or even demonic.

Returning to the question of how a person's religious practices might interact with neurological functioning, a good place to start is with fear-based religion. Religious activities that focus on fear may have an effect on the area of the brain known as the anterior cingulate (Newberg hypothesizes that it is possible that even damage could occur to this part of the brain), and the person will tend to lose interest in other people's concerns or even act aggressively toward them. Additionally, in the case of fear-based religions, it has been found that these

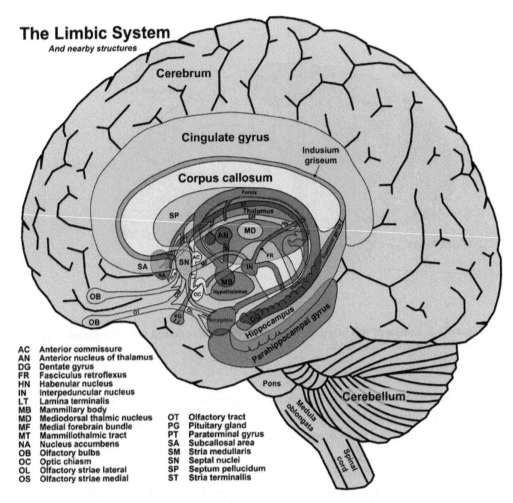

The Limbic System
And nearby structures

AC	Anterior commissure
AN	Anterior nucleus of thalamus
DG	Dentate gyrus
FR	Fasciculus retroflexus
HN	Habenular nucleus
IN	Interpeduncular nucleus
LT	Lamina terminalis
MB	Mammillary body
MD	Mediodorsal thalmic nucleus
MF	Medial forebrain bundle
MT	Mammillothalmic tract
NA	Nucleus accumbens
OB	Olfactory bulbs
OC	Optic chiasm
OL	Olfactory striae lateral
OS	Olfactory striae medial

OT	Olfactory tract
PG	Pituitary gland
PT	Paraterminal gyrus
SA	Subcallosal area
SM	Stria medullaris
SN	Septal nuclei
SP	Septum pellucidum
ST	Stria terminalis

Figure 5.4: The limbic system is part of the brain that is associated with emotions and memories, including those that are religious.

beliefs may actually produce symptoms that are similar to post-traumatic stress disorder (PTSD), a psychological disorder characterized by anxiety, depression, flashbacks, sleep disorders, angry outbursts, and difficulty concentrating. Brain scan studies indicate that once a person anticipates a negative event, activity in the amygdala increases, whereas activity in the anterior cingulate is turned down. The result is that this generates high levels of neuroticism and anxiety (i.e., intense fear or dread that lacks a specific cause).

The specific images of God a person holds are found to be correlated with either increased or decreased activity in different parts of the brain. Thus, envisioning God as either authoritarian or critical activates the limbic areas of the brain; these areas generate fear and anger. Consequently, the brain is then primed to fight; interestingly, the strongest advocates of an Authoritarian God frequently refer to themselves as "God's warriors" and use battle images. On the other hand, if God is seen as benevolent, then the prefrontal cortex is stimulated;

loving and compassionate images or thoughts tend to stimulate the part of the brain known as the anterior cingulate. When the anterior cingulate is stimulated, there is a suppression of the impulse to be frightened or get angry, as well as an increase in feelings of empathy toward those who suffer or are hurt. Finally, with atheists, it was found that frontal lobe activity increased, which shows they were thinking about God in an abstract way; there was little stimulation in other parts of the brain that are related to meaning, value, pleasure, or comfort.[49]

Crime and Deviance

What is the effect of religiosity on deviance and criminal behavior? Does it have a deterrent effect? Over the years, there has been great interest in the possibility that religiosity might discourage criminality; initially, most of the research focused on young people, but has now expanded to adults. The results are sometimes contradictory and confusing, but some interesting trends come to light. In this section, we'll review some of the research that has explored the effects of religion upon crime.

In 1969, Rodney Stark and Travis Hirschi conducted a study of the effect of religiosity (i.e., attendance at church services and Sunday school, as well as belief in hellfire or punishment in an afterlife). Stark notes that they "were unable to find any correlations between religiousness ... and delinquency" among the high school students he studied. This result surprised scholars, as it was not expected; soon, other research would contradict Stark and Hirschi's findings.[50]

Rohrbaugh and Jessor (1975) investigated the effect of religiosity on "personal control against transgression, social problem behavior, or deviance" by administering questionnaires to subjects who were drawn from high school and college populations. The authors' measure of religiosity includes these four dimensions: ritual religiosity (e.g., attending church services or praying); consequential religiosity (e.g., the influence of religion on decision making); ideological religiosity (e.g., beliefs about God and the afterlife); and experiential religiosity (e.g., experiencing a feeling of religious reverence or devotion). The results of their study provide strong support for the hypothesis that religiosity "functions as a personal control by regulating problem behaviors" (such as premarital sex and marijuana use) among both high school and college students. They conclude that the religious person has the characteristic of "a general conventionality, a relative acceptance of social institutions as they are, and a set of values that sustain conformity and eschew self-assertion and autonomy."[51]

Albrecht et al. (1977) studied Mormon teenagers and conclude that religious attitudes are "not strongly related to engagement to non-engagement in deviance" for either boys or girls. But participation in religious activity (e.g., attending Sunday meetings and other church activities and personal prayer) are "strongly related to an absence of deviance." Religious variables (i.e., behavior and attitudes) act "as more of an inhibitor for victimless than victim deviance." The authors also found that a young person's perceptions of peer behavior and his or her relationship to parents were also important factors in explaining deviance.[52] Similarly, in what Argyle refers to as a classic study, Jensen and Erickson studied over 3000 high school students in Arizona and "found small negative correlations for eighteen types of crime and deviance and four types of religiosity." Further, church attendance was "the strongest predictor and the effect was greatest for alcohol and marijuana … theft and violence were effected less."[53]

Elifson et al. (1983) also found that attendance at church was important in inhibiting delinquent behavior, but concluded that even more important was religious salience (i.e., how important religion is to a person), belief in the power of personal prayer, and orthodoxy as factors in discouraging delinquency. However, the impact of religiosity on deterring delinquency seems to be limited by what Argyle refers to as the "Stark" effect. Research by Stark et al. (1982) shows that "religion effects serious crime and delinquency only in communities where organized religion is strong;" this is an ecological solution to the problem posed when some researchers in other parts of the country were finding a deterrent effect for religiosity that did not appear among students in California.[54] Thus, Stark and associates found that religiosity did not deter delinquency on the West Coast of the United States because the communities in those areas are not strongly religious; but in other areas of the country, where religious practice is strong, there are significant deterrent effects for religiosity.[55]

Another interesting effect of religion was reported by Peer et al. (1985) in a study which examined the effect of religiosity on deviance deterrence and deviance amplification. The authors found that "higher levels of religiosity" are modestly to weakly associated with lower levels of self-reported delinquency, but more significantly, they report finding that earlier religiosity appears to amplify or increase later deviance if a young person then becomes less religious.

A study conducted by Cochran et al. (1994) examines the question of whether the effect of religiosity on deterring delinquency is spurious (false); some scholars argue that other factors related to social control such as low arousal level and general social control may actually be what was deterring delinquency. The authors concluded that the effect of religiosity on deterring behaviors such as assault, theft, vandalism, illicit drug use, and truancy is insignificant; but religiosity remains significant as a deterrent to the use of legalized substances like alcohol or tobacco.[56]

Other, more recent studies suggest religiosity is either a limited factor in explaining why some people do not act deviantly or criminally, or not a factor at all. Perrin (2000) reports that approximately 41 percent of religious students in a university who participated in a study were honest when given a chance to cheat on the scoring of a quiz; but this finding was bracketed by the reality that the majority of religious students who participated in the study were dishonest about the same task.[57] Cretacci (2003) studied the effect of a social bond that includes religion on violence among adolescents in grades 7–12. The author concludes that there is no significant effect for religion; he hypothesizes that the reason there is no effect is that the sample was "drawn from an advanced, hetero-geneous, perhaps secular society ... it may be that less advanced, more closely knit, perhaps agricultural societies are centers for strong effects of religion on deviance" and that "highly advanced, loosely knit, industrial societies such as the United States are places where only minimal effects exist."[58] However, this finding of Cretacci's may be a recent example of the Stark effect; Wallace, Moak, and Moore (2005), noting recent concerns about school violence, looked at the effect of religion on school delinquency in Kentucky and found that religion did have a mediating effect on school delinquency.[59]

Finally, given that religion seems to be waning while spirituality gains popu-larity, it may be that spirituality will prove to be a significant factor in deterring crime. Hodge, Cardenas, and Montoya (2001) did a study examining the effect of religious participation and spirituality on substance abuse among youth in the rural Southwest. They conclude that, while religious participation does have an effect on the probability of never using alcohol, increased spirituality "predicted greater probability of never using marijuana and hard drugs." Thus, spirituality is a separate construct from religion and refers to a person having "an existential relationship with God," while being religious refers to participating in the external structures of ritual and religious practices; one can be "spiritual" and not religious, or vice versa. The authors account for the discrepancy between religion and spirituality by hypothesizing that religion is "expressed in a social context" and spirituality is "more internal, reflecting an individual's relationship with God."[60]

Studies of the effect of religion on adult criminality show a deterrent effect, too. Bainbridge (1989) reports that his analysis of the 1980 Religious Ecology Dataset indicates that church membership negatively correlated with suicide, assault, burglary, and larceny; he suggests that "acts of larceny may be more read-ily deterrable by religious beliefs" than the other crimes.[61] Evans et al. (1995) found that "participation in religious activities was a persistent and noncontin-gent inhibiter of crime."[62] Baier and Wright (2001) conducted a meta-analysis of 60 studies and conclude that "religious beliefs and behaviors exert a moderate deterrent effect on individuals' criminal behavior."[63] They also observe that the effect is less powerful for white subjects than for blacks.

Research among prisoners indicates that there are positive effects of religiosity on inmates' behavior. Wiernik (2007) reports on the results of a study of a national sample of 420 inmates and states that "religious beliefs lead to fewer adherences to prison norms when violence is called for, but more adherences to the norms in the case of racial segregation, stealing for profit, and inmate guard relations."[64] Results of the study by Kerley et al. (2005) indicate that "religiosity directly reduces the likelihood of arguing and indirectly reduces the likelihood of fighting."[65] Clear and Sumter (2002) conducted a nonrandom sample of 769 inmates in 20 prisons and conclude that inmate religiousness is associated with higher levels of prison adjustment, better psychological adjustment, and fewer self-reported disciplinary confinements.[66]

But not all studies find that religion has a positive effect on criminality; there are some adult crimes that are not discouraged by religiosity or by certain kinds of religiosity. Delamontagne (2010) proposes examining the relationship between membership in evangelical Protestant fundamentalist sects and hate group membership; this is a significant question, as there was a 54 percent increase in the number of hate groups in the United States between the years 2000–2008. Delamontagne notes that "several and various relationships between the Hate Group Representation Rate (HGRR: measures rate of Hate Groups in different states) and religiosity measures within the Gallup Poll and the Pew Forum of Religion and Public Life has revealed numerous and consistent statistically significant association between Hate Group Representation and indicators of religiosity." Another problematic area relates to homicide: Bhattacharya (2013) reports that studies by Fox, Levi, and Quinet (2008) and Fajnzylber et al. (2002) found that "all the nations with high homicide rates were extremely religious, and that the nations with the lowest homicide rates tended to be relatively non-religious." Bhattacharya also reports finding an "inverse relationship between rate of assaults and religiousness."[67]

There may be denominational difference in the deterrent effect of religiosity on crime. According to Argyle, the "greatest effect of religion on crime is for Mormons ... the lowest crime rates are for Mormons and Jews, the highest for Catholics, with class held constant, though this may be due to the effects of Irish and Italian culture." He concludes: "the effect of religion on crime and deviance is quite weak, compared with religion's other effects" and that the effect "has almost certainly declined in America, and this may be part of the process of secularization there."[68]

SUMMARY

In this chapter, we have examined research related to religion, developing a portrait of the religious person, as well as what religious experiences are like. We have seen there are different ways that persons visualize God—some see a loving, parent-like figure, while others see an angry, authoritative deity. Interestingly, these images have implications for a person's political views and his or her neurological functioning. Finally, we reviewed some of the research that has been done on the effect of religiosity on crime. Most of the research has been conducted on young people, and while the results are sometimes contradictory, the trend is that there seems to be some measureable effect of religiosity on deterring crime; similar patterns exist for adults, too. However, there are some crimes such as homicide that appear to increase as religiosity does.

KEY TERMS

+ **Authoritarianism**
+ **Authoritative God**
+ **Benevolent God**
+ **Critical God**
+ **Deconversion**
+ **Distant God**
+ **Dogmatism**
+ **New religious movements**
+ **Numinous experiences**
+ **Religious orientations**

REVIEW QUESTIONS

1. What is religious orientation, according to Allport?
2. Explain authoritarianism and dogmatism. How are they important in understanding religious behavior?
3. What is deconversion? Explain the process.
4. What are the four perceptions of God (e.g., Authoritative God, etc.) that Americans hold? Explain each one.
5. Discuss the relationship between religion and criminality.

END NOTES

1. Cavalli-Sforza, L. L., et al. "Theory and observation in cultural transmission." Science 218, no. 4567 (October 1982): 19–27. Quoted in Michael Argyle, *Psychology and Religion* (New York: Routledge, 2000), 16.
2. Danso, Henry, Bruce Hunsberger, and Michael Pratt. "The role of parental religious fundamentalism and right-wing authoritarianism in child-rearing goals and practices." Journal for the Scientific Study of Religion 36, no. 4 (December 1997): 496–511. Quoted in Michael Argyle, *Psychology and Religion* (New York: Routledge, 2000), 16.
3. Argyle, Michael. *Psychology and Religion* (New York: Routledge, 2000), 17.
4. Allport, Gordon W., and J. Michael Ross (1967). "Personal religious orientation and prejudice." *Journal of Personality and Social Psychology* 5, no. 4: 434. PsycINFO, EBSCOhost (accessed Oct. 16, 2014).
5. Allport and Ross, 434.
6. Adorno, T. W., E. Frenkel-Brunswick, D. Levinson, and R. Sanford. *The Authoritarian Personality* (New York: Harper & Row, 1950). Quoted in Michael Argyle, *Psychology and Religion* (New York: Routledge, 2000), 34.

7. Altemeyer, Bob, and Bruce E. Hunsberger. "Authoritarianism, religious fundamentalism, quest, and prejudice." *International Journal for the Psychology of Religion* 2, no. 2 (1992): 113–133. PsycINFO, EBSCOhost (accessed Oct. 16, 2014). Quoted in Michael Argyle, *Psychology and Religion* (New York: Routledge, 2000), 34.

8. Shaffer, Barbara A., and Brad M. Hastings. "Authoritarianism and religious identification: Response to threats on religious beliefs." *Mental Health, Religion & Culture* 10, no. 2 (2007): 157. PsycINFO, EBSCOhost (accessed Oct. 16, 2014).

9. Rokeach, Milton, Warren C. McGovney, and M. Ray Denny. "A distinction between dogmatic and rigid thinking." *Journal of Abnormal and Social Psychology* 51, no. 1 (July 1955): 87–93. PsycARTICLES, EBSCOhost (accessed Oct. 16, 2014).

10. Argyle, 35.

11. Rokeach, Milton. The Open and Closed Mind. (Oxford, England: Basic Books, 1960). Quoted in Michael Argyle, *Psychology and Religion* (New York: Routledge, 2000), 35.

12. Argyle, 145; 154.

13. Shariff, Azim F., and Mijke Rhemtulla. "Divergent effects of beliefs in heaven and hell on national crime rates." PLoS ONE 7, no. 6 (June 18, 2012): PsycINFO, EBSCOhost (accessed Oct. 16, 2014).

14. Galen, Luke W. "The complex and elusive nature of religious prosociality: Reply to Myers (2012) and Saroglou (2012)." *Psychological Bulletin* 138, no. 5 (September 2012): 918–923. PsycARTICLES, EBSCOhost (accessed Oct. 16, 2014).

15. Ferraro, Kenneth F., and Cynthia M. Albrecht-Jensen. "Does religion influence adult health?" *Journal for the Scientific Study of Religion* 30, no. 2 (June 1991): 193–202. PsycINFO, EBSCOhost (accessed Oct. 16, 2014).

16. Seybold, Kevin S., and Peter C. Hill. "The role of religion and spirituality in mental and physical health." *Current Directions in Psychological Science* 10, no. 1 (February 2001): 21–24. PsycINFO, EBSCOhost (accessed Oct. 16, 2014).

17. Argyle, 17.

18. Hood, R. W., B. Spilka, B. Hunsberger, and R. L. Gorsuch (1996). The Psychology of Religion: An Empirical Approach, 2nd ed. (New York: Guilford). B. Spilka, and D. N. McIntosh, eds. Quoted in Michael Argyle, *Psychology and Religion* (New York: Routledge, 2000), 20.

19. Köse, Ali (1996). "Religious conversion: Is it an adolescent phenomenon? The case of native British converts to Islam." *International Journal for the Psychology of Religion* 6, no. 4: 253–262. Quoted in Michael Argyle, *Psychology and Religion* (New York: Routledge, 2000), 20.

20. Argyle, 20–21.

21. Kirkpatrick, Lee A., and Phillip R. Shaver (1990). "Attachment theory and religion: Childhood attachments, religious beliefs, and conversion." Journal for the Scientific Study of Religion 29, no. 3: 315–334. Quoted in Michael Argyle, *Psychology and Religion* (New York: Routledge, 2000), 22.

22. Argyle, 22–23.

23. Paloutzian, Raymond F. (1981). "Purpose in life and value changes following conversion." *Journal of Personality and Social Psychology* 41, no. 6: 1153–1160. Quoted in Michael Argyle, *Psychology and Religion* (New York: Routledge, 2000), 24.

24. Paloutzian, Raymond F., James T. Richardson, and Lewis R. Rambo (1999). "Religious conversion and personality change." *Journal of Personality* 67, no. 6: 1047–1079. PsycINFO, EBSCOhost (accessed Oct. 16, 2014).

25. Argyle, 24.

26. Barbour, J. D. *Versions of Deconversion: Autobiography and the Loss of Faith* (Charlottesville: University of Virginia Press, 1994). Quoted in Henri Gooren, 2011. "Deconversion: Qualitative and quantitative results from cross-cultural research in Germany and the United States: A review essay." *Pastoral Psychology* 60, no. 4: 609–617. PsycINFO, EBSCOhost (accessed Oct. 16, 2014).

27. Janet L. Jacobs. *Divine Disenchantment: Deconverting from New Religions* (Bloomington: Indiana University Press, 1989). Quoted in Michael Argyle, *Psychology and Religion* (New York: Routledge, 2000), 24–25.

28. Argyle, 47.

29. Hay, David, and Ann Morisy. "Reports of Ecstatic, Paranormal, or Religious Experience in Great Britain and the United States—A Comparison of Trends." *Journal for the Scientific Study of Religion* 17, no. 3 (September 1978): 258; 260. Psychology and Behavioral Sciences Collection, EBSCOhost (accessed Oct. 17, 2014).

30. Argyle, 50.

31. Andrew M. Greeley. *The Sociology of the Paranormal* (Beverly Hills, CA: Sage Publications, 1975). Quoted in Michael Argyle, *Psychology and Religion* (New York: Routledge, 2000), 51 & 60.

32. Argyle, 58–59.

33. Argyle, 67.

34. Hay, David, and Ann Morisy. "Reports of Ecstatic, Paranormal, or Religious Experience in Great Britain and the United States—A Comparison of Trends." *Journal for the Scientific Study of Religion* 17, no. 3 (September 1978): 255.

35. Hay, David. "The Spirituality of Adults in Great Britain: Recent Research." *Scottish Journal of Healthcare Chaplaincy* 5, no. 1 (2002), 4–9.

36. Argyle, 70.

37. Argyle, 70.

38. Pfeifer, Samuel, and Ursula Waelty. "Anxiety, depression, and religiosity—A controlled clinical study." *Mental Health, Religion & Culture* 2, no. 1 (May 1999): 35–45. PsycINFO, EBSCOhost (accessed Oct. 17, 2014).

39. Drinnan, Ange, and Tony Lavender. "Deconstructing delusions: A qualitative study examining the relationship between religious beliefs and religious delusions." *Mental Health, Religion & Culture* 9, no. 4 (September 2006): 317–331. Academic Search Premier, EBSCOhost (accessed Oct. 17, 2014).

40. Ng, Felicity. "The interface between religion and psychosis." *Australasian Psychiatry* 15, no. 1 (February 2007): 62–66. Academic Search Premier, EBSCOhost (accessed Oct. 17, 2014).

41. Dein, Simon, Christopher C. H. Cook, Andrew Powell, and Sarah Egger. "Religion, Spirituality, and Mental Health." *Psychiatrist* 34 (2010): 63–64.

42. Rashed, M. "Religious Experience and Psychiatry: An Analysis of the Conflict and Proposal for the Way Forward." *Philosophy, Psychiatry, and Psychology* 17, no. 3: 185–204. Quoted in Mona Gupta, "Religious Beliefs and Psychiatric Beliefs: Worlds Apart and Perhaps Best Left That Way." *Philosophy, Psychiatry, & Psychology* 17.3 (2010): 205–207. *Project MUSE*. Web. 17 Oct. 2014. http://muse.jhu.edu/

43. DeHoff, Susan L. "Distinguishing mystical religious experience from psychotic experience in the Presbyterian Church (U.S.A.)." Dissertation Abstracts International Section A, 2013. PsycINFO, EBSCOhost (accessed Oct. 17, 2014).

44. Argyle, 68.

45. Gorsuch, Richard L. "The conceptualization of God as seen in adjective ratings." *Journal for the Scientific Study of Religion* 7(1), 1968, 56–64. Quoted in L. L. Brown, *The Psychology of Religious Belief* (London: Academic Press, 1987), 80.

46. Grossman, Cathy Lynn. "Americans' Views of God Shape Attitudes on Key Issues." *USA Today*, October 7th, 2010. http://usatoday30.usatoday.com/news/religion/2010-10-07-1Agod07_CV_N.htm

47. Grossman, Cathy Lynn. "Americans' Views of God Shape Attitudes on Key Issues."

48. Grossman, Cathy Lynn. "Americans' Views of God Shape Attitudes on Key Issues."

49. Berger, Rose Marie, and Jonathan Mendez. "America's Four Views of God." *Sojourners*, July 2007. http://sojo.net/magazine/2007/07/americas-four-views-god

50. Newberg, Andrew, and Mark Robert Waldman. *How God Changes Your Brain: Breakthrough Findings from a Leading Neuroscientist* (New York: Ballantine Books, 2010).

51. Stark, Rodney. "Religion and the Moral Order Reconsidered." *IARCA Journal on Community Corrections* 6, no. 6 (June 1995): 6–9. Criminal Justice Abstracts with Full Text, EBSCOhost (accessed Oct. 20, 2014).

52. Rohrbaugh, John, and Richard Jessor. "Religiosity in Youth: A Personal Control Against Deviant Behavior." *Journal of Personality*, vol. 43(1) March 1975, 136–155.

53. Albrecht, Stan L., Bruce A. Chadwick, and David S. Alcorn. "Religiosity and Deviance: Application of an Attitude-Behavior Contingent Consistency Model." *Journal for the Scientific Study of Religion* (1977): 16 (3), 263–274.

54. Jensen, Gary F., and Erickson, Maynard L. "The Religious Factor and Delinquency: Another Look at the Hellfire Hypothesis." *The Religious Dimension*, ed. Robert Withnow (New York: Academic Press, 1979). Quoted in Michael Argyle, *Psychology and Religion* (New York: Routledge, 2000), 187.

55. Stark, Rodney. "Religion as Context: Hellfire and Delinquency One More Time." *Sociology of Religion* (1996): 57:2, 163–173.

56. Stark, Rodney, Lori Kent, and Daniel P. Doyle. "Religion and Delinquency: The Ecology of a 'Lost' Relationship." *Journal of Research in Crime and Delinquency* 18 (1982): 4–24. Quoted in Michael Argyle, *Psychology and Religion* (New York: Routledge, 2000), 187.

57. Arneklev, Bruce J., John K. Cochran, and Peter B. Wood. "Is the religiosity-delinquency relationship spurious? A test of arousal and social control theories." *Journal of Research in Crime and Delinquency* 31.1 (1994): 92+. *Academic OneFile*. Web. 20 Oct. 2014.

58. Perrin, Robin. "Religiosity and Honesty: Continuing the Search for the Consequential Dimension." *Review of Religious Research*, 2000, vol. 41:4: 534–544.

59. Cretacci, Michael A. "Religion and Social Control: An Application of Modified Social Bond on Violence." *Criminal Justice Review*, vol. 28:2 (autumn 2003): 254–276.

60. Wallace, Lisa Hutchinson, Stacy C. Moak, and Nathan T. Moore. "Religion as an Insulator of Delinquency in Schools." *American Journal of Criminal Justice* 29, no. 2 (spring 2005): 217–233. Criminal Justice Abstracts with Full Text, EBSCOhost (accessed Oct. 20, 2014).

61. Hodge, David R., Paul Cardenas, and Harry Montoya. "Substance Use: Spirituality and Religious Participation as Protective Factors Among Rural Youths." *Social Work Research*, vol. 25: 3 (Sept. 2001): 153–161.

62. Bainbridge, William Sims. "The Religious Ecology of Deviance." *American Sociological Review*, vol. 54:2 (Apr. 1989): 288–295.

63. Evans, T. David, Francis T. Cullen, R. Gregory Dunaway, and Velmer S. Burton Jr. "Religion and Crime Reexamined: The Impact of Religion, Secular Controls, and Social Ecology on Adult Criminality." *Criminology* 33:2 (1995): 195–224.

64. Baier, Colin J., and Bradley R.E. Wright. "'If You Love Me, Keep My Commandments': A Meta-Analysis of the Effect of Religion on Crime." *Journal of Research in Crime and Delinquency*, vol. 38:1 (Feb. 2001): 3–21.

65. Wiernik, Craig. "Walking the Walk and Talking the Talk: The Influence of Religious Beliefs on Inmates' Behavioral Intentions." Conference Papers, *American Society of Criminology* (2007 Annual Meeting 2007): 1. Criminal Justice Abstracts with Full Text, EBSCOhost (accessed Oct. 20, 2014).

66. Kerley, Kent R., Todd L. Matthews, and Troy C. Blanchard. "Religiosity, Religious Participation, and Negative Prison Behaviors." *Journal for the Scientific Study of Religion* 44, no. 4 (Dec. 2005): 443–457. Psychology and Behavioral Sciences Collection, EBSCOhost (accessed Oct. 20, 2014).

67. Clear, Todd R., and Melvina T. Sumter. "Prisoners, prison, and religion: Religion and adjustment to prison." *Journal of Offender Rehabilitation* 35, no. 3-4 (2002): 127–159. PsycINFO, EBSCOhost (accessed Oct. 20, 2014).

68. Fox, J. A., J. Levin, and K. Quinet. *The Will to Kill: Making Sense of Senseless Murder* (Boston: Pearson, 2008) and P. Fajnzylber, D. Lederman, and N. Loayza. "What Causes Violent Crime?" *European Economic Review*, 47:7, 1323–1357. Quoted in Sonali Bhattacharya, "A Global Spiritual Index, Its Predictors and Relationship to Crime." *Journal of Human Values*, vol. 19:1 (2013): 83–104.

69. Argyle, 188.

Part II

6. Christianity

By Timothy Oslovich

OVERVIEW

Christianity claims more adherents than any other religion on earth. Almost one third of the world's 7 billion people are Christian.[1] In many ways, Christianity is similar to the other great world religions—Christianity has doctrines, rituals, and moral rules. Christianity has holy people, holy places, and a holy book (the Bible). And yet, these distinctly religious things are not the center of Christianity. The center of Christian faith is a person: Jesus Christ. Christianity is ultimately not about believing the right doctrines, performing the correct rituals, or even following the proper moral rules. Christianity is about trusting the right person, Jesus Christ.

This chapter will explore the history of Christianity from its beginning almost 2,000 years ago until the 21st century, including a brief overview of the different branches of Christianity. The key doctrines (incarnation, atonement, resurrection, Jesus' return, and the Trinity) and rituals (baptism, Holy Communion, and prayer) will be described, and contemporary trends in Christianity (such as the growth of Christianity in the developing world and increasing secularization in the developed world) will be briefly explored.

Figure 6.1: *Pantocrator*: This icon is an image depicting Jesus as "The Ruler of All."

HISTORY

The Life of Jesus

Christianity is rooted in Judaism. Jesus was a Jew, and all of Jesus' earliest followers were Jews. Jesus grew up worshipping in the local synagogue (the Jewish place of worship in a local community) and traveling to Jerusalem for the Jewish holy days. The Jewish scriptures were the scriptures of the first Christians and are part of the Christian Bible today.

Christianity began in the province of Palestine in the Roman Empire in the first half of the first century of the Common Era (CE). The Common Era begins with the year many believe Jesus of Nazareth was born in Bethlehem, a small town in Judea. The Western calendar is divided into two periods—the Common Era and Before the Common Era. Traditionally, these divisions were known as AD (Anno Domini, "in the year of our Lord") and BC (Before Christ). This is worth noting because it is an example of how deeply Christianity has influenced Western culture, including the culture of the United States. Understanding Christianity is necessary to understanding much of Western thought, politics, and law.

Most of the information we have about Jesus is contained in works called gospels, literally, "good news." Until the Christians adopted the word gospel to describe the "good news" about Jesus, the word was primarily used by officials of the Roman Empire to describe news that came from or about the emperor. It was no accident that Christians used this word to describe the news about Jesus. In their minds, Jesus' coming was a monumental event that would have vast implications, not only for individuals, but also for the way empires and nations were organized as well. Jesus did not come merely to show individuals how to lead a moral life or how to get to heaven. Jesus came to inaugurate the Kingdom of God—God's rule over everyone and everything. Although only Christians believed that Jesus' coming had this much significance, some non-Christian sources also mention Jesus briefly. Jesus is mentioned in the *Antiquities of the Jews* by Josephus, a Jewish historian, and in the *Annals* by a Roman historian, Tacitus. Most scholars acknowledge that Jesus of Nazareth was a historical person.

Jesus came from humble beginnings. The account in the Gospel of Luke tells us that Jesus was born in a stable with a feeding trough as his first crib. The first people to visit him were shepherds—people who were at the bottom of the social and economic scales in first-century Palestine. This was not what one would expect for the one who would later be recognized by many as the Messiah (the long-expected king who would free the Jewish people from the oppression of the Romans and rule the whole world with justice). However, there were indications that Jesus was no ordinary baby. The shepherds had seen angels who told them where Jesus could be found and who had revealed to them that Jesus was the Messiah. A new star (perhaps a comet) also appeared when Jesus was born, and astrologers from the East came to revere the newborn "King of the Jews."

However, by all accounts that we have, Jesus grew up as an ordinary Jew, learned his father's trade of carpentry, and lived an unremarkable life until around the age of 30. At that time, Jesus went out to the Jordan River and was baptized (submersed in the water as a symbol of cleansing and a new beginning) by a man named John. John was calling for his fellow Jews to repent (transform their hearts and minds so that they could follow God authentically). When Jesus was baptized, a voice came from heaven identifying him as God's Beloved Son. Immediately after his baptism, Jesus spent 40 days in the wilderness, fasting, praying, and overcoming temptation. He then began his public ministry.

Jesus' ministry focused on three things: teaching, healing and other miracles, and sharing meals with everyone, especially those who were considered outcasts. Jesus' teaching centered on the "Kingdom of God," which he saw as already breaking into this world. The Kingdom of God meant that God's rule of perfect peace, justice, and love would be the new reality. In Jesus, this new reality was beginning to be realized. Jesus taught about this new reality primarily through stories called parables. Parables are brief stories using ordinary things to disclose the truth about spiritual things. Jesus used stories about farmers and seeds, fathers and sons, and pearls and weddings to invite people to see God and God's world in new ways. Many of these stories helped people see God as a loving father, rather than as a distant king.

Jesus' healings and other miracles were ways of showing that God's reign was breaking into this world. In God's kingdom, there is no sickness or pain or hunger, and Jesus began to show people what God's reign looked like by healing the sick, feeding the hungry (on several occasions, he miraculously multiplied a few loaves of bread and a few fish into enough to feed thousands of people), and showing his power over nature. According to the Gospels, Jesus raised at least three people from the dead in order to show that even death would be overcome in God's kingdom.

Finally, Jesus gave people a picture of the inclusiveness of God's kingdom by eating with all sorts of people, especially people who were seen as outcasts—tax collectors, prostitutes, and other "sinners." In a culture that divided people into "clean" (good) and "unclean" (bad), Jesus' willingness to eat with those who were considered unclean was radical. In Jesus' culture, eating with someone was one of the most profound ways to demonstrate respect, acceptance, and love. His message was clear: there was room in God's kingdom for all, for the poor, the sinner, the outsider—all those despised by the religious authorities. Jesus invited all to repent and enter God's kingdom.

As a result, Jesus encountered some opposition from the Jewish religious leaders. (Remember that Jesus was a Jew, so the leaders were trying to correct one of their own and prevent him from leading others in what they believed was a dangerous direction.) They felt that God's law made it clear that sinners, especially certain kinds of sinners such as prostitutes and tax collectors, should be excluded and punished, not welcomed. Of course, the Jewish religious leaders believed that God was forgiving, but God's law also had to be obeyed. The fact that Jesus took it upon himself to offer forgiveness to sinners (something only God could do) and welcome them made it clear that Jesus was a blasphemer. In other words, he was someone who disrespected God by claiming to have God's power to forgive sin. Therefore, he deserved to be executed. The fact that Jesus was always talking about the kingdom of God also made the religious leaders nervous because the Romans, who ruled Palestine, didn't like talk of any king or kingdom except the Roman emperor and the Roman Empire. The religious leaders (rightly) believed that Jesus' talk about the kingdom of God could provoke the Romans to act even more brutally toward the Jews. Eventually, Jesus was seen as a threat by both the Jewish religious authorities and the Roman governor. He was arrested, brutally beaten by Roman soldiers, and crucified. Crucifixion was the most painful form of execution reserved for the worst criminals, especially those people who were seen as a threat to the Roman Empire. After asking God to forgive the people who crucified him, Jesus died and was laid in a tomb by some of his followers.

This sounds like the end of the story. A good man goes against the power of the empire and is killed. His followers scatter, and nothing else is heard from them. But that is not what happened with Jesus. Christians believe that Jesus was raised from the dead three days after his execution. He appeared to his followers who were, at first, very reluctant to believe that he was alive again. Jesus' resurrected body was not the same as his body before he died. Although Jesus demonstrated that he had a body (by eating with his followers), his new body was no longer subject to pain, death, or decay. After spending 40 days with his followers, he ascended into heaven.

The Early Church

All of the first followers of Jesus were Jews, and it was only gradually that they came to see themselves as part of a new religion. They gradually accepted that Jesus' message should be shared with non-Jews as well. Just before he ascended, Jesus instructed his followers to wait in Jerusalem until they received power from the Holy Spirit. Fifty days after Jesus' resurrection, his followers had a powerful experience of the Holy Spirit, which gave them the courage to tell others about Jesus and the kingdom that he was bringing into existence. (See the discussion of the doctrine of the Trinity below to see how the Holy Spirit fits into the Christian conception of God.) They began sharing the good news about Jesus with their fellow Jews. They told people that Jesus had been crucified and that he had also been raised from the dead, proving that he was the Messiah and that his message was true. They told people not only in their native land of Judea, but also soon spread out all over the Roman Empire to tell others. Many people responded to the good news about Jesus Christ.

A Jewish man named Paul, who had violently opposed Christianity, had an encounter with the resurrected Jesus and became the most important missionary for the Christian faith. He traveled all over the Mediterranean, telling people about Jesus and founding communities of Christians—churches. By the end of the first century CE, churches could be found in just about every major city of the Roman Empire, and the vast majority of Christians were Gentiles (non-Jews).

However, the growth of Christianity was complicated by the fact that Christianity was illegal. Christians were often seen as a threat to the Roman Empire because they refused to worship the emperor. Offering a sacrifice to the emperor (who saw himself as a god) was seen as a necessary demonstration of loyalty to the empire. If someone refused to offer the sacrifice, that person was seen as opposing the emperor and was often imprisoned or executed. Many Christians died because they refused to worship any king except Jesus.

Despite Christianity's illegal status and the persecution of Christians, Christianity spread throughout the Roman Empire. The Christian message of hope in a suffering Savior who overcame death was appealing to many, especially many of the poor. Sociologist Rodney Stark contends that another reason Christianity spread so rapidly was because of the Christians' way of life. Christians cared for one another and also cared for their neighbors in need. The practice of Christians loving one another and loving their neighbors was demonstrated powerfully when epidemics struck major cities. According to Stark (who cites contemporary sources), pagan religious leaders and anyone with means to flee would escape from a city with an outbreak of disease. Christians (including Christian leaders) would remain, caring for the sick who were Christians and caring for their sick neighbors as well. In the ancient world, there were no hospitals, and most people who became infected during epidemics died as a result. However, since Christians believed in a crucified and resurrected Savior who had overcome death, they did not fear death. Jesus had promised to raise from death all who trusted in him, and Jesus had cared for the sick when he walked the earth. It made sense for Christians to care for the sick, even at the risk of their own lives. Their bravery and compassion impressed many people. Also, since people who receive care and remain hydrated have a much better chance of surviving an illness, Christians also became known for saving lives. Christianity became known as a religion that offered benefits for this life and for the afterlife. It was a combination that enabled Christianity to experience huge growth.[2]

Christendom

In 313 CE, the Roman emperor Constantine made Christianity legal in the Roman Empire. Not long after this, Christianity became the official religion of the Roman Empire, and all of the pagan temples that had been part of traditional Roman religion now became Christian places of worship. Christian religious leaders (priests) became the beneficiaries of government support. It was no longer dangerous to be a Christian. In many ways, it was advantageous to be identified with the religion the emperor favored. It was a dramatic change for Christianity.[3] It was the beginning of Christendom, a period in which the Church and the state supported one another to maintain order, promote what the leaders considered to be the common good, spread the Christian religion, and preserve their power.

With its new status as the official religion of the Roman Empire, the Church became more structured and more uniform in belief and practice. In 325 CE, a council (meeting of Church leaders) was called to determine how the relationship between Jesus (the Son of God) and God the Father should be understood. The result was what is now called the Nicene Creed, which makes it clear that God the Father and God the Son (Jesus) are "of the same substance." In other words, Jesus is fully God (as well as being fully human). This creed (a succinct statement of fundamental beliefs) is still used by the majority of Christians today as a way to state the essentials of their faith.

The Bible is the book that contains the story of God's interactions with the people of Israel, the story of Jesus, and the story of the beginning of the Christian Church. Although Christians differ considerably in the ways they interpret the Bible, all Christians consider the Bible to be central to their faith and the main way that they learn about God. From the beginning, Christians had considered the Jewish scriptures to be sacred for them as well. Christians often call the Jewish scriptures the Old Testament, since these writings existed long before Jesus was born or the Church existed. As the Church defined itself, four gospels (books about Jesus), a book about the early Church (Acts of the Apostles), and various letters (many of them written by the missionary, Paul) were recognized as sacred scripture for Christians in addition to the Jewish scriptures. In 367 CE, a Christian leader (bishop) named Athanasius sent out a letter that clarified which writings should be included in what became known as the Christian New Testament. The New Testament, along with the Old Testament, constitute the Christian Bible.

For almost a thousand years, the Church was unified. (There were other expressions of the Church such as the Nestorian Church in Persia, the Coptic Church in Ethiopia and Egypt, and others, but the vast majority of Christians were part of what was known as the Catholic Church.) In 1054, the Church split into the (Western) Roman Catholic Church and the (Eastern) Orthodox Church. Differences in doctrine and disputes over authority caused the rift, which still exists today.

The Roman Catholic Church remains the largest group in Christianity. More than one billion people identify themselves as Roman Catholic.[4] The leadership of the Roman Catholic Church is based in Vatican City, located within the city of Rome. Vatican City is the world's smallest independent country. The pope is the leader of the Roman Catholic Church and has a great deal of power within the Church and a vast amount of influence outside it. Roman Catholics look to the pope for guidance on religious and moral matters, and popes have written and spoken about topics as diverse as the role of Mary (the mother of Jesus), labor unions, and nuclear weapons. Roman Catholic religious life centers on the Mass, a worship service that includes the Eucharist or Holy Communion (the sharing of bread and wine consecrated by a priest), as well as readings from the Bible, singing, prayers, and usually a sermon. In many parishes (local Roman Catholic communities), Mass is celebrated daily, and Catholics are required to attend Mass on Sundays.

The Orthodox Church claims approximately 260 million members throughout the world.[5] Although the Orthodox Church has much in common with the Roman Catholic Church in terms of doctrine and practice, Orthodox Christians do not recognize the authority of the pope. The Orthodox Church is organized into independent national churches such as the Russian Orthodox Church, the Greek Orthodox Church, Ethiopian Orthodox Church, etc. Orthodox Christians follow a liturgy (order of worship) that has remained relatively unchanged since the fifth century CE. Participation in the Divine Liturgy (Sunday worship service) is vital for Orthodox Christians. As one Orthodox teacher puts it, "I believe that participation in the Eucharistic Divine Liturgy is the most important thing one can ever do. It characterizes, defines, and constitutes the true Christian ... ."[6] For Orthodox Christians, participating in the Divine Liturgy brings them into communion with God and empowers them to work to make the world better.

Later, in the 16th century, the Roman Catholic Church was further split by what became known as the Protestant Reformation, and the third major group in Christianity was formed. There are about 801 million Protestants in the world.[7] Protestants are really not a single group, but many groups, the first of which began when some Christian leaders criticized practices of the Roman Catholic Church and ended up forming new Christian groups. The Reformation began with a Catholic priest named Martin Luther challenging Roman Catholic practices and beliefs. Luther protested against corruption and abuses in the Roman Catholic Church such as the selling of indulgences. In Luther's time, a person could purchase "indulgences" from the Church, which, according to the Church's teaching, would enable the person's deceased relatives to go directly to heaven. Luther saw no basis for this practice in the Bible, and he saw it as a way that the Church authorities manipulated common people to enrich themselves.

Luther believed that much of this corruption resulted from a misinterpretation of the gospel. He insisted (following the New Testament Letter to the Romans) that people are justified (made right with God) solely by the grace of God, which the believer appropriates through faith in Christ. The Roman Catholic Church countered with the teaching from the New Testament Letter of James that "faith without works is dead" (James 2:26, NRSV),[8] and insisted that proper belief had to be expressed by right action. Almost 500 years later, Roman Catholics and Lutherans signed a document (the Joint Declaration on the Doctrine of Justification) that declared that the arguments of the 16th century were exaggerated, and they affirmed that both churches never really disagreed on the essence of the doctrine of how people are made right with God. Both affirmed that God's grace, which people receive through trusting Jesus Christ, is what enables people to come back into a right relationship with God. And both affirm that this restoration of relationship will result in faithful people doing good in the world.

After Luther, many others also challenged some of the Roman Catholic Church's teachings and practices. Each leader interpreted the Bible differently, and many began their own sects or denominations. For example, a man named John Calvin started what became known as the Reformed Church in Geneva, Switzerland, shortly after Luther began his protests against the Roman Catholic Church. Calvin influenced many other Christian thinkers, and his ideas about human nature ("total depravity"—people are completely evil and are incapable of doing the right thing without God's help) and predestination (God has already decided who will be saved and who will not) have deeply influenced American Christianity. Many people who followed Calvin's teachings (Calvinists) believed that evidence that one was predestined to go to heaven would be shown in the lives of believers. For example, those who were predestined to be saved were often expected to live moral, successful, and economically prosperous lives. As a result, Calvinists were often very hard working, frugal, and successful.

Today, there are thousands of different denominations based on different interpretations of the Bible. Nevertheless, almost all Christians hold to the core doctrines of Christianity, despite the differences. Different Protestant groups emphasize different doctrines, but most have an emphasis on the grace of God and on the individual's right and duty to read and interpret the Bible. After the Reformation, both the Protestant Churches (those who split from the Roman Catholic Church), the Roman Catholic Church, and the Orthodox Churches faced challenges from societies that relied more and more on science and reason and less and less on received tradition and religion.

ESSENTIAL DOCTRINES AND PRACTICES

Doctrines–The Central Beliefs of Christians

The key doctrines of Christianity are incarnation, atonement, resurrection, Jesus' return, and the Trinity. Incarnation is the belief that God took on human form in Jesus of Nazareth. This was a radical idea. The Jews had always believed that God was Spirit and that, although God did interact with humans, God was not bound by flesh. Christians believe that, in Jesus, God and humanity are united. Jesus is considered to be fully God and fully human. This is a paradox because logic tells us that one being cannot be 100 percent God and 100 percent human, but that is how Christians came to understand Jesus. Those who had contact with him saw that he had the power of God: he healed people, stilled storms, walked on water, and even raised the dead. But he also shared the vulnerability of humans—he got tired, hungry, and thirsty, he felt pain, and he even died. For Christians, the incarnation means that God truly understands the human condition because God has experienced human weakness and pain in Jesus.

Atonement is the word used to refer to what Christians understand happened when Jesus died on the cross. There are several different atonement theories that have been accepted by Christians. Perhaps the most common is substitutionary atonement. This theory states that Jesus died on the cross to pay the penalty for humanity's sins. The sin of human beings violated God's just commands, and someone needed to pay the penalty. Since Jesus was sinless, he was able to die in the place of all human beings who have sinned against God. All those who trust in Jesus' sacrifice are freed from sin and the punishment that results from sin. Substitutionary atonement has been the predominant way of understanding Jesus' death on the cross in American Christianity.

However, there are other ways that atonement has been explained. Many Christians affirm what has been called the Christus Victor (Christ the Victor) theory of the atonement. Many scholars think this was the predominant understanding of the atonement in the early Church. Christus Victor sees Jesus' death as the key moment when all the forces that subjugate human beings—sin, death, and all the supernatural evil forces in the world—were defeated by Jesus. On the cross, through his death, Jesus overcame the powers of sin, death, and evil and set humanity free to live as God's beloved people.[9] The resurrection of Jesus proves the victory.

Although Jesus' sacrifice on the cross is often presented as the center of Christian preaching and teaching, there is no Christianity without the resurrection. After three days in the tomb, Jesus was resurrected (raised from the dead) by God. He rose in a new body that was no longer subject to disease, injury, pain, or death. Jesus' resurrection is the first of many. Christians believe that everyone who trusts in Jesus will also be resurrected. One day in the future, when Jesus returns, God will give everyone a new body like Jesus' resurrection body. His death and resurrection are at the core of Christian faith. Jesus' death is understood to set humanity free from sin and death, but without resurrection, his death is merely the death of another person who opposed the Roman Empire. The resurrection of Jesus validates his life and teaching, shows that he is divine, and gives Christians confidence for the present and hope for the future.

After his resurrection, Jesus spent 40 days with his disciples, but after that short time, his resurrected body left the earth. Christians believe that someday Jesus will return and complete the work that he began and fully manifest the Kingdom of God. In other words, when Jesus returns, all evil, disease, poverty, and death will be eliminated. Many Christians believe that this will be a time of great struggle and terrible conflict as Jesus subdues all the evil forces in the world. The final end, however, is a new heaven and a new earth. In the words of the last book of the Christian Bible, "He will wipe every tear from their eyes. Death will be no more; mourning and crying and pain will be no more, for the first things have passed away" (Revelation 21:4, NRSV).

Perhaps the most difficult Christian doctrine to grasp is the Trinity, the idea that God is somehow simultaneously three and one. The first followers of Jesus were all Jews who had a strong faith in one God. In a world where the vast majority of people acknowledged a wide variety of deities, Jews maintained that there was only one God, the all-powerful Creator of heaven and earth. However, as the first followers of Jesus came to understand him more and more, they came to realize that in some way, when they were in the presence of Jesus, they were in the presence of God. Jesus did and said things that could only be from God. Later, after Jesus ascended into heaven, they experienced the Holy Spirit, not just as a force from God, but as a personal reality. Over the first few centuries of Christianity, the doctrine of the Trinity was formulated to explain how the Father, Son (Jesus), and Holy Spirit are all God. Yet, there are not three Gods, but one God. The Father, Son, and Holy Spirit have always existed as God and in a relationship of love to one another. Traditionally, the Trinity has been described as "One God in Three Persons." Father, Son, and Holy Spirit are so deeply united as to be one God, yet they remain distinct so that it makes sense to speak of them using three

Figure 6.2: *Trinity Icon* shows the three persons (Father, Son, and Holy Spirit) of the One God.

different words. Although difficult—if not impossible—to comprehend, the Trinity is one of teachings of Christianity that most distinguishes it from other religions. The Trinity means that at the center of reality, there is not a singular, all-powerful being or a force without personality, but a relationship of mutual love. One way of concisely expressing Christianity is to say that the Son came to earth in Jesus in order to invite human beings to join the eternal relationship of perfect love that has always been shared by the Father, Son, and Holy Spirit. (Note: Referring to God as "Father" does not mean that Christians believe that God is male. Christians believe that both men and women reflect God's qualities and that God is beyond gender.)

Key Christian Practices

Although there are many different styles of Christian worship and a wide variety of Christian rituals, there are several aspects of Christian worship that the vast majority of Christians share. Most Christians gather for their primary worship service on Sunday. The service includes readings from the Bible, an explanation of the biblical readings (a sermon), singing, prayers, and sometimes baptism or Holy Communion.

One of the simplest definitions of prayer is talking with (which includes listening to) God. For Christians, this means talking with God as Jesus talked with God. "We [Christians] begin by expressing the confidence that we stand where Jesus stands, and we can say what Jesus says."[10] Thus, the most common prayer among Christians is one that Jesus taught his disciples, and it begins with the words, "Our Father." Jesus called God "Father," and he invites his followers to do the same. For Christians, prayer is talking with a loving Father who has their best interests at heart. This does not mean that Christians believe that all requests made in prayer will be fulfilled. Prayer is not magic. But Christians do believe that prayer changes the world; just as importantly, prayer changes the one who is praying, helping the person praying to know, trust, and love God more.

Baptism is the ritual by which a person becomes a Christian and joins the Church. Baptism involves water—a person is immersed in water or has water poured over him or her. The immersion or pouring is often accompanied by words similar to these: "You are baptized in the name of the Father and of the Son and of the Holy Spirit." Baptism conveys the forgiveness of sins (as water washes) and adoption into God's family. As noted above, Jesus was baptized, and at his baptism, the voice of God was heard proclaiming him God's Beloved Son. Similarly, at an individual's baptism, God claims a new Christian as God's son

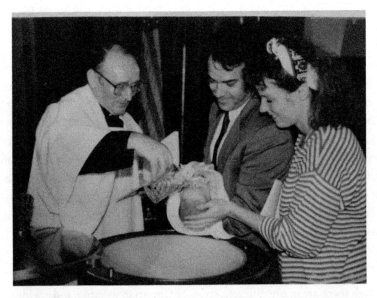

Figure 6.3: Baptism is a ritual in which a person becomes a Christian.

or daughter. "And just as Jesus came up out of the water, receiving the Spirit and hearing the voice of the Father, so for the newly baptized Christian the voice of God says, 'You are my son/daughter,' as that individual begins his or her new life in Jesus."[11]

The final ritual we will discuss here is the sacred symbolic meal of bread and wine (or grape juice) that Christians share. This symbolic meal is called Holy Communion, the

Figure 6.4: Pentecostal worship. Pentecostals are Christians who emphasize the power of the Holy Spirit to bring gifts such as miraculous healings.

Lord's Supper, or the Eucharist. It is a ritual that reminds Christians of the Last Supper, the meal Jesus had with his disciples on the night before he was crucified. It also reminds Christians that one day, Jesus will return to usher in the Kingdom of God and the everlasting feast at which all are welcome. Holy Communion involves the recitation of Jesus' words from the Last Supper, which are recorded in the New Testament. Jesus identifies the broken bread with his body, which will be broken on the cross, and the wine with his blood, which will be shed. After Jesus' words are read, the bread and wine (or grape juice) are shared. Each person only receives a small amount of bread or wine. This sacred meal serves to draw believers closer to Jesus and closer to one another. "For Christians, to share in the Eucharist, the Holy Communion, means to live as people who know that they are always guests—that they have been welcomed and that they are wanted."[12]

CONTEMPORARY DEVELOPMENTS

Christianity, like many of the world's religions, is undergoing a time of great change in the 21st century. For hundreds of years, Christianity has been the dominant religion in Europe and in many of the areas settled and colonized by Europeans: North America, Australia, New Zealand, and much of Latin America. However, by the end of the 20th century, Christianity fell into decline in most of Europe, Australia, New Zealand, Canada, and the United States. Although the United States remains predominantly Christian (about

78 percent of the U.S. population self-identifies as Christian[13]), the fastest growing "religious" group in the United States is the people who self-identify as having "no religious preference."[14] On the other hand, Christianity is growing is Latin America, Africa, and some parts of Asia. The majority of the world's Christians now live outside Europe and North America, and the margin of this majority will continue to grow. This will no doubt bring changes to how the Christian faith is expressed.

In the United States, the rapidly growing number of people who are not Christian—or even religious—has challenged Christianity to change and adapt to new cultural realities. The Protestant Christians who had enjoyed predominance in American Christianity since the founding of the country were rapidly declining in numbers and influence by the late 20th century. However, there are some Christian groups that are growing or at least maintaining their numbers. Many Pentecostal churches are faring much better than the traditional Protestant churches and the Roman Catholic Church. Pentecostal churches emphasize the power of the Holy Spirit and experiences such as speaking in tongues, prophecy, and miraculous healing. Speaking in tongues refers to an experience in which a person, under influence of the Holy Spirit, speaks or prays in an unknown language. This is part of many Pentecostal worship services. Prophecy refers to a person receiving a message from God for the gathered community of believers. Miraculous healing refers to a person with an illness being healed by the power of God, usually as the result of prayer by a person who is understood to have the gift of healing. The Pentecostal movement began in the early 20th century in the United States, and the number of Pentecostal believers continues to grow, especially in Africa and Latin America. Many people, especially the poor and marginalized, are attracted to Pentecostal churches because of the experience of God that is part of the Pentecostal worship. There are approximately 279 million Pentecostals in the world.[15] (Pentecostals are included in the Protestant category.)

Another group of Christians that is trying to adapt to the changing culture is called the Emerging Church. The Emerging Church is very loosely organized, and it is very difficult to determine the number of Christians who would identify themselves as "Emerging." (Emerging is not a category in Pew religion surveys.) However, the leaders of this movement seek to make the Christian faith more relevant to young people in the United States who are disaffected by traditional Christianity. More participatory worship (e.g., discussions of what the Bible means rather than a sermon by one leader, multiple people leading the worship, a return to ancient Christian practices such as chanting and contemplative prayer) is one of the hallmarks of this movement. It is too early to tell if this movement will have a lasting impact on American Christianity, but many of the leaders in the movement are hopeful about the future.

CHAPTER SUMMARY

Any short description of a major world religion is bound to have major gaps. One paragraph on each of the three major forms of Christianity (Roman Catholicism, Eastern Orthodoxy, and Protestantism) is obviously inadequate, and there are many aspects of Christianity that are not even mentioned. Some suggestions for further reading are listed below. It is also true that many of the effects of Christianity—both good and bad—are not discussed in this chapter. For example, Christian beliefs have inspired wars and violence, but Christian convictions have also been responsible for the construction of countless hospitals. However, this brief chapter gives the reader some insights into the beginning of the Christian faith, its central figure (Jesus Christ), and some of Christianity's most important history, practices, and doctrines. Christianity, at its core, is a religion that focuses on love and relationship. Jesus expressed great love for all people during his ministry and called on his followers to do the same. At their best, Christians continue to invite others to look forward to the Kingdom of God, where there will be no evil. They also make that kingdom a little more real even today by following Jesus' instructions to "[L]ove the Lord your God … and love your neighbor as yourself" (Matthew 22:37, 39, NRSV).

KEY TERMS

+ **Atonement theory.** A way of explaining what happened to God and/or humanity when Jesus died on the cross. The substitutionary atonement theory states that Jesus acted as a substitute for all humanity on the cross. All human beings have sinned (broken God's law) and deserve to die. Jesus died in our place on the cross, satisfying God's justice and opening the way for human beings to be reconciled to God. The moral exemplar atonement theory states Jesus shows us in his life and death on the cross how to live in the best way possible (having compassion for the poor, forgiving enemies, even being willing to die for the sake of others). The Christus Victor theory states that, through his death on the cross, Jesus defeated the power of sin and death and opened the way for human beings to be free to be reconciled to God. The mimetic atonement theory (espoused most clearly by René Girard) states that through his sacrifice on the cross, Jesus exposed the bankruptcy of sacrifice and the violence that it exemplifies, freeing people to reject violence and evil and be reconciled with God.
+ **Bible.** The Christian Bible consists of books considered sacred by Jews and Christians (which Jews call the Tanakh and Christians call the Old Testament). These books tell the story of creation and of God's interactions with the Jewish people. The second part of the Christian Bible consists of books that are considered sacred by Christians (the New Testament),

which tell the story of Jesus and the early church. "The Bible is the territory in which Christians expect to hear God speaking."[16]

- **Eastern Orthodox Church.** The Eastern Orthodox Church consists of a number of independent national churches such as the Greek Orthodox Church and the Russian Orthodox Church. The Orthodox churches preserve an ancient liturgy (order of worship) and stress the idea that believers, through prayer, worship, and service, become more and more like God. This process is called *theosis*.

- **Eucharist.** Also called Holy Communion, the Lord's Supper, and the Blessed Sacrament, this is the sacred meal that Christians share as part of their worship. It consists of bread and wine (or grape juice). The meal points back to the Last Supper, the meal Jesus shared with his disciples before he died; it is a place where most Christians experience the presence of Christ and fellowship with other believers and look forward to the day when Christ will return and redeem the world.

- **Incarnation.** The belief that God took on human form in Jesus. Christians believe that Jesus was completely human (and thus shared in all of humanity's weakness and suffering, except that he did not sin) and completely divine (and thus could clearly and accurately reveal God's nature). In the Christian view, if one wants to know what God is like, one should look at Jesus.

- **Jesus' Return.** Christians believe that Jesus will return someday to complete the work that he began—inaugurating the Kingdom of God. This includes the resurrection of the dead and the establishment of peace and justice and the end of disease, violence, and death.

- **Messiah.** The long-expected deliverer and king who would free the Jewish people from oppression and rule the whole world with justice. Christians believe that Jesus of Nazareth is the Messiah.

- **Protestantism.** In the 1500s, Martin Luther and others protested that the Roman Catholic Church had become corrupt and no longer taught the truth. Stressing that human beings were reconciled to God through faith in (trusting) Jesus, they rejected the idea that the religious rituals of the Roman Catholic Church were necessary to be faithful followers of Jesus. They also rejected the authority of the pope. As a result, they were expelled from the Roman Catholic Church (or left the Roman Catholic Church) and formed their own groups. Today, there are thousands of different Protestant denominations.

- **Resurrection:.** In the Christian tradition, resurrection does not mean a simple return to life after having been dead. After his resurrection, Jesus was not exactly the same as he was before the resurrection. In some ways, he was the same Jesus: He had a body. He ate and drank. However, Jesus' resurrected body was not subject to disease, decay, or death. Likewise, when people are resurrected when Jesus returns, they will have bodies that are not subject to such things.

+ **Roman Catholic Church.** The largest body of Christians, numbering about one billion worldwide, the Roman Catholic Church traces its origins back to Peter, the leader of the original disciples of Jesus. The head of the Roman Catholic Church is the pope. The pope has great power in the Roman Catholic Church and great influence over much of the rest of Christianity.

+ **Trinity.** Traditionally, the Trinity has been described as "One God in Three Persons." Over the first few centuries of Christianity, the doctrine of the Trinity was formulated to explain how Father, Son (Jesus), and Holy Spirit are all God. Yet, there are not three Gods, but one God. The Father, Son, and Holy Spirit have always existed as God and in a relationship of love.

REVIEW QUESTIONS

1. What proportion of the world's population is Christian? What percentage of the population of the United States is Christian? Why is this significant for politics, law, and ideas about justice?

2. What is one indication that Christianity has had a significant influence on Western culture?

3. What were some of the emphases of Jesus' teaching?

4. Why did the Jewish religious authorities and the Romans see Jesus (and later, Christians) as a threat?

5. How did Christianity change after it became legal and later became the official religion of the Roman Empire?

6. What are the three major branches of Christianity? How did Christianity come to have these three major expressions?

7. What caused the Protestant Reformation?

8. What are the key doctrines of Christianity? Which doctrine do you think shapes Christian practice the most?

9. What are the central Christian practices? How do they influence the lives of Christians?

10. What are some of the changes that Christianity is currently undergoing?

11. What do you think will happen to Christianity in the future?

END NOTES

1. Pew Research Center (2011). Accessed at http://www.pewforum.org/2011/12/19/global-christianity-exec

2. Stark, Rodney. *The Rise of Christianity: How the Obscure, Marginal Jesus Movement Became the Dominant Religious Force in the Western World in a Few Centuries* (Princeton, NJ: Princeton University Press, 1996), 73–94.

3. Shelley, Bruce L. *Church History in Plain Language*, 5th ed. (Nashville: Thomas Nelson. 2013), 102.

4. Pew Research Center (2011). Accessed at http://www.pewforum.org/2011/12/19/global-christianity-traditions

5. Pew Research Center (2011). Accessed at http://www.pewforum.org/2011/12/19/global-christianity-traditions

6. Farley, Father Lawrence. *Let Us Attend: A Journey Through the Orthodox Divine Liturgy* (Chesterton, IN: Conciliar Press, 2007), 7.

7. Pew Research Center (2011). Accessed at http://www.pewforum.org/2011/12/19/global-christianity-traditions

8. References to passages in the Bible note the name of the book in which the passage occurs, the chapter number, and the verse number. All scripture quotations in this chapter are from the New Revised Standard Version of the Bible. Copyright © 1989 the Division of Christian Education of the National Council of the Churches of Christ in the United States of America. Used by permission. All rights reserved.

9. See Gustav Aulen. *Christus Victor: An Historical Study of the Three Main Types of the Idea of Atonement* (Eugene, OR: Wipf and Stock. 2003).

10. Williams, Rowan. *Being Christian: Bible, Baptism, Eucharist, Prayer* (Grand Rapids, MI: Eerdmans, 2014), 62.

11. Williams, 2.

12. Williams, 41.

13. Pew Research Center (2012). Accessed at http://religions.pewforum.org/reports

14. Pew Research Center (2012). Accessed at http://www.pewforum.org/2012/10/09/nones-on-the-rise

15. Pew Research Center (2012). Accessed at http://www.pewforum.org/2011/12/19/global-christianity-exec

16. Williams, 23.

SUGGESTIONS FOR FURTHER READING

Father Lawrence Farley. *Let Us Attend: A Journey Through the Orthodox Divine Liturgy* (Chesterton, IN: Conciliar Press, 2007).

Brian McLaren. *Finding Faith—A Search for What Makes Sense* (Grand Rapids: Zondervan, 2009).

Gerard O'Collins. *Catholicism: A Very Short Introduction* (Oxford, UK: Oxford University Press, 2008).

Bruce L. Shelley. *Church History in Plain Language*, 5th ed. (Nashville: Thomas Nelson, 2013).

Huston Smith (2009). *The World's Religions*, 50th Anniversary Edition (New York: HarperOne, 2009).

Rodney Stark. *The Rise of Christianity: How the Obscure, Marginal Jesus Movement Became the Dominant Religious Force in the Western World in a Few Centuries* (Princeton, NJ: Princeton University Press, 1996).

Rowan Williams. *Being Christian: Bible, Baptism, Eucharist, Prayer* (Grand Rapids, MI: Eerdmans, 2014).

Linda Woodhead. *Christianity: A Very Short Introduction*, 2nd ed. (Oxford, UK: Oxford University Press, 2014).

7. Islam

Submission to God

By Steven Blackburn

OVERVIEW

Islam grew in a part of the world where stories of the Hebrew prophets like Abraham and Moses were part and parcel of the spiritual consciousness of a number of important Arab tribes.[1] In addition, Jesus of Nazareth and John the Baptist were also known to many in the Arabian Peninsula. In fact, a number of the clans of the area before 600 CE identified themselves as Jewish or Christian, though most worshipped the gods and goddesses of the desert. As a major shrine and pilgrimage site of pre-Islamic paganism, the Ka`bah was said to have contained over 300 icons, idols, and other representations of these deities. None other than the Virgin Mary, the mother of Jesus, was one of these whose image was on display. A god of the polytheistic pantheon was called Allah, which simply means "God," or more literally, "the God," in Arabic.

Arabia is a long distance from the centers of Judaism and Christianity, and geographical isolation often leads to practices that "headquarters" might not recognize as being correct. So, despite the major trade connections between Arabia and the Roman and Persian empires, the Judaism and Christianity as practiced by these Arabs were somewhat unconventional. For example, the Hebrew prophet Ezra was apparently held by some Arabian Jews to have been the son of God, while among Arabian Christians, the status of Jesus was not always clear—was he fully God, or something less?

The religious records of the time are few. Added to the mix was a belief held by some non-Jewish and non-Christian Arabs in a single supreme God, even if most followed in the polytheistic ways of their forebears.

Into this world was born Muhammad, who would become the greatest and final prophet of the Islamic religion. Islam sees itself as standing in a long prophetic tradition, beginning not just with Abraham, the first monotheist of the Hebrews, but with Adam himself.

Muhammad, at first, was not conscious of beginning a new religion: prayers were directed to the Holy City of Jerusalem, Jesus was called "Messiah" and was born, miraculously, to a virgin, and the values to which Muhammad called his neighbors were not unlike those preached by Jews and Christians: compassion for the widow, the orphan, and stranger within one's gates; the necessity of truthfulness in one's dealings with one's fellows; the centrality of refraining from evil while encouraging a consciousness of God; tempering a sense of self in favor of exalting the worship of the One God, to whom all should submit.

In the following pages, the influence that Islam has had through the ages will be explored, looking at the impact the religion of Muhammad has had in any number of fields—history, literature, politics, art, education, mysticism, etc.

HISTORY

Muhammad was born around the year 570 CE in the city of Mecca, a major commercial and social center of what is now western Saudi Arabia.[2] As an orphan, Muhammad fell under the protection of his uncle, a respected elder (*sheikh* in Arabic) of one of the most powerful tribes of the region: the Quraysh. This protection would become very important once Muhammad began calling his kin and fellow townspeople to abandon their paganism and "lawless" ways in favor of a belief in One God, the God of Abraham. But before he began preaching, Muhammad was employed in the caravan trade, working for an older woman named Khadijah, who would subsequently become his wife. Khadijah owned a number of caravans, with Muhammad as her most trusted lieutenant. When Muhammad experienced his first vision, it was to Khadijah that he ran for refuge out of fear. Khadijah comforted him and encouraged him to continue to seek out God's presence.

Muhammad's early preaching fell largely on deaf ears, and despite the protection of his uncle, Muhammad and his followers were increasingly persecuted. His declaration that there was only one God was interpreted as an attack on commercial interests connected with the Ka`bah. Muhammad also threatened some long-held practices, such as female infanticide—unwanted girl babies were buried alive soon after birth. One group of his followers fled to Ethiopia, a Christian kingdom of east Africa. The Muslims were given asylum on the basis that what they taught, and what Christianity taught, were declared

Figure 7.1: Sultan Ahmed Mosque in Istanbul was built during the days of the Ottoman Empire in the 17th century and is also known as the "Blue Mosque."

to be essentially identical. This was determined by a recitation of Muslim teachings about Mary and the birth of Jesus. Not long afterward, the remainder of the Muslims in Mecca immigrated to another important center of the caravan trade, the city of Yathrib, now known as Medina (*Medinat al-Nabi*, Arabic for City of the Prophet).

Muhammad and his followers were welcomed with open arms in Medina, a diverse city of pagans, Jews, and Christians. The services of Muhammad as a mediator among various factions led to an agreement called the Constitution of Medina, allowing each tribe to continue to practice their own religion (as Islamic scripture proclaims, "Let there be no compulsion in religion") while uniting the various tribes under the political leadership of Muhammad. Conflict between Medina and Muhammad's hometown of Mecca led to a number of battles and skirmishes, with the forces of Islam gaining the upper hand for the most part. While there was an element of commercial rivalry here, Muhammad's claims to be a prophet of God also fueled the competition. Demanding permission to

Figure 7.2: Muslims praying in mosque. Devout Muslims pray five times each day in a practice known as Salat, which is one of the "Five Pillars of Islam."

return to Mecca to perform the annual pilgrimage (Arabic: *Hajj*, pilgrimage) to the Ka`bah, Muhammad's followers eventually wore down the pagan opposition, and Muhammad entered Mecca without a shot being fired; the city yielded to him peaceably.

Within a couple of years, Muhammad had died. Some tribes insisted that with Muhammad's death, his constitution was no longer in force. If political Islam was to survive, the Islamic community, or Ummah, had to quickly choose a successor to keep recalcitrant clans within the fold. Settling on Muhammad's father-in-law (who would live only two years more than Muhammad), the figure of Ali, Muhammad's cousin, was passed over, setting the stage for centuries of intra-Islamic conflict: the "partisans of Ali" came to be known as Shi`ites, while the majority party, or Sunnis, continued to pass over Ali as leader (*caliph*) of the Ummah in favor of figures such as Omar and Uthman, members of Muhammad's Quraysh tribe. At best, this was ironic in the eyes of many Muslims, but most of the Quraysh had opposed Muhammad to virtually the last minute before his triumphal entry into Mecca only a few years before. By contrast, Ali had been one of Muhammad's earliest followers; his rejection by the pre-Islamic old guard was considered by many to be a grave injustice.

One of the major differences between the Sunni majority and the Shi`ite minority is the nature of leadership of the Ummah.[3] While Sunni caliphs, as members of Muhammad's Quraysh tribe, were invested with political authority, their religious power was limited to a somewhat passive sense of "leading by example." The Ummah operated under a principle of consensus (*ijma*). Muhammad is said to have declared that his Ummah would never agree on error. So, in a sense, the community of Sunni Islam is invested with a type of infallibility. On the other hand, in Shi`ite Islam, infallibility is found not in a community, but in a figure, the *imam*. As the Shi`ite equivalent of a caliph, the imam had to come from Muhammad's line of descent through his daughter, Fatimah, the wife of Ali. Theoretically, these infallible imams held not only political authority, but also exercised religious leadership that was proactive in nature. While Shi`ite imams were clearly not prophets—Muhammad having been the "seal of the prophets"—they were divinely appointed by God.

The Sunni caliphs were not always known for their piety. After the first four successors to Muhammad, a civil war led to the creation of Islam's first dynasty, the Umayyads, who ruled from Damascus. They reigned less than 100 years, with discontent so strong that they were overthrown by a broad coalition of non-Arab Muslims, Shi`ites, and the lower classes in general. The second dynasty, the Abbasids,[4] moved the capital to Baghdad. In the popular imagination, Abbasid rule is identified with the literature and imagination of *One Thousand and One Nights*, with stories of flying carpets, genies and lamps, and grand viziers. The Abbasids have a much better reputation than the Umayyads in several areas: piety, cultural and scientific advancement, and social reforms. It was during the Abbasids that so much of the Greek heritage, including Plato and Aristotle, were preserved in translation and ultimately reexported to Europe. It was also during the Abbasids that an Islamic theological consensus was reached, and a widespread system of education was put in place. In effect, the consensus resolved all potential conflicts or differences in favor of the divine over the human: divine revelation trumps human reason, divine predestination outweighs human free will, the Qur'an (the scriptures of Islam) are uncreated, and only God can know who is "saved" and who isn't, since no human can discern the inner heart and intentions of another.

This consensus was built upon six basic beliefs or articles of faith: that God is One, that God sends angels as messengers to humanity, that angels speak to prophets, that prophets convey the word of God to humanity, that God ultimately sits in judgment of humanity based on their response to the word of God as recorded in the scriptures, and that God's decrees are final.[5]

Clearly, the Abbasid caliphate (750–1258 CE) witnessed great advances, not only in theology but in education, the sciences, literature, and philosophy. But as centuries passed, Abbasid caliphs lost much of their power to their grand viziers (roughly equivalent to a prime minister). The entire system collapsed with the Mongol invasions: Baghdad was sacked in the mid-13th century CE.

With a few notable exceptions, Shi`ites have not held political power within the Ummah. Ali, who eventually became the fourth successor to Muhammad, was beset by civil war. He died after a very short period of rule. One of his sons was subsequently killed, while the other went into internal exile. The Fatimids, a Shi`ite dynasty, founded the city of Cairo in the 10th century CE during their heyday in northern Africa. Another Shi`ite dynasty, the Safavids, ruled Iran for close to a quarter millennium in the 16th, 17th, and early 18th centuries CE. Despite the collapse of the Safavid state, Iran has remained Shi`ite to the present day. The present regime in Iran, headed up by the ayatollah, is explicitly Shi`ite in nature.

The religious leadership vacuum at the top in Sunni Islam was filled not by a person such as a caliph or an imam, but by a class of self-appointed experts in Islamic law, or Shari`a. This class of experts is called the *Ulama* (the learned).[6] Although their powers are unofficial, they have exercised varying measures of prestige through the centuries. The members of the Ulama can often issue legal opinions (*fatwa*) that do not carry the force of law, but which are usually held in high esteem by the Sunni population at large (fatwas are also a feature of Shi`ite Islam).

The growth of a legal class paralleled the growth of Islamic mysticism, also known as Sufism. The earliest mystics in Islam had a strong puritanical streak. But the Islamic injunction against monkery assured that celibacy would not take hold within an Islamic system. Sufis sometimes operated outside the system, given that they were thought to have a direct line to God, as it were. The more extreme and outspoken Sufis were sometimes executed for their failure to conform to standard Islamic rites and rituals; most Sufis today are fairly moderate in their outlook. Without an infallible imam to guide the Sunni community, there is a belief that every hundred years or so, a figure will appear who will guide the Ummah back to the right track. This figure, called the renewer (*mujaddid*), is only recognized through community consensus. While there is a notable lack of consensus in the modern period as to who these personages actually are, there is remarkable agreement among Sunnis regarding the earlier ones. These include Umar ibn Abd al-Aziz, an early caliph who not only reformed Islamic rule, but also led in the collection and preservation of stories and sayings of the Prophet (*hadith*); al-Shafi`i and ibn Hanbal, two early jurists who founded two of the great schools of Islamic law; al-Ghazali, a theologian and philosopher who did much to bring Sufism into the system; and al-Razi, one of the most masterful commentators on Islamic scripture.

Islamic armies erupted out of the Arabian Peninsula under the second and third caliphs. Sweeping across northern Africa, Muslim generals were soon poised to cross the Straits of Gibraltar to enter western Europe. To the north, Arab armies took Jerusalem, Syria, and large portions of what is now Turkey from the Byzantine Empire. The Byzantines would survive, however, till the 15th century CE, after which Constantinople fell, opening the way to southeast

Figure 7.3: Hajj pilgrims travel to Mecca in a ritual of self-renewal that reminds a person of having to stand before God's judgment at the end of life.

Europe. By the time of Martin Luther (early 16th century CE), Muslim armies were besieging Vienna. To the east, the Sassanid Empire in Persia (now Iran) collapsed in short order, opening the way for Islamic armies to march through Afghanistan and into the Indian subcontinent.

This did not mean, however, that the local populations were quickly converted to the religion of Muhammad. The process was gradual, taking a few centuries. In some areas such as India, the task was never completed. And other countries today recognized as Muslim such as Indonesia (the country with the largest Muslim population in the world) never experienced a military invasion from Islamic forces. Instead, Islam spread through commercial contacts and was carried by many Sufis, who found in the mystical Hinduism and Buddhism of Southeast Asia a form of spirituality that was consistent with mystical Islam.

The spread of Islam was not uninterrupted. The Crusades of the 12th and 13th centuries CE brought Christian armies into the heart of Islamic territory. The 13th century also saw the arrival of the Mongols from the east, sacking the city of Baghdad, the seat of the Sunni caliphate. Both of these incursions did not lead to permanent setbacks, however: Christian armies were eventually ejected from the Holy Land by the fabled general, Saladin, while the Mongol hordes were eventually absorbed by the Ummah and converted to Islam. In the wake of these crises, the Ummah no longer had a single, unified caliphate. Instead, there grew to be four major Muslim empires: the Mughals in India, the Safavids in what is now Iran, the Ottomans in what is now Turkey, and the Mamluks centered in Cairo. These empires—only one of which had Arabic as its common language—had varying degrees of fortune over the coming centuries. But until the early 19th century, these Muslim empires were largely free from outside interference, despite military engagements (such as the naval battle of Lepanto in 1571, when Catholic maritime forces bested an Ottoman fleet off the western coast of Greece).

One notable reversal of Islamic military fortunes occurred in what is now Spain. The Islamic term for this area is al-Andalus, or Andalusia. Muslim overlords governed for centuries, and often their subjects were beneficiaries of benevolent rule, tolerating both Jewish and Christian subjects.[7] However, a program of Reconquista by Spanish Christian forces, notably under Queen Isabella and King Ferdinand, eventually put an end to Islam in Spain. In 1492, the last Muslim forces were ejected, with portions of the Jewish and Muslim populations fleeing to the relative safety of Muslim-controlled northern Africa.

The arrival of Napoleon Bonaparte in Egypt in 1798 proved fateful for both the Ummah and Europe, even though Napoleon withdrew his armies within a relatively short time (French forces departed the region in 1801). European powers would increasingly hold sway over vast areas of the Ummah: Indonesia became a Dutch colony, British, French, and Portuguese forces contested control of the Indian subcontinent, the British came out on top in Egypt, while France, Italy, and Spain held sway in the rest of northern Africa. Russia challenged the Ottomans to the north, and restless European populations under Turkish control repeatedly rebelled with increasing success. The military fortunes of Islam were in decline, and the decision of the Ottomans to join forces with Germany in World War I cemented the fate of their empire, which was dismembered, with France and Britain carving spheres of influence in former Ottoman lands: France, in addition to her earlier ascendency in northwest Africa, now looked after Syria and Lebanon, while Britain added to her privileged position in Egypt and now held sway in Iraq, Jordan, and Palestine.

ISLAMIC PRACTICES

The Muslim day of worship is Friday, and gathering at the mosque (from the Arabic for place of prostration) is compulsory for males; women are exempt due to duties in the home, but are no strangers to mosques. While many mosques are large and ornate, the idea is simply to have a place set aside for getting together with fellow Muslims at prayer time, whether on Friday or any other day of the week. Muslims, though, are free to carry out the prescribed prayers (five times per day) anywhere they happen to be. Traffic has been known to come to almost an entire stop, even in large downtown cities, when the call to prayer is heard. Cars pull over to the side of the road, occupants emerge with their prayer carpets, and pray. The effect can be quite dramatic.

If women are in attendance, they are expected to pray behind male worshippers out of a sense of modest decorum. In many mosques, the women pray in an upstairs gallery from which they can observe the rest of the worship service. Some mosques set aside space for women to one side, much as churches in colonial America had men sitting on one side of the central aisle and women on the other.

Prayer is the center of Muslim worship. However, scripture is recited, and a sermonic reflection is delivered. There is no singing, though prayers and scripture are chanted. Before entering the prayer hall, worshippers are required to remove their shoes and perform ritual ablutions of the face, arms, and feet.

Islamic dress varies regionally. Men generally wear some kind of robe, though Muslims in Western-style clothing, from suits to more casual wear, are very common. Women's dress also runs the gamut. While covering one's hair is often seen as the minimally acceptable Islamic veiling, some women wear Western-style clothing. Others veil themselves more completely, covering themselves from head to foot.

Major holidays in Islam include Eid al-Adha, commemorating the sacrifice of a ram in place of Abraham's son. Today, many carry out the practice of killing a ram, distributing portions of the meat to the poor. The holiday falls at the opening of the annual pilgrimage to Mecca. Another holiday is Eid al-Fitr, marking the end of the month of Ramadan, during which Muslims fast from sunup to sundown. During the Ramadan fast, Muslims eat a ritualistic meal after sundown to break their fast in an orderly and decorous manner. After consuming some dates, a few nuts, and perhaps some dried fruit, believers undertake the preparation and consumption of a more lavish meal.

Mawlid al-nabi, or the birthday of the Prophet, is a relatively late development in Islam: during the Prophet's lifetime, it was not known to have been celebrated, and the occasion is not mentioned until the 12th century CE. The status of the Prophet in Islam is more like that of Moses in Judaism than Jesus in Christianity: Muhammad is not worshipped, is not considered in the least bit divine, nor is he considered the founder of Islam. Still, many Muslims (especially Sufis) mark the occasion of the Prophet's birth by the recitation of religious poetry, distribution of alms, and expressions of love for the person of Muhammad. In many areas, the atmosphere of celebration is quite festive, sometimes carnivalesque or even profane. This practice is frowned upon by modern conservatives, who see the entire concept as yet another indication of heretical innovation, corrupting the Ummah.

While there are bound to be variations in a religion of over one billion adherents who speak many languages living on all the continents of the Earth, certain basic features are clear. Given that one Muslim cannot discern the heart of another, theological belief, while important, effectively takes a backseat to Islamic practice and ritual: after all, one can clearly observe what someone is doing, while one never knows what another person is thinking. So being seen to observe commandments often puts one in good standing with the rest of the community.

Islamic practice is based on five pillars of action, with minor differences due to the Sunni-Shi`ite split.[8] The first of these pillars is giving witness, or testimony (shahadah) to one's faith. This is highly formulaic, consisting of a simple declaration: "There is no god but God, and Muhammad is his messenger," to which the Shi`ites would add in their call to prayer a third phrase: "and Ali is his vicegerent." Recitation of this sentence marks one's entry into the Ummah, which then requires the believer to engage in four other practices, or pillars: prayer five times a day facing Mecca; fasting from sunup to sundown during the holy month of Ramadan; giving alms (at least 2.5 percent of one's entire wealth annually); and engaging in a pilgrimage to Mecca at least once in one's lifetime, unless doing so brings economic hardship on oneself and/or one's dependents.

There is a disputed sixth pillar of Islam: engaging in jihad (struggle). Part of the difficulty is the definition of this activity. According to Islamic tradition, the Prophet said there were two kinds of jihad—the higher and the lower. The lower jihad is fighting physically in the cause of God. This lower jihad has been variously defined by Islamic thinkers through the centuries. The classical definition insists that jihad can only be waged under the leadership of the Ummah's caliph (there has been no caliph in Islam for almost a hundred years now), and the lower jihad must be defensive in nature and be directed only at armed combatants. The higher jihad, which Muhammad said was more important, refers to the struggle within: the battle to do good instead of evil, to entertain only pure thoughts, to subjugate one's baser instincts to nobler pursuits.

With the exception of the first, all the pillars are communal in nature. Muslim mystics, however, are highly individualized: it is difficult to be in direct contact with God except as an individual, though a group of individuals may gather to encourage each other in the individuals' mystical quest. As a result, Sufis have traditionally gathered in mystical orders which assist in the training of novices and suggest certain practices that facilitate closer contact with God. Some of these groups strike non-Muslims as colorful (the whirling dervishes of Turkey come to mind), while others seem more than unconventional, such as orders that engage in various forms of self-mutilation. However, the vast majority of Sufis—the huge Qadiri and Shadhili orders are good examples—appear like their neighbors and do not perform any outward rituals or dress in any way that would call attention to their mystical bent.

Sufism is not held in universal high regard throughout the Ummah. For example, when the founders of the state of Saudi Arabia came to power in the 18th century CE, they effectively outlawed Sufism and destroyed Sufi shrines in areas under their control. The reason for this hostility was the perception that shrines, based on tombs of holy men, were a religious innovation in Islam. And innovation, when used in a religious context, is roughly equivalent to the idea of heresy. Many Muslims of a more conservative outlook view Sufism with varying degrees of hostility, while Muslims with a modern view of the world tend to see Sufism as superstitious. Sufis are also accused with emphasizing the individual too much at the expense of the collective good, and of having a quiescent view when it comes to politics or industriousness. Historically, Sufis, with their personal connections to the divine, have not always been meticulous in their religious observations. This has also led to suspicions among some that Sufis are not "good" Muslims. Still, Sufism (at least in its conventional varieties) remains widespread throughout most portions of the Ummah.[9]

Muslims' views of other religions also display much variety. Muhammad explicitly saw himself in a line of prophetic and religious figures stretching back to Abraham and beyond.[10] Accordingly, Islam holds that revelations from God include not only the Qur'an, but also the Gospels, as well as the Torah and the Psalms. However, Muslims hold that these pre-Islamic writings have been corrupted over time (this corruption can be one of interpretation of texts or actual alteration of what the original texts originally said), and that only the Qur'an has been preserved from textual tampering.

CONTEMPORARY DEVELOPMENTS

Islam as a world religion continues to spread and grow. Today, there are over 1.5 billion Muslims, making up between one-fifth and one-quarter of the world's population. From its birthplace in the Arabian Peninsula, Islam has spread beyond the Islamic heartland (roughly the areas of the Umayyad and Abbasid caliphates) into regions such as sub-Saharan Africa (for example, there are almost 80 million Muslims in Nigeria), as well as the United States and Canada (4 million and 150,000, respectively). Even China's Xinjiang province, north of Tibet, has a substantial Muslim population (9 million out of 22 million). Clearly, Islam is not just a religion of the Arabs. In fact, Arabs make up less than one-fifth of the entire Muslim population: there are almost as many Indonesian Muslims as there are Muslims from the 22 nations of the Arab League.

The end of the age of colonialism after World War II led to independence for many nation-states, including places where Islam is strong. Indeed, the fight against colonialism was particularly pronounced among Muslims from the 19th century onward. The liberation of many territories has led to what is called an Islamic revival. However, the revival (also sometimes called the awakening)

Figure 7.4: Famous American Muslims.

is more than political. It includes a reexamination of religiosity as well as an evaluation of the dangers, not to mention the potential usefulness, of the West in relation to the Ummah itself.

Islam confronted this situation over a thousand years earlier when it encountered Greek thought in the translated works of Plato, Aristotle, and others. Islam, by consensus, decided to use the tools of foreign thinkers—logic, rhetoric, and so on— but rejected the actual content of that foreign thought. This appears to be the conclusion that modern Islam is ready to take once again. Whether Islam can adapt to Western technology while refusing to adopt Western thought patterns remains to be seen, but if history repeats itself, Islam should be successful.

Since innovation is heretical, then one suggested approach is to go "back to the future," with attempts to restore the Ummah to its supposed pristine purity during the days of the Prophet. Whether this can actually be achieved is doubtful, given that Islam is now a worldwide, multilingual, and cross-cultural phenomenon, rather than a linguistically and culturally homogeneous system of a relatively small number of urban Arabs with a seventh-century CE outlook. These modern restorationists, if they can be called that, who wish the Ummah to return to a simpler yesteryear, are generally called *Salafis* (from the Arabic for ancestral).[11] Salafi was first used in 19th-century CE Egypt by a famous reformer, Muhammad ʿAbduh. It does not mean "fundamentalist," though this is sometimes the term Western journalists employ to label these modern conservatives. Among such groups is the Muslim Brotherhood,[12] whose victorious candidate for president of Egypt in 2012, Mohammed Mursi, was toppled in an anti-Islamist military coup barely a year after taking office.

Salafis, however, are not unchallenged. Not only do they have to contend with Sufi mystics and traditionalist Ulama, they are often challenged (most often unexpectedly) by modern Muslim feminists. The talk of Islam and feminism strikes many as contradictory.[13] However, Muhammad himself can be viewed as something of a seventh-century CE feminist, with his attacks on female infanticide, his legislation ensuring that women could inherit estates from their family, limiting polygamy by not only allowing four wives per husband, but also by effectively eliminating it altogether through his insistence that if a man were to have more than one wife, each wife had to be treated completely and totally equally. There were to be no favorites. Muhammad's own comment on this stricture was that it was virtually impossible to carry out. Thus, Muhammad may have meant this virtually impossible undertaking to be the death knell of polygamy. Whatever the intent, the vast majority of Muslims adhere to the one-man-one-woman arrangement in the building of the family.

Evidence that women had legal rights in 19th-century Islam can be found at the heart of the Ottoman Empire. Women not only had the right to sue men in court, but according to the records of the time, women succeeded in their lawsuits more often than not. During the same period in Victorian England, such rights for women were unthinkable. The collapse of the Ottoman Empire arrested this evolution in gender attitudes in Islam, much as the impact of colonialism had a disturbing effect on the application of Shari`a: in those areas of the world where Shari`a was abrogated by the colonial experience, the tendency has been to reintroduce it by applying it literally, since the traditions of how the law was to be applied in increasingly modern contexts were lost. Hence, we hear about women in sub-Saharan Africa being stoned to death for having sex outside of marriage—because they were raped. This causes revulsion no less in most portions of the Muslim world than it does in more "progressive" societies.

The fact that women have served Muslim-majority countries as prime minister and head of state is often overlooked, since non-Muslims often see Saudi Arabia as setting the standard for what is "correct Islam." But women reaching the highest pinnacle in the political sphere are not anomalies: women have succeeded each other in their country's highest office, and one Muslim country, Bangladesh (population 150+ million), has been run by women longer than by men.

Of course, feminism is not to be measured simply by who sits in the local version of the Oval Office. Historically, Muslim women have run educational academies, even in areas where the education of women was not yet mainstream. And while the thought of having women lead men in prayer at the mosque is an idea not yet ready for prime time, women are allowed to serve as prayer leaders of congregations that are entirely made up of females (think of single-sex educational settings where the chaplain—a Christian term, to be sure—is also a woman).

SUMMARY

From its beginnings in an out-of-the-way desert area of southwest Asia, Islam has grown to be the world's second largest religion, present on every single continent. While the liturgical language of the religion and of its scriptures, the Qur'an, remains Arabic, most Muslims are not native speakers of the language of Muhammad. While there is core agreement on common practices—the Five Pillars of witness, prayer, fasting, charitable giving, and pilgrimage—as well as core theological concepts on the Oneness of God, Angels, Scriptures, Prophets, Divine Judgment, and Divine Sovereignty, Islam as it is lived shows remarkable diversity, not too surprising for a religion that boasts over one and a half billion adherents.

KEY TERMS

- **Allah.** The Arabic word for God
- **Caliph.** The political leader of the Ummah, seen as a successor to Muhammad
- **Hajj.** The annual pilgrimage to Mecca
- **Ijma.** Consensus (of the Ummah)
- **Imam.** For the Shi`ites, an infallible successor to Muhammad; among the Sunnis, a prayer leader
- **Jihad.** Striving or struggling in God's cause; this effort may be personal, or communal
- **Ka`bah.** The shrine central to the annual Islamic pilgrimage to Mecca
- **Mosque.** Place of worship where the community gathers for midday prayer on Friday
- **Prophet.** One who receives revelations from God and transmits them to the rest of humanity
- **Qur'an.** The scriptures of Islam, revealed to Muhammad through the Archangel Gabriel
- **Shari`a.** Islamic law, the sources of which are considered divine
- **Shi`ite Islam.** Made up of followers of Ali, Muhammad's son-in-law
- **Sufism.** The Islamic version of mysticism, wherein a person can be in direct touch with God
- **Sunni Islam.** These Muslims place final authority in the consensus of the Ummah
- **Ulama.** The class of experts in matters of Shari`a and other Islamic fields of knowledge
- **Ummah.** The entirety of the Islamic "commonwealth"

REVIEW QUESTIONS

1. Who was Muhammad, and what were his role and position in the coming of Islam?
2. What are the Five Pillars, or basic practices, of Islam?
3. What are the Six Articles of Faith, or basic beliefs, of Islam?
4. What is the historic relation of Islam to Judaism and Christianity?
5. What is Sufism, and how is it regarded within Islam?

END NOTES

1. Speight, R. Marston. *God Is One: The Way of Islam* (New York: Friendship Press, 2001), 13–15.
2. Cragg, Kenneth. *The Call of the Minaret*, 3rd ed. (Oxford: OneWorld, 2000), 61–82.
3. Dabashi, Hamid. *Authority in Islam* (New Brunswick: Transaction Publishers, 1989), 71–93.
4. Esposito, John L. *Islam: The Straight Path* (New York: Oxford University Press, 2011), 55–61.
5. Sarwat, Sadoon. *Grains of Sustenance: A Study of the Faith and Practice of Islam* (2012), 8–17.
6. Hughes, Aaron W. *Muslim Identities* (New York: Columbia University Press, 2013), 141–142.
7. Menocal, Maria. *The Ornament of the World: How Muslims, Jews and Christians Created a Culture of Tolerance in Medieval Spain* (Boston: Little, Brown, 2002), 28–44.
8. Denny, Frederick M. *An Introduction to Islam*, 4th ed. (Boston: Prentice Hall, 2011), 110–128.
9. Hammond, Andrew. *Pop Culture Arab World!* (Santa Barbara, CA: ABC CLIO, 2005), 194–199.
10. *A Common Word between Us and You* (Jordan: Royal Aal al-Bayt Institute for Islamic Thought, 2009).
11. *Encyclopaedia of Islam*, 2nd ed. (Leiden: Brill, 1995), 900–909.
12. Campo, Juan E. *Encyclopedia of Islam* (Facts On File, 2009), 506–508.
13. Lyons, Jonathan. *Islam through Western Eyes* (New York: Columbia University Press, 2014), 155–190.

8. Judaism

By William J. Cook Jr.

OVERVIEW

Judaism is different from other religions, which we will discuss in this section of the book, because being Jewish can refer both to being a people or a cultural group, as well as being the practitioner of a religion known as Judaism. Though Judaism is the smallest of the world's great religions, it has had a very significant influence upon the development of culture in the Western world, not to mention having been an important wellspring for two other major world religions, Christianity and Islam. As we have seen earlier, in the chapter describing the history of criminal justice, the development of our system of justice occurred at the hands of individuals who drew much of their inspiration from their study of Jewish law and traditions.

Historical records reveal that Sephardic Jews (those practicing a type of Judaism that follows a Babylonian tradition of Jewish law and ritual) first came to the North American colonies in the 1600s and established their first synagogue (a house of worship) in 1692. Later, in the 1880s, very large numbers of Ashkenazi Jews (those who come from Europe, especially Germany, and combined Babylonian and Palestinian traditions of Jewish law and ritual) immigrated to the United States.[1] During the 19th century, Jews participated in the western expansion in the United States and became part of the saga

Figure 8.1: *Abraham and Isaac* by Marc Chagall is the artist's depiction of the Patriarch, Abraham, being stopped by an angel as he prepares to sacrifice his son, Isaac.

of the American West.[2] There were additional waves of immigration during the early and mid-20th century.

Today, the percentage of adults in the United States who state they are Jewish has dropped to about two percent (approximately 4.2 million persons). The percentage of Americans who have Jewish ancestry or culture and state they are Jewish, but are also atheist, agnostic, or have no particular religion—in other words, not religious at all—now ranges about .5 percent. Among the youngest generation of adult Jews, the millennials, about 68 percent indicate they are Jewish by religion, while 32 percent report they are Jewish by ancestry, ethnicity, or culture, but not by religion. About 43 percent of the population of American Jews resides in the Northeast.[3]

The Jewish people trace their religious and ethnic heritage back about 4000 years ago to the ancient world of Palestine. Fundamental to their religion is the conviction that God made covenants (i.e., a covenant is a relationship of commitment between God and God's people) with Abraham, Moses, and David, who were leaders of different generations of the Jewish people in the ancient world. Never a large group and subjected to conquests, persecutions, and slavery, the Jewish people have had to overcome great suffering; it is extraordinary that the Jewish people have survived to this day and have achieved such significance in history. In the opinion of Huston Smith, one of the foremost scholars of religious studies, "what lifted the Jews from obscurity to permanent religious greatness was their passion for meaning."[4] Next, we'll turn to the history of the Jewish people and later come back to examine the ways in which the Jewish people found meaning in life and in their relationship to God.

HISTORY

To speak of the history of the Jewish people, one must bear in mind the importance of the idea of a *story*. For those who are Jewish, history is not simply a set of facts, but the story of their people. And in remembering this story, there results a sense of unity as it is studied, handed down from generation to generation, and sometimes relived.[5] It is "the story of a God who acts in time and leads his people through time to a final fulfillment."[6]

It is through the pages of the Hebrew Bible that one comes to understand the *story*. In the first part of the Hebrew Bible, one finds the Book of Genesis, which tells how God created the world and its creatures and people by His words. As the story unfolds, one is introduced to the early leaders, or patriarchs, of the Jewish people, about how they came to hold a unique set of beliefs, and how this people eventually became a nation, living in a land given to them by their God. According to Cohn-Sherbok, "on the basis of ancient documents found at the Mesopotamian sites of Mari and Nuzi, the accounts of the Hebrew patriarchs accurately reflect the conditions of the Middle Bronze Age period (2000–1500 BCE)."[7]

In the Book of Genesis, which is where the beginnings of the history of the Jewish people are related, the idea of a **covenant**, or "contract of mutual obligation," between God and the people is a fundamental part of the story. After the great deluge, God established a covenant (known as a *berit* in Hebrew) with Noah and his offspring never again to destroy the world with a flood. The sign of the covenant was a rainbow in the sky.[8]

Patriarchs

Abraham is the patriarch from whom the Jewish people descend. The events of the story of Abraham have been estimated to be about 1800 BCE.[9] A descendant of Terah, he was called Abram (but later known as Abraham) and is considered the father of many nations. Abram lived in Mesopotamia, and at 75 years old, was called by God and told to "go from your country and your kindred and your father's house to the land that I will show you."[10] Then, he was given five blessings: God promises to make of Abram a great nation, bless him, make his name great, bless those who bless him and curse those who curse him, and in him, to bless all the families of the earth.

So, Abram left and traveled to the land of Canaan. And there, God appears to Abraham and promises to give the land to his offspring. After a period spent in Egypt during a famine, Abram continues his life as a prosperous nomad with "flocks and herds." His nephew, Lot, is taken captive, but Abram rescues

Figure 8.2: *Moses* by Chagall shows the story of the infant Moses being saved from the river by the Pharoah's daughter.

him. Soon, Abram becomes concerned that he has no son to be an heir. But God comes to Abram in a vision, promising him that "his very own issue would be his heir." God said: "Look toward heaven and count the stars ... so shall your descendants be." And Abram believed, and "the Lord reckoned it to him as righteousness."[11]

But Abram's wife, Sarai, bore Abram (now in his eighties), no children, so she offered him her Egyptian maidservant, Hagar, to be his concubine. Hagar conceived a child by Abram, and "she looked with contempt upon her mistress." Thus, Sarai was harsh to Hagar, who then ran away. But later on by a well, an angel appears to Hagar and tells her to return to Sarai and "submit to her"; and that she would have a son who was to be named Ishmael. The angel promises to "so greatly multiply your offspring that they cannot be counted for multitude."[12] (Today, Muslims see Ishmael as the progenitor of 12 tribes in North Arabia and "recognize Arabs as the descendants of Ishmael."[13])

When Abram was 99 years old, God again appears to him and says, "I am God Almighty; walk before me and be blameless." God then promises: "And I will make my covenant between you and me, and make you exceedingly numerous ... no longer shall your name be Abram, but your name shall be Abraham." The covenant requires that "every male among you shall be circumcised when he is eight days old." God also changes Abram's wife's name to Sarah (from Sarai). And God gives his word that Abraham would have a son by Sarah and that his name would be Isaac; God also pledges for Isaac to "establish my covenant with him as an everlasting covenant for his offspring after him." Additionally, God promises to make of Ishmael a great nation, too.[14]

One day, God tests Abraham by telling him to take his son, whom he dearly loved, to a mountain in the land of Moriah and "offer him there as a burnt offering." Abraham travels to that land and places a bundle of wood on Isaac, as he carries a knife and fire, and together they walk to the place of offering. Arriving at the place of offering, Abraham builds an altar, binds his son, and places him on the pile of wood that is on the altar. As Abraham takes his knife to kill Isaac, an angel calls to him, saying, "Do not lay your hand on that boy or do anything to him; for now I know that you fear God since you have not withheld your son, your only son, from me." At that point, Abraham sees a ram caught in a thicket and offers it as the sacrifice. After this event, God again promises to bless Abraham.[15] To this day, Abraham is considered a model of faithfulness. And the story of the binding of Isaac, because the boy offered himself as a willing victim, has been seen by later generations as an example to be emulated, in that one should prefer martyrdom than deny allegiance to God.[16]

The story continues with the life of Isaac, the second patriarch, his wife, Rebekah, and his sons, Jacob and Esau. Isaac is often seen as a model of willingness to sacrifice one's life rather than violate Jewish law.[17] His son, Jacob, would become the third patriarch.

Jacob acquired the birthright of his older brother, Esau, through devious means. At the suggestion of his mother, he fled to the land of his mother. As he travels away, he comes to a place where at night, he puts a stone under his head and has a dream of a ladder, from Earth to heaven, on which angels are ascending and descending from heaven. And God stands next to him and says, "I am the Lord, the God of Abraham, your father, and the God of Isaac; the land on which you lie I will give to you and your offspring." God foretells that Jacob would have many offspring and promises to be with him and keep him wherever he goes. Jacob names the place Bethel, which means "the House of God."[18]

Jacob arrives in his mother's land, and after being deceived in his first marriage, he finally marries Rachel. He fathers children, one of whom is by Rachel and known as Joseph. Finally, he returns home. On the night before Jacob sees his brother, Esau, whom he fears will still be vengeful, he is alone "and a man wrestled with him until daybreak." During the encounter, Jacob's hip was put out of joint, and yet Jacob would not let this man go until he received a blessing. The man said: "You shall no longer be called Jacob, but Israel, for you have striven with god and with humans and have prevailed." The man blessed Jacob, who decided to name that place Peniel, because he said, "I have seen God face to face, and yet my life is preserved."[19]

Jacob had 12 sons, who would become the progenitors of the 12 tribes of Israel. However, Jacob, (of course, now known as Israel), loses his son, Joseph, whom he believes to be dead, but who was actually sold into slavery by his brothers. Taken to Egypt, Joseph ends up imprisoned after being falsely accused of rape by his master's wife. Joseph, because of his ability to interpret dreams, is freed and soon becomes valuable to the pharaoh; eventually, he becomes wealthy and powerful because he is also a wise administrator. It seems that the events described in the story of Joseph might have happened around 1700 BCE because archaeological evidence suggests that people from Palestine may have traveled to Egypt around that time.[20]

There is a famine, so Joseph's brothers come to Egypt to get food, and, though they do not recognize him, he realizes who they are and helps them, thereby saving his people. Finally, Joseph is reunited with his father, Jacob. The significance of what happens in the story of Joseph is that it shows that "the God of Israel was a god who acted in history on behalf of his people and thus could be counted on to keep the covenant established with Abraham and reaffirmed with Isaac and Jacob." And, most importantly, it can be said that "Joseph represents the covenant in action."[21]

But there is an ominous note in the story of Joseph helping his family. It is what brings "the twelve tribes to Egypt and sets the scene for the story of the slavery in the land of the Pharaohs and for the Exodus that brought that slavery to an end."[22] After Joseph's death, his family remained in Egypt because they were able to live well there. But when a new pharaoh, one "who did not know Joseph," came to power, the Hebrew people were "oppressed and persecuted and forced to work as slaves on the construction of the royal cities of Pithom and Ramses."[23] The new pharaoh also decrees that all newborn Hebrew males are to be killed.

The biblical narrative continues with the story of the deliverance of the Hebrew people from Egyptian slavery in the Book of Exodus. The story begins with the birth of a male child to a family of the house of Levi. When he was three months old, the parents tried to save their son by placing him in a basket that was hidden among the reeds along the river. They left his older sister to watch what happened. Soon, the pharaoh's daughter saw the basket and had her servant bring it to her. She "took pity on the child because he was crying," and realizing he was a Hebrew child, decided to get a nurse for him after Noah's sister suggested she could find one (who in reality would be the child's birth mother). Later, the child was brought to live with the pharaoh's daughter, and she named him Moses (which means "I drew him out of the water"). He was raised as an Egyptian prince.[24] Moses was destined to become "the most important figure in Judaism."[25]

When he was older, he saw a Hebrew slave being abused—and about to be murdered—by an Egyptian overseer. Angered at the injustice, Moses intervened, saving the life of the Hebrew slave and killing the Egyptian. Moses fled to Midian, where he became a shepherd for Jethro, the priest of Midian, and married his daughter, Zipporah. It was while tending flock at the Mount of Horeb, known as "the mountain of God," that "the angel of the Lord appeared to him in a flame of fire out of a bush; he looked and the bush was blazing, but it was not consumed."[26] God calls to Moses, declaring, "I am the God of your father, the God of Abraham, the god of Isaac, and the God of Jacob." Moses, fearing to look at God, hid his face. Then, God said that he would deliver his people from the Egyptians and bring them to the "land of milk and honey" and

Figure 8.3: Jewish people praying by the Western Wall of the destroyed Temple in Jerusalem. This wall is all that remains of the Jewish Temple site, which was the holiest place in Judaism.

that "I will send you to Pharaoh to bring my people, the Israelites, out of Egypt." But Moses questions his ability to do such a task, saying, "Who am I?" But God answers: "I will be with you" and gives a sign to Moses: that he will worship on that very mountain after bringing the people out of Egypt.[27] Subsequently, Moses asks God's name; God replies: "I AM WHO I AM," and "Thus, you shall say to the Israelites, I AM has sent me to you."[28] (Jewish practice is never to pronounce the name of God; it is usually written as the **tetragrammaton YHVH**, and, instead, when referring to God, it is customary to use "the Lord" or "Adonai"; among Christians, the name of God is written as "Yahweh.")

To convince the pharaoh, who was possibly Ramses II (1290–1224 BCE), God sent ten plagues against the Egyptians.[29] The last plague was to slay the first-born sons of the Egyptians, but the Israelites' first-born males were spared by the Angel of Death because their parents smeared the blood of a slaughtered lamb on their doorposts. This was the first Passover.

The pharaoh did let the people leave, which they did so quickly that they did not take time to let bread rise, and "the Lord went in front of them in a pillar of cloud by day to lead them along the way, and a pillar of fire by night to give them light."[30] However, the pharaoh changed his mind and pursued the escaping Hebrew slaves with his chariots. When Hebrews came to the sea and were about to be overtaken by pharaoh's men, they complained to Moses, saying, "What have you done to us?" But Moses reassured them, and God instructed

Moses to "lift up your staff, stretch out your hand over the sea and divide it."[31] The Israelites escaped through the parted sea, and there, all of the pursuing Egyptians drowned when the waters returned.

The Israelites entered the wilderness and were given food (i.e., "bread rained from heaven") and water (from a rock that Moses struck with his staff) through miracles done through Moses's intercession for his people. Coming to Mount Sinai, Moses alone climbed the mountain and remained there 40 days, during which he had neither food nor drink. When Moses returned to the people, he carried the two tablets on which were inscribed God's laws (the Ten Commandments and other laws), but he smashed them when he found the people had been unfaithful during his absence. Later, he carved new tablets with the laws, known as the *Torah*, which he taught the people. Moses was thus the mediator of God's covenant and the Torah to God's chosen people.[32]

For 40 years, Moses led the Israelites in the wilderness until they finally reached the border of the Promised Land, the Land of Canaan, where he died. The religious scholar Louis Jacobs observes that very few scholars deny that Moses was a historical figure, but the more important issue is "not so much the question of the historical Moses, but the role this towering figure occupies in the life and thought of the Jewish religion."[33]

The Book of Joshua describes the Israelites crossing the River Jordan, then entering and conquering the Land of Canaan; this happened sometime around the end of the 13th century BCE, as "there is archeological evidence that a people known as 'Israel' was already established in the Land of Canaan by 1220 BCE."[34] Joshua was an assistant to Moses and was named by God to be his successor; he is "the prototype of the faithful disciple."[35] Under the leadership of Joshua, the Israelites enter into a "solemn covenant to reject other Gods, serve Yahweh alone, and to observe the laws of the covenant."[36]

Judges and Monarchy

After Joshua dies, there comes the reign of Judges, which is described in the Book of Judges. There are 12 judges, among whom the major ones are Othneil, Ehud, Deborah, Gideon, Jephthah, and Samson. They "were tribal and attached to particular regions; their fragmented reign continued for more than 150 years during the twelfth and eleventh centuries BCE."[37] Samuel was the last of the judges and warned the people against foreign gods. He also anointed Saul as the first king of Israel, and later anointed David as king when Saul died in a battle.

David enters the biblical narrative as the courageous shepherd boy who faces the giant, Goliath, and fells him with a slingshot in a battle with the Philistines. He is also said to have been a talented musician, whose playing of the lyre was able to soothe King Saul when he was distressed; David is also said to the be the composer of the Psalms. Treated unfairly—that is to say, marked for death—by King Saul, David remains loyal. Eventually, David is anointed king of Judah, and then becomes king of Israel around 1000 BCE, reigning for about 40 years. He captures Jerusalem, names it the City of David, and decides to build a temple there, but is told by the prophet Nathan that he cannot because he "is a man of war." David was in many ways a very good king, but he did have weaknesses such as his lust for Bathsheba, the wife of another man. According to Jacobs, "it is not the historical David that is important for the Jewish religion [instead, it is] the David of tradition, David as the proto-type of the saintly psalmist who pours out his heart in supplication to God on his own behalf, but especially on behalf of his people." Jacobs also notes the contrast between Moses, the "stern lawgiver" and David, "the graceful singer of God's praises."[38]

Solomon is the next king of Israel, and is, of course, David's son. Solomon is remembered for his wisdom and for being visited by the queen of Sheba. It was Solomon, who, when he became wealthy, built the first temple in Jerusalem and a royal palace. He placed the Ark of the Covenant, which contained the two tablets with the law, in the temple.

Divided Kingdom and Conquest

After the death of Solomon in 922 BCE, there was a split in the kingdom when ten tribes in the north broke way and appointed a king of their own. The northern kingdom was known as Israel, and the southern kingdom was known as the kingdom of Judah. The kingdom of Judah was composed of the remaining two tribes, Judah and Simeon, and kept Jerusalem as its royal city. The northern kingdom, Israel, had Samaria as its royal city. The people of Samaria were conquered by the Assyrians in 722 BCE and exiled, while Babylonians and others were sent to live in their land. Thus, the northern kingdom disappeared; the conquest of the Israelites was seen as a punishment for worshipping false gods and "for the peoples' lack of allegiance to Yahweh and not following His law." It happened that there was to be continuing antagonism between the Samaritans and the Jewish people later.[39]

The kingdom of Judah survived because its king, Ahaz (735–715 BCE), paid tribute to the Assyrians and encouraged the worship of Assyrian gods. But the prophet, Isaiah, who believed that the northern kingdom of Israel collapsed because of its unfaithfulness to God's law, warned against idolatry and of a similar fate for the kingdom of Judah.[40] Later, when Josiah (640–609) is king, the prophet Jeremiah warns "that the southern kingdom would eventually be devastated by foreign powers" and that "Jerusalem and the temple itself would be destroyed."[41] In 597 BCE, Nebuchadnezzar, king of Babylon, conquers Jerusalem, plundering the temple and palace, and Judah's king, Jehoaikim, and many of its citizens are taken into captivity in Babylon. In 586, the new king of Judah, Zedekiah—against the advice of the prophet, Jeremiah—rebels, but Nebuchadnezzar returns, lays siege, and conquers Jerusalem, destroying the temple. The king (who was blinded) is exiled to Babylon. The disastrous event is commemorated on the ninth of Ab (during July-August) each year.

Persian Period

The time of captivity in Babylon is described in the lament of Psalm 137: "By the waters of Babylon, there we sat down and there we wept when we remembered Zion." Nevertheless, the exiles, though persecuted in Babylon, still seem to have prospered there and kept "the faith alive in synagogues." The priest, Ezekiel, who had been among the exiles, began to prophesy that God "would restore the fallen nation."[42] Eventually, this did happen when the Babylonians had been conquered by the Persians. The king of Persia, Cyrus, allowed the exiles to return home in 539 BCE.

Second Temple Period

When the exiles return to Jerusalem, they set about rebuilding the temple. It is completed sometime around 515 BCE and is known as the Second Temple. The leaders do not allow any Samaritans to assist in building the temple. The people are having difficulties, even though they had returned home. Two important leaders arose. First, Nehemiah was the Jewish governor of Judea who rebuilt the walls of Jerusalem and addressed problems of laxity in the community that included intermarriage with non-Jewish people and the rich exploiting the poor.[43] The second important person was Ezra, who was a scribe, and instructed the people in the law in 458 BCE. His goal was to bring people back to the covenant, as they had become lax about worshipping; Ezra had the law read to the people in a language they could understand.[44] Ezra adapted the law to new circumstances, which led the people to accept it as a "constitution"; this, in turn, caused Persia to recognize Judah as a legal community.[45]

During this same time, there continued to be a Jewish community in Babylon, as well as one in Egypt because, when Jerusalem fell in 587 BCE, there was a group of Jews (including the prophet Jeremiah) who had fled there. Wherever they were, the Jews were distinctive because they followed the law, or the Torah. It is during this period that one sees the beginnings of the Diaspora (this is the name for the Jewish communities that were located outside of Palestine).[46]

Hellenistic (Greek) Period

The Persian Empire fell to Alexander the Great (356–323 BCE) of Macedonia, but when he died, control of Judea passed to the Ptolemaic dynasty. The Jewish community appears to have been treated fairly under the Ptolemys' control. Greek became the language used in all of the areas conquered by Alexander, and during the third century BCE, a Greek version of the Torah, known as the Septuagint, appeared. However, in 198 BCE, control of Judea was taken over by the Seleucid king, Antiochus III (241–187 BCE). When he died, his son,

Seleucus IV (218–175 BCE), plundered the Jerusalem Temple. When Seleucus IV was murdered, he was replaced by Antiochus IV Epiphanes (215–164 BCE) who, after a Jewish rebellion, banned circumcision, Sabbath observance, and reading of the Torah, and rededicated the Temple to Zeus, sacrificing pigs there. These actions brought about a revolt by the Jewish people, who were led by a group known as the Maccabees. Known also as the Hasmoneans, the Maccabees won their battle for independence, restored Jewish Law, rebuilt the altar, and again dedicated the Temple to the God of the Jews on December 14, 164 BCE, which is commemorated today by the Festival of Lights, Hanukkah.[47]

Other developments at this time were the formation of Jewish groups with different political and religious views, among which were the Pharisees and the Sadducees; the Sanhedrin, "or council of leaders, was established as the central authority for all legal decisions involving the different groups."[48] The Pharisees, whose name may mean "separatists," believed that Israel was given an oral Torah (known as the *Mishnah*, and which will be discussed later) by God and also that there was a world to come (i.e., an afterlife). The Sadducees appear to have been aristocratic priests and wealthy landowners who controlled temple worship.[49]

Roman Period

In 63 BCE, the Hasmonean rule of Judea ended with the conquest of Jerusalem by the Roman general, Pompey. The Romans appointed Herod, an Idumite whose family had converted to Judaism under the Hasmoneans, as king of Judea. He rebuilt the Temple to gain the favor of the Jewish people.[50] The Romans ruled in this way: there was a Roman governor who supervised Roman concerns in the area, but the Jewish people were ruled by a Jewish king (Herod) and the Sanhedrin. After Herod's death, the rule of Judea was divided among his three sons by the Romans.

It was during this time that Christianity began. Initially, "the Way," as it was then known, was a sect within Judaism, and its early members were all Jewish. However, as large numbers of pagans converted to Christianity, the nature of the sect changed, so as to become an independent religion.

There was a series of rebellions by the Jewish people against Roman rule, one of which occurred between 66–70 CE and was led by a group known as the Zealots. The Romans crushed the rebellion, and then the Roman emperor Titus disbanded the Sanhedrin, destroyed Jerusalem, and tore down the Temple in 70 CE. Many of the Jewish people in Judea were enslaved by the Romans. Later, in 132 CE, there was another rebellion led by Simon bar Kochba, which was "inspired by the belief that God would empower the Jews to regain control of their country and to rebuild the temple."[51] Nevertheless, the Romans suppressed the rebellion, killing about half a million Jews and devastating much of Judea; the rebellion was over by 135 CE. The emperor Hadrian outlawed Judaism in the land (though this law was rescinded later after he died), and Jews "were forbidden to enter the now pagan city of Jerusalem under penalty of death."[52]

Rabbinic Judaism

After the destruction of the Temple, Jews could no longer worship in the traditional ways (i.e., sacrificial offerings) that had been handed down through the generations. A group of scholars assembled at Yavneh, located west of Jerusalem, and developed a form of Judaism that was not dependent on sacrifice or Temple worship. After the defeat of bar Kochba, this community of sages moved to Usha in Galilee, and thus began the development of Rabbinic Judaism (rabbi is the name for a teacher of Judaism qualified to render decisions in Jewish law[53]). The rabbis' work consisted of "interpreting Jewish law and formulating norms that would govern every aspect of Jewish life as it developed in new social, political and cultural circumstances."[54] The rabbis taught that there were 613 commandments revealed by Moses: "365 prohibitions according to the number of days in a solar year, and 248 positive precepts corresponding to the parts of the human body."

The rabbi known as Judah the Prince compiled the Mishnah around 200 CE. This was a digest of oral Torah, and it "consisted of discussions and rulings of teachers that had been transmitted orally." It covers such topics as benedictions and prayers, tithes, the Sabbath, Passover, marriage, civil law and criminal proceedings, temple matters, and ritual purification.[55] Then, rabbis in Jerusalem and Babylon produced commentaries based on extended discussions of the Mishnah, which were known as the Talmud; the Jerusalem Talmud appeared around 400 CE, while the Babylonian Talmud was produced around 500 CE and has been the more influential of the two. Lastly, there is the type of text known as Midrash. This is a searching of scripture and includes "sermons and other explanations of the Bible ... (that was) compiled between 300–600 CE."[56]

Middle Ages

During the Middle Ages, the majority of Jewish people were living away from Palestine in communities in Europe, North Africa, the Middle East, and even in such distant places as India and China; most were living in lands controlled by either Muslim or Christian rulers. It was during this time that Jewish people were forced to live in restricted zones, or ghettos, in many localities and suffered many persecutions.

An important figure from this period was Moses Maimonides (1135–1204), a physician, Talmudic scholar, and philosopher. He showed that Greek philosophy was compatible with Jewish thought and also compiled the *Mishnah Torah*, a "great code of Jewish Law" and wrote *The Guide for the Perplexed*, which showed how the Bible has to be interpreted "not to be in conflict but in harmony with reason."[57]

Age of Enlightenment and the Modern Era

The Age of Enlightenment began in Europe in the late 17th century and brought with it a rejection of tradition in favor of reason, with an emphasis on the individual. Modern states such as France and Germany, as well as England, began an era of religious tolerance and welcomed Jews into a secularized society, if they were willing to compromise on some of their practices, which had kept them separated. But the emancipation of Jewish people from ghetto life also meant that the subsequent assimilation to a more secular life became a threat to the Jewish community.

In the 1800s, there was a movement among educated Jews in Germany to make changes in the practice of Judaism to bring the religion into the modern era. This approach became known as **Reform Judaism** and was rooted in an assumption that there are elements of the Torah that are eternal, but other legal customs developed over the centuries in response to different situations faced by the Jewish people. Among the changes were a relaxed attitude toward the Sabbath, less observance of dietary regulations, disavowal of a messiah and the hope of returning to Jerusalem to rebuild the Temple. The Reformists emphasized the ethical precepts of Judaism more than the rituals, conducted services in German, and incorporated music from pipe organs. The movement spread to other countries and was well received in America.[58] In 1873, Isaac Mayer Wise (1819–1900) organized the Union of American Hebrew Congregations in Cincinnati, and two years later, instituted the Hebrew Union College to train Reform rabbis. However, at a banquet celebrating the graduation of the school's first graduates, shellfish (forbidden by traditional Jewish dietary law) was served. Some guests reacted with horror, which helped lead to the development of Conservative Judaism (to be discussed later).[59] Nevertheless, the majority of Jews in the United States today are members of Reform Judaism.

Orthodox Judaism is the name for a movement started in response to the development of Reform Judaism in Europe. The Hungarian rabbi Moses Safer (1762–1839) argued against Reform Judaism, proclaiming that "anything new, any innovation in Jewish life is forbidden by the Torah."[60] Eventually, Orthodox Judaism developed in America, too. The word orthodox actually comes from Christian theology and means right opinion or doctrine. Thus, those who practice Orthodox Judaism "concur that the entire Torah, oral and written, comes from God, in exactly the words in which we now have it, and that everything in the Torah happened exactly as it is said to have happened." Today, there is variety in orthodoxy, with the neoorthodox, the orthodox, and the ultra-orthodox. It is estimated that about one in seven Jews in the United States follows Orthodox Judaism, but the number is growing.[61]

Conservative Judaism also has roots in 19th-century Europe in what was called the Historical School, which was an effort to "try to conserve the traditional Jewish life in the modern world"; it was an attempt "to steer a middle course between Reformers and the Orthodox."[62] The leader of the Historical

Figure 8.4: The Bar Mitzvah is a "coming of age" ritual for Jewish males at age thirteen, when they are then considered responsible for what they do.

School was Rabbi Zechariah Frankel (1801–1873), originally from Prague, who was a theologian and scholar of the Talmudic period. He held that "while freedom to investigate the origins of Jewish beliefs and institutions is granted … this does not affect the need for strict observance of the precepts since such observance belongs to the living religion."[63] However, Frankel and his followers also argued that "although the essentials of Judaism have always remained, some aspects of Jewish life have been modified down through the centuries," and so, "some elements must be considered essential today, other elements may be discarded or modified."[64] This movement, when it came to America, was to be referred to as Conservative Judaism. It happened that "a number of prominent Rabbis and laymen became increasingly disturbed by the excesses of American Reform." These leaders founded the Jewish Theological Seminary to train a modern, but "strictly traditional Rabbinate" and founded the Synagogue of America in 1913.[65]

In America, most Jews are members of either Reform temples or Conservative synagogues. Neusner notes that the differences between the two groups "do not strike outsiders as very weighty" because they concur on most basic questions. He also states that the differences on religious observance among ordinary people will be insignificant, but "their rabbis may differ since Conservative Jews who do not observe dietary laws or the Sabbath and festivals, expect that their rabbis will, while Reform Jews do not [expect their rabbis to do so]."[66]

KEY IDEAS AND PRACTICES

Some of the beliefs of the Jewish people have changed over the many centuries, but others have not changed at all. As Huston Smith observes, "the basic contribution of Judaism to the Middle East (and, it might be added, to the world) was monotheism."[67] Jews believe that there is only one God, who created the universe and who controls the events of history. This God is concerned about people and has revealed God's self to God's people and is the God of all nations. God formed a covenant with the Jewish people, and they were able to strengthen their bond to God by faithfully observing God's law. They believe that God entered history and has intervened in human affairs, and therefore, people must treat each other well; this is to do good works and observe God's Law. In ancient times, the famous Rabbi Hillel once summarized the Torah, or Law, for a person who would convert to Judaism, saying "That which is hateful unto you do not do to your neighbor. This is the whole Torah. The rest is commentary."[68]

The *Shema*, or *Shma*, is a prayer that is "the Jewish declaration of faith."[69] It is this verse (Deuteronomy 6:4): "Hear (*Shema*) O Israel, the Lord our God, the Lord is One." In the book of Deuteronomy, it says that this prayer should be said "when lying down and when rising up." So, a pious Jew should say this prayer in the morning after daybreak and at night; it is also said before one dies, and is recited by martyrs for the faith. The Shema leads to the way that Jews should live: that is, to love God and care for each other by observing the Torah.

Concepts about resurrection and immortality emerged in Jewish thought around the time of the development of Christianity. Prior to that time, "longings for immortal life among the Jews had been satisfied by the belief that the individual would find his fulfillment by merging his personal destiny with the immortal life of his people." The rabbis acknowledged that man had a soul, but never agreed on what happened to the soul when he died. The belief in the resurrection was that one day God would rejoin the souls to the bodies of those who had died.[70]

The coming of a **Messiah**, "the Anointed One," who was to be a person sent by God to bring about a new era of peace on Earth, was a belief that went back to the Prophets, though the term was not used for a redeemer until after the biblical age.[71] Today, Orthodox Jews continue to pray for the coming of the Messiah and hold the belief that "the redemption of the world awaits his advent." Some imagine him as a kind of "mysterious superman," while others see him as "a gifted leader of men and nations." This messiah is a personal messiah, or a person, and all see the Messiah as "God's messenger, endowed with the power and authority to cleanse the world of evil." Generally speaking, Conservative and Reform Jews do not believe in a personal messiah; but they see the idea of messianism as a "human symbol of the divine," which has more to do with the quality of human life, and "it helps project mankind forward, toward a Golden age yet to come." They do have the religious hope that "men must labor together to bring about the Kingdom of God on earth."[72]

The original forms of worship of the Jewish people involved ritual sacrifices of animals by priests at the Temple in Jerusalem. After the destruction of the Temple, this form of worship was no longer possible, and another form developed during the period of Rabbinic Judaism. The location for worship since that time has been the synagogue, a place where Jews come together to study Torah, pray, and listen to sermons at services under the leadership of rabbis and sometimes cantors (religious singers). Services are held on the Sabbath (Saturday) each week and on the Holy Days of each year.

Strictly observant Jews follow the dietary laws (*Kashrut*). Clean food (known as *kosher*, or proper, food) comes from animals that are considered "clean": they have a cloven foot and chew their cud. Food from unclean animals (such as pork, or fish without fins or scales like shellfish) cannot be eaten. The blood must be drained from the clean animal and not consumed. Fruit and vegetables are considered clean, as long as they are free of bugs. Milk cannot be consumed with meat; if one has eaten meat, she or he must wait about seven hours before drinking milk. Also, one may not use utensils that were in contact with meat for dairy.

Time was an important dimension in which God acted, so the Jewish people have consecrated time. There is the Sabbath, or day of rest, taken on the seventh day of the week, as God did in the story of the creation of the world related in the Book of Genesis. The Sabbath is meant for leisure and study of the Torah. For strictly observant Jews, on the Sabbath, there must be no work, travel, chores, or exchange of money. On Friday evenings, as the Sabbath begins, there is a ritual that is followed. Jewish women light two candles and speak a blessing. Then there is the Sabbath meal, during which the father presides over the *Kiddush*, a sanctification of the Sabbath, by saying a benediction over a cup of wine. Then a prayer, the Kiddush, is recited. After drinking the wine, there is a benediction said over the bread (*challah*), and the family has the Sabbath meal.

Judaism also observes feasts according to a lunar calendar cycle. Originally, these three observances were agriculturally based. There is Passover (*Pesach*), which recalls the Exodus from Egypt and which happens at the beginning of the planting season. Passover recalls the Exodus meal eaten on the night Jews fled from Egypt with Moses. Special foods such as unleavened bread, bitter herbs, a mixture of nuts, apples, raisins, and cinnamon, parsley in salted water, and lamb are eaten as a way of recalling the sufferings of the Jewish people under the pharaoh. Then, there is the Feast of Weeks (*Shavuot*, or Pentecost), which commemorates the giving of the Torah to Moses on Mount Sinai, and which happens at the end of the barley harvest, usually around May-June. Thirdly, there is the Festival of Booths (*Sukhot*, or Tabernacles), commemorating the wandering of the Hebrews in the desert before they arrived in Canaan; this takes place at the end of the agricultural season, before winter.

The Days of Awe are especially holy days for the Jewish people. The New Year (*Rosh Hashanah*) is celebrated in the fall, just before the Feast of Booths. Ten days later is the Day of Atonement (*Yom Kippur*), and on this day (which occurs in September-October), Jews confess their sinfulness before God and do penance. During these days, a ram's horn (*Shofar*) is blown to remind the Jewish people of their calling to the Covenant with God. Four days after Yom Kippur is the Festival of Booths (described already in the preceding paragraph), which lasts a week, and is a time of confidence and hope in the future. In November-December is the Feast of Lights (*Hanukkah*), which lasts eight days and recalls the relighting of the candelabra in Jerusalem by Judas Maccabeus in 165 BCE, who regained the Temple and purified it after it was desecrated by Antiochus IV.

Time is also made sacred in the life cycle of a Jewish person through different rituals. At birth, males are circumcised (the ceremony is called a *bris*) on the eighth day after birth, so that the child will bear in his flesh a sign of the Covenant. At puberty, a boy becomes a "son of the Commandment" through a ceremony known as a *Bar Mitzvah* and reads aloud from the Torah in the synagogue. There is now a similar ceremony for girls in Conservative and Reform congregations known as a *Bat Mitzvah*. When a couple marries, they stand under a canopy, and the marriage contract is read. There are seven blessings, and they drink from the cup of betrothal. The glass is then smashed to recall the destruction of the Temple. At the end of life, there is the practice of a bereaved family sitting *shiv'ah*, or mourning for seven days after the burial. On the one-year anniversary of a person's death, the mourning family lights a candle which burns for twenty-four hours, gives a donation to charity in the name of the deceased, and prays the *Mourner's Kaddish*, a prayer that sanctifies God's name, acknowledging that God created the world according to His will and praying for the coming of God's kingdom; though the Kaddish does not mention death, the custom of reciting the prayer when someone dies began in the Middle Ages in Germany and spread to other parts of the world.

CONTEMPORARY DEVELOPMENTS

During the 20th century, two events have had an enormous impact on contemporary Judaism. First, there is the *Shoah* (annihilation, or sometimes called the Holocaust) during World War II, during which Nazi Germany attempted to obliterate the Jewish people; this horrific moment in human history brought about the killing of six million Jewish men, women, and children, and the suffering of many others . As Jews struggled with this immensely evil event, some lost their faith in God, while others wondered if it was a punishment, and still others could just not understand God's ways. Today, in the Jewish community, there is a resolve never to forget what happened, and those lost in the Shoah are remembered on *Yom HaShoah* (Holocaust Memorial Day, which occurs during April-May).

The second major development was the establishment of the State of Israel, which in some sense was a consequence of the Holocaust. The roots of the dream of a Jewish homeland emerged in the 19th century with the development of Zionism, a movement to create a Jewish state in Palestine. Not all Jews accepted Zionism, as they believed that God must be the one to restore the nation of Israel. Nevertheless, at the end of World War II, it was clear that the need for Jews to have their own homeland was paramount. In 1947, the United Nations endorsed a plan to partition Palestine to create an Arab state and a Jewish state. In May 1948, the State of Israel was officially established. In the years since, Israel has encountered wars and other forms of violent resistance to its existence. Yet, it can be said that "the essential fact for Jews is that Israel exists and has withstood all onslaughts against it … . and represents for many Jews a redemption of two thousand years of powerlessness and exile."[73]

In discussing the state of modern American Judaism, Cohn-Sherbok argues that "the modern period has witnessed the fragmentation of the Jewish community into a variety of sub-groups ranging from Ultra-Orthodox Hasidism to progressive Reform Judaism." He then notes these current problems: some Jews have abandoned their belief in God; many do not follow the code of Jewish law; other Jews question the Torah and "choose which laws have a personal significance"; also, there is confusion about what constitutes a Jewish identity— are Jews members of a nation? Or are they a civilization? Are they a religious community?[74] Other questions the Jewish community wrestles with are related to intermarriage with non-Jews, sexuality, and the ordination of women rabbis by some congregations. A last question might be: Should one see himself as an American Jew or as a Jewish American? Regardless of these questions, as Jacob Neusner notes, it can be said that "the very diversity of American Judaism itself expresses the shared life and social dreams of this country."[75]

CHAPTER SUMMARY

Judaism is a religious tradition with a rich history, and it continues to be a vibrant source of faith for many people in the world. Essential to understanding Judaism is to bear in mind that it involves a story—the story of God's care and involvement in history with God's people. It is a story that includes all the ugliness and all the splendor in human nature as a people learn to love their God and to love each other. In the early stages of the story, there are the patriarchs who lead the people as they join in covenants with God and agree to obey God's law, or the Torah. Later, there is the period of the Judges, and then the monarchs, the most famous of whom was King David. There are the periods of slavery in Egypt and the Exodus led by Moses freeing the Hebrews from the clutches of the pharaoh. Then, the captivity in Babylon, the destruction of the Temple built by Solomon, and its later restoration. There were other times when the Jewish people would be subject to Persian, Greek, and Roman overlords. There would be rebellions by the Jewish people, and the final destruction of the Temple by the Romans, which was then followed by the exile of the Jewish people from Palestine to other lands, where they would suffer many persecutions. But through it all, the Jewish people were unified in their commitment to the Covenant with their God through obedience to the Torah.

KEY TERMS

- Covenant
- Conservative Judaism
- Messiah
- Midrash
- Mishnah
- Orthodox Judaism
- Patriarchs
- Reform Judaism
- Shema
- Talmud
- Tetragrammaton
- Torah

REVIEW QUESTIONS

1. Who were the Patriarchs?
2. Who is Moses? What is the Torah?
3. Explain the development of Rabbinic Judaism.
4. Discuss Reform Judaism, Orthodox Judaism, and Conservative Judaism.
5. Discuss contemporary developments in Judaism.

END NOTES

1. Albanese, Catherine L. *America: Religions and Religion* (Boston: Wadsworth, Cengage Learning, 2007), 41.

2. Marks, M. L. *Jews among the Indians* (Chicago: Benison Books, 1992). (The author acknowledges his debt to Eddie Ginsburg for sharing stories about the west.)

3. "A Portrait of Jewish Americans." The Pew Research Center, Religion and Public Life Project, Oc. 1, 2013, http://www.pewforum.org/2013/10/01/jewish-american-beliefs-attitudes-culture-survey/, paragraphs 1–5.

4. Smith, Huston. *The World's Religions* (New York: HarperOne, 1991), 272.

5. Gafni, Isaiah M. *Great World Religions: Judaism* (Chantilly: Teaching Co., 2003), 10.

6. Esposito, John L., Darrell J. Fasching, and Todd Lewis. *World Religions Today* (New York: Oxford University Press, 2006), 21.

7. Cohn-Sherbok, Dan. *Judaism: History, Belief, and Practice* (New York: Routledge, 2003), 21.

8. Jacobs, Louis. *The Jewish Religion: A Companion* (New York: Oxford University Press, 1995), 103.

9. Maher, Michael. *Judaism: An Introduction to the Beliefs and Practices of the Jews* (Blackrock: Columba Press, 2006), 14.

10. Genesis 12:1.

11. Genesis 15 1:6.

12. Genesis 16 1–11.

13. "Ishmael." In *The Columbia Encyclopedia* (New York: Columbia University Press, 2013). http://scroll.lib.westfield.ma.edu:4826/content/entry/columency/ishmael/0 (accessed Nov. 6, 2014).

14. Genesis: 17 1–22.

15. Genesis: 22 1–19.

16. Maher, 15.

17. "Isaac." In *The New Encyclopedia of Judaism* (New York: New York University Press, 2002). http://scroll.lib.westfield.ma.edu:4826/content/entry/nyupencyjud/isaac/0 (accessed Nov. 6, 2014.)

18. Genesis: 28 10–17.

19. Genesis: 32 22–32.

20. Maher, 16.

21. Hollis, Susan. "Joseph." In *Encyclopedia of Jewish Folklore and Traditions* (London: Routledge, 2013). http://scroll.lib.westfield.ma.edu:4826/content/entry/sharpejft/joseph/0 (accessed Nov. 6, 2014).

22. Maher, 16.

23. Cohn-Sherbok, 21.

24. Exodus 2: 1–10.

25. Cohn-Sherbok, 353.

26. Exodus 3: 1–2.

27. Exodus 3: 3–12.

28. Exodus 3:13–14.

29. Maher, 16.

30. Exodus 13:21.

31. Exodus 14:16.

32. Maher, 18.

33. Jacobs, 353.

34. Maher, 16.

35. Jacobs, 290.

36. Maher, 20.

37. Cohn-Sherbok, 32.

38. Jacobs, 113.

39. Maher, 22.

40. Cohn-Sherbok, 61.

41. Cohn-Sherbok, 68–70.

42. Cohn-Sherbok, 74.

43. Cohn-Sherbok, 80.

44. Cohn-Sherbok, 80.

45. Morrison, Martha, and Stephen F. Brown. *Judaism World Religions* (New York: Facts On File, Inc., 1991), 44.

46. Morrison and Brown, 45.

47. Cohn-Sherbok, 88.

48. Morrison and Brown, 47.

49. Jacobs, 376, 438.

50. Maher, 27.

51. Cohn-Sherbok, 115.

52. Morrison and Brown, 48.

53. Jacobs, 401.

54. Maher, 29.

55. Cohn-Sherbok, 116.

56. Morrison and Brown, 49.

57. Jacobs, 32.

58. Maher, 34–35.

59. Jacobs, 416.

60. Jacobs, 473.

61. Neusner, Jacob. "Judaism in the World and in America." In *World Religions in America*, ed. Jacob Neusner (Louisville: Westminster John Knox Press, 2009), 138.

62. Maher, 38.

63. Jacobs, 172–173.

64. Maher, 38.

65. Jacobs, 92.

66. Neusner, 139.

67. Smith, 274.

68. Jacobs, 241.

69. Jacobs, 460.

70. Rosenberg, Stuart E. *Judaism* (Glen Rock: Paulist Press, 1966), 139.

71. Jacobs, 342.

72. Rosenberg, 147–148.

73. Esposito, et al., 125.

74. Cohn-Sherbok, 336.

75. Neusner, 140.

9. Hinduism

By William J. Cook Jr.

He who is rooted in oneness realizes that
I am in every being. Wherever he goes,
He remains in me.

Bhagavad Gita

OVERVIEW

Hinduism is a religion that began long ago, around 1500 BCE, in the Indus Valley in India, developing over many centuries. It is now the oldest and third largest of the world's major religions. There is no known founder as in Buddhism or Christianity, and there is still no overall leader today. Hinduism is the result of a blending of different spiritual traditions from south Asia. Known for its diversity, Hinduism nevertheless still provides its followers with "a shared scripture (the Vedas), a shared sacred symbol (Om), and a sacred center (Varanasi in North India)."[1] Major traditions in Hinduism are Vaishnavism (its followers are devoted to the god Vishnu), Shaivism (devoted to the god Shiva), Shaktism (its followers are devoted to the goddess Devi), and Smartism (devoted to one of these gods: Ganesha, Siva, Shakti, Vishnu, or Surya).

Today, there are about one billion Hindus around the world, constituting 15 percent of the global population. Nearly all Hindus (i.e., 99 percent) live in the Asian Pacific region, while just about one percent of the total population of Hindus can be found living in other parts of the world. Most Hindus (about 94 percent) live in India, followed by Nepal (2 percent) and Bangladesh (1 percent). Hindus are slightly younger (median age is 26) than the rest of the global population (median age is 28).[2]

There are about two million Hindus living in the United States, comprising about one percent of the total population, yet only about one-quarter of Americans know someone who is Hindu. A survey conducted by the Pew Research Religion and Public Life Project suggests that most Americans are "neutral" in their attitudes toward Hindus.[3] Still, there have been sporadic hate crimes committed against them.

Prior to 1965, there were few Asian Hindus who were able to settle in the United States because of restrictive immigration policies; but since the relaxation of those policies, the population of Hindus of Asian heritage has increased dramatically in the past 50 years. As a group, they tend to be well educated, with 57 percent of American Hindus attaining postgraduate education, as compared to 12 percent of the general population.

Most Asian American Hindus (85 percent) tend to worship at a temple a few times a year, but almost an equal number (78 percent) have a religious shrine in their homes. About three-quarters of Asian American Hindus see yoga as more than just exercise, as a spiritual practice. About half believe in astrology (i.e., that the position of the stars can affect people's lives), with a slightly smaller percentage (46 percent) reporting that they believe there is spiritual energy in physical things; about 34 percent believe in ancestral spirits. Almost all Asian American Hindus celebrate Diwali, the Hindu Festival of Lights. Only about one-third of Asian American Hindus (whose heritage is almost invariably Indian) report that "religion is very important in their lives"; this percentage is rather low compared to that of Hindus living in India, among whom about 69 percent indicate that religion is very important when asked the same question. Nearly all American Hindus (91 percent) do not hold that only theirs is "the one true faith" and accept that there is more than one way to interpret the teachings of Hinduism. They say that many religions can lead to eternal life. It appears that Asian American Hindus are open to adapting to other religious traditions in America: about one-third of them report that they sometimes go to services of other religions, and about three-quarters also celebrate Christmas.[4]

It is difficult to know how many non-Asian Hindus there are among the citizens of the United States. Certainly, since the 1960s, a number of Americans have studied the teachings of Hindu masters and converted to Hinduism, joining groups such as Hare Krishna or the Self-Realization Fellowship. Many more persons informally have come to adopt Hindu beliefs such as reincarnation; a Gallup Poll in 2004 found that about 25 percent of all Americans (i.e., 72 million) believe in reincarnation. A Harris Poll conducted in 2005 reports that 16.5 million Americans practice yoga regularly.[5] Thus, it is certain that Hinduism is now influencing American life in a variety of significant ways.

HISTORY

There are several ways that different scholars have found to organize the history of Hinduism. In this chapter, we draw upon the work of Gerald James Larson, who describes the development of Hinduism using these six historical periods: (1) the Indus Valley period; (2) the Brahmanical period; (3) the Buddhist and Shramana period; (4) the Classical period; (5) the Muslim period; and (6) the Modern period.[6]

The Indus Valley Period extends from approximately 3000–1500 BCE. Archaeologists who have studied sites from this time have found religious artifacts suggesting there was a fertility cult with a belief in a Mother Goddess; there are also what appear to be bathing areas (it will be seen later that ritual bathing is part of the practice of Hinduism, as well as a belief in a powerful goddess). Modern Hinduism thus seems to have deep roots that extend into the Indus Valley Culture. The Brahmanical period ranges from approximately 1500–600 BCE. It was then that nomadic tribes from areas in Europe and Asia migrated into the Indus Valley and joined with the people there, eventually forming a ruling class known as the Aryans; later, those who had come into India would come to be referred to as Indo-Aryans. They developed a culture that had a tripartite social structure of priests or **Brahmins**, warriors, and food gatherers or commoners; there was one more group, the *shudras*, who were the pre-Aryan peoples and at the bottom of society.

The Brahmins offered sacrifices of milk, honey, ghee (a type of clarified butter), and animals to the gods of the sky and Earth, so as to "feed them" and ensure that the people would be blessed with such things as prosperity and longevity that would bring happiness. Their gods included *Agni* (god of fire), *Indra* (the warrior god), *Soma* (god of a psychoactive drink used at rituals), and *Varuna* (the god of rewards and punishments). In order to do the sacrificial rituals, the Brahmans utilized instructions found in the *Brahmanas*, chants and hymns (*mantras*) known as the **Vedas**. They also wrote philosophical works, which came to be known as the **Upanishads**. The Vedas are known as *shruti* (scriptures), and these were considered sacred and from the gods. Sometimes, the periods during which these scriptures arose is referred to as the "Vedic period." The first of the three Vedas is the *Rig Veda*, or "Knowledge of Verses," and was written in ancient Sanskrit in northwest India around 1500 BCE; it describes many gods such as Indra (king of gods and king of rain and a warrior), Varuna (god of the heavens and moral law), Agni (the god of fire; our word ignite is related to this name). These gods are like human beings. The gods want "love, wealth, fame and praise."[7]

The Buddhist and Shramana period ranges from approximately 600 BCE to 300 CE. The word *shramana* means "one who strives or exerts himself," so this was a time of searching for inner truth among mendicants who were not priests, as well as among some of the priestly class (Brahmins). One example of a shramana group is those who followed Siddhartha Gautama, who is known as the Buddha, or "the Awakened One." (Buddhism is discussed in detail in the next chapter.)

During this time, there was dissatisfaction with the sacrificial system of the priests; among those who rejected this system of sacrifice by Brahmins, there was a shift toward the inner life with the practice of meditation, also known as *yoga* (*yoga* comes from the word for yoke and can refer to joining mind and body together through concentration). It was also during this period that the pair of famous Indian epics, the *Ramayana* and the *Mahabharata* were written. The Ramayana tells the story of Rama (a manifestation of the Hindu supreme god, Vishnu), whose wife, Sita, is abducted by the king of Lanka. Sita is rescued by Lord Rama, who is helped by Hanuman, the monkey god. The Mahabharata is the longest known epic and is about the Kurukshetra War. It contains the famous *Bhagavad Gita*, a song describing a battlefield dialogue about selfless duty between a prince, Arjuna, and his charioteer (who turns out to be the god-king Krishna). The prince is faced with the moral dilemma of whether he can kill enemies who also happen to be his relatives.

A significant development during the Shramana period was the emergence of devotional cults. For example, the Shaivas belonged to a devotional cult to the god known as Lord Shiva, while those known as the Vaishnavas were devoted to the god Vishnu. Both of these gods absorbed attributes of local gods from different areas. It was during this time that *bhakti*, or devotion to a personal god, begins. Part of the devotion includes worshipping images of the gods, a practice known as *puja* (later, we'll see the continuation of the devotional cults, bhakti, and puja in modern Hinduism).

The *devas* (gods) of the ancient Vedas (and the later gods that developed) are not "God" as people in Western culture conceive of the divine. Instead, they are more powerful than humans, live longer lives, and know much more. They are divinities, but "they are not supreme." Still one must be respectful of them because they are "active forces in the world" and are even associated with natural phenomena.[8]

Classical Hinduism dates from about 300 CE through 1200 CE. At this time, the first Hindu temples were dedicated. There is also attention given to the *Trimurti*, or the three gods who form the Absolute or Brahman (the Supreme Cosmic Spirit). These three forms are: Brahma, the creator god; Vishnu, the preserver god; and, Shiva, the destroyer god. Vishnu has other *avatars*, or manifestations, as Lord Krishna and Lord Rama.

There is also a feminine side to the Absolute or Brahman; this is known as the *Devi* or *Shakti*. Thus, the Absolute can also have three female forms, known as the *Tridevi*, such as Saraswati, goddess of knowledge, arts, and music. She is associated with Brahma, the creator god. Lakshmi is another female form, and she is the goddess of wealth, health, and fortune. Lakshmi is a consort of Vishnu, the preserver god. Then there is Parvati, goddess of spiritual fulfillment (or as Durga, who fights demons); she is associated with Shiva (the Destroyer). Those who are devoted to the Devi are known as *Shaktas*.

In the Hindu concept of time, there are unending cycles of life, death, and rebirth; this is known as **samsara**. These endless cycles are painful for those who must endure them. The future rebirths that a person must experience are determined by *karma*, a form of natural law. It means that someone's life is ruled by what one does; that is to say, that what a person does in this life will determine what he or she will become in the next life or some other future life. Doing good deeds will bring a good destiny; doing evil will bring evil consequences. The consequences can be seen in the social status one has when he or she is born. There can be release from this endless cycle of samsara, and it is known as *moksha*. One may attain moksha in two ways. One method is through disciplined meditation, which leads to wisdom. Another is through what is called bhakti yoga, which involves devotion to a deity who will aid the devotee in attaining moksha.

It was during this time that the **Code of Manu** was produced; it was part of a group of texts on the law known as the *Dharmashastras*. The Code of Manu deals with the king and the state, lists religious and legal obligations, and discusses ethical behavior and punishments for crimes, as well as the social structure (known as *varnas*) and the stages of life.

We'll look at the social structure described in the Code of Manu, which consists of four levels of social status (**varnas**) that involve social groupings of families based on rules about what occupation one could follow and whom someone could marry, as well as with whom he or she could dine. Perhaps you have heard the word *caste*, which comes from a Portuguese word that was used to describe such a social grouping. It was believed that being born into a higher social grouping was a reflection of good karma. The most respected group with the highest social standing was the **Brahmins**, who were priests and teachers. Next come the *Kshatriyas*, who were the warrior class and were responsible for maintaining social order and governing. The third group was known as the *Vaishyas* and were the families involved in business or commerce. The group with the lowest social status was known as the shudras, who were the servants of the higher varnas. There was no upward mobility within the groupings; one's only chance of "moving up" would have to come in a future rebirth.

The first three varnas (Brahmins, Kshatriyas, and Vaishyas) were known as "twice-born" because only they were allowed to study the Vedas, the sacred scriptures. The system of varnas, though it might seem oppressive to someone raised in Western culture, represents a certain type of justice, since the privileges of each varna were proportionate to their responsibilities. For example, a Brahmin would be punished more severely than a lower varna who committed the same offense; for "the punishment of the *vaishya* should be twice as heavy as that of the shudra, that of the kshatriya twice as heavy again, and that of the *Brahmin* twice or even four times again." As Huston Smith notes, "within each caste there was equality, opportunity, and social insurance."[9]

Figure 9.1: This Hindu temple near Atlanta, Georgia has a fountain with images of Ganesha, the Hindu deity with an elephant's head who is associated with wisdom and is considered the remover of obstacles.

There was a fifth group—the "untouchables"—who were truly the social outcasts. They were the families who were considered to be impure because they were tasked with butchering, cleaning up refuse and human waste areas, and removing dead animals. Those who were untouchables had strict social limitations placed on them; for example, they could not enter the house of a member of a higher social group, use common trails, or eat among those of a superior social standing, just to name a few. (In modern India, these practices have been outlawed, but there still seem to be some lingering influences of this stigmatization of one group of people.)

At this point, one might wonder what the aim or purpose of life is to a Hindu. There are four purposes (called *Purusarthas*) in living outlined in the *Dharmashastras*. The first is *Dharma* (righteousness or law) and refers to doing one's duty as a member of a particular varna or caste. The next is *artha* (wealth, work), to devote oneself to work in order to be wealthy and successful. Then, there is *kama* (pleasure), which is the pursuit of play, music and dance, as well as sexual pleasure. Finally, there is moksha (release), which is release from the cycle of rebirth. Thus, this means utilizing spiritual practices to attain release from samsara (the continuing cycles of rebirth and transmigration).

There are four stages of life outlined in the Code of Manu that are called *Ashramas*. The first stage is *Brahmacharya* (student), which is when a young person lives as a celibate with a teacher (known as a *guru*) and learns about sacred knowledge by studying the *Vedas*, as well as other skills. The next stage, *Grihastha* (householder), happens when the young man returns to marry and raise a family; women were expected to remain under the protection of a male, so they stayed at home until married, after which they were subject to their husbands. The householder is expected to provide for his wife, children, parents, and holy men who visit. The third stage is *Vanaprastha* (forest dweller) and is retirement from the responsibilities of the householder and engaging in more religious practices and contemplating moksha (this is release from samsara). The fourth stage is known as Sannyasa (ascetic); this is when someone decides to renounce all worldly attachments and become a wandering ascetic (someone

who engages in self-denial) who does pilgrimages to Hindu sacred sites and practices spiritual
disciplines while seeking moksha. There is no
obligation for a person to proceed through to the
third or fourth stages—someone could simply
decide not to become a "forest dweller" or ascetic.

The Muslim period (1200–1757 CE) was
characterized by contact between Hindus and
Muslims, who came to India as traders and
military invaders. Once Hindu areas were under
Muslim control, sometimes the living conditions
of the conquered peoples were difficult, as there
was antagonism toward their religion. But other
Muslim rulers were more tolerant, and Hindus
were given more freedom to practice their
religion. Generally speaking, the two religious
traditions, Islam and Hinduism, coexisted with

Figure 9.2: Roundel of Brahma, who is
the Hindu god of creation.

little reciprocal influence of one upon the other, with the exception of the work
of some scholars.

A conquered people must find ways to preserve their identity. Hindus
accomplished this during the Muslim period by reaching back into their traditions and reemphasizing the practices that made them different. Hindus began
to emphasize vegetarianism, nonviolence (known as *ahimsa*), and devotion to
a god (known as bhakti). The symbol around which this emphasis on Hindu
identity was rooted was the Sacred Cow, a tradition that began in the Vedic period. The cow, associated with the goddess Shiva, represents divine and natural
beneficence, or kindness. In the Code of Manu, it is forbidden to slay a cow; it
was seen as tantamount to killing a Brahmin and was a capital offense. A cow
also represents the concept of ahimsa, as it symbolizes nonviolent generosity,
as well as Mother Earth or motherhood because it provides nourishment.[10] To
this day, veneration of the cow differentiates Hindus from others.

The Modern period (1757 CE–present) brought English control over
India, which introduced many facets of modernity: new ideas, new technology,
increased commerce, and education. Today, India is an increasingly important
nation-state and has been experiencing significant economic growth. With
respect to Hinduism, there have been reform movements and the successful
exportation of an adapted Hinduism to Europe and North America.

There are several important personages who have been influential Hindus in
the modern era. First is the reformer, Swami Vivekananda, then Paramahansa
Yogananda, an important international proponent of Hinduism, and Mohandas
Gandhi, the great political leader. Each will be discussed in the next section
because of the significance and influence of their ideas and practices within
modern Hinduism.

KEY IDEAS AND PRACTICES

Born in Calcutta to a wealthy family, Swami Vivekananda (1863–1902) was originally named Narendrath Dutta. He was studying at college, expecting to become a lawyer, when he encountered a famous religious teacher, Shri Ramakrishna (1836–1886), and had a powerful religious (mystical) experience. He then became a disciple of Ramakrishna, who taught a philosophy known as monism, a view that maintains there is no separation of the self from the universe. Ramakrishna taught that there is a oneness of self with the *Brahma*, the universal whole. When Ramakrishna died, Narendrath became a Sannyasin (ascetic) and took the name Vivekananda (joyous mind); he also had the title *swami*, which means an ascetic teacher. He and his companions traveled throughout India as mendicants. Eventually, Swami Vivekananda is said to have come to the ocean, which he entered to swim to an island where he meditated for three days. When he returned, it is said that he had a new vision of the divine oneness of humanity.

Vivekananda came to the World Parliament of Religions, held in 1893 in Chicago. A powerful orator, he gave speeches that introduced the attendees of the conference to Hinduism, explaining such concepts as reincarnation and that a person's goal should be to realize the divinity that lies within and express that through concern for others. He argued for religious tolerance and quoted from the *Bhagavad Gita*: "As the different streams having their sources in different places all mingle their water in the sea, so, O Lord, the different paths which men take through different tendencies, various though they appear, crooked or straight, all lead to Thee."[11]

Vivekananda remained in the United States for a few years and taught the philosophy of Vedanta (which is based in the *Vedas*), and then returned to India. Before his departure, he established centers for the study of Vedanta philosophy in New York and London. The philosophy that he taught is manifest in his addresses to the World Parliament of Religions, where he said that the whole object of Hinduism is "by constant struggle, to become perfect, to become divine, to reach and see God." He also argued that Hindu thought was consistent with science by saying that: "Science is nothing but the finding of unity." Vivekananda also said that, "by the study of different religions, we find that in essence they are one" because, having examined Buddhism, Christianity, and Islam, he found that "the same foundational principles taught in my religion [i.e., Hinduism] were also taught by all religions." It is not through books that one finds salvation, but through who we become and that we must understand that the "end of all religions is the realizing of God in the soul."[12] His ideas appealed to many American people, who found them reminiscent of some of the ideas in Christianity.

The next important proponent of Hinduism in the United States was known as Paramahansa Yogananda (1893–1952). Born in Calcutta to a Kshatriya family, he was named Mukunda Lal Ghosh. He attended college, and a disciple of Sri Ramakrishna named Mahendra Nath Gupta was his first mentor. One day, after both had seen an early version of a movie, Mahendra placed his finger upon Mukunda's chest, and immediately "all noise on the busy street stopped for Mukunda. He saw the pedestrians and vehicles, but all was silent, and he observed a luminous glow emanating from

Figure 9.3: Swami Vivekananda was a powerful orator and teacher who brought the philosophy of the Vedanta to the United States at the end of the 19th century.

all phenomena." From this experience, Mukunda drew the conclusion that "the physical world has the reality of a motion picture or a dream."[13] He eventually would find his master, Sri Yukteswar, who foretold that Mukunda would travel to America to teach.[14]

Later, Mukunda took the vows of Sannyasa and the name Yogananda. He started a school for boys, but soon came to America in 1920 to speak at the International Congress of Religious Liberals. He then proceeded to travel about the United States teaching about Hinduism. After a few years, he established the Self-Realization Fellowship (SRF) in Los Angeles, which grew to more than 500 temples, retreats, ashrams, and meditation centers around the world. Members of the Self-Realization Fellowship venerate images of Krishna and Christ, who are seen as the sources of the teachings of Self-Realization Fellowship.[15] His work in America was rewarded with a new title, Paramahansa, which means Supreme Swan. This title was given to him after he came to America by his master, Sri Yukteswar; the title is honorific, indicating that Yogananda attained enlightenment.

Yogananda taught a method known as *kriya yoga*. He started by teaching physical exercises (*hatha yoga*), in which a person uses different postures (*asanas*) to facilitate the movement of energy from one part of the body to another. Those who have been initiated into the SRF system of kriya yoga are required to pledge that they will not reveal it to someone who has not been officially initiated. Nevertheless, it is known that kriya yoga involves "awakening an energy—*kundalini*—thought to lie at the base of the spine and directing it upwards" toward the crown of the head, which would energize the seven energy centers (called *chakras*) of the body. Then, using the mind, one moves the energy, while practicing breathing techniques and repeating a mantra (an incantation); "the yogic practitioner hoped to reach a superconscious state."[16]

Mohandas Gandhi (1869–1948) was born to a family in India who were Vaishnavas and devoted to the Lord Krishna. He later traveled to England to do legal studies in London (where he was also exposed to Christianity), and then practiced law for about two decades in South Africa. He returned to India around

Figure 9.4: George Harrison in Vrindaban. Harrison was one of the Beatles, the famous rock group of the 1960s, who found enlightenment through Hinduism.

1914 to join in the nationalist movement. Though a famous political leader, Gandhi is also remembered for his spirituality which was rooted in a reformed Hinduism, with some Christian influences, too. One of his key ideas was *satya*, which means truth; he "equated truth with God, implying morality and spirituality are the same." Another important one was ahimsa, nonviolence, "which was broadened by Gandhi to include any form of coercion or denigration."[17] Gandhi was also initiated into kriya yoga by Paramahansa Yogananda. The effects of Gandhi's vision were far-ranging in India and in Europe, as it was influential upon the German Christian theologian Dietrich Bonhoeffer, who resisted Hitler, and in the United States, where it inspired Martin Luther King Jr., the civil rights leader.

There are two other Indian spiritual masters who came to American and had great influence: these are Maharishi Mahesh Yogi and Swami Prabhupada.

Maharishi Mahesh Yogi was born in India in 1911 as Mahesh Prasad Varma. He completed a college degree in physics and math and also lived in a monastery for more than ten years studying with a famous master. In 1958, he left India and traveled to several countries, including the United States, to present his ideas. His method, formally known as the Science of Creative Intelligence (SCI), was said to be a scientific response to the stresses of modern life; he claimed that it was not a religion, but a court later rejected that assertion.

The technique taught by Maharishi Mahesh Yogi was called transcendental meditation (TM) and was derived from Vedic traditions, but in a newer form, that suggested that "an unchanging reality is opposed to an ever-changing phenomenal world." A person can access the unchanging reality, or being, through her or his "breath (Prāṇa), which is an expression of Being in the sense that it ... represents the latent power of Being within a person." The technique is basically for a person to meditate for about 20 minutes, attending to the breathing and using a mantra. He or she can then move through different levels of consciousness to the highest level, which is one of unity.[18]

Maharishi became quite a celebrity in the 1960s when the Beatles and the Beach Boys studied with him. TM was advertised as a technique that could be scientifically proven to lower blood pressure and lower stress and increase intelligence, as well as lower the crime rate in areas where it was intensively practiced.[19] There were centers at many colleges, as students were drawn to TM, expecting it would facilitate their success in school, and hence in their future careers. Today, in the Midwest, there is the Maharishi International University, now known as the Maharishi University of Management, which offers undergraduate and graduate degrees. The institution is based on the principle of "consciousness-based education," so every student is immersed in TM.

A. C. Bhaktivedanta Swami Prabhupada (1896–1977) came to New York City in 1965 as a 70-year-old *sadhu* (saintly person), with no money except for 40 rupees (about seven dollars), but in fulfillment of his master's wish that he teach to the whole world bhakti yoga, which holds that one can reach spiritual realization through devotion to Krishna (God).[20]

Prabhupada was born in Calcutta. When young, he completed studies for a college degree and become a householder, working as a manager for a company. Eventually, he found a spiritual teacher, who tasked him with a missionary effort to teach others in foreign lands about bhakti yoga. In his sixties, Prabhupada took the vows of Sannyasa (renunciation) and lived in a monastery. He translated some of the important writings of his spiritual tradition.

After Prabhupada was in New York for about nine difficult months, he established the International Society for Krishna Consciousness (ISKCON), with his first temple in a poor Manhattan neighborhood known as the Lower East Side. Within two years, he had between 150–200 followers. He then went to San Francisco, which was a hippie focal point for psychedelic drugs and music at that time. He acquired followers there by convincing young people there that they would get a better "high" from the technique of chanting Hare Krishna than by using illegal drugs. Prabhupada then continued to travel to other places in the world, and by the time he died 12 years later, he had an estimated 5000 disciples worldwide.[21]

Members of the International Society for Krishna Consciousness were easily recognizable because they would often appear in groups, clad in saffron robes and sporting mostly shaved heads with a kind of ponytail remaining, dancing along a city street singing chants and using finger cymbals. They claimed that the Hare Krishna chants brought about altered consciousness and states of bliss. When some of these followers went to India with Prabhupada, people referred to his Western disciples as "dancing white elephants." Those who lived at the temples as "students" followed a strict monastic life that included rising at 4:00 AM, chanting, attending a daily lecture, and abiding by rules such as being vegetarian and celibate. Those disciples who wished to be "householders" and intended to marry were allowed to follow a modified set of vows.[22]

When Prabhupada died, the number of disciples declined in the United States, and the group was rocked by scandals. There were individuals accused of drug trafficking, others were accused of child abuse, and the organization itself was attacked by some outsiders as a cult. The group did not dissolve, however, because the Hare Krishna temples attracted ethnic Hindus who had moved to the United States.

SUMMARY OF KEY IDEAS OF HINDUISM

1. Hindus believe that reality is one and that separation is an illusion.
2. It is believed that there is an impersonal power behind the material world: this is called Brahman.
3. In each person, there is a spirit, *Atman*, which connects the person to Brahman.
4. When a person becomes a realized person, he or she will realize that Atman is Brahman.
5. There is reincarnation and samsara, the endless cycle of rebirth.
6. There is karma, the natural law governing the effects of one's good or evil actions upon one's destiny.
7. There can be moksha, or release from samsara.
8. Since more than one religion can lead to salvation, one should be tolerant.

WAYS TO THE DIVINE

There are three paths which a person can take to come to the divine described in the *Bhagavad Gita*. These different paths, known as yogas, reflect the difference in the types of people and their needs:

1. *Puja:* This is the path of devotion and ritual. Family members daily greet, bathe, clothe, and feed a god by means of images of that divinity (i.e., statues). The Indian word for devotion is bhakti, and this path means that one directs her or his love toward the god, to adore that god. Part of this practice includes repeating the god's name and worshipping that god in a particular *ishta*, or adopted form, such as Rama or Krishna.
2. *Jnana:* The way of knowledge. This path appeals to the reflective, who, learning techniques of meditation and bodily positioning from teachers, or gurus, can come to higher states of consciousness—mystical states. Thus, jnana is really having acquired insight—that is, knowledge of the ultimate.
3. *Karma:* The way of action. This path teaches that a person must live according to his varna, or caste, and faithfully perform the actions required, without being concerned with results or personal rewards. This leads one to rebirth in a higher state. The point of life is "to transcend the smallness of the finite self."[23]

Robinson sums this up by saying that "Hinduism is made up of three great religious forms and three broad streams that continually flow and mingle together." The three great forms are (1) *polytheism* (the worship of many gods); (2) *monism* (the concept of seeking union with the "One Spirit" that is beyond the self and the world; and (3) *monotheism* (worship that concentrates on "One Personal God." The first great stream is the *way of devotion*. The second is the *way of knowledge*, and the third is the *way of works*.[24]

CONTEMPORARY DEVELOPMENTS

The trend among Hindus in the United States is now to define their place in society. The first people drawn to Hinduism in America were a small group of intellectuals and religious liberals who were interested in the teachings brought here by the missionary gurus Vivekananda and Yogananda. Then, in the 1960s, many young people were attracted to forms of Hinduism such as TM or the International Society for Krishna Consciousness because they rejected their parents' religious traditions, which so many found uninspiring. Hinduism was novel and had popular appeal with the likes of the Beatles and the Beach Boys seeking gurus. The difference today is that the growing voice of Hinduism in the United States is that of ethnic Hindus and their children, many of whom were born in America.

Hindu culture is becoming better known as the general public becomes aware of such celebrations as Holi, which celebrates the arrival of spring, with participants dousing each other in colored powders while enjoying food and music. A Holi celebration in Potomac, Maryland, last year drew about 3000 celebrants and was covered by the *Washington Post*.[25] And in Southern California, the *Los Angeles Times* reported on the celebration of Diwali, the Hindu Festival of Lights that celebrates the lunar New Year, which took place there. The story reports that a young woman, "one of thousands of Hindus gathered at homes and in temples for the occasion," said that the "entire community comes together on this auspicious day and we get to celebrate light, we get to celebrate good over evil, and we get to do that together, in unity. Everybody is full of hope."[26]

Among ethnic Hindus, there is an effort now to teach their children the traditions of their religion. One creative method was held in Chicago, where there was a "dharma bee," which tested about 3000 students' knowledge of Hindu leaders such as Vivekananda.[27] Another way is through the use of classes patterned on the Sunday school so familiar to Christians. In addition, there are questions being explored such as, "What language should be used for religious services? Can English be a liturgical language for Hindus?" In Minnesota, there is a Hindu community that has been carving out its identity, attempting to teach its children and answer those questions, and yet it was also dealing with victimization as a result of a hate crime—an occasional problem for ethnic Hindus. That Hindu community "reached out and befriended the vandals, who are now college students, and even included them in a ceremony at which the destroyed icons were buried."[28]

Probably the best bellwether of change is in the appearance in 2010 of the "Take Back Yoga" campaign. About 15 million Americans practice yoga, virtually all of them doing it for reasons other than religion such as better health, peacefulness, and better cognition. But the issue involves ownership: Who owns yoga? Most Americans would probably say that it obviously does not "belong" to anyone. But those who have organized the "Take Back Yoga" campaign argue that "the philosophy of yoga was first described in Hinduism's seminal texts and remains at the core of Hindu teaching." Dr. Aseem Shukla, cofounder of the

Hindu American Foundation, writes that "Hinduism has become the victim of 'overt intellectual property theft', made possible by generations of Hindu yoga teachers 'who had offered up a religion's spiritual wealth at the altar of crass commercialism.'" On the other hand, prominent Indian American physician and author Deepak Chopra responded to the campaign, saying that "Hinduism was too 'tribal' and 'self-enclosed' to claim ownership of yoga." However, another Indian American leader supports the campaign and sees it as "a coming of age for Indians in the United States" and that Indian civilization "has made contributions to the world, and these should be acknowledged."[29]

And there is evidence now that the complaint about yoga belonging to Hinduism seems to have been heard: in 2014, the Smithsonian Institution presented an exhibit entitled *Yoga: The Art of Transformation*. The exhibit was intended to highlight the Hindu roots of yoga.[30]

CHAPTER SUMMARY

Hinduism is the world's third largest and oldest religion. Though rather new to American society, some of its significant concepts have very much become a part of mainstream usage—Hindu terms such as reincarnation, karma, cremation, and hatha yoga are familiar to all. Hinduism presents a view of life as being endlessly cyclical, with persons being subjected to rebirth and transmigration. This causes distress, for which Hinduism has a solution: moksha, or release. One can find moksha through attaining enlightenment. Traditionally, there are three paths one can follow: *puja* (path of devotion), *karma* (duty), and *jnana* (knowledge).

Famous proponents of Hinduism who came to the United States during the 20th century adapted the religion so that it would be more suitable for American tastes and emphasized the tolerant aspects of Hinduism. The religion drew much interest during the 1960s and 1970s, as young people were drawn to Hinduism because it was so individualized and different from the institutional religions of their childhoods. However, that period of growth was followed by a decline in American participants in Hinduism, which was soon overshadowed by an influx of ethnic Hindus as immigration patterns changed. Today, Hinduism is still not well understood by most Americans, but that is certain to change over the next few decades.

KEY TERMS

- Brahmins
- Bhakti
- Devas
- Jnana

+ **Karma**
+ **Moksha**
+ **Puja**
+ **Samsara**
+ **Upanishads**
+ **Yoga**

REVIEW QUESTIONS

1. What are the six periods in the development of Hinduism?
2. What are the Vedas?
3. What is the Hindu concept of time?
4. Discuss the societal structure (varnas) outlined in the Code of Manu.
5. Explain these concepts: samsara and moksha, as well as bhakti, jnana, and puja.

END NOTES

1. Prothero, Stephen. *God Is Not One* (New York: HarperCollins, 2010), 134.
2. Pew Research Religion and Public Life Project, "Hindus," Dec. 18, 2012, http://www.pewforum.org/2012/12/18/global-religious-landscape-hindu/
3. Pew Research: Religion and Public Life Project, "How Americans Feel About Religious Groups," Jul. 16, 2014, http://www.pewforum.org/2014/07/16/how-americans-feel-about-religious-groups/
4. Pew Research: Religion and Public Life Project, "Asian Americans: A Mosaic of Faith," Jul. 19, 2012, http://www.pewforum.org/2012/07/19/asian-americans-a-mosaic-of-faiths-overview/
5. "So How Many Hindus Are There in the United States Today?" *Hinduism Today*, Jan.-Mar. 2008, 61. accessed on Oct. 29, 2014, http://hafsite.org/sites/default/files/HT_Census_USA_Jan08.pdf
6. Larson, Gerald James. "Hinduism in India and in America." In *World Religions in America*, ed. Jacob Neusner (Louisville: Westminster John Knox Press, 2009), 179–196.
7. Doniger, Wendy. *On Hinduism* (New York: Oxford University Press, 2014), 10.
8. Robinson, James B. *Hinduism* (Philadelphia: Chelsea House Publishers, 2004), 43.
9. Smith, Huston. *The World's Religions* (New York: HarperCollins, 1991), 57–58.
10. Britannica School, s.v. "sanctity of the cow," accessed Nov. 1, 2014, http://scroll.lib.westfield.ma.edu:3291/levels/referencecenter/article/26665
11. "Vivekananda, Swami." *World Religions Reference Library*, ed. Julie L. Carnagie, et al. Vol. 4: Biographies (Detroit: UXL, 2007), 383–390. *Gale Virtual Reference Library*. Web. Nov. 1, 2014.

12. Vivekananda, Swami. *The Collected Works of Swami Vivekananda*, vol. 1 (Calcutta: Sri Gauraga Press, 1915), 1–30.

13. Wessinger, Catherine. "Yogananda." *Encyclopedia of Religion*, ed. Lindsay Jones, 2nd ed., vol. 14 (Detroit: Macmillan Reference USA, 2005), 9902–9903. Gale Virtual Reference Library. Web. Nov. 1, 2014.

14. Yogananda, Paramahansa. *Autobiography of a Yogi* (Dakshineswar: Yogoda Satsanga Society of India, 2006), 120.

15. Wessinger, Catherine. "Self-Realization Fellowship." *Religions of the World: A Comprehensive Encyclopedia of Beliefs and Practices*, ed. J. Gordon Melton and Martin Baumann, 2nd ed., vol. 6 (Santa Barbara, CA: ABC-CLIO, 2010), 2569–2570. *Gale Virtual Reference Library*. Web. Nov. 1, 2014.

16. Albanese, Catherine L. *America: Religions and Religion* (Boston: Wadsworth, Cengage Learning, 2007), 215.

17. Juergensmeyer, Mark. "Gandhi, Mohandas." *Encyclopedia of Religion*, ed. Lindsay Jones, 2nd ed., vol. 5 (Detroit: Macmillan Reference USA, 2005), 3271–3273. *Gale Virtual Reference Library*. Web. Nov. 1, 2014.

18. Olson, Carl. "Transcendental Meditation." *Encyclopedia of Religion*, ed. Lindsay Jones, 2nd ed., vol. 14 (Detroit: Macmillan Reference USA, 2005), 9289–9292. *Gale Virtual Reference Library*. Web. Nov. 1, 2014.

19. Albanese, 215.

20. Rochford, E. Burke Jr. "Prabhupada, A. C. Bhaktivedanta." *Encyclopedia of Religion*, ed. Lindsay Jones, 2nd ed., vol. 11 (Detroit: Macmillan Reference USA, 2005), 7354–7355. *Gale Virtual Reference Library*. Web. Nov. 1, 2014.

21. Rochford, *Gale Virtual Reference Library*. Web. Nov. 1, 2014.

22. Shinn, Larry D. "International Society for Krishna Consciousness." *Encyclopedia of Religion*, ed. Lindsay Jones, 2nd ed., vol. 7 (Detroit: Macmillan Reference USA, 2005), 4521–4524. *Gale Virtual Reference Library*. Web. Nov. 1, 2014.

23. Smith, 38.

24. Robinson, 9.

25. Lyford, Chris. "Transcending Cultures." *Washington Post*, Apr. 06, 2013. http//search.proquest.com/doc.view/1324206127

26. Silverstein, Stuart. "L.A. Area Hindus Celebrate the New Year; With Food, Prayer and Gift, Adherents of the World's Third Largest Religion Fete the Triumph of Good Over Evil." *Los Angeles Times*, Oct. 23, 2006. http:// search.Proquest.com/docview/422105935

27. Smith, Mitch. "Young Hindus Embrace Their Heritage at Dharma Bee." *Chicago Tribune*, Jun. 1, 2013. http://search.proquest.com/docview/1367928716

28. "Hindu Americans Face Challenges, Growth in Their Faith." *Boston Globe*, Sep. 20, 2009. http://search.proquest.com/docview/405187484

29. Vitello, Paul. "Hindu Group Stirs Debate Over Yoga's Soul." *New York Times*, Nov. 28, 2010. http://search.proquest.com/doview/814406963

30. Shukla, Suhag A. "Smithsonian's Yoga: The Art of Transformation Brings to Light Yoga's Hindu Roots … Almost." *Huffington Post*, Jan. 1, 2014. http://www.huffingtonpost.com/suhag-a-shukla-esq/smithsonians-yoga-the-art_b_4691008.html

10. Buddhism

By William J. Cook Jr.

Two Monks were arguing about a flag.
One said: "The Flag is moving." The other said: "The wind
is moving."
The sixth patriarch happened to be passing by. He told them:
"Not the wind, not the flag; mind is moving."

—*Zen Koan from The Gateless Gate*

OVERVIEW

Buddhism is fairly new to America, first introduced here in the 19th century, but it is an ancient religion that is well over 2000 years old and is mostly concentrated in Asia. Buddhism started in India (but was later diminished there by the resurgence of Hinduism) and spread to Sri Lanka, Thailand, and Tibet, where it dominates; it also extended into Korea, China, and Japan, where it has influenced the culture. Buddhism can also be found in Burma, Laos, Cambodia, Nepal, Vietnam, Bhutan, and Mongolia. According to the Pew Research Religion and Public Life Project, there are 488 million Buddhists worldwide, representing about 7 percent of the world's population, with approximately 99 percent of all Buddhists living in Asia. The country with the largest population of Buddhists is China, where virtually half of all Buddhists reside. In Asian countries, the term Buddhism is not generally used; instead, it is referred

Figure 10.1: American Buddhist monk Claude AnShin Thomas is a Vietnam veteran who teaches Buddhist meditation and practice and has completed thousands of miles in walking on peace pilgrimages.

to as the *Dharma*, or teaching, or *Buddha-sasana*, or the Teachings of the Buddha.

In North America, there are approximately 3.9 million Buddhists, and many are found within immigrant communities of Japanese, Chinese, Vietnamese, and Laotian people. Other Buddhists are generally middle-class whites who have converted. There are an additional 1.3 million Buddhists who reside in Europe.[1]

Buddhism is not a religion in the sense that there is a belief in a God, as one finds in Christianity, Judaism, or Islam; however, in some of its traditions, it does recognize gods and spirits. Nevertheless, Buddhism does fit well within a broader understanding of religion that was developed by the religious studies scholar Ninian Smart (1927–2001). He held that a religion should have these seven dimensions or aspects: practical and ritual; experiential and emotional; narrative and mythical; doctrinal and philosophical; ethical and legal; social and institutional; and material. Buddhism meets all of these criteria, as it has rituals; emphasizes experience as a way to enlightenment; has mythical stories about the Buddha's past lives; has a set of teachings known as the Dharma; has ethical principles (known as the Eightfold Path) to guide life; has social institutions such as monasteries for monks and nuns; and in the material dimension, it has places as holy sites and temples.[2]

Buddhism came to the United States with the arrival of Chinese immigrants in the mid-18th century. A significant milestone in the transmission of Buddhism to North America occurred in the 1890s, when a Japanese Zen master (i.e., a teacher of a type of Buddhist practice known as Zen) named Soyen Shaku (1860–1919) spoke at the World's Parliament of Religions. Later, when he returned to Japan, one of his students, D. T. Suzuki (1870–1966), came to America and was responsible for educating a wide audience of Westerners about

Buddhism. Suzuki translated important Buddhist texts into English, wrote, and taught at schools such as Columbia University; his written works quickly became very popular and are considered classics today.

In the 1950s, young Americans who were drawn to the "Beat" culture were fascinated by Zen Buddhism. The famous "Beat" poet and novelist, Jack Kerouac (1922–1969), published a novel called *The Dharma Bums*, which was very successful and introduced a new generation to ideas about Buddhism. In the 1960s, as another group of young people rebelled against traditional, institutional religion, Buddhism enjoyed renewed and expanded interest as the baby boomers turned inward in their search for inner transformation, peace, and wisdom, something that Buddhist practice could well facilitate. As that generation has matured, many have remained devoted to Buddhism (though some have blended it with their Judaism or Christianity) and have now passed it along to their children and grandchildren. They are also a highly educated and successful group, with about one-quarter completing postgraduate studies (as compared to one-tenth of the general population).[3] American Buddhists also have found novel applications of Buddhist practice and psychology to be used in education, clinical psychology and psychiatry, corrections, and business management, to name a few areas, and they have been underpinning these applications with research and clinical studies. Indeed, in a little more than a century, Buddhism has become a very significant part of the American cultural landscape.

HISTORY

It can rightly be said that "Buddhism begins with a man."[4] That man is **Siddhartha Gautama** (566–486 BCE, though some believe he died in 410 BCE), who was born near the Himalayas, in an area that is in the modern country of Nepal. His family belonged to the Shakya tribe and is believed to have been of an aristocratic warrior class (known as Kshatriyas), although the extent of their wealth and power may have been exaggerated in later stories about his life. Siddhartha Gautama eventually came to be known as the Buddha, but this is a title that means "the Awakened One," and also as Shakyamuni, or "Sage of the Shakyas."

A clear historical record does not exist for Siddhartha's life, as ancient peoples did not write biographies as we know them today. However, there is a basic chronology of his life that is generally accepted. He was married at the age of 16 to a woman named Yasodhara; she bore him a son. Soon after the birth of his son, when Siddhartha was about 29 years old, he left home in search of religious wisdom. At the age of 35, he attained enlightenment, and then proceeded to become an itinerant spiritual teacher until his death at age 80.[5]

There are four events in the life of Siddhartha Gautama which Buddhists recall in their myths, literature, rituals, and pilgrimages. These are: (1) the Birth of Siddhartha Gautama; (2) his Enlightenment; (3) his First Sermon; and (4) his Death.[6]

Birth: The story is told that Siddhartha's mother dreamed that a white elephant had entered her side when he was conceived. This was considered a portent of great significance about her child's future. The interpretation of the dream was that he was destined to be a Turner of the Wheel (known as a *chakravartin*) as either a great emperor (thus, turning the "Wheel of Conquest") or a great religious teacher (turning the "Wheel of Dharma" or the "Wheel of Teaching"). Siddhartha, the name this child was given, means "one who has achieved his aim."

As the time of her child's birth drew near, Siddhartha's mother traveled toward her family's home, but she did not get there in time, so the baby was born near a tree. But there was a "miraculous shower and the earth shook," again, portents of cosmic significance; the infant stood up, took seven steps, and declared "that this would be the last time that he would be born."[7]

His mother died seven days after his birth, but he was raised by his mother's sister, who became his stepmother when she married Siddhartha's father. His youth was said to be sheltered and privileged. His father attempted to protect him from the ugly side of life—that is, he made sure that the streets were populated with healthy and happy people—in the hope that his son would not be upset and drawn in the direction of becoming a spiritual teacher, but instead, would become a great temporal leader. Thus, his palace life was comfortable, but he did feel a need for something deeper, a spiritual life.

One day, when he had left the sheltered world of the palace, he saw an old man on the street. This troubled him, for he did not know about aging, so he returned to the palace to contemplate aging. On a second trip, he happened upon a sick man; again, this troubled him, as he did not know about sickness. Then, on the third trip, he saw a corpse being carried to cremation; he was disturbed by this, as he had not known about death. Finally, on the fourth trip, he met a religious mendicant (one who has rejected ordinary life in favor of the lifestyle of an itinerant beggar seeking wisdom).

Meeting this fourth man, the religious mendicant, Siddhartha was inspired to seek spiritual answers to the problems of humankind that he had recently come to know. That night, he took a last look at his child and wife and left the palace so that he could take up the life of a homeless mendicant. He gave away his jewelry and cut off his hair.

Keown argues that this "simple, poignant story" about Siddhartha leaving the palace is "unlikely to be true in the literal sense," as he believes it is unlikely that anyone could be so naive, nor would he come to such a state of dissatisfaction with his life so suddenly. Instead, he proposes that the story be viewed as a kind of parable that depicts the palace life as representing complacency and the four persons he meets as "the dawning of a realization about the nature of human life."[8]

Figure 10.2: *Prince Siddharta Shaves His Head*: This ancient images depicts the moment when Siddhartha renounces his privileged life so that he might search for enlightenment.

Enlightenment: Siddhartha sought out spiritual teachers so he could attain the wisdom that he now sought. The first teacher he found taught him how to meditate in such a way that he could go into a trance, or a state of absorption known as the "sphere of Nothingness." Eventually, Siddhartha found this practice unsatisfactory, as it was not a permanent solution; one still had to return to ordinary experience, and the problems of aging, sickness, and death still remained.

Then, he found a second teacher who taught him an advanced meditation technique that brought him to a place of "neither perception, nor non-perception." Here, one has the experience that consciousness seems about to disappear. But Siddhartha was dissatisfied with this method as well, since it did not bring about a permanent solution to the problems of life he sought to address.

Next, Siddhartha began to learn techniques of austerity as a way of controlling his desires and emotions. One such technique was to hold his breath for longer and longer periods. He found that this only gave him headaches. Another technique he tried was to cut down on the amount of food he consumed, so that eventually, he would hardly be eating anything. As it happened, he finally reached a point at which he was having just one spoonful of bean soup each day; this; however, left him in an emaciated state in which his hair fell out, and he was even too weak to sit up. Finally, he decided that he needed to eat sufficiently to nourish himself.

From his experience of the negative effects of these different austere practices, Siddhartha concluded that extremes of any kind were not good. He began a new approach that he called "the Middle Way," which means to avoid the extremes of self-denial and self-indulgence. This means that one should live a life of moderation, one not given over to seeking pleasure or pain. He then sat under a tree and began to meditate.

KEY IDEAS AND PRACTICES

Enlightenment: Siddhartha then sat down under a tree known as the Bodhi Tree and began to meditate. One night, while he was meditating, he encountered temptations, but was able to overcome them. Then, as the night unfolded, he attained the enlightenment that he sought.

The ancient texts say that during the first part of that night, he acquired the power to look back through his previous lives. Then, during the second part of the night, he received the clairvoyant (i.e., the ability to perceive things usually inaccessible to human senses) power to see the end and rebirth of all types of beings according to their good and bad deeds. Thirdly, he attained the knowledge that he had rooted out craving and ignorance once and for all.

In this night, Siddhartha had attained *nirvana*, which means an end to the endless cycle of rebirths that is the destiny of all creatures; it is important to recognize that being reborn endlessly was not considered a good thing—we'll see more about why this was so in a later section of this chapter. And it was through this experience that Siddhartha became the Buddha, or Enlightened One. A Buddha is one who has come to understand the causes of suffering and "blown them out" (**nirvana** means "to extinguish," so this is just like blowing out the flame of a candle).

After his enlightenment, the Buddha stayed for some seven weeks at the place, known as Bodh Gaya, where it had happened. He considered what to do next. At first, he was inclined to live a life of privacy and seclusion. However, a god appeared and appealed to him to share his teaching with others. So, moved by compassion for the suffering of other people, he decided to leave Bodh Gaya and go forth to share his teaching.

First Sermon: The Buddha traveled to a deer park near a holy place called Varanasi, also known as Benares, as he knew, through his new psychic powers, that his two first teachers were now dead and that some of his old friends who were also spiritual seekers would be found there. When he met his friends, they were initially skeptical of his claim that he was now a *Tathagata*, or "one who has attained what is really so."

The Buddha's first sermon—that is to say, his first teaching—is known as "the first turning of the wheel of Dharma" and is the beginning of the Buddhist tradition being set in motion. The **Dharma** is also called the teaching (the Dharma is symbolized by a wheel in Buddhism and is frequently depicted in sculptures and other Buddhist art; the wheel is also used to symbolize Buddhism).

In the first sermon, the Buddha outlines his essential teaching, which is known as the **Four Noble Truths.** The first Noble Truth is the Truth of Suffering, or *Dukkha.* The second Noble Truth is the Truth of the Origin of Suffering. The Third Noble Truth is the Truth of the Cessation, or End, of Suffering. The Fourth Noble Truth is the Truth of the Path that leads to the Cessation of Suffering, known as the "Eightfold Path."

The First Noble Truth proclaims that "all is suffering." This is to say that suffering is an intrinsic part of human life—it is part of the human condition. This precept can be understood in three ways. The first is that there is suffering that is physically or mentally painful; an example of this kind of suffering might be a toothache that is physically painful or a loss of a loved one that is mentally painful.

The second way that suffering occurs is when it is due to change. This refers to the human propensity to try to hold on to something that brings pleasure, even though it will eventually bring pain. For example, when someone gets a new ring or other piece of jewelry, he or she will enjoy how attractive it is and try to keep it that way; but sooner, or later, change occurs: it will get scratched and start to look old.

The third way that we experience suffering is when it results from what are called conditioned states. This means that pleasurable things can bring pain, too, even while they still bring us pleasure. This is a familiar experience to every adolescent who has experienced that first "crush," which can be both exhilarating and heartbreaking. A good way of describing this experience is evident in the title of a very popular song from the 1950s: "Why Must I Be a Teenager in Love?"

The Second Noble Truth, also known as the "Truth of Arising," or samudaya, teaches that suffering arises from desire (not desire in the ordinary sense), which comes from ignorance. It is a wrongful craving or thirst that can take three different forms: (1) a craving for satisfaction through objects of the senses; (2) a thirst for existence, which could be described as a "will to be"; and (3) a desire not to possess, but to destroy.

The word desire, or craving (*Tanha*), really suggests a desire that has become perverted or misdirected. Tanha—that is, desire or craving—means the three roots of evil: greed, hatred, and delusion. These three roots are often depicted as a rooster, a pig, and a snake chasing each other's tails in a circle. This may be considered craving; craving gives rise to more craving, so the cycle of rebirth goes round and round. In a more general way, this is also saying that the universe is characterized by cyclic change.

The Third Noble Truth is the Truth of Cessation, or nirvana. As Huston Smith notes, the third Noble Truth is logically concluded from the Second Noble Truth. He says, "(i)f the cause of life's dislocation is selfish craving, its cure lies in overcoming such craving." Now, by "dislocation," Smith means that a person feels a sense of being "out of joint"—like "bones that have slipped from their sockets."

He continues, saying that, "(i)f we could be released from the narrow limits of self-interest into the vast expanse of universal life, we would be relieved of our torment."[9] Thus, this teaching tells us that, when craving is removed, suffering ends, and nirvana is attained. So, what is extinguished? The greed, hatred, and delusion. The resulting state is one of peace, joy, and compassion.

One question that may arise about what gets "blown out" in nirvana is whether one's soul is extinguished. In Buddhism, there is no concept of a soul, so there is no soul to be extinguished. However, when the greed, hatred, and delusion are extinguished, then the person is no longer concerned with ego—in other ways, concerned with "me and mine." There is then a sense of connectedness to others. Smith notes that when we coddle "our individual identities, we lock ourselves inside 'our skin-encapsulated egos' and seek fulfillment through their intensification and expanse." He compares the ego to a "strangulated hernia," which, "the more it swells, the tighter it shuts off the free-flowing circulation on which health depends," so the result is that "the more pain increases."[10] Buddhists say that we have no self, either; what we think of as "self" is "actually nothing more than a conventional name attached to an ever-changing combination of separate parts called the five *skandas*." It is "these five 'aggregates'—matter, sensations, perceptions, thoughts and consciousness—[that] create the illusion of 'I' and 'me'. But this illusion is all there is to 'myself.'"[11]

The Fourth Noble Truth is the Path. A good analogy to help understand this is offered by Huston Smith. The symptom of the disease, as described in the First Noble Truth, is dukkha (suffering). If the Second Noble Truth is the diagnosis of the disease (i.e., craving), the Third Noble Truth is the prognosis (i.e., the disease can be cured by overcoming ego), then the Fourth Noble Truth is the prescription to cure the disease. The Path is something that one must follow—that is, to train oneself; it is not something that happens passively.

Before saying more about the Path, it is useful to mention another of Huston Smith's observations. He points out that he believes that the Buddha presupposed one thing for the Path: that one needs to associate with others who already know and follow the Path in order to learn it effectively because "virtue is contagious," and this will help a person overcome discouragement and doubt.

The Path has eight parts, so it is commonly known as the *Eightfold Path*; the eight parts are divided into three categories. The Eightfold Path explains how one can make the transition from the state of *samsara* (repeated rebirths) to nirvana. By following the Eightfold Path, a person achieves the highest form of life, one that leads to the development of virtue and knowledge. It is also a "Middle Way," which seeks a balanced life (between indulgence and austerity).

The initial category involves **wisdom** and includes these two steps: (1) **Right View**; and (2) **Right Resolve**. Right View means that one should accept and experience Buddhist teachings. As Huston Smith observes when talking about Right View, the Four Noble Truths can be thought of as a blueprint or map for the mind that one can trust as she or he embarks on this journey.[12] But a different perspective on Right View is provided by Zen Master Seung Sahn, who says it means "put down all your thinking and opinions and see this world exactly as it is"; and it means "understanding that actions based on desire, anger, or ignorance will always lead to suffering, both for us and others."[13] Right Resolve, or Right Intent, means that one should make a serious commitment to the effort to become enlightened; one must become single-minded about pursuing it.

The next category describes the steps that involve **morality**. These are: (3) **Right Speech**; (4) **Right Action**; and (5) **Right Livelihood**. Right Speech means to tell the truth and to speak thoughtfully. In order to tell the truth, we must become aware of how often we tend to dissemble, and then work to correct that. This benefits us because it allows us to be more genuine with others because, when we deceive them, "the walls of our egos thicken to further imprison us."[14] Seung Sahn says that "(i)n Zen, we say that 'the tongue has no bone' … because the tongue can say one thing in one sentence, and in the next breath say an entirely different thing … this is the source of all lies and gossip."[15] The other aspect to Right Speech is to avoid harmful speech because it is slanderous, idle, or abusive of others.

Right Action involves conducting oneself in such a way as to not harm others; an essential principle in Buddhism is known as *ahimsa*, which means to not harm. So, Right Action means no killing, no theft, no lying, no abuse of sex, no using intoxicants. The goal of avoiding these behaviors is to become more self-less and charitable to others. Right Action means "being aware of how our actions affect other beings because that also affects our minds."[16] Right Livelihood is rooted in the same perspective that one should not harm others: thus, one should not engage in an occupation that is harmful to others. For those who are totally dedicated to seeking enlightenment, this is a call to join a monastery, where one would be with monks or nuns dedicated to seeking enlightenment; for a layperson, the Buddha taught that Right Livelihood entails avoiding work that harms others such as poison peddling, slave trading, or prostitution, to name just a few.[17]

The last category describes steps related to **meditation** (*Samadhi*). These are (6) Right Effort; (7) Right Mindfulness; and (8) Right Meditation. Right Effort is to gain control of one's thoughts and to cultivate positive states of mind.[18] This requires determined exertion of willpower; in describing how one should do Right Effort, the Buddha uses the image of an ox that is carrying a load through mud: he keeps moving forward at a steady pace, not letting up until he is through it.[19]

Right Mindfulness means to cultivate constant awareness. We tend to move through life missing much that is happening, somewhat unconsciously. So, Right Mindfulness means to train oneself to attend to what is happening each moment: the thoughts, feelings, and actions. If one is drinking a glass of water, then it means to really attend to the water, the sensations of drinking it, and so forth. One pays attention to the content of the stream of consciousness, not judging, just noticing what comes to mind, and not reacting. Through this practice, one learns that these sensations, thoughts, and feelings pass by constantly; eventually, it happens that "the belief in a separate self-existent self begins to dissolve."[20]

Right Meditation, or Concentration, means developing deep levels of mental calm through techniques of meditation that can also be used to concentrate the mind and can bring integration to the personality. One type of concentration or meditation, "Calming Meditation" (*samatha*) is to follow one's breath—how it comes in and how it goes out. Thus, a simple way to meditate is: "to sit down in a stable posture and concentrate on the movement of the breath." But before long, one will find that "thoughts and distractions rise in the mind." Hence, to practice Right Concentration or Meditation, "you observe them (i.e., thoughts and distractions), let them gently pass away, and bring your concentration back to the movement of your breath."[21] The Vietnamese Buddhist monk Thich Nhat Hanh teaches another version of a "Calming Meditation," a walking meditation that incorporates conscious breathing while one walks "in the present moment."[22] Seung Sahn teaches that Right Meditation means to "keep a mind that is clear like space, yet functions as meticulously as the tip of a needle."[23]

There is also the technique of Insight, or Mindfulness, Meditation, known also as *vipassana*. The Buddha developed this practice so that the meditator could gain insight. In this type of meditation practice, one does not focus on the breath, but instead "you follow your feelings or thoughts or sensations. If you are bored, observe that you are bored. If your back aches, observe that your back aches." In doing Mindfulness Meditation, one sets as her goal to "simply be mindful of things as they are, to watch how all conditions arise and pass away and so to observe ... that 'no feeling is final' and no thought or sensation either."[24]

Another Buddhist meditation practice is known as **Metta**, or "loving-kindness" meditation. One begins by focusing loving-kindness on oneself; then, he or she "cultivates unconditional love for a friend ... then ... for someone you neither like nor dislike ... then for someone you dislike or even hate." Eventually, the meditator extends loving-kindness to everyone in the world.[25] From a Buddhist perspective, this makes sense, as all are related; one's enemy today could be her mother or daughter in another lifetime.

Two more important concepts for Buddhism are **karma** and the *sangha*. Karma is the term for the belief that future rebirths are determined by the moral deeds that a person does in this life. It is not meant to be seen as a kind of divine system of rewards and punishments; rather, it is more like a natural law such as gravity. Because of the existence of karma, which can be either good or bad, it can be said that "individuals are the sole authors of their good and bad fortune." Further, as Buddhists believe that human beings have free will, then "in the exercise of free will they engage in self-determination." One may experience these consequences in this lifetime or later lifetimes because karma "that has accumulated but not yet experienced is carried forward to the next life or even many lifetimes ahead."[26]

Buddhists believe in six realms of rebirth, which are depicted in what is known as the Wheel of Life. Therefore, one can be reborn into the animal realm, or the realm of ghosts, or into hell as the result of negative karma. On the other hand, if one has earned merit, then she or he could be reborn into the realm of humans, the realm of titans, or the realm of gods. The best realm is that of the gods, but this is not a permanent abode and is not nirvana. So, even the gods will be reborn.

There is also the term sangha, which is the Buddhist community. There are two categories of members: (1) monks and nuns; and (2) laypeople. Originally, the sangha was focused on the monks and nuns, but expanded later as Buddhism developed along the lines of the Mahayana tradition (to be explained soon). Buddhist monks and nuns are people who have given up possessions and social responsibilities so they can be totally devoted to seeking

Figure 10.3: *Shakyamuni Buddha*: This image shows the Buddha after attaining liberation and enlightenment.

nirvana. They live in monasteries and abide by strict rules, which include requiring that they beg anew each day for their food, that they not save any food for tomorrow, and that they not eat after noon. Monks and nuns are not allowed to touch gold or silver, either. The laypeople follow the Buddha's basic teachings, but do not renounce their ordinary lives. Therefore, they are unable to be completely devoted to seeking nirvana because of their daily responsibilities, but they can earn merit, or good karma, by providing food to begging monks and nuns, as well as annually providing cloth for new robes for monks and nuns and funds to care for shrines and monasteries.

Development of Buddhism

After the death of the Buddha, traveling monks spread the teachings of the Buddha. However, some disagreements eventually developed among Buddha's followers, and along with that came new traditions within Buddhism; most of these have disappeared, so that today one finds three major traditions: **Theravada** Buddhism, **Mahayana** Buddhism, and **Vajrayana** Buddhism.

Theravada Buddhism, the Buddhism of Southeast Asia, is really the oldest of the extant traditions and preserves much of the earliest teachings of the Buddha; it is known as "the Teaching of the Elders." The Theravada school emphasizes that the Buddha is an example of "what each person could achieve," that the "Buddha always remained human, never divine," and that there is no god.[27]

Mahayana Buddhism, also known as "the Great Vehicle," developed after the Theravada school and is larger; this second school of Buddhism is found in China and Japan. While the Theravada tradition emphasizes the individual taking responsibility and seeking her own enlightenment, it is the community that is important in Mahayana Buddhism.

The texts associated with Mahayana Buddhism appear to have been written about four centuries after the Buddha's death and are largely a "radial reinterpretation of the story of the Buddha." The texts speak of "a second turning of the wheel of "Dharma" as a result of the Buddha bringing forth a new teaching. One of the major texts of the Mahayana is the Lotus Sutra. In this tradition, Buddha is seen as having to bring a second teaching, as the first was too simple or primitive because people were not ready to accept a more developed understanding of the Dharma; but this is now presented in the Mahayana.

The focus shifts to the previous lives of the person who would become the Buddha to a time when he was a *bodhisattva*.[28] Bodhisattva is the term for a person "who takes a vow to work tirelessly over countless lifetimes to lead others to nirvana."[29] Thus, instead of being focused on saving oneself—that is, working for one's own nirvana—the bodhisattva selflessly works to save all others before proceeding to a state of nirvana.

The major effect of this change in emphasis in Buddhism is that it meant one did not need to become a monk or a nun to be devoted to the Dharma and that laypeople could become bodhisattvas, too. It meant that the focus was no longer just on wisdom, but now on wisdom and compassion, known as *karuna*. Thus, it was not only "important to see reality clearly, but it was also important to put that insight into practice—to act ... for the welfare of others."[30]

People also looked at the bodhisattvas as buddhas and celestial beings who had developed powers to help them. The Bodhisattva of Compassion, Avalokitesvara, is a being who helps people if they fall into danger and call upon him for help; in China, this same being is seen as having a female form and is known as Kuan-yin. There is also Amitabha, who is called Amida Buddha in Japan, and is a compassionate bodhisattva associated with the Pure Land, or the Western Kingdom (but it is not nirvana). Those devoted to Amida believe that, if they call upon him at the time of death, he will come to take them to the Pure Land, where they could then experience enlightenment.

In the Mahayana school, the Buddha was described as having three expressions, or Buddha bodies. This first was the "body of appearance" or physical

Figure 10.4: Sitting *zazen* (meditation). Practitioners of Zen sit in a meditation posture that affords stability and strength as they follow their breath or meditate upon *koans*.

body of the Buddha; the second was the "body of Bliss" that was surrounded by light and was seen as resulting from enlightenment; finally there was the "body of essence" or "the true being of the Buddha as an absolute beyond space and time." In the last two forms, the Buddha came to be seen as having "functioned in certain ways like a god—and so did others who became buddhas."[31]

The third major school is known as Vajrayana (Tantric) Buddhism, which developed out of Mahayana; it is the type of Buddhism associated with Tibet, where it appeared between the eighth and the 11th centuries. *Vajra* means thunderbolt or diamond, so this tradition is known as the thunderbolt or diamond vehicle. According to Prothero, the Vajrayana school "combined Theravada-style monasticism, the study and contemplation of Mahayanist texts, the magical and ritualistic traditions of Tantra (these are ancient Indian writings that include magical words and mystical diagrams known as mandalas), and the shamanistic [a shaman is a kind of priest or medicine man] beliefs and practices of the indigenous Bon religion."[32] In Vajrayana, the many buddhas of the Mahayana were "seen as visualizations of the passions in each human being," and using symbols, the followers of the thunderbolt vehicle, "aimed to transform their inner passional forces" so that they could then "merge them into a oneness at the center of the self ... (and this was) the mystical goal of union with a divinity within."[33]

CONTEMPORARY DEVELOPMENTS

In the United States in the 18th century, ethnic Buddhists built some temples to serve their communities. After many years, in the mid-20th century, a group known as the Buddhist Churches of America joined structures familiar to Christians such as Sunday school and Sunday services to their Buddhist practice; in this way, they hoped to preserve their tradition in a form that would blend well into American society.[34] This amalgamation of Christian and Buddhist practices is common among immigrant communities and has happened among other immigrant groups such as Jews, and even among some Christian groups such as Lutherans, who adapted more "Protestant" and less "Catholic" ways in the face of anti-immigrant sentiment in the days of the First World War.

There was also the growth of a type of Buddhism known as Zen. Originally known as Chan Buddhism (in China), but eventually known as Zen in Japan, it draws from both the Theravada and Mahayana traditions, emphasizing meditation as a way to enlightenment. One of the major proponents of Zen practice in the United States was D. T. Suzuki, who was sent to America by Zen Master Soyen Shaku, whom we have earlier noted had spoken at the World's Parliament of Religions in 1893. As you will recall from the introduction to this chapter, Suzuki translated important Buddhist texts into English, taught at universities, and authored popular books about Zen that helped many Americans in the 1960s and 1970s become involved in the study and practice of Buddhism.

Two Japanese Zen traditions are actively practiced in the United States. The first is the Rinzai school, which works with *koans* while doing *zazen* (sitting meditation). A koan is a teaching tool used by a Rinzai Zen master to teach his students; it is a puzzle that can't be solved logically. A famous example is: "Two hands clap and there is a sound. What is the sound of one hand clapping?" Other examples are: "Does a dog have Buddha nature?" "If you meet the Buddha on the road, kill him." Hence, the point is that one does not come to enlightenment by using reason; it is a spontaneous event. The Zen tradition is known as the Soto school. In this form of Zen, one sits in meditation and "just sits" while the mind becomes clearer and uncluttered by thoughts. Eventually, enlightenment happens. There is also a Korean tradition of Zen that has followers in the United States, as well.

A third form of Buddhism very popular today derives from Tibetan traditions. The 14th Dalai Lama, Tenzin Gyatso, is considered to the spiritual and temporal leader of the Tibetan people; he lives in exile in India, but is truly a "world citizen." The Dalai Lama is a Buddhist scholar, holding the highest degree in Buddhist philosophy, and has worked tirelessly for human rights, international peace, scientific exploration, and interfaith dialogue. Many of the recent scientific studies that show amazing benefits in the utilization of meditation and Buddhist psychology have been the product of scientific conferences sponsored by the Dalai Lama. Ethnic Tibetan masters such as Tarthang Tulku, as well as

North American masters like Pema Chodron, have greatly popularized Tibetan Buddhism, which involves meditation, but also has some very practical suggestions for living a healthy life psychologically.

The Buddhist group known as Soka Gakkai International-USA derives from a Japanese tradition known as the Nichiren Shoshu school and has grown markedly in the United States. The Nichiren Shoshu school is based on the views of a 13th-century Japanese Buddhist monk named Nichiren (1222–1282), who rejected the development of the Pure Land school in Buddhism. He "founded a new religious movement which made the Lotus Sutra the centre of practice rather than the Buddha Amida."[35] The Lotus Sutra is a text that was popular with the Mahayana and is a discourse of the Buddha; Nichiren told his followers that, by turning to the Lotus Sutra, they could achieve their spiritual goals, as well as gain material prosperity.

In the modern world, there was a lay movement that was an offshoot of the Nichiren Shoshu school known as Soka Gakkai. The group was known for its aggressive recruitment; this is different from other Buddhist groups, which often take the attitude about membership that could be stated as "if one comes, he is welcome; if he leaves, we do not follow." Though originally led by priests in Japan associated with Nichiren Shoshu, there was a split that led to the formation of Soka Gakkai International-USA (in America, the group has always had a lay leadership, and that continues). Nevertheless, people were attracted to the group because of the belief that they could find peace and become prosperous, too. Soka Gakkai claims an international membership of 12 million, with approximately 350,000 members in the United States.[36] It also counts some famous people among its members such as movie star Orlando Bloom and singer Tina Turner.

Today, there are also Americans who are lay Buddhists who have become leaders in the application of Buddhist thought, especially Buddhist psychology, to health concerns and to living a balanced and engaged life. An example is Jon Kabat Zinn, a scientist who served on the faculty of the University of Massachusetts Medical School, who found that he could help many medical patients with their coexisting psychological and existential suffering by training them in the use of mindfulness techniques; he wrote a seminal book about his work, *Full Catastrophe Living*, which introduced people all over the world to his work and led to many new applications and discoveries related to mindfulness. Another example is Mark Epstein, a psychiatrist who published the book, *Thoughts Without a Thinker*, which examines psychotherapy from a Buddhist perspective.

CHAPTER SUMMARY

In this chapter, we have reviewed the history of Buddhism and examined its essential teachings. Beginning in India, Buddhism became one of the major religions in Asia and the West. Its founder, Siddhartha Gautama, was a nobleman who rejected a comfortable life in order to search for an answer to the problem of the human condition. Becoming a mendicant, he studied with different teachers, learning various techniques that were useful in advancing along the spiritual path; but none of these techniques provided the answer he sought. Finally, during an amazing night of meditation, he became enlightened—that is to say that he found the answer and soon began to teach others. The teaching, or Dharma, is seen in the Four Noble Truths. Buddhism has evolved over the centuries and continues to bring wisdom to those who search for an answer to the question of human suffering.

KEY TERMS

- Bodhisattva
- Dharma
- Dukkha
- Eightfold Path
- Four Noble Truths
- Karma
- Nirvana
- Sangha
- Siddhartha Gautama
- Vipassana

REVIEW QUESTIONS

1. How did Siddhartha Gautama's enlightenment occur?
2. What are the Four Noble Truths?
3. What is the Eightfold Path?
4. What is the sangha?
5. Explain these terms: Dharma, dukkha, karma, and nirvana.

END NOTES

1. Pew Research Religion and Life Project, "Global Religious Landscape: Buddhism," accessed Oct. 23, 2014, http://www.pewforum.org/2012/12/18/global-religious-landscape-buddhist

2. Keown, Damien. *Buddhism: A Very Short Introduction* (Oxford, UK: Oxford University Press, 2013), 5–16.

3. Pew Research Religion and Life Project, "Global Religious Landscape: Buddhism," Summary of Key Findings, accessed Oct. 23, 2014. http://religions.pewforum.org/reports

4. Smith, Huston. *The Illustrated World's Religions.* (New York: HarperCollins, 1994), 60.

5. Keown, 20.

6. Keown, 20.

7. Keown, 20.

8. Keown, 22.

9. Smith, Huston. *The World's Religions* (New York: HarperCollins, 1991), 101–103.

10. Smith, *The World's Religions*, 103.

11. Prothero, Stephen. *God Is Not One* (New York: HarperCollins, 2010), 184.

12. Smith, *The World's Religions*, 106.

13. Sahn, Seung. *The Compass of Zen* (Boston: Shambala Publications, Inc., 1997), 100.

14. Smith, *The World's Religions*, 107.

15. Sahn, 101.

16. Sahn, 102.

17. Smith, *The World's Religions*, 106.

18. Keown, 59.

19. Smith, *The World's Religions*, 109.

20. Smith, *The World's Religions* 111.

21. Eckel, Malcolm David. "Buddhism in the World and in America." In Jacob Neusner, ed., *World Religions in America* (Louisville: Westminster John Knox Press, 2009), 205.

22. Nguyen, Anh-Huong, and Thich Nhat Hanh. *Walking Meditation* (Boulder: Sounds True, Inc., 2006).

23. Sahn, 103.

24. Prothero, 178.

25. Prothero, 178–179.

26. Keown, 41–43.

27. Albanese, Catherine L. *America: Religions and Religion* (Boston: Wadsworth Cengage Learning, 2007), 220.

28. Eckel, 208.

29. Keown, 62.

30. Eckel, 208.

31. Albanese, 220.

32. Prothero, 197.

33. Albanese, 220.

34. Albanese, 221.

35. Keown, 88.

36. "Who We Are" at Soka Gakkai International, accessed Oct. 28, 2014, http://www.sgi.org/about-us/sgi-facts/sgi-membership.html

11. New Agers, Neo-Paganism, New Religious Movements, and Other Religions

By William J. Cook Jr.

OVERVIEW

Since the 1960s, there have been some seismic changes in the religious landscape in America; it could be argued that "moral authority for most Americans was increasingly located in the self rather than in the family, church, or nation."[1] One of these changes that has happened over the past 50 years involves the growth of religions that have either not been traditionally accepted by mainstream society, or are, in actuality, new creations; or they are religions that have existed in other parts of the world, but which have only recently appeared here. Additionally, there are many people who describe themselves as spiritual, but not religious. Those who are dissatisfied with their experience of traditional religion and are exploring alternatives are known as religious seekers. One estimate of the number of religious seekers is that they constitute about 20 percent of the population;[2] however, no one really knows for sure what the actual demographics are for these individuals, since, generally speaking, they are not affiliated with any institutions, and when they meet in groups, they are usually informally organized. It also happens that some people are rooted in a traditional religion such as Christianity, but mix it with another, newer practice: for example, there are now what are known as "Quagans"—these are persons who are Quakers (a group most see as a denomination of Christianity) who also practice paganism.

Interestingly, the roots of the New Age movement are found in the 19th century; paganism and forms of witchcraft have long histories, extending back through the colonial days in America to the ancient world. **New Religious Movement** (NRM) is a term that refers to religious groups that were more pejoratively described as "cults" in the recent past; originally, the Latin word cultus meant "worship" or "reverence," but in modern times, the word cults was used to refer to religious groups that had adopted some unusual theological ideas and were called heretics. During the mid-20th century, the word began to have implications that a religious group demonstrated highly deviant behavior, in addition to holding unacceptable theological beliefs. Another characteristic of the religious groups that were labeled as cults included what was seen as the objectionable behavior of the group's leader—for example, being excessively controlling of the group's members and demanding that they be worshipful of the leader, isolating and bullying the members and requiring them to strictly follow his or her teachings uncritically; that is to say, the members had been "brainwashed."[3] During the 1970s and 1980s, there the phenomenon of "cult busters" arose, whose goal was to deprogram young persons who had become members of a targeted cult. The behavior of the cult busters was controversial and in some cases illegal, even though their motives may have been good, with the intention of helping to free those whom they saw as victims of a cult and its leader.

Therefore, it is currently popular to use the term "New Religious Movements" (NRMs) instead of cults; New Religious Movements tend to have some novel religious beliefs and perhaps some unusual patterns of behavior or dress. Some new religious groups that have been included in this category of NRMs are definitely not cults (in the pejorative sense) and have presented no threat to either the group's individual members or to society, but there are other groups that have been problematic or dangerous. Among this latter category, one could include the Branch Davidians, Christian Identity, Heaven's Gate, or the Rajneesh movement, to name a few. In the world of criminal justice, it is important to be able to distinguish between benevolent and malevolent NRMs so as to protect the religious rights of those that are innocent and harmless in their religious practice and to recognize those that are not.

NEW AGE MOVEMENT

If you happen to pick up a newspaper that is directed toward those who are interested or involved in New Age practices, the following are some topics you would find being discussed and some of the services you'd find being advertised. There are Reiki masters who utilize a Japanese art involving the healer laying on hands to balance another person's internal energies in the expectation of better health. Other healing modalities offered in advertisements include using crystals to strengthen one's immunity and to ward off negative energy from other people or electronic devices. Another provider will use light and sound to promote vibrational healing. If a person feels a need for more celestial support, there is the possibility of attending an "angel school," where the student can learn about "angel attunement," as well as how to use the four main archangels and how to receive messages. Should an individual be curious about the meaning of her life, there are astrologers who will examine the stars for clues about a person's destiny, but there is also a training session offered that will teach her to read the "Akashic Record" (a term from Theosophy, a movement from the 19th century, for the ethereal record of our thoughts, feelings, and life events). On the other hand, if reading the Akashic Record seems daunting, but you still want to try to know about the future, there are advertisements for psychic tarot readings and psychic mediums, who promise to tell a person about her past lives, but also communicate telepathically with angels and spirit guides for the client, too.

Social scientists have estimated that about ten million Americans have engaged in the kinds of practices favored by New Agers.[4] The New Age community appears to be composed of middle- and upper-middle-class persons who are educated and not alienated from society; typically, they are females who are middle-aged or young, urban, and from the East and West coasts.[5]

The term New Age derives from the Age of Aquarius, the new astrological age that was anticipated to arrive, possibly with the millennium, and which was expected to bring freedom; the prior age was Pisces, which some associated with traditional patriarchal religion. So what is the New Age movement? It is difficult to say exactly, as there are many ideas and practices that are included under the New Age tent. But essentially, as one can conclude from the various advertisements and stories listed above, New Agers are "committed to transforming both the self and society through a host of practices."[6] They believe in angels, miracles, clairvoyance, channeling of spirits, and yet, "they combine such practices [and] beliefs with other elements such as Asian religious tradition, the human potential movement, American Indian beliefs, and holistic healing practices."[7] Those drawn to the New Age movement don't meet weekly to perform a ritual like a church service, as is common among followers of traditional religions. Instead, they are more likely to engage in "specialist-client" relationships, such as when an individual engages the services of a Reiki master. The goal of all of this is to bring about spiritual and physical healing so as to "facilitate the shift to a new level of consciousness." But it is important to note that the New Age movement does not appear to be hostile to traditional religion.[8] Some people blend traditional and new approaches to spirituality.

For New Agers, salvation is possible; it depends on discovering the "divine inner self." By cultivating the divine inner self, a person who meditates or does yoga or uses various techniques (such as we saw in the advertisements) that can be learned, can draw on his own psychic powers to bring about physical or psychological healing.[9] This approach is rooted in the assumption that positive

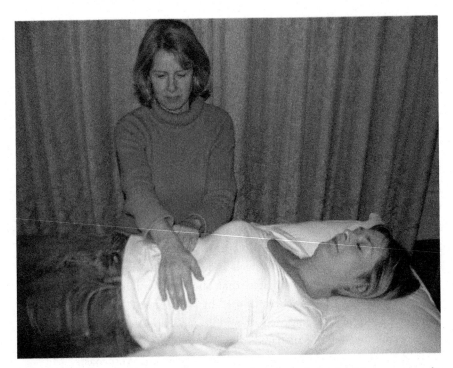

Figure 11.1: Reiki practitioner places her hands to transfer *ki*, or energy, in order to promote healing.

thinking is essential in bringing about change. Two fundamental assumptions held by New Agers are that human consciousness has an unlimited potential and that people have a connectedness to all of life, especially to Earth, which is seen as a living being (called the **Gaia hypothesis**). People therefore have a responsibility to the Earth.[10]

The New Age movement evolved from various philosophies, beliefs, and approaches to spirituality such as transcendentalism, spiritualism, Theosophy, and New Thought that were popular in the 19th century. A major influence at that time was metaphysical religion, which focused on the mind as a "saving force." This approach diverged from traditional religion; thus, there was the influence of someone like Ralph Waldo Emerson (1803–1882), who was recognized as the leader of **transcendentalism**, a popular religious and philosophical movement that mixed Asian (e.g., Hindu) religious ideas and Neoplatonism. In Emerson's view, the person must turn inward to "cultivate the qualities that would lead to harmony with the self and universe."[11] **Spiritualism** was another popular practice in that same era. Spiritualism involved holding séances, where a human medium (usually a woman) would contact and communicate with the spirits of the dead in order to answer questions, prophesy, or engage in healing by transmitting a force through their fingers.

In the latter part of the 19th century, the Theosophical Society developed. It was founded in New York City by an immigrant, Helen Blavatsky (1831–1891), and a lawyer, Henry S. Olcott (1832–1907), who shared an interest in occult research—this is to acquire secret knowledge about the nature of the universe and the divine. The Theosophists also provided "the first organized channel for the introduction of Asian religious thought to the United States."[12]

New Thought, which was called the Mind Cure Movement, is attributed to the teaching of Phineas P. Quimby (1802–1806), who was healed through a mesmerist (someone who used hypnotic trances with a patient), but decided that what really happened was that the mesmerist was able to get the person to be healed to change his or her belief. Warren Felt Evans (1814–1889) was healed by Quimby. Though he had been a minister, he became a healer, too. Evans concluded that what was essential was both the power of suggestion and that the patient made a conscious affirmation of health and an affirmative prayer. Later, one sees the influence of New Thought on the development of Christian Science in the mid-20th century in the work of Norman Vincent Peale (1898–1993), who wrote the famous book *The Power of Positive Thinking* (1952).

What is New Age religion like? Albanese gives a twofold model to answer this question. First, she notes that some New Agers are inclined to be social thinkers who are concerned about the environment, holistic health, and transformation. She finds that this group is inclined toward ordinary religion (in conjunction with their New Age interests), and "evidence suggests strong participation by Catholics, Protestants and Jews."[13] The second group is described by Albanese as "individually oriented actors" who engage in practices such as channeling or working with crystals. This group is drawn to extraordinary religion, as they are "spiritual seekers who want direct evidence of and contact with the extraordinary." And while members of more conventional religions speak of God, New Agers tend to speak of the universe. Thus, it can be said that, for New Agers, "the universe has become the source of life's many events and coincidences, and it also possesses an intelligence that guides and guards people."[14]

In summary, one can see that the emphasis in New Age religion is on the therapeutic—healing the self and the world. The self is seen as divine, but still not complete; it needs to be "integrated" or "expanded" or "true." This happens through a process of self-discovery and healing. Nevertheless, the self does have godlike powers and can do miraculous things. For example, one woman believes that a person can regenerate bones or teeth, while another is sure that "by reversing the flow of energy," she will be able to bring new vitality to an old mill town in her vicinity. Additionally, like New Age practitioners, New Age gods are nonjudgmental, so there is "no universal supreme being who exercises his authority over humans. Instead, people describe having their own gods and spirits who are like friends, providing assistance when needed." The fundamental characteristics of the New Age movement are individuality, fluidity, and equality.[15] The benefit that New Age spirituality brings to contemporary society is the "emphasis on health and healing and on interconnectedness, which provides a balancing force for stress and specialization in the modern Western world."[16]

NEO-PAGANISM

The term **neo-paganism** is one that can refer to different belief systems and traditions such as Celtic druidism (i.e., sun worshippers), Wicca, or witchcraft, ceremonial magic, and shamanism (involving a medicine man who leads an initiate through a journey to the spirit world). In the United States, neo-paganism is an effort to revive and re-create ancient nature religions. Because there really is no continuity with that ancient past, neo-pagans draw from Native American traditions, Greek, Roman, and Egyptian mythologies, and even fictional writings such as *Lord of the Rings*. Neo-paganism has been described as created to be "egalitarian, individualistic, [as well as] influenced by **Apocalypticism** [i.e., a belief that the world will end soon] and social change movements."[17]

Neo-paganism and modern Wicca are two of the fastest growing spiritualities; in surveys conducted during the decade extending between 1990–2000, the "number of people identifying themselves as Wiccan or Pagan grew faster than any other religious category."[18] In 2005, the American Religious Identification Survey (ARIS) reported that there were an estimated 307,000 Wiccan, druid, and pagan adults in the United States. Another study suggests that most pagans are white, of European descent, and middle-class and many are female; it is theorized that more females are attracted to paganism because of the emphasis

Figure 11.2: Druids at Stonehenge, an ancient site in England, conduct a modern pagan ceremony.

on worship of the female divinity (the goddess). Nevertheless, it is difficult to know exactly how many people practice paganism today, as there is hesitancy to speak about their participation for fear of negative reactions such as rejection or even reprisals, as has happened in the case of some women who lost custody of their children in divorce cases because they were witches or practitioners of Wicca.[19]

In her classic work, *Drawing Down the Moon: Witches, Druids, Goddess-Worshippers and Other Pagans in America*, Adler explains that "most Neopagans sense an aliveness and 'presence' in nature."[20] Neo-pagans often define their sacred spaces by the four powers (e.g., the directions of north, east, etc.) and have altars with statutes of their deities and symbols of the four elements (water, air, fire, and Earth). Life passages are marked through rituals for blessing newborns, marriage vows, and death rites. There are neo-pagan rituals and festivals for seasonal celebrations that "include retelling of myths, theater, ritual performances, music, feasting and storytelling." The purpose of the rituals is to link the celestial world with the human world and to celebrate the cycles of life and death and the change of seasons.[21]

A participant's description of a neo-pagan ritual is reported by Pike in her book, *New Age and Neopagan Religions*. Here is a description of the ritual and the rationale underpinning it:

> *We draw spirals in the dirt. We have feathers, yarn, a shell:*
> *our altar. We release the snake from her bucket. She is beautiful,*
> *the scales on her back glistening in diamond shape, her tail crowned*
> *with many rattles … . When we go, she will coil her body into a spiral*
> *and remain, a fitting guardian for this land … This is how it works:*
> *someone has a vision that arises from a fierce and passionate love.*
> *To make it real, we must love every moment of what we do. Impermanent*
> *spirals embed themselves in asphalt, concrete, dust. Slowly, slowly, they*
> *eat into the foundations of the structures of power. Deep transformations*
> *take time. Regeneration arises from decay.*[22]

Neo-pagans may practice alone (known as "solitaries") or in small groups known as either covens or circles. A coven is a committed group that has a long-term involvement with one another; it is a stable, cohesive group whose members maintain a degree of intimacy. A circle is a group that has more variable and fluid membership, with a consequent decrease in intimacy among the members. The groups (e.g., circles and covens) are autonomous and decentralized; there is networking through websites and some national organizations that promote neo-paganism.[23]

Unlike traditional religions, there are no set beliefs that one must hold to be considered a neo-pagan. It can be said that, "Witchcraft is a mystery religion in which participation in rituals is more important than adherence to particular beliefs or myths."[24] However, Yardley outlines some of the most common beliefs among neo-pagans. The first is that nature is sacred and that all creatures are interconnected. The second most common belief is that the divine is both male and female, or god and goddess, who are represented in different forms within the different cultures such as Egyptian, Celtic, or Norse). Wiccans envision the goddess as a moon goddess who has three aspects: maiden, mother, and crone (i.e., a young, middle-aged, or elderly woman), represented by the waxing, full, and waning moon. The god is seen as the horned god of nature and wildlife. The fourth common belief is that nature is composed of four spiritual elements (Earth, air, fire and water). The pentacle (a five-pointed star in a circle) represents the four elements plus the spirit and is often worn (e.g., as jewelry) as a sign of one's spiritual path. Finally, there is the belief that people can make changes happen in their lives by practicing magic; this means to focus intention and energy toward a goal through the enactment of rituals. Magic can be worked for such practical purposes as getting a new job or home or for psychological reasons such as curing addiction or for acquiring greater self-confidence. It happens that most neo-pagans believe that working harmful magic will bring back harmful results to the one who does this.[25] (There is an example of this perspective in the Wiccan Rede, which cautions: "An it harm none, do what ye will.") Adler explains that "magic is a convenient word for a whole collection of techniques, all of which involve the mind ... the use of the imaginative faculties, particularly our ability to visualize how other beings function in nature so we can use this knowledge to achieve necessary ends."[26]

Holidays typically celebrated by neo-pagans include the solstices in winter and summer, the equinoxes in spring and fall, and four other holidays: Samhain (October 31st), Imbolc (February 2nd), Beltane (May 1st), and Lammas (August 2nd). Other celebrations occur with the arrival of new moons and full moons. The major festivals of neo-paganism are called *Sabbats*, and they celebrate the changing seasons. Changes in the moon cycle are celebrated during the *Esbats*; the moon is "viewed as a female deity which moves from maid at the quarter moon, to mother at the full moon, and to the crone, or wise old woman at the new moon."[27]

Witches comprise the largest group among the neo-pagans. Some are extreme separatist feminist witches who worship the great goddess in women-only covens. Others are more traditional, Gardnerian witches, who learn rituals from teachers and who worship a male god and female goddess; this emphasizes the dual nature of divinity.[28] Gerald Gardner (1884–1964) was a British civil servant who claimed to have made contact with a genuine coven of witches in New Forest, England, and later wrote several books detailing the beliefs and practices of what he claimed was an ancient tradition. He called it Wicca. Though Gardner had great influence on the development of Wicca, his approach has also been criticized by some, saying that "much of Wicca was made up, while the rest was a mix of nudism and freemasonry ... . Gardner may sincerely have worshipped nature, but the rituals and laws of his religion were made up."[29] Ceremonial magicians are more inclined to draw from 19th-century occultists or from the writings of the British occultist Aleister Crowley (1875–1947). Crowley was educated at Cambridge University and wrote a book, *The Book of Law*, which he claimed was dictated to him through a messenger of the ancient Egyptian god Horus. Ceremonial magicians also draw from the Kabbalah, which is a tradition of esoteric Jewish mystical teachings. Crowley describes magic as the "science and art of causing change to occur in conformity with will."[30]

Figure 11.3 Starhawk is an author and activist who is a modern pagan concerned about issues related to feminism and ecology.

A group of neo-pagans that has evoked societal concern over the past 50 years involves satanism among some of them; in fact, most neo-pagans disavow any involvement with satanism. Anton LaVey, leader of the Church of Satan, became famous in the 1960s when he published his book, *The Satanic Bible*. In that book, he enunciated principles of satanism, such as that Satan represents indulgence, wisdom, vengeance, kindness to those deserving it, and the view that man is really just another animal.

Petersen describes satanism as involving "black magic, demonology, and dark occultism." There is a "self-'centrism' and measured antinomialism … . The Prince of Darkness is the Lord of Matter and he is a rebellious individualist." There appear to be two types of Satanists: "those who emphasize Satan as a symbol of the naturalized self" and another group "who maintain a more idealistic framework, with Satan being a force or entity outside the purely natural (as in carnal and material)." Further, he concludes that the satanic rituals are actually psychodramas that "are actively *transforming* guilt, stigma, and repression into benefits through emotional catharsis … the controlled transgression elicits an emotional response, exorcising whatever 'demons' are holding the Satanist back."[31] An example would be a young fellow who is so shy that he cannot talk to women, but after participating in satanic rituals, he overcomes his inhibitions and is able to speak easily with women.[32]

Edward Moody explores the question about why people are drawn to satanism. He argues that Satanists find that something they call "magic" works for them, and they accomplish many of the goals they set out to achieve. Moody observes that there has been a growth in such magical groups today because of an "attempt by various people to regain a sense of control over their environment and their lives."[33]

During the 1980s and 1990s, there was a "moral panic" in America and Great Britain in relation to what was termed "satanic ritual abuse" by cults that were alleged to have engaged in "sexual abuse, infant sacrifice, perverse ceremonies and mind control." Hundreds of persons, many of them day-care workers, were accused of satanic rituals that were criminal. The evidence brought forth was "almost entirely of 'memories': those extracted from small children by anxious adults." But as the inquiries continued, the evidence collapsed; the memories proved not to be reliable. As David Frankfurter observes: "it is important to realize that actual, historically tenable forensic evidence for the alleged Satanic cults and the crimes has *not* yet appeared, a fact that many law-enforcement experts, psychologists, sociologists, and journalists noted already in 1991."[34]

NEW RELIGIOUS MOVEMENTS

As explained earlier in the chapter, New Religious Movements is the term used to describe religious groups that have adapted novel or unusual theological principles, usually in conjunction with a lifestyle some might consider deviant. There appear to be two generic styles of New Religious Movements. The first type has been called "antimodern" in character and protests the changes in social life related to modernity. An example of an antimodern NRM is the International Society for Krishna Consciousness (ISKCON). The second type is actually modern in their "form and functioning ... even in some aspects of their beliefs." An example of this second grouping might be Transcendental Meditation or Scientology.

New Religious Movements are very diverse in the ways they are structured and function. Some NRMs are highly structured with multiple levels of organization, while others are not; some are local and small, but some are large and international. There are NRMs that require a great commitment on the part of their members: they invest much of their time, money, and professional expertise, as well as their marriages and families. Other NRMs are seen to have more desultory members who invest little in the organization. There are NRMs that have been founded by self-styled prophets or messiahs such as the Branch Davidians, and yet, there are other NRMs that grew more spontaneously out of a movement; an example of this latter type is the Christian Identity Movement.

Some NRMs offer new interpretations of traditional sacred scriptures such as the Bible, while others offer new sacred writings.[35]

Some hypothesize that now people are drawn to NRMs because they are experiencing a sense of **dislocation** in modern society. This dislocation can be attributed to three themes in modern society: (1) changes in values; (2) changes in social structure; and (3) changes in the role and character of religious institutions (i.e., secularization). Hence, membership in an NRM can help an individual cope with the changes that have caused them to feel dislocated.[36] The NRMs can be said to "provide areas for theological and social experimentation. Some of these experiments are successful and result in lasting religious organizations that exert broad theological and cultural influences." Some are not successful and eventually disappear, while other religious experiments "produce groups whose beliefs and practices are deemed utterly abhorrent by the wider society."[37]

You may be wondering how it happened that, what was once called a cult is now referred to as a New Religious Movement. To answer, we'll need to look back about 50 years. In the 1960s, many religious groups with Asian roots such as the Hindu International Society for Krishna Consciousness or the Transcendental Meditation of Maharishi Mahesh Yogi were called cults and thus eyed suspiciously; during the period extending from the 1970s to the 1990s and later, there were Christian groups such as the Peoples' Temple and the Branch Davidians that were labeled as cults. Sociologists of religion sought the use of a new term—New Religious Movements—for such atypical religious groups, so as to reduce the prejudice and negative consequences of a label such as a cult. The consequences of a negative label can be disastrous because it tends to influence media reporting about such groups, which, in turn, can affect the response of the government to the group. Hill et al., in discussing these effects, argue that:

> The civil government, by misunderstanding the world-
> views of new religious movements, contributes to the
> sense of persecution on the part of these movements.
> In times of tension, this sense of persecution further
> polarizes the situation and can actually encourage the
> group to engage in violent behavior. The classic example [of]
> this occurrence is the standoff between Federal officials
> and the Branch Davidians in Waco, Texas in 1993.[38]

In their content analysis of news stories about religious groups labeled as cults, Hill et al. found that the "most influential reporting on religion … fails the standards of an 'evenhanded, non-judgmental and fair approach' to new religious movements, at least in the language used to describe them." They discovered that characterization of a new religious group as a cult was invariably then linked "to

Figure 11.4: The Wiccan altar has ritual implements such as an athame (ceremonial dagger), a chalice, candles, a pentacle, and a statue of a goddess with Pan.

violence, actual or potential." The authors then ask why this would happen and suggest that the answer is that "the media accepted uncritically the assessments of civil governments" because news reporting on "unpopular or marginal religions are frequently predicated on unsubstantiated allegations or government actions based on faulty or weak evidence occurring at the front-end of an even[that is, when the event begins]."[39]

The problem of unfair characterizations of New Religious Movements is not new. In 1978, the prominent theologian Harvey Cox wrote about his interest in the "'recurrent deep structures' with which mainstream writers and critics do characterize, caricature and condemn marginal movements." He identifies four themes or myths that were used in this way.

The first myth is what he called the "subversion myth"—that "a movement, whatever its religious intentions, is thought to pose a threat to the civil order." Cox notes that sometimes the religious movements are seen as "religious fronts" for politically subversive movements, or that the movement will endanger civil authority. As an example of a group where this had happened, Cox points to the treatment of Quakers by the Puritans in Boston; he says, "Simply being a Quaker was enough to get someone deported or finally hanged in Boston Common."

The second myth is the accusation that "behind the walls of these movements exists a form of sexual or behavioral deviancy." The third theme Cox notes is what he refers to as the myth of dissimulation. He states, "It runs this way: 'You can't talk to these people because they are taught to dissimulate. They are carefully coached in not telling the truth and misleading you ... their doctrine itself teaches them to lie to you.'" Cox points out that, at one time, this canard was used against the Jesuits (an order of Roman Catholic priests who are known for their intellectual acuity).

Cox calls the fourth typical characterization the myth of the evil eye. He says this myth holds that "no sane person would possibly belong to a movement 'like this'. And, therefore, the participant must be there involuntarily." He then notes that this perspective is based on the expectation of the "existence of some kind of coercive, manipulative, or magical activity—or witchcraft—is inferred." He then observes that the "term, 'brainwashing' has come into currency recently as a more psychologically acceptable way of expressing what was expressed previously in other ways." Further, Cox states that "the brainwashing version of the evil eye myth holds that 'these people' are the victims of prophets, spell-binders, witches, or hypnotists."[40]

So, one might ask: If Harvey Cox is correct in his incisive assessment of the myths used to criticize them, *what are the people who join cults really like?* First of all, it has been consistently shown in research that people who join New Religious Movements are not mentally ill and that belonging to such a group generally seems to be more beneficial than harmful to the mental health and well-being of those belonging to the NRM. However, there is evidence that members do pay a price in terms of rigidity and restriction of autonomy.[41] Apparently, those who join NRMs may have "a fragile past" characterized by "an insecure attachment history, high need for closure and depressive tendencies." But as members of the NRM, they seem to have a "positive present" with "positive world assumptions, security in adult attachment, and no depression," and a "positive future," according to their own self-perceptions.[42]

The last issue to consider with regard to NRMs involves violence. As noted earlier in Cox's critique of the myths used to caricature New Religious Movements, one is that the NRMs are violent by nature. The reality is that most are not violent at all. But when violence does occur, it can be said to be "*interactive in nature.*" Wessinger argues that it is "the quality of interactions of people in mainstream society—law enforcement agents and other government officials, reporters, psychologists and social workers, citizens, concerned relatives, and anticultists—with members of a new religion helps determine whether or not tragic violence occurs."

Wessinger identifies three categories of NRMs in relation to violence. First, there is the "assaulted NRM," which describes a situation where the NRM did not initiate the violence, but has been attacked by others. Depending on the values of the group (i.e., are they pacifists?), they may or may not defend themselves. The second group is referred to as a "fragile NRM". These are groups that become fragile in reaction to internal weaknesses and experiencing societal opposition. In this kind of an unstable situation, the NRM may initiate violence in order "to preserve their endangered religious goal. Their violence may be directed outwardly toward those whom they see as enemies, or inwardly against members, or both." An example of this occurred when 920 people belonging to the Peoples' Temple died through murder or suicide in Jonestown, Guyana, in 1978. The third group identified by Wessinger is called the "revolutionary NRM," and it is the most dangerous. These NRMs are revolutionary millennial movements that have a goal of achieving collective salvation on Earth; however, even with these groups, the potential for violence is related to how persecuted by the mainstream the group feels because this will confirm their conviction that violence is necessary "to achieve a collective salvation for those who are identified as worthy of being included in the 'elect.'" A contemporary example is al Qaeda.[43]

CHAPTER SUMMARY

In this chapter, we have examined three types of religious movements that are found along the margins of religious practice. First, there was a discussion of the New Age movement. New Agers are people who, either to some degree or completely, have rejected mainstream religions in search of a more personalized spiritual experience. Some people drawn to the New Age movement mix a nontraditional practice such as using crystals for healing with an adherence to a mainstream religion. Others have no interest in mainstream religion, but still seek a spiritual experience and may instead go to a shaman so as to be led on a quest that will bring inner knowledge. The goals for most New Agers are inner growth and healing.

Neo-paganism is an attempt to return to a more "natural" religion—the type of religion believed to have been practiced in the days before the monotheistic religions prevailed. Neo-pagans see nature, the body, sexuality, and imagination as holy; they believe that divinity is immanent in nature. Neo-pagans may also practice Wicca, or witchcraft, in order to bring about changes according to what it is that they will.

New Religious Movements are, in a real sense, religious experiments. These are groups of believers who may have modified the teachings of a mainstream tradition such as Christianity, or even blended several traditions together. The beliefs held by NRMs can range widely: for example, there have been NRMs devoted to contact with Unidentified Flying Objects (UFOs) and extraterrestrials; there are other NRMs who believe that the end of the world is imminent and that they have a special role to play in the end times; and there are some NRMs that are rooted in Asian religious traditions such as Hinduism. What all NRMs have in common is the experience of being marginalized by society. For most, this is just a painful rejection, but for a small subset, this can be a factor in eliciting violence.

KEY TERMS

+ Apocalypticism
+ Celtic druids
+ Dislocation
+ Gaia hypothesis
+ New Age
+ Neo-paganism
+ New Religious Movements (NRMs)
+ Transcendentalism
+ Spiritualism
+ Wicca

REVIEW QUESTIONS

1. What is the New Age movement?
2. What is neo-paganism?
3. Why is the term New Religious Movements (NRMs) used instead of cults?
4. What have been common societal reactions to New Religious Movements?
5. Discuss Wessinger's model of the development of violence in some New Religious Movements.

END NOTES

1. Pike, Sarah M. *New Age and Neopagan Religions in America* (New York: Columbia University Press, 2004), 74.
2. "Spirit Wars: American Religion in Progressive Politics."
3. Cleaver, Ken. "The Practical and Ethical Considerations in Labelling a Religious Group as a 'Cult.'" *Journal for the Study of Religions and Ideologies* 11.33 (2012): 164–181. ProQuest. Web. Nov. 13, 2014.
4. Tucker, James. "New Age Religion and the Cult of the Self." *Society* January/February 2002 (46–51).
5. Albanese, Catherine L. *America: Religions and Religion* (Boston: Wadsworth, Cengage Learning, 2007), 236.
6. Pike, 22.
7. Pike, 22.

8. Flere, Sergej, and Andrej Kirbis. "New Age is Not Inimical to Religion and Traditionalism." *Journal for the Scientific Study of Religion*, March 2009, 48(1): 179–184.

9. Pike, 23, 73.

10. Pike, 23.

11. Albanese, 184.

12. Albanese, 189.

13. Albanese, 236.

14. Albanese, 232, 234.

15. Tucker, 48–50.

16. Woodside, Lisa N. "New Age Spirituality: A Positive Contribution." In *New Age Spirituality: An Assessment*, ed. Duncan S. Ferguson (Louisville: Westminster/John Knox Press, 1993), 145.

17. Pike, 19.

18. Jensen, Gary F., and Ashley Thompson. "Out of the Broom Closet: The Social Ecology of American Wicca." *Journal for the Scientific Study of Religion* (2008) 47 (4):653–766.

19. Yardley, Meg. "Social Work Practice with Pagans, Witches, and Wiccans: Guidelines for Practice with Children and Youths." *Social Work* (October 2008) 53(43): 329–336.

20. Adler, Margot. *Drawing Down the Moon: Witches, Druids, Goddess-Worshippers and Other Pagans in America* (New York: Penguin Books, 2006), 3.

21. Pike, 19.

22. Pike, 160.

23. Yardley, 330.

24. Berger, Helen. "The Routinization of Spontaneity." *Sociology of Religion* (1995) 56 (1): 49–61.

25. Yardley, 330.

26. Adler, 7.

27. Berger, 54.

28. Pike, 19.

29. Stanley, Tim. "Give Me That Old Time Religion." *History Today* (August 2013) 63(8): 50.

30. Adler, 8.

31. Petersen, Jesper Aagard. "The Seeds of Satan: Conceptions of Magic in Contemporary Satanism." *Aries* (2012) 12: 91–129.

32. Adler, 478.

33. Adler, 477.

34. Frankfurter, David. "The Satanic Ritual Abuse Panic as Religious-Studies Data." *Numen* (2003) 50: 108–112.

35. Wessinger, Catherine. "New Religious Movements: An Overview." *Encyclopedia of Religion*, ed. Lindsay Jones, 2nd ed., vol.10 (Detroit: MacMillan Reference USA, 2005), 6513–6520. *Gale Virtual Reference Library*. Web. Nov. 6, 2014.

36. Dawson, Lorne L. "The Cultural Significance of New Religious Movements and Globalization: A Theoretical Prolegomenon." *Journal for the Scientific Study of Religion* (1998) 37 (4): 580–595.

37. Wessinger.

38. Hill, Harvey, John Hickman, and Joel McLendon. "Cults and Sects and Doomsday Groups, Oh My: Media Treatment of Religion on the Eve of the Millennium." *Review of Religious Research* (2001) 43(1): 24–38.

39. Hill, et al., 34.

40. Cox, Harvey. "Deep Structures in the Study of New Religions." In *Understanding the New Religions*, ed. Jacob Needleman and George Baker (New York: Seabury Press, 1978), 122–131.

41. Buxant, Coralie, and Vassilis Saroglou. "Feeling Good, but Lacking Autonomy: Closed-Mindedness on Social and Moral Issues in New Religious Movements." *Journal of Religion and Health* (2008) 47: 17–31.

42. Buxant, Coralie, Vassilis Saroglou, Stephania Casalfiore, and Louis-Leon Christians. "Cognitive and Emotional Characteristics of New Religious Movement Members: New Questions and Data on the Mental Health Issue." *Mental Health, Religion and Culture* (May 2007) 10(3): 219–238.

43. Wessinger.

Part III

12. Religion, Retribution, and Rehabilitation

By Gordon S. Bates

INTRODUCTION

Justice has had many faces over the centuries. It has taken the form of revenge, sometimes by individuals acting as vigilantes or by families in feuds that lasted months or years. Justice can be sought through retaliation by one nation or another for perceived harms suffered, or to appropriate desired resources and land. Justice for the wealthy is often different from that given to the poor. Similarly, the face of justice that minorities perceive can be very different from the face that appears to the majority race, and the justice handed out to immigrants can differ greatly from that bestowed on citizens. Justice can appear to be, and in fact is, very different to different people, depending on the circumstances.

This chapter argues that there are two primary faces of justice; that is, two ways justice is implemented in practice. The first, and perhaps the most basic to human nature, is retributive justice.[1] This first face of justice is an approach that places direct and retaliatory punishment for crimes above all else. The purpose of the punishment is to pay the offender back for the harm done to society and the victims. Originally, the term had two dimensions. It meant a recompense for evil or a tribute for an achievement. It has been suggested that the restriction of retribution to a payback for evil dates to the 16th century and the publication of "The Day of Retribution," a Christian summary of the final Day of Judgment by God. Although the document also deals with God's rewards for good deeds, its lasting emphasis is on the divine penalties for acts of evil.[2]

The second face of justice, rehabilitation, is an approach that focuses on the restoration and reintegration of offenders back into society, whether the punishment is a simple fine or lengthy incarceration. Rehabilitation means to change someone or something back to an original—or at least improved—state of mind and behavior. Many have argued that the term is misleading because the majority of offenders were never "habilitated"; that is, they were criminally inclined from birth (the theory of the bad seed) or that they were never socialized, from birth onward, to be law abiding. Supporters of rehabilitation argue in turn that though there may be genetic factors involved in criminal activity, the bad seed theory is not confirmed by research; and that deficiencies in family environment, early education, and subsequent exposure to antisocial behavior can be rectified with proper discipline and assistance, together with the indispensable cooperation of the offender.[3]

RELIGION'S ROLE IN THE HISTORICAL STRUGGLE TO ACHIEVE JUSTICE

The Abrahamic faiths (Judaism, Christianity, and Islam) have provided the chief repository of values that interact to produce either retributive or rehabilitative justice. After the 18th century and the impact of the Enlightenment era, these religious values were rationalized to be more broadly acceptable and less dangerous. The religious core remains. The rationalization of retribution is seen in the many legal and moral arguments to justify the death penalty. The rationalization of rehabilitation is seen in the realization that beyond the Abrahamic traditions, even religions without a belief in a transcendent or supernatural divinity (such as Buddhism and Taoism), have developed their own versions of the Golden Rule: Do to others as you would have them do to you. World religions have rich and complex traditions about the need to control every form of violence in every community and achieve harmony within the individual and the community.[4]

The desire for some kind of punishment for the offender is arguably the most natural response to a violation of the law, the destruction or theft of property, and an injury to or the act of killing, whether it is a single individual or a larger group. From the beginning of time, religion has played a key role in the desire for all aspects of retribution.

RELIGION'S INFLUENCE ON COLONIAL JUSTICE

The colonists who crossed the Atlantic in the early 17th century came for a variety of reasons. Some came for adventure and economic profit, some for religious freedom, and some because they were enlisted, or forced, by the English Crown to serve the needs of those looking for financial gain. Some, consisting of clergy, lawyers, or business representatives, were highly educated. All came out of the religious culture of Great Britain and carried with them experiences and assumptions that were part of that world. The Puritans and other Christian dissenters from the Anglican Church of England expressed in the actions and writings their convictions about God, about the Bible, and about human nature's tendency to sin and need of salvation. John Winthrop, the Puritan leader of the Massachusetts Bay Colony, proclaimed their mission. It was to form a community that could be a symbol of God's love and judgment, a "city set on a hill," so just and faithful that all nations might be drawn to emulate them.[5]

The New Haven Colony Code provides us with an excellent example of one of the first legal codes and its focus on retribution. The Code of 1650 reveals that not all colonists were law-abiding, and the code outlines the punishments that each offender was to be given.[6] The crimes listed began with robbery, followed by theft, pilfering, heresy, rebellion against parents, fornication, forgery, and gaming. The punishments included whipping, sitting for a time in the stocks or pillories, and mutilation by branding (for example: B for burglary). Capital punishment was ordered for murder, but also for idolatry, witchcraft, blasphemy, or copulation with animals. The Bible provided chapter and verse for each crime and penalty. It is notable that the Puritans and most other Christian groups in early America saw salvation of the soul as supremely important. If the body was made to suffer, perhaps the soul would eventually respond to rescue the sinner and preserve society. If repentance was not achieved, however, the punishment was still justified by divine commandment.

A horrendous example of religiously justified retribution, one that left the principle of *Lex Talionis* far behind, occurred in the Connecticut Colony in the 17th century, shortly after the settlements along the Connecticut River were established. Indian attacks were not common, but they occasionally happened as settlers cleared land for farming and became intrusive within the hunting grounds of the local tribes.

Reaction to Native Americans was the first great moral challenge of America. Reaction to the economic potential of slavery was the second. After the suppression and elimination of Native American resistance, slavery was the parallel decision that ultimately influenced criminal justice policy. Both were rooted in religious assumptions and teachings. Each of the 13 original colonies participated in the benefits of slavery—a doorway to cost-efficient manpower—as early as 1620.

The treatment of the Native Americans and the implementation of slavery exemplify two of the more extreme occasions of the retributive face of colonial justice. It is important to note, however, that while the idea of rehabilitation was not entirely absent, it was seen almost exclusively in the continued proclamation of the Christian message of personal redemption from sin. The desire to reclaim offenders was genuine and deep in the Puritan psyche and the governments of other colonies. In Pennsylvania, the land granted William Penn by the Duke of York, a massive resettling of Quakers made their tolerant faith supreme. The public policies put into effect by the elder Penn as the first governor of Pennsylvania were revolutionary.

In other words, colonial religion cut both ways, seeking to punish and to restore. The fact that retribution was dominant does not negate the fact that the original colonies set the standard and tone for all subsequent generations in continuing a focus on restoration as well.

AMERICAN JUSTICE AFTER THE REVOLUTION

John Howard, an English sheriff, examined jail and prison conditions in his shire and in other parts of England. His testimony in 1874 before the English Parliament led to legislation that improved the hygiene, diet, and medical care of all inmates. Up to that time, men, women, and children were crowded together in unsupervised, filthy enclosures. Rape, child abuse, and extortion were common, unchecked, and never penalized. Howard's full report, published in 1877 as *The State of the Prisons in England and Wales*, started a movement to further reform criminal justice in England.

The prison reform movement reached America in 1800, sparking the wholesale transformation of prison construction and purpose in Pennsylvania, Connecticut, and several other states. In 1870, a national congress on prisons was held in Cincinnati, Ohio, chaired by the governor of Ohio, Rutherford B. Hayes. Hayes, the 19th president of the United States and one of the few politicians who paid any attention to criminal justice, was a leading supporter of prison reform. The focus of this historic conference was almost entirely on reforming America's prisons to be primarily reformatory institutions, in which punishment and treatment combined for the purpose of rehabilitation. There were ample reasons just in American history for that emphasis.

At the end of the 19th century, retribution in all of the state prisons faced serious problems. One is its propensity to multiply and intensify punishments. In theory, the judicial penalty for crime is the loss of freedom and time, first through probation, then incarceration, and finally through parole. The capacity of official custodians to amplify the punishment in a variety of ways is often unbelievable to modern sentiments.[7] When the first prison in America was created, it was in one of the most inhumane settings imaginable. Now located in Granby, Connecticut, but originally in the rural town of Simsbury, Old Newgate Prison was formed in 1773 from the shafts of an abandoned copper mine. With a steady temperature of 55 degrees, with groundwater dampening the walls and floors of the shafts and with light provided only occasionally by candles, it was hard enough on those who dug copper out of the bedrock. It was unbearable for those subsequently held there for months or years. The prison was marked by attempts to escape from the first month.

The Connecticut General Assembly had actually authorized the use of the mine shafts in 1772 as a progressive alternative to the corporal punishments of the time, such as the whipping post, the stocks and pillories, and branding. Public objection to such shaming techniques had grown, along with a renewed desire to regain offenders as regular law-abiding citizens. The use of the mine as a prison had two other supposed benefits. It was less expensive than building a state prison, and it would isolate offenders. The punishment of isolation, it was assumed, would generate a willingness within the offenders to change. The two shafts of the prison, one 25 feet into the hillside and one 67 feet down, offered such isolation. In the summer of 1773, a lodging room 16 feet square was cut out of the rock at the bottom of the first shaft. It was considered secure enough to hold anyone from horse thieves to murderers.

General Washington commandeered Newgate Prison later in 1773 for Americans supporting England (called Tories) and prisoners of war. After the war ended, it held a variety of convicted offenders from all over Connecticut. It ultimately gave the state a lasting and unwelcome reputation for confining prisoners in ways that were savage and brutal. Connecticut was accused of creating a modern dungeon. The political fallout was too much to bear. In 1829, Newgate's remaining convicts were taken to a new prison in the town of Wethersfield, one intended to be a model of restorative justice. By 1870, the Wethersfield State Prison was again being condemned for its abominable conditions and use of corporal punishment.

The cells [at the state prison in Wethersfield] are three feet and a half in width by seven in breadth, and about seven in height … . They are without ventilation, the little orifices in the rear failing to show any current of air when a lighted match is held in them. The lower tier is damp, especially in the summer … . In the morning, after the cells have been occupied by one hundred and ninety men for the night, the effluvia in the cells and in the corridor is reported to be exceeding offensive … .[8]

Even when it wasn't intended, retributive justice had a way of rising from the ashes to a position of dominance. Its inability to police itself and to contain its tendency to multiply punishments was a deficiency rarely overcome.

Another problem with retributive justice is that the amount of discretion available at each level of a justice system greatly complicated the integrity of the concept of deserved punishment. Unlike the English justice system, built initially around the religious concept of the divine right of kings, American justice was built from the bottom up, with ordinary citizens serving as police officers, prosecutors, judges, prison staff, and wardens, all under the rule of law. As a consequence, a high degree of trust was placed in these officials to do the right thing in administering justice. That trust, though badly tarnished over the years, is still very much in evidence. We see that tradition of discretion, for example, in our current justice systems. The police officer as the first official responder must decide whom to arrest and on which charge when making an arrest. Although there are many regulations to be followed in most law enforcement units, the discretion of the arresting officer is often very broad, and in the heat of controlling a crime scene, personal biases can affect who is arrested and the decision as to what crime has been committed. In addition, the testimonies of witnesses can vary immensely in the struggle to describe exactly what happened at the scene of the crime.

A third problem with retributive justice is that it has proven to be counterproductive most of the time. It rarely satisfies the victims, and there is ample evidence that it does not increase public safety. In the words of Miriam Rodgers McClure: "The upshot is this: if retributive justice is a sound form of *justice*, it must aim at correcting injustice; one must exhibit the virtue of justice in doing retributive justice and one should make the world a better, or at least no worse, place by doing so."[9] In fact, however, studies continue to show that recidivism (the return to crime) remains high after release from prison, and that the public still does not feel safe in most areas of the nation. A study in Connecticut concludes that "well over half of releases from Connecticut's prison are rearrested within two years and almost half of the releases end up back in prison within two years."[10]

A fourth problem with retributive justice is its potential to corrupt those empowered to apply the punishments ordered by Crown or court. A modern example of that potential is the prison experiment of Professor Philip Zimbardo in 1971 at Stanford University.[11]

Historically, when religion is involved to complement custodial power, punishment imposed with the express purpose of saving the individual offender's soul has had the effect of removing all equally moral restrictions on the bodily measures used to accomplish that end. Witness the excesses of the Crusades of the 11th century, the Spanish Inquisition in the 16th century, and the New England witch trials or the massacre of Native Americans in the 17th century. When such a tradition of retributive punishment is then written into law, it can set off an astonishing sequence of depersonalization and brutal behavior in its quest for justice. Witness, above all, the mass incarceration that occurred in the last quarter of the 20th century in America.

RELIGIOUS SUPPORT FOR MASS INCARCERATION: THE FOREMOST RESULT OF RETRIBUTIVE JUSTICE

Over the last 50 years, American prisons have compiled one of the most striking examples of excessive retribution in United States history. The generative pressure for such a punitive response to crime was the chaos of the 1960s. Urban riots in the streets of Los Angeles and dozens of other cities took place, most of it with a heavily racial character. The "war on poverty" initiated by President

Lyndon Johnson, for all the assistance programs that emanated from it, had not changed the ratio of minorities locked into poverty or below poverty incomes. Lack of job opportunities, lack of education, and lack of health services had taken a toll on the patience of black and Latino populations. The eruption of violence in the streets was mirrored by riots in prisons across America, by political assassinations, and amplified by the unpopularity of the war in Vietnam.

In the 1970s, the chaos continued, with increasing anti-authority outbursts among America's young adults. Draft-card burnings shared the spotlight with feminist resistance to classic household traditions of male chauvinism and the Victorian sense of a woman's place being in the home raising children. In 1971, President Richard Nixon declared a "war on drugs." Nixon himself was a firm believer in law and order. He was raised within a Quaker Christian framework by his mother and never lost that perspective. The crackdown on drug abuse is not always highlighted among the key events of his term in office, but Nixon's war on drugs was revolutionary. It set in motion a pattern of retributive justice that has characterized the nation for the last 40 years.

Nixon found consistent and enthusiastic support for his anti–substance abuse campaign from almost all segments of society, but none matched the fervor found within the conservative, evangelical forms of Christianity that became known as the "moral majority" and the "religious right."

Among those attracted to Nixon's antidrug theme (besides the moral majority) were many other Americans who were suspicious and frightened by the masses of black citizens who rioted in the Watts area of Los Angeles in 1965. In addition to a desire for law and order, racial prejudices have been a covert, unresolved issue among Americans since the end of the Civil War. After the 1960s, it became a visible reaction within the national body politic, especially in the Deep South. Racial issues, of course, have a religious history that is thousands of years old, rooted in the biblical narratives of the Book of Genesis. Racial prejudice also became a political tool. John Ehrlichman, special counsel to President Nixon, declared in 1968 that Nixon's election campaign needed a boost to put it over the top. His prescription: "We'll go after the racists!"[12] That statement, indicating the motivational power of racial prejudice, expressed the racial assumption of white superiority and black inferiority. The Reagan revolution, in particular, politicized national criminal justice and many local systems to a degree never before experienced in America.

In the mid-1970s, at the beginning of the war on drugs, an equally dramatic shift occurred in legislatures across the country on two fronts, consisting of a relatively sudden loss of faith in rehabilitation. Academic studies had long questioned the claims of rehabilitation programs within prisons. In 1974, one study, entitled "What Works"[13] by Robert Martinson, caught the attention of correctional leaders and the media across the nation. It had the effect of putting a decisive question mark above all such efforts for adults or juveniles to reform individual offenders while incarcerated.

The resulting loss of faith in rehabilitation programs among academic experts coincided with a growing number of correctional professionals who were convinced that the rehabilitative sentencing process was producing grossly unfair results. The result was a nationwide return, starting in 1981, to deliberately punitive legislation. The new laws were designed to send offenders of all types to prison for longer sentences; and to decrease both reductions in sentences for good behavior and the release of inmates on parole.

During Reagan's term, as part of a strategy to increase public safety, his reprise of Nixon's war on drugs capitalized on the use of the metaphor of "war." The repeated image of a pitched battle against evil on the streets of America replicated what previous presidents had known: that the majority of religious people believed in the morality of war when facing a threat that most considered undeniably evil.[14] The war against drugs was considered just as valid as a war against another nation. Pressure to do so came from many groups, but the most consistent and vocal advocate was the religious right, supported by other conservatives. Surprisingly, pressure also came from liberal factions in the community and in correctional circles, who found it difficult to argue that the rapidly rising substance abuse was a major contributor to crime. White suburban communities, as well as minority neighborhoods in the cities, were united in their concern about the toll being taken by drug traffic.

Two facts became apparent to those deeply involved in criminal justice agencies, public and private. One was that major sellers of illicit drugs were from the minority cultures, while the major buyers were from the suburbs. The other fact was that there were at least as many white people involved as users and providers as there were from black and Latino communities. The war on drugs, however, focused on the urban minorities. Karim Ismaili, currently dean of the College of Graduate Studies of Bridgewater State University, concluded his study of the situation in these words:

African Americans and Latinos are over-represented at each stage of the criminal justice process. Studies show that this disparity is not due to differing rates of offending or differences in criminal activity across race and ethnicity ... . The reasons for this are complex, systemic and not easily isolated or dismantled. The social costs are also alarming, including a discredited criminal justice system that reinforces and perpetuates racism.[15]

Despite an awareness among experts that the drug war was very selective in its decisions about whom to prosecute, both Democrats and Republicans came to believe it would be political suicide to appear soft on crime. Support from the conservative religious activists, who used talk radio as well as church pulpits, became a powerful factor in making that strategy work.

The war on drugs quickly became a campaign to keep the streets clean of the sellers of drugs, particularly cocaine and heroin. The stated strategic principle enunciated by President Reagan was that if the supply could be dried up, substance abuse would dry up also. That logic proved to be very wrong—and disastrous. The demand continued, and as soon as a street corner was cleared of providers, others stepped in to succeed them. Marc Mauer, a lead investigator in the Sentencing Project, titled his book on the drug war *The Race to Incarcerate*.[16] In the book, he detailed the negative facts about the "get tough" and "Just Say No" policies that were so appealing in political campaigns.[17]

Three-strike laws were passed in states from California to Connecticut during the 1990s. Federal support was given in massive doses to improvements (usually more armaments and SWAT team equipment, much of it drawn from military inventories) in law enforcement. Prison and jail building became the growth industry of the last 20 years of the 20th century as communities vied to have such facilities for the jobs they created and the virtual guarantee of continued existence. Few religious denominations spoke out against the push for safe streets and public safety. It was a criticism-proof political strategy. Saying nothing can be just as powerful a force for the status quo as any verbal or demonstrative advocacy can be for changes in policy.

The result of the drug war and the barrage of legislation that characterized 1980 to 2000 was a bloated prison system. Although crime rates had decreased several times during that period, the incarceration rate continued to rise. By the turn of the century, the total number of those imprisoned in state and federal facilities reached over two million. When those in halfway houses and on probation or parole are counted, the number exceeded five million people. America had become the world leader in the number of people incarcerated. When the ratio of those imprisoned per 100,000 in the general population is considered, the ratio in the 1920s had been 100/100,000 persons. By 1997, the ratio had more than quadrupled to 445/100,000.[18]

Of even greater import, the incarceration rate of minority persons has increased dramatically compared to their proportion of the population. The drug war, intentionally or not, has had the effect of turning the prisons into a modern version of slave plantations. As Michelle Alexander phrases it, in a deliberately controversial way:

> *The great debate over whether black men have been targeted by the criminal justice system or unfairly treated in the War on Drugs often overlooks the obvious. What is painfully obvious, when one steps back from individual cases and specific policies, is that the system of mass incarceration operates with stunning efficiency to sweep people of color off the streets, lock them in cages, and then release them into an inferior second-class status … . The first step is to grant law enforcement officials extraordinary discretion regarding whom to stop, search, arrest and charge for drug offenses … . Then … close the courthouse door to all claims by defendants and private litigants that the criminal justice system operates in a racially discriminatory fashion.*[19]

Other scholars such as Todd Clear have extended the effect of mass incarceration from the prison system to the local neighborhoods from which offenders come and to which they return.[20] The fact is that once processed through the criminal justice system, the offender loses almost all his privileges and rights as a free citizen and, in most states, has a very difficult time reclaiming them. Gone is the right to vote, access to public housing, access to health care among others. Being hired proved to be an illusion for many, except by lying about one's arrests or convictions. If the lie was discovered, it almost always resulted in being fired. It was not unusual, between 1990 and 2010, to find two and sometimes three generations of a family in prison or with prison records as misdemeanants or felons. The result was that whole neighborhoods were decimated, with both male and female ex-offenders unable to function successfully, except by returning to crime.

Was religion the only factor inducing mass incarceration with a high percentage of minorities represented in the criminal population? Clearly it was not. Political agendas and criminological theory also played a huge part. Most religious people who supported "lock-them-up-and-throw-away-the-key" would probably deny any direct intention to be deliberately harsh on black or Latino people. Yet there can be little doubt that religious biases and assumptions at work about the evils of drug abuse and the untrustworthiness of minorities provided a large part of the cultural demand for more prisons. On the one hand, support for public safety and streets free of crime based on maintaining public morality is high in the polling of public opinion. On the other hand, the religious basis of retributive justice and racism is well documented in the history of slavery itself, a set of attitudes that did not disappear after slavery was abolished. America's dependence on slavery became the elephant in the criminal justice venues where policies were discussed and formed.

Religious arguments provided a bridge between practical justifications based on slavery's necessity and more far-reaching theories predicated on its desirability. Religious idioms pervaded the proslavery literature, in part because Protestant ministers played a leading role in the defense of slavery and in part because such language was well calculated to appeal to antebellum Southerners. Indeed, historian Drew Gilpin Faust suggests that "'the Bible indeed served as the core' of the 'pro-slavery mainstream.'"[21]

Millions of Americans, including many politicians, business leaders, and criminal justice professionals, take the same Bible referred to by these authors literally today. One has to assume that their voting patterns, political views, and even their professional judgments are shaped at least in part by the teachings of the same scriptural passages that motivated the defenders of slavery in the past two or more centuries, since that is the constant affirmation of biblical literalists on the religious right. Slavery may have been abolished, but the attitudes that sustained it are still operative and implemented in American society on every level.

The bottom line is that American slavery traditions were built on, and shaped by, a commitment to retributive justice. If Michelle Alexander and others are correct in referring to the current retributive prison policies as the basis for a new Jim Crow era (that is, a new form of plantation slavery based on racial prejudice), then it is clearly possible—and highly probable—that it has a religious foundation in scriptures that are still considered divinely inspired by such a large proportion of American citizens.

RELIGIOUS ROOTS OF THE SCAPEGOAT THEORY

There is another recent and provocative point of view on religious influence on retributive justice. It has arisen from the scholarly work of René Girard, a French sociologist and philosopher who recently retired from Stanford University. His theory uses a metaphor of the scapegoat. While Girard is not an easy read, his work is well worth the effort required.

The scapegoat is an ancient religious practice, used by the South American Mayans and other nativist religions, as well playing a role in the Hebrew tradition. Girard connects religion and violence in ancient or primitive religions and suggests that violence, especially retributive violence, is not simply an occasional factor in the formation of religious beliefs about guilt, fear, and salvation, but is a central and controlling factor.[22]

The book of Leviticus in the Hebrew Torah (the first five books of the Bible) contains the best-known version of the scapegoat story. It occurs in Leviticus 16:21–22 and reads as follows in the revised King James translation:

And Aaron shall lay both his hands upon the head of the live goat, and confess over him all the iniquities of the children of Israel, and all their transgressions in all their sins, putting them upon the head of the goat, and shall send *him* away by the hand of a fit man into the wilderness.

Historically, of course, the scapegoat was an actual goat, chosen annually by the religious leaders to act as a substitute. René Girard's suggestion, that virtually every ancient religion had a scapegoat concept within it, is being debated increasingly in academic circles. The value of the image, however, is that it is applicable to many topics where wrongdoing and healing intersect. The scapegoat is a very useful metaphor in criminal justice, and serves to link religion in a new way to the community's response to crime, where victims and society search constantly for justice.

Responding to crime invariably involves looking for a cause to take the blame for whatever is threatening public safety and causing harm to property or persons. The blame can be placed on an individual, a group, an institution, or a source of crime such as drugs or guns. Laws can be blamed, as can legislators, law enforcement, the courts, or prison management. Any of those can become a scapegoat, a way to remove blame and shame from society, the nation, and religion.

Politics, in its turn, helped shape diffuse middle-class anxieties into a more focused set of attitudes and understandings, identifying the culprits, naming the problem, setting up scapegoats. As the middle classes found themselves becoming regular victims of crime, they were simultaneously encouraged to view themselves as victims of big government, of tax-and-spend policies, of irresponsible welfare programs, of union-led inflation, and in the United States, of affirmative action programs. All of these were said to work against the interests of "decent, hard-working middle-class people, and to benefit the undeserving and increasingly disorderly urban poor … . If the middle classes were now the new victims, their victimizers were obviously an undeserving underclass, fostered by wrongheaded welfare policies, social service professionals with vested interests, and out-of-touch liberal elites who did not live in the real world."[23]

The wide scope of arrests and convictions of Black and Latino men for lengthy prison sentences can certainly be interpreted, in a broad, cultural sense, as part of a politics of reaction, whose hidden purpose was to cover the guilt and fear that was afflicting millions of Americans for a national problem of illicit drug use that went far beyond those who were arrested, prosecuted and sent to prison. It can also be interpreted to represent another form of scapegoating that arises out of America's combined civil and traditional religion. Rene Girard's theory argues that when people feel drastically threatened, they "blame either society as a whole, which costs them nothing, or other people who seem particularly harmful for easily identifiable reasons." (see end note # 22) It is a potential way to understand the influence of religion on retribution that is worthy of more exploration.

RELIGION'S INFLUENCE ON REHABILITATION

Rehabilitation is an ancient concept, perhaps as old as the felt need to punish wrongdoers. In some ways, the choice of primacy between punishment and rehabilitation is a chicken-and-egg controversy. Whether the first humans conceived of punishment first and then of rehabilitation in prehistorical times cannot be proved one way or the other. Both were ancient reactions to wrongdoing or the breaking of taboos.

During the colonial period, the early colonists' initial response to crime had the double purpose of punishing and redeeming the offenders. However, even after crime was distinguished from sin in the 19th century, the religious desire to minister to those in need continued to compel a societal appreciation of mercy and compassion. With that in mind, here are four major ways in which religion has impacted rehabilitation and kept it visible as the other primary face of justice.

<u>First,</u> **religion provided the concept of cellular space, in which personal reform can be undertaken in a concentrated way.** Medieval Christian monasteries and convents had for centuries been constructed in a cellular architectural style. In the 18th century, English philosopher Jeremy Bentham, among others, noted that setting aside certain cells for rebellious or troublesome monks and sisters was ingenious. It enabled them to be isolated, to do penance quietly through spiritual reading and meditation. Cellular structure was gradually co-opted for prison architecture, first on the continent, then in England, and finally in America. The religious rationale for such isolation was to achieve repentance; hence the decision to borrow the term, penitentiary, to describe the purpose of many of our current prisons.

Unfortunately, the cellular structure of prisons may also have to be considered as one of the most destructive of religion's contributions. It may also provide a myriad of examples of unintended consequences. The individual cell, so similar to the cages of animals in zoos, automatically reinforced the idea that the criminal is little more than an intelligent animal and undeserving of humane treatment. It also tended to make the inmate react like a caged animal, affecting his or her psyche and reducing the inmate's self-respect. The fact that most new prisons and jails that have been built in America during the last 40 years continue to use cellblocks indicates that the psychological impact of such incarceration has either not yet been fully appreciated or that the use of cells is assumed to be totally appropriate to house offenders.

<u>Second,</u> **the rehabilitation ideal, though not officially an American principle, is a humanitarian ideal rooted in religious compassion and the belief that all humans are children of God.** Advocacy for offender rehabilitation is an attitude that derived, at least in part, from biblical teachings such as Matthew 25, a parable of Jesus that describes visits to those in prison as an essential example of Christian discipleship. Jewish and Muslim traditions have equivalent teachings about caring for others. In addition, it is arguably more likely a religious than a secular assumption that even offenders who seem to have no positive value to the community deserve at least respect and empathy during their incarceration. The religious basis for compassionate care was clearly exemplified in my own work with the Connecticut Prison Association's prison volunteer program.[24] The agency was a private, secular agency, and its program did not advertise for religious volunteers. The agency itself had no official tie to any existing religious group or denomination. Its charter did not mention religion or God, yet it adopted the rehabilitation ideal as its guiding principle.[25]

<u>Third,</u> **religion has been the sparkplug for prison reform.** The English reformer John Howard came from a Quaker family. He formulated the beginnings of the modern concepts of prison reform in the 18th century. Howard is credited with recommending single-cell occupancy to reduce the prisoner-on-prisoner violence that was rampant in the prisons and jails of his day. The

John Howard League was established to honor his name. Its first leader, William Tallack, was a Quaker, and like his successors, a practical philanthropist.

The prison reform movement found expression in the first quarter of the late 18th century when Quaker leaders active in the Pennsylvania Prison Society in Philadelphia, Pennsylvania, established the Walnut Street Jail in 1790 to demonstrate reformed humanitarian conditions. Forty years later, the Eastern State Penitentiary was built just outside of Philadelphia. It was the most expensive correctional institution in the nation, and it was dedicated to rehabilitation. Its three penal disciplines were total silence (to enhance reflection), individual labor in large cells (to inculcate good work habits and avoid idleness), and meditation (to engender repentance). All three were drawn from the medieval church precedent, along with cellular architecture.

Silence was to be the hallmark of reformatory prisons. To make the silence within the prison even more pronounced, the guards at the Eastern State Penitentiary wore slippers to cushion their steps while walking the cell corridors. No sounds by the inmates were allowed, either verbal or singing. Even humming drew a penalty. A sermon delivered once a week constituted the only human sounds heard by the inmates. Within a decade, the imposition of absolute silence and individualized labor had a lasting effect, one totally unintended by the designers. It not only failed to produce the desired penitence; it drove many of the inmates insane. Eastern State Penitentiary had no choice but to modify its disciplines to include more socialization, but the overall structure remained the same. Rehabilitation had become retributive.

Religious persuasion was also behind the creation of a different approach in New York's Auburn State Prison and Connecticut's State Prison in Wethersfield. Both were built in 1829 to incorporate a rehabilitative environment (as the primary purpose of the institution) through silence, labor, and meditation, just as in Pennsylvania's model. However, in Auburn and Wethersfield, the silence was imposed only at night in the cellblocks to facilitate meditation. The day labor was called "congregate" (another religious term) and took place in workshops where moderated communication could take place. The Auburn model was quickly emulated across the nation, as it cost less to build, was more productive, and earned the prison a profit through prison labor.

A visionary national congress of prison reformers in America was held in 1870 in Cincinnati, Ohio. The congress published a list of over 40 rehabilitative "principles," describing features that every custodial facility should have to foster a reformatory environment. Almost every participant that spoke at the congress and the annual meetings that followed for the next 80 years articulated a religious foundation for their involvement.[26]

Fourth, **religion, through the rehabilitative ideal, shaped the sentencing and the incarceration disciplines, as well as the political perspective of the United States from the American Revolution through most of the 20th century.** Rehabilitation was the primary face of justice, more in theory than in reality. It was honored and applauded in correctional conferences, academic studies, and news media coverage. In practice, however, it was used often as a cover for retributive punishments.[27]

Probation and parole were a part of the rehabilitative process from 1840 on. The concept of probation became an official part of the penology vocabulary and spread across the nation.[28] Parole, on the other hand, originally called "conditional release," had come into use as part of the reformatory prisons that were established in England, Ireland, and Australia during the 19th century. It was based on the concept of indeterminate sentences, which, unlike definite sentences, usually had a minimum and a maximum term.

Halfway houses originated around 1970, with much of the enthusiasm and persistence arising out of church and synagogue members, who saw a need for transitional housing for offenders as they prepared to reenter the community. They faced the same kind of resistance that arose in communities selected for group homes for the mentally challenged, orphans, or wayward young women who have made the mistake of getting pregnant. The acronym, NIMBY (not in my backyard), summarized the refusal of neighborhoods to allow halfway houses.

Rehabilitation managed to stay the most visible face of justice until 1980, when, as related above, the tide changed abruptly; faith in rehabilitation faltered, and retribution was reinstated nationally and locally. Both faces of justice continue to be in a relationship that is both symbiotic and antagonistic, with retribution still the predominant factor in the search for criminal justice.

FIFTH, THE REHABILITATIVE IDEAL PUSHES SOCIETY TO CHOOSE HEALING OVER VIOLENCE

Perhaps the leading example of this pressure comes from a relatively new approach called restorative justice. Like reintegration, restorative justice is an old idea that has taken new forms in the 21st century. It seeks to explore and heal whatever relationships have been broken between the victim, the community, and the offender. Whereas the existing justice system assumes that crimes are committed against the state, represented by the victim, restorative justice assumes that, in reality, the local community—not the state—is the second victim. Consequently, the goal is to restore harmony between the victim, the offender, and the community. It does so by seeking to construct face-to-face meetings between the offender (sometimes while a prisoner, but usually after release) and the victim, and the offender and community representatives.

THE SHIFTING TIDE IN THE 21ST CENTURY

Several forces have been at work since 1990. One is that the crime rate has been in decline for the past two decades. A second is the cost of criminal justice has become prohibitive and disproportional to other state issues. States like Connecticut now are spending more on prisons than on higher education. A third is a fresh appreciation of rehabilitation's potential. A fourth is that, in religious circles, compassion seems to be gaining ground at the expense of judgmentalism. There are others, but these four are sufficient to suggest that the tide may be turning away from retribution as the primary solution to the problem of crime.

In Connecticut, for example, a state branch of a historic Christian religious order, the Knights of Malta,[29] has begun a private initiative to reassess the effectiveness of the approach that has had the helm of criminal justice since 1980. Its assessment and findings are contained in *The Justice Imperative: How Hyper-Incarceration Has Hijacked the American Dream*. Its argument is a combination of moral justice, economics, and the latest research on crime and crime prevention. It is carefully documented, showing that the state of Connecticut can no longer tolerate a system that is inefficient, counterproductive, costly, and unjust. It lifts up the recent reforms in the area of juvenile crime as an indicator:

> *The Connecticut Justice Imperative draws its evidence from the latest data now available. It is not a unique situation, but mirrors what is happening in most other states. It summarized the findings on recidivism, public safety, prison populations and the practical reality that 95% of offenders eventually are released back into the community, most unprepared and disabled by restrictive policies to survive in the free world. Too often, their only recourse is to return to crime. The evidence demonstrates that the present prison and court systems are not cost-effective. It also shows that rehabilitation could provide a better investment.[30]*

Rehabilitation, of course, makes sense only as long as the causes of crime are found not just in the individual offender's free choice, but within the total environment that surrounded the offender before her crime was committed, during her decision-making process, and which continues to envelop her after release. Retributive justice, on the other hand, is based on the premise that since the factors at work in the environment are legion, it is better to simply punish the crime and not worry about the possible causes. The mounting evidence indicates that the retribution premise is usually ineffective, costly, and counterproductive. The individual offender does not operate in a vacuum.

Francis Cullen and Shannon A. Santana articulate the assessment of the current status of criminal justice regarding the choice between retribution and rehabilitation. There is a good reason, they say (quoting Todd Clear's work), why rehabilitation deserves a new look, because it appeals to a core theme in American culture—one present across time—that offenders, especially young ones, are not beyond redemption. We are, after all, the very people who founded the "penitentiary," reaffirmed rehabilitation in the "new penology," and chose to call our prisons "correctional" institutions. We are perhaps more skeptical than our predecessors about the extent to which criminals can be reformed. Even so, we share their vision that we lose something as a people when we reduce the correctional enterprise to inflicting pain, warehousing offenders, and depleting the system of all hope and compassion (Clear). There is, in the end, something ennobling about rehabilitation—something that calls us to do good for offenders not because we must but because such action symbolizes the kind of individuals and nation we wish to be.[31]

Religion, as we stated at the beginning, is not the only factor in the decisions being made in America regarding the face of justice that will be dominant in our criminal justice systems. The foregoing analysis is intended to summarize how religion has already deeply influenced criminal justice at every level and continues to play a major role.[32] In the aftermath of mass incarceration, both retribution and rehabilitation are being seriously reexamined by scholars and by practitioners. The choice up to now has been how to combine these two faces of justice in the search for justice after a crime has been committed. With appropriate changes, it just might be possible to invest our national and local resources more wisely toward the neglected goal that both methods claim to seek: the prevention of crime.

END NOTES

1. Human nature is a complex topic that sciences such as anthropology, psychology, and biology have struggled to understand for well over a hundred years. Every religion also has expressed in sacred writings, or the interpretation of those texts, widely varying beliefs about the origins of humanity and what it means to be human. This chapter reflects the author's view that, on the one hand, humans have evolved from other animal species and contain, as part of the human brain and DNA, both the competitive urge to survive if threatened or harmed and the inclination to retaliate for harm done. It also reflects his conclusion that respect for others and a sense of kinship to family and others have also evolved from living in community and religious insights. Cf. *Criminal Behavior: A Psychological Approach*, by Curt R. Bartol and Anne M. Bartol (Upper Saddle River, NJ: Pearson Education, 2014), Chapter 1, Introduction, and Chapter 6, Juvenile Delinquency. Cf. also *Morality and Beyond*, by Paul Tillich (New York and Evanston, IL: Harper & Row Publishers, 1963), 17–20.

2. Zenon Jr., Lotufo. *Cruel God, Kind God: Psychology, Religion, and Spirituality* (Kindle edition) (Praeger Publishing: Amazon Digital Services, Inc., 2012), 93–99.

3. Cf. *Juvenile Justice: Process and Systems*, by Gus Martin (Thousand Oaks, CA: Sage Publications, 2005), 76–77.

4. Cf. Karen Armstrong's study of the Golden Rule across all religious traditions in *Twelve Steps to a Compassionate Life* (New York: Anchor Reprint edition, 2011).

5. The "city on a hill" symbolism was drawn from the Gospel of Matthew, chapter 5, verse 14 ff. "You are the light of the world, a city set on a hill cannot be hidden; nor does anyone light a candle and put it under a basket but on a lampstand, and it gives light to all that are in the house." It is ironic that the early colonies of Puritans in New England were as harsh in their treatment of dissenters within their own communities as they had been treated by English authorities. How the light is received and interpreted can make the difference between judgmentalism and being merciful. Once an absolutist framework is established with Holy Scriptures that cannot be questioned, the tendency is to be exclusive rather than inclusive, dictatorial rather than open-minded.

6. *The Code of 1650: A Compilation of Some of the First Laws in America, to which Is Added Some Extracts from Actual Court Proceedings of the New Haven Colony* (Hastings, MN: Hungry Point Farm, 1972). The crimes listed appear in the index, with page numbers for the law itself, pp. 11–12. Original spellings are maintained in quotations from colonial writings.

7. Consider the kinds of punishment that eventually were used at Eastern State Prison during the late 19th and early 20th centuries: There was the water bath, in which inmates were dunked, then hung out on a wall in winter until ice formed on the skin. The mad chair, which bound an inmate so tightly that circulation was cut off, later necessitating amputations. The iron gag, in which an inmate's hands were tied behind the back and strapped to an iron collar in the mouth, so that any movement caused the tongue to tear and bleed profusely. And "the Hole," a dank underground cell where unfortunate souls had no light, no human contact, no exercise, no toilet, and little food and air. http://www.npr.org/2013/10/24/232234570/is-eastern-state-penitentiary

8. *Hartford Courant*, May 28, 1872, Charles D. Warner, Gurdon W. Russell, and Francis Wayland, "The Prison Commission: Report of the General Assembly."

9. McClure, Miriam Rodgers. "On Retributive Justice," http://www.academia.edu/192866/On_Retributive_Justice, p. 11. Rodgers McClure states her purpose thus: "The paper concludes that retributive justice does not give the state a reason to introduce further suffering into the world to punish wrongdoers, but the fact that a wrongdoer deserves to suffer is a reason for reallocating victims' existing, compensable losses, for which the wrongdoer is culpable, to that wrongdoer in the form of civil liability because the wrongdoer deserves to bear the loss in the place of his or her victim," p. 2.

10. *The Justice Imperative: How Hyper-Incarceration Has Hijacked the American Dream* (The Justice Initiative, 2014), p. 20. The use of "Alternatives to Incarceration" in the decades following 1985 in Connecticut and elsewhere reduced recidivism significantly, but touched only a small percentage of convicted offenders.

11. http://www.prisonexp.org—Zimbardo's own website; http://www.bbcprisonstudy; and also the website: http://psychology.about.com/od.classicpsychologystudies/a/Stanford-prison-experiment.htm

12. Cf., among other sources for this quotation, *The New Jim Crow: Mass Incarceration in the Age of Color Blindness*, rev. ed., by Michelle Alexander (New York: New Press, 2012), 44.

13. Martinson, Robert. "What Works: Questions and Answers About Prison Reform," *Public Interest* 35 (spring 1974).

14. Pew Research Document. "Different Faiths, Different Messages: Americans Hearing About Iraq from the Pulpit, but Religious Faith Not Defining Opinions," MARCH 19, 2003. "A solid majority of the public (77%) believes that, in general, war is sometimes morally justified, while just one-in-five say it is never morally justified. Opinion on this issue has changed only slightly since November 2001, when 83% felt war is sometimes morally justified and 12% said it is never warranted."

15. *U.S. Criminal Justice Policy: A Contemporary Reader*, ed. Karim Ismaili (Sudbury, MA: Jones & Bartlett Learning, 2011), 259.

16. Mauer, Marc. *The Race to Incarcerate* (New York: New Press, 1999).

17. *Race to Incarcerate*, op. cit. See especially, Chapter Four: "Crime as Politics."

18. Rafter, Nicole Hahn, and Debra L. Stanley. *Prisons in America*, (Santa Barbara, CA: ABC-CLIO, Inc., 1999), 1.

19. *The New Jim Crow: Mass Incarceration in the Age of Color Blindness*, 103.

20. Cf. *Imprisoning Communities: How Mass Incarceration Makes Disadvantaged Communities Worse*, by Todd Clear (Oxford: Oxford University Press, 2007), especially Chapters Four, "Communities, Coercive Mobility and Public Safety" and Five, "Death by a Thousand Little Cuts."

21. Kolchin, Peter. *American Slavery: 1619–1877* (New York: Hill and Wang, 1993), 191–193. Kolchin is quoting from The *Ideology of Slavery: Proslavery Thought in the Antebellum South, 1830–1860*, by Drew Gilpin Faust (Baton Rouge: 1981), 10.

22. Girard, René. *The Scapegoat* (Baltimore: Johns Hopkins University Press, 1989); and *Violence and the Sacred* (Baltimore: Johns Hopkins University Press, 1972). These are only two of dozens of books by Girard.

23. Garland, David. *The Culture of Control: Crime and Social Order in Contemporary Society* (Kindle edition) (Chicago: University of Chicago Press, 2001, Chapter 6, "The Crime Complex: The Culture of High Crime Societies," under the part labeled Increased Salience of Crime. Once again, the spellings of various words is the British style.

24. In my role as director of the Connecticut Prison Association's Volunteer Sponsor Program for 11 years, my status as a clergyman undoubtedly made it easier to recruit volunteers from churches and synagogues. Yet, at least 50 percent of our volunteers came from other sources, and most of those who came from a religious context did not cite biblical passages or claim to be volunteering for religious reasons. Most simply wanted to help offenders get back on their feet in free society. They believed in second chances for reasons apart from their faith.

25. *The Connecticut Prison Association Annual Report of 1880*. The goals of the organization, which was incorporated in 1875, were to: 1) benefit society by the reformation of criminals; 2) assist prisoners in the work of self-reform; 3) promote reformatory systems of prison management; 4) aid discharged convicts to live honorably; and 5) cooperate in the repression of crime.

26. The annual reports of the National Prison Association provide ample evidence of the influence of religion on both the ministries that were being offered to inmates across America and the rehabilitation policies that were promoted.

27. For example: The local newspaper coverage of the Willie Horton crime while on parole was instrumental in undermining the campaign of Michael Dukakis, the Democratic challenger to George H. W. Bush in 1988. Hundreds of articles appeared locally and were syndicated nationally by the Republican campaign to keep the focus on both the use of parole release and the fact that Willie Horton was African American. Despite the fact the Massachusetts record of successful parole release record was superb, the impression given was of excessive crime being committed by parolees. The fact that the parolee was a black man served to heighten prejudicial fears of black people, whether criminal or not. One of the Republican campaign themes was a call for more prisons, harsher penalties, elimination of parole, and curtailed use of probation.

28. *Criminal Justice in America*, op. cit., 229–230.

29. According to its official website: The Sovereign Military Hospitaller Order of St. John of Jerusalem of Rhodes and of Malta, better known as the Sovereign Order of Malta, has a two-fold nature. It is one of the most ancient Catholic Religious Orders, founded in Jerusalem in around 1048. At the same time it has always been recognized by nations as an independent subject of international law. The Order's mission is summed up in its motto "Tuitio Fidei et Obsequium Pauperum": nurturing, witnessing and protecting the faith (*tuitio fidei*) and serving the poor and the sick representing the Lord (*obsequium pauperum*).

30. Ibid, Chapter 3, "The Staggering Cost of Mass Incarceration," 15–18.

31. Dressler, Joshua. *The Encyclopedia of Crime and Justice*. Article on rehabilitation by Francis T. Cullen and Shannon A. Santana (New York: Macmillan Reference USA©2002). An E-book found at the website: http://www.encyclopedia.com/topic/Rehabilitation.aspx

32. Cf. Karen Armstrong's new book, *Fields of Blood: Religion and the History of Violence* (New York: Knopf, 2014). Armstrong affirms the reality that religion, especially prior to the Enlightenment, played a key role in the justification of violence and retributive justice. Since the 18th century, economics, political strategies, and environmental factors have been increasingly involved. Nevertheless, she strongly makes the case that religion is the primary motivation behind the evidence of compassion in the world, the search for alternatives to violence, and the desire to reduce retribution wherever possible to make room for the rehabilitation of both individuals and nations.

13. The Myth of Redemptive Violence, or The Myth of Redemptive Love

By Wayne G. Rollins

Where love stops, power begins, and terror and violence.
—C. G. Jung

INTRODUCTION

Analytical psychologist Jung once commented that when a scholar in white shirt and tie, with degrees from the best of universities, contributes to a technology to create a weapon of mass destruction, his unconscious is up to more than scientific advance. Violence has its finger in the pie (Jung, 99–100). When President George W. Bush, recent born-again Christian, tells us on the one hand that Jesus is his favorite philosopher, but on the other hand that a bullet is faster than a war in dealing with Saddam Hussein, you know that violence, rightly or wrongly, is at least an option and perhaps an imperative for the White House.

Violence holds archetypal attraction for the human soul and is readily activated whenever the scent of threat or conflict is at hand. It is ready for action in everyday experience from domestic conflicts to tribal, national, religious, and social class wars. It clearly has its advocates and practitioners in the pages of the Bible.

The dividing line in the Bible between violence and nonviolence is not to be found, as commonly as thought, between the Old and

New Testaments. The fault line does not lie between two documents, but between two psychic attitudes that run longitudinally through both Testaments, and by inference through every stratum of the history of the human race. In the Old Testament (Hebrew Bible), for example, we find Samuel slaying Agag, King of the Amalekites, before the Lord (1 Sam. 15:33), and we read of Joshua slaughtering sheep, oxen, asses, men, women, and children to deliver Israel from the Canaanite religion (Josh. 6:21). But we also find the poet Isaiah envisioning swords being turned into ploughshares and spears into pruning hooks (Isa. 2:4) and Hosea preaching to Judah that deliverance does not lie in bow, sword, horse, horseman, or war (Hos. 1:7).

The antithesis persists in the New Testament. On the one hand, we find the command to love our enemies (Matt. 5:44) and to forgive until it hurts (Matt. 18:22), and on the other, the story of Ananias and Sapphira struck dead by God for failing to pay their full tithe of goods to the nascent Christian community (Acts 5:1–11). Also, in the Book of Revelation, we find Christ portrayed as the innocent lamb who was slain (5:6), but at the same time, as the one presiding over the machinery of heaven bent on the violent destruction of the enemy (6:1ff.). At one point, Christ sits astride a white battle steed, leading a heavenly army "to tread the wine press of the fury of the wrath of God" (19:11–16).

Within the later religious traditions that spin off from both Testaments, Judaism and Christianity, we find the same contradictory leitmotifs: acts of mercy, benevolence, and healing, profound spirituality, and lofty moral standards, combined with the crusades and inquisitions, the systematic and often violent oppression of Palestinians by Zionist zealots, and the black irony of the cross-burning Ku Klux Klan. Violence is a frightful, but predictable, aspect of human behavior in the best of company, as native to the human scene as the white-steepled church to the New England village green.

EXPOSITION

Whence the resort to violence? The answer is a family secret of the human race with profound and complex psychological, biological, sociopolitical, economic, demographic, and possibly genetic roots. But the more profound questions may be, Whence the justification of violence among a people who think of themselves as decent, law-abiding, respectably religious and moral people? Whence the defense of violence within a tradition that values the prophetic warning against reliance on tanks and missiles, while trying to take seriously the command to love one's enemies? Why the tolerance of violence in families of nations that regard themselves as civilized, high-minded, and fundamentally on the right track?

One answer comes from biblical scholar Walter Wink in a brilliant exposition of the history and amplification of the myth of redemptive violence in biblical and Western culture. Wink advances this thesis in a superb one-volume summary of his trilogy on the biblical image of the principalities and powers titled *The Powers That Be: A Theology for the New Millennium* (Wink, 1998). Wink is not ignorant of the psychodynamic factors that contribute to the violent programs of "good people," such as repression, denial, projection, displacement, and rationalization. But his primary emphasis is on a mythic construct he has discovered operative in the collective consciousness of the West for over three thousand years that has been able for centuries to put a virtuous mask on the face of violence. His detection of this construct began with his preoccupation with the biblical image of the "powers," a first-century metaphor for a perennial phenomenon; namely, systems of domination and the violence they breed.

THE "POWERS" AND VIOLENCE

Wink tells us that he has been poring over the mystery of systems of domination and violence for three decades, beginning with his research on the New Testament metaphor of the "powers," or "principalities and powers" (Rom. 8:38; Eph. 1:21, 3:10, 6:12; Col. 1:16, 2:10, 2:15; Titus 3:1). Even though the New Testament tradition portrayed these powers as celestial, angelic, or demonic forces, Wink found behind their "gross [heavenly] literalism ... the clear perception that spiritual forces impinge on and determine our [earthly] lives" (3). This led him to suspect that this biblical metaphor represented something true about ourselves and our society, an idea that Wink elaborated in three volumes over the course of eight years. Their titles virtually tell the story of his gradual discovery: *Naming the Powers: The Language of Power in the New Testament* (1984), *Unmasking the Powers: The Invisible Forces that Determine Human Existence* (1986), and *Engaging the Powers: Discernment and Resistance in a World of Domination* (1992).

What are the powers? One of the first facts about the powers is that they are trans-individual. Individuals participate in the powers and exercise their authority, but individuals do not comprise the powers. The powers are rather "the systems themselves, the institutions and structures that weave society into an intricate fabric of power and relationships" (Wink, 1998, 1). They have the capacity for "unmitigated evil," but also for surprising good, though Wink's immediate goal is to explore the former.

Wink found himself fascinated also with the New Testament suggestion that the powers are invisible, which seemed to imply metaphysical as well as physical aspects. Wink noticed, for example, that "the letters to the seven churches" in the Book of Revelation are addressed to the "angels" of those churches. What does "angel" mean? Wink speculates that it refers to the idiosyncratic inner spirit, character, or disposition of each of the churches. Powers are not "simply people and their institutions ...; they also include the spirituality at the core of those institutions" (Wink, 1998, 4). Changing these systems accordingly requires dealing not only with outer forms but also with the inner core, whether with a corporation, the federal government, a political party, or an ecclesiastical institution.

Out of a desire to better understand the dark side of the powers, Wink traveled with his wife, June, on a sabbatical leave to Chile in 1982 to experience firsthand the military dictatorship of General Augusto Pinochet in Chile. He visited other parts of South and Central America as well, to see the *barrios*, the notorious *favelas*, and to speak with nuns and priests who were working for human rights and with defense lawyers searching for the "disappeared ones."

Wink's reaction was one of devastation. He found himself overwhelmed with despair, even physically ill. "The evils we encountered were so monstrous, so massively supported by our own government ... that it seemed nothing could make a difference" (6–7). He began to wonder "how the writers of the New Testament could insist that Christ is somehow, even in the midst of evil, sovereign over the Powers." Only in time was he able to find any hope in it all, and then only by holding tenaciously to Paul's pronouncement in Romans 8:38–39 that "neither death, nor life, ... nor principalities ... nor powers ... will be able to separate us from the love of God in Christ Jesus," in the hope of excavating the truth that might be anchored in those words.

A question Wink wrestled with throughout was how to combat the institutionalized violence by which "unjust systems perpetuate themselves" (7); by violent or nonviolent means. Wink began as an advocate of qualified nonviolence: "Try nonviolence, but if it fails, try violence." But, he writes, "I began to realize that if violence was my last resort then I was still enmeshed in the belief that violence saves" (8).

To test the waters of nonviolence, Wink spent a second sabbatical in 1986 in South Africa. Taking exception to antiapartheid allies who denounced nonviolence as ineffectual, Wink "discovered a remarkable variety of effective nonviolent actions that many people there were employing in perhaps the largest grass roots eruption of diverse nonviolent strategies in a single struggle in human history" (8). The outcome was a new book by Wink, *Violence and Nonviolence in South Africa* (1987), later published as a modestly bound South African version under the title *Jesus' Third Way*, mailed out to 3,200 black and white clergy in South Africa and 800 Roman Catholic priests and pastoral workers.

Out of the encouragement that came from seeing the contribution of nonviolent strategies to the "fall of the Berlin Wall, the collapse of Communism in the Soviet Union and Eastern block [sic], and the transformation of South Africa" (1987, 10), Wink was motivated to examine further the psychocultural roots of violence. This route of inquiry led him to the realization that a mythos operative for 5,000 years in Western culture has provided the rationale for "good people" to allow themselves and their cultures to be violent in the service of a higher cause: the myth of redemptive violence.

THE MYTH OF REDEMPTIVE VIOLENCE

Wink tells us that he first became aware of the myth of redemptive violence while reflecting on children's TV shows, pondering the "mythic structure of cartoons," and the ingenuous and gratuitous violence that plays across the screen, from the Teenage Mutant Ninja Turtles to Captain America, Batman and Robin, Tom and Jerry, cowboy-and-Indian westerns, and even the demolition of the monster Bluto by a spinach-eating Popeye. Wink tells us "the format never varies" (1987, 44). The hero brings the world back into order with violent exhibitions of power.

These shows for the young are reprises of an old, old story, native to systems of domination, where, as in the case of Mesopotamian culture of 3000 BCE, the perennial challenge was to maintain the power of the dominant patriarchy over the enemy, and over the women, children, slaves, and hired workers as well. The law declared, "If a woman speaks … disrespectfully to a man, that woman's mouth is crushed with a fire brick" (40). "It is one of the oldest continually repeated stories in the world." The story "enshrines the belief that violence saves and that war makes peace" (42). As Havelock Ellis observes, it is that "insidious delusion" whispered in the ears of mankind for centuries: *Si vis pacem para bellum* (Seldes, 1972, 958).[2] It does not appear in the least as mythic to those who hold it as true. It is simply "the nature of things. It's what works. It seems inevitable, the last and, often, the first resort in conflict" (Wink, 1987, 42).

Wink reports that the mythic scenario he found playing out in children's movies, cartoons, and Nintendo games suddenly "rang familiar" (44). It dawned on him that the same mythos was rehearsed in a story dating from 1250 BCE in the *Enuma Elish*, the Babylonian Creation story. It could have been produced in Hollywood, yet it comes from a pre-biblical era, and like the biblical myths, it has been rehearsed for generations, reinforcing the same values of the system of domination that engendered its promulgation.

The Babylonian Creation story opens with Apsu, the father god, and Tiamat, the mother god, dragon of chaos, giving birth to a host of younger gods. The plot immediately thickens when the younger gods proceed to generate so much noise in the heavens that the older gods plot to liquidate them. When the fledgling gods catch wind of the plan, they murder their father, Apsu. Tiamat, outraged, pledges vengeance against them. Terrified, they turn to the youngest among them, Marduk, and promise him unqualified power over them if he will protect them from the wrath of Tiamat.

Marduk accepts. He catches Tiamat in a net, driving an "evil wind" down her throat. He bursts her belly with an arrow and pierces her heart. Her skull is split with a club and her blood scattered. He then stretches out the corpse, dismembers it, and from the pieces creates the world. Simultaneously, with the aid of Ea, Marduk imprisons the older assembly of gods associated with Apsu.

He executes one of them, and from his blood Ea creates the human race as servants of God.

What are the truths conveyed by this myth? The human race and the whole creation are the progeny of violence and have violence written in their bones; the gods, that is, the "voices" at the heart of the universe, are violent; women are the mythic embodiment of chaos and are to be controlled, if need be, violently. Over against the Creation myth in Genesis 1, which holds that men and women are equally enjoined to be fruitful and multiply and are made in the image of a beneficent creator God, we hear another story:

> The myth of Redemptive violence is the story of the victory of order over chaos by means of violence. It is the ideology of conquest ... The gods favor those who conquer. Conversely, those who conquer must have the favor of the gods ... the king, the aristocracy, and the priesthood. Religion exists to legitimate power and privilege. (Wink, 1987, 48)

This same mythic taste for violence permeates the Bible. Wink cites (1998, 84) biblical scholar Raymund Schwager, who points out 600 passages of violence in the Hebrew Bible, 1,000 instances of God meting out violent punishment, 100 passages where Yahweh orders to kill, and several stories of God's inexplicable desire to kill someone, such as his attempt at Moses' life in Exodus 4:24–26. "Violence," Schwager concludes, "is easily the most often mentioned activity in the Hebrew Bible" (1987, 209).

Wink finds this mind-set duplicated in a contemporary admonition from a member of the religious right:

> That it is a privilege to engage in God's wars is clearly seen in the Psalms, perhaps nowhere better than in Ps. 149:5–7, where the saints sing for joy on their beds while they contemplate warring against God's enemies, or Ps. 58:10. "The righteous will rejoice when he sees the vengeance; he will wash his feet in the blood of the wicked." Those who cannot say "Amen" to such sentiments have not yet learned to think God's thoughts after him ... The righteous ... are called by God's law to exercise a holy "violence" against certain of the wicked, thereby manifesting God's wrath. (1987, 59)

Wink finds the Babylonian myth alive and well also in contemporary culture in general—in media; in foreign policy; in the Super Bowl; in *Rambo* movies; in vigilantism; and in spy thrillers where murder, lying, stealing, illegal entry, and seduction are justified in the service of "national security" (48–51). He cites an astonishing parallel to the Apsu-Tiamat tale resurrected in the movie *Jaws*. The police chief encounters a gigantic shark, read by critics as a symbol of consummate evil, and "kicks an oxygen tank into the attacking shark's throat, then fires a bullet that explodes the tank, thus forcing into the shark's body a wind that bursts it open." Though there is no procreation of a universe or of human beings from the shark's corpse, Brody, the police chief, becomes a superhero. "Chaos is subdued, and the island is restored to a tourist's paradise" (51).

THE MYTH OF REDEMPTIVE LOVE

"I believe that Jesus' gospel is the most powerful antidote to the myth of redemptive violence that the world has ever known" (62). With these words, Walter Wink voices the conviction that appears across his writing, that the "third way" that Jesus teaches and walks is the model for sane human behavior on the planet. It is also the cure for the spiral of domination and violence dramatized in the Apsu-Tiamat myth that is replayed literally millions of times in the stories that 21st-century American culture and much of world culture tell themselves and their young. The antidote to the myth of redemptive violence is another story, the myth of redemptive love. The life and death of Jesus pen this mythos on the consciousness of those who hear and follow him.

Were we to locate any single word from the library of Jesus' utterances that provides the fulcrum on which his attitude toward violence and domination turns, it would be the stunning challenge in the Sermon on the Mount that we are to love our enemies and pray for those who persecute us (Matt. 5:44), matched by the contrapuntal echo in Paul's spiritual arsenal, "Do not be overcome by evil, but overcome evil with good" (Rom. 12:21). Nowhere in religious or political history have these enjoinders been advanced as the foundation stones for a way of living in a world marked by domination and violence.

With his unique angle of vision, Wink sees that these words and every piece of Jesus' life and teaching are dedicated to undermining systems of domination and the violence that germinates within them. "The kings of the Gentiles lord it over them, … but no so with you; rather the greatest among you must become like the youngest, and the leader like one who serves" (Luke 22:24–27). Jesus subverts every system and structure of domination—economic domination, the domination and repression of women, religious and cultic domination with exclusivizing codes of purity and holiness, the domination of ethnicity and racial identity, and the domination of family that can so insidiously thwart change and new possibilities. Jesus, in fact, announces his identity with a new family: "Whoever does the will of God is my brother and sister and mother" (Mark 3:35). Jesus' death, as well as his life, succeeds further in unmasking the violence at the heart of the religious and political systems of domination that put him to death.

"Jesus' Third Way" is the title of a chapter in *The Powers That Be*, and also the popular title, as mentioned earlier, of Wink's book *Violence and Nonviolence in South Africa*. The "third way" is a third option to the two standard, competing approaches to the question of violence. The first is the acceptance of the inevitability of and need for violence to secure the peace, the myth of redemptive violence. The second is a nonviolent route that is passive and nonresistant and refuses to coerce or resist in any form. The third way of Jesus, as Wink discerns it, is a resistant nonviolence, one that is confrontational and coercive without being lethal. It is the nonviolence of Gandhi, Dorothy Day, Leo Tolstoy, Martin Luther King Jr., and Cesar Chavez. It is the resistant nonviolence that Witness for Peace initiated in the warring environments of Nicaragua, El Salvador, Guatemala, and Haiti (1987, 117). It is the resistant nonviolence forged by the collaboration of Catholics and Protestants that challenged the Marcos dictatorship in the Philippines (121ff.); that brought an end to the genocide inaugurated by the Soviets in Lithuania (151); and that resisted the Nazi pogroms in Finland, Norway, Denmark, Holland, and Bulgaria (152ff.). It is the resistant nonviolence that is imagined in the enjoinders to turn the other cheek and walk the extra mile, designed to confront, disarm, and raise the consciousness of the oppressor and demean his power and authority (98–111).

At the heart of the command to love one's enemy and pray for one's persecutor is the conviction that the Holy is all-inclusive and at work in every individual. This means that no one is beyond the pale of regeneration and transformation. As Wink puts it, "Loving enemies is a way of living in expectation of miracles" (178). I recall Cesar Chavez once telling a group of theological students that on the mornings of those days on which he would be meeting about workers' rights with the owners of the huge grape farms, he would rise at 4 AM to meditate and pray, preparing to love everyone in the room that he would enter that day; "It changed me and changed them."

Wink adds a series of stories that demonstrate the real possibility of the aggressive, resistant nonviolent approach to enemies (145–179). The stories demonstrate the imagination, the daring, the originality, and the hope that informs the Promethean will to love one's enemies and to resist the myth of redemptive violence.

The most astonishing of these stories takes place at the home of Cantor and Mrs. Michael Weisser in Lincoln, Nebraska, in 1991. No sooner had they moved into their new home on a new assignment than the Weissers received a phone call. The voice said, "You will be sorry you ever moved into 5810 Randolph Street, Jew boy." The call was followed by a mailing that included the message "The KKK is watching you, scum." The envelope included pictures of Hitler and caricatures of Jews and blacks.

The police told Cantor Weisser that they knew the culprit—Larry Trapp, the state head of the KKK who had terrorized Jews, Asians, and blacks in Iowa and Nebraska. They regarded him as dangerous: "We know he makes explosives." An irony is that Trapp, 44 years old, was physically ill, in the late stages of diabetes, confined to a wheelchair. He lived in a small apartment festooned with Nazi artifacts, pistols, and shotguns.

Weisser followed Trapp's activities on television as a white supremacist TV showman. After one particularly odious show, Weisser left a message on Trapp's KKK hotline: "Larry," he said, "do you know that the very first laws that Hitler's Nazis passed were against people like yourself who had no legs or who had physical deformities or physical handicaps? Do you realize you would have been among the first to die under Hitler? Why do you love the Nazis so much?"

Weisser continued the calls until Trapp finally picked up personally and bellowed, "What the f____ do you want?" "I just want to talk to you," said Weisser. "You black?" Trapp demanded. "Jewish," Weisser answered. "Stop harassing me," said Trapp, who asked him why he was calling. Weisser remembered a suggestion of his wife's. "Well, I was thinking you might need a hand with something, and I wondered if I could help," Weisser extemporized. "I know you're in a wheelchair and I thought maybe I could take you to the grocery store or something."

Trapp was speechless, mumbled something about Weisser's "niceness," but refused help. Weisser ignored his rebuff and called again, several times. At one point, Trapp suggested he was rethinking a few things, but in his next show reverted to the same old hatreds. Weisser called again, furious, denouncing him as a liar and hypocrite.

To Weisser's surprise, Trapp began to backtrack. "I'm sorry I did that. I've been talking like that all of my life … . I can't help it … . I'll apologize!" That evening with his congregation, the cantor offered prayers for the grand dragon.

The next night, Cantor Weisser answered his phone. It was Trapp. "I want to get out," he said, "but I don't know how." When the Weissers offered to go over to Trapp's home to bring him some food, he hesitated, but then told them to come. When they walked into Trapp's small apartment, Trapp began to cry and threw his two rings with swastika symbols to the ground. All three cried, laughed … and hugged for the first time.

Trapp soon after renounced his racist activities and penned apologies to those he had threatened over the years. Weeks later, when his physicians gave him only a month to live, he accepted an invitation from the Weissers to move into their home. It had two bedrooms. They had three children. As Trapp's physical state worsened, Weisser's wife, Julie, gave up her nursing job to care for Trapp, for a period of over nine months. Three months before he died, he converted to Judaism (1998, 172–175).

Wink interjects, "Most people who are violent have themselves been the victims of violence. It should come as no surprise, then, to learn that Larry Trapp had been brutalized by his father and was an alcoholic by the fourth grade." And he adds, "Loving our enemies may seem impossible, yet it can be done … . No miracle is so awesome" (175).

REFERENCES

Jung, C. G. (1958). *The undiscovered self*. Boston: Little, Brown.

Schwager, R. (1987). *Must these be scapegoats?* San Francisco: HarperSanFrancisco.

Seldes, G., ed. (1972). *The great quotations*. New York: Penguin Pocket Books.

Wink, W. (1984). *Naming the powers: The language of power in the New Testament*. Philadelphia: Fortress.

Wink, W. (1986). *Unmasking the powers: The invisible forces that determine human existence*. Philadelphia: Fortress.

Wink, W. (1987). *Violence and nonviolence in South Africa*. Philadelphia: New Society.

Wink, W. (1992). *Engaging the powers: Discernment and resistance in a world of domination*. Minneapolis: Fortress.

Wink, W. (1998). *The powers that be: Theology for a new millennium*. New York: Doubleday.

END NOTES

1. This chapter had appeared earlier in *The Destructive Power of Religion: Violence in Judaism, Christianity, and Islam*, vol. 4, ed. J. Harold Ellens (Westport: Praeger Publishers, 2004). The editor gratefully acknowledges the generosity of Dr. Rollins and Dr. Ellens in permitting republication of the chapter in this volume.

2. Translation: "If you want peace, prepare for war."

14. Restorative Justice

By Thomas Roscoe

Restorative justice provides a new vision of how to go about the task of sanctioning those who have violated collective norms. This chapter will describe what this vision is, and how it relates to our traditional system for sanctioning criminal offenders. We will then review the main types of restorative justice programs that currently exist, along with information on their effectiveness. The chapter will conclude with main issues that should be considered in deciding whether to adopt this new vision.

Readers should keep in mind that restorative justice is a broad concept with supporters of diverse political persuasions and with very different views as to the nature and scope of desired changes. We will direct our attention to the specific dilemma of sanctioning criminal offenders, though we should realize that restorative principles are also being applied in schools, workplaces, and even at the international level (Van Wormer & Walker, 2013). Restorative justice is a broad concept, as is the concept of justice itself. There is not a precise definition that would be satisfactory to all of its wide range of supporters. We will define a basic vision of restorative justice, and how it may serve to augment the current sentencing process.

DEFINING RESTORATIVE JUSTICE

According to Van Ness and Strong (2015), definitions of restorative justice usually focus on (1) the concept of encounter, among those involved in the offense (stakeholders); (2) a concept of reparation or repayment; and (3) a concept of transformation, away from conflict and toward living in harmony with each other. Van Ness and Strong define restorative justice as "a theory of justice that emphasizes repairing the harm caused or revealed by criminal behavior. It is best accomplished through cooperative processes that include all stakeholders" (2015, p. 43).

Howard Zehr (2002), a chief architect of the recent restorative justice movement, defines restorative justice as "a process to involve, to the extent possible, those who have a stake in a specific offense and to collectively identify and address harms, needs, and obligations, in order to heal and put things as right as possible" (p. 37). Zehr reminds us that beyond any legal violation involved, crime is a violation of people and relationships. Such violations create obligations to put things right. Victim and community needs in light of crime and offender accountability for addressing these needs should form the focus of criminal sanctioning.

Restorative justice is essentially a critique of our contemporary system of sanctioning offenders, where questions center on either what to do *to* (retribution), or do *for* (rehabilitation) the offender. Should we punish the offender, or instead do something to help the offender stay out of further difficulty? The rehabilitation advocate may fail to grasp the seriousness of the offense, due to a shortsighted focus on perceived offender needs or societal causes (Wright, 1991). On the other hand, according to Moore (1993), "The retributivist paradigm, always claiming to be strong on morality, is weak on logical rationale" (p. 6). Moore sees the need for an alternative to both the rehabilitation and retributive traditions that is intellectually satisfying, as is the argument that we need to treat the addict, but is also strong on values, though in a way that is constructive rather than destructive.

BRIEF HISTORY OF RESTORATIVE JUSTICE

The beginning of the restorative justice movement in North America is associated with an initiative in Kitchener, Ontario, in 1974. Two teens pled guilty to 23 counts of property damage due to a vandalism spree. A probation officer who was an active participant in the Mennonite Church proposed that the two offenders meet with all their victims in order to work out a restitution plan. The actual encounter, rather than the restitution itself (which was paid in full), was the novel idea. The victims now had the chance to express their feelings about the offense directly to those responsible. The offenders had the opportunity to demonstrate that they are better than the offense and capable of making amends. In short, stereotypes are challenged, and fears are reduced (Zehr, 1990).

This initiative set the stage for similar such efforts. The first Victim Offender Reconciliation Program (VORP), staffed in part by the Mennonite Central Committee, was established in Elkhart, Indiana, in 1978. Similar initiatives quickly took hold in Europe, especially Germany, and have continued to the present. Although still new, restorative justice has certainly been widely embraced in many quarters worldwide (Umbreit & Armour, 2011).

As interest in restorative justice grew, it was recognized that many of these presumably new ideas were actually well entrenched in earlier societies outside the Western sphere of influence. Japan has a tradition of sanctioning that emphasizes confession, repentance, and absolution. The offender negotiates for the victim's pardon. If there is a confession, sincere repentance, and forgiveness from the victim, the case is dropped from any continued formal process (Haley, 1989).

In the moots of Tanzania, a mediator is chosen by the complainant. The public is allowed to attend the proceedings, which are orderly, but informal. Once the case is resolved to the satisfaction of victim and offender, the matter is closed and cannot be raised again, for fear that the dispute will be renewed (Wright, 1991).

In Confucian China, mediation was seen as superior to adjudication, since it was less coercive. Social order depended on moral and customary principles of behavior. *Yang*, or yielding, was regarded as virtuous in that it prevented conflict. These principles dissolved in 1911 with the establishment of the republic (Wright, 1991).

Earlier communities had considerably more stable populations, with a high level of interdependence among residents. Given that victims and offenders and their families were likely to live in close proximity to each other, probably for the entirety of their lives, community well-being—and even survival—required a means of assuring peaceful relations. Those in leadership positions needed to assure that the outcomes prescribed for a given offense would be within the limits of acceptability for both victim and offender. Otherwise, a single offense could result in an endless series of vendettas that could compromise the community's well-being (Van Ness & Strong, 2015).

Western traditions of sanctioning offenders largely emanate from transitions in England, following the Norman Conquest of 1066. The control of this new territory by the French required a means of consolidating the power of the crown and establishing the hegemony of William the Conqueror. Criminal law would overrule both Church law and local forms of dispute resolution. Judges representing the crown would be sent out from central locations into remote areas for the purpose of administering the king's law. Written law would facilitate this control by affording consistency and expediency in settling disputes (Van Ness & Strong, 2015).

Those acts that were previously viewed as local disputes were now viewed as crimes against the state, to be punished similarly, regardless of local concerns or circumstances. Restitution payments previously made by the offender to the victim would now be shared between the victim and the Crown, with increasing shares going to the throne as time went on. Eventually, victims were pretty much left out of the process entirely, and the notion of crime as a matter to be resolved by the offender and the state was firmly entrenched. State control usurped local means of resolving problems in ways that made sense to the community and which served to clarify and promote the community's moral sensibilities (Wright, 1991).

Nils Christie (1977), an early advocate for restorative justice, points to the cold, stark architecture of court buildings as typifying the remoteness of the criminal justice system from the lives of the people. Intimidation is intended in the setting and the processes of the criminal court. Resolution to human conflict is conveyed as beyond the grasp of those lacking appropriate credentials.

Means of introducing more humane approaches are limited due to the adversary model underlying the American system and its focus on securing convictions and imposing punishments. Ironically, only a small percentage of cases actually require the advantages gained through an adversary system, given the tendency toward plea bargaining rather than trial. Though the adversary model may be an optimal means of arriving at the truth, it is the processing of cases that is the more typical function of courts (Umbreit, 1985). Within this framework, the focus is on the offender, with the victim's role "shadowy and indistinct" (Wright, 1991). Zehr and Umbreit (1982) quote a criminal court judge, "I don't care what the victim or offender needs or wants, this crime (an assault) was against the state, and I'll take care of it as I see fit" (p.64).

As a result, victims often experience frustration in being left out of their own cases and in their inability to get answers. Courts may not understand how questions such as "Why did you destroy my child's toys?" weigh so heavily on the victim's mind. Victims are left without the means to "deal with their fears, phobias, and stereotypes" (Wright, 1991, p. 20). Civil remedies, even when available, deal only with the monetary aspects of victimization. What is lacking is "a ceremonial means to resolve the indignation—the righteous anger of the immediate victim" (Moore, 1993, p. 16). The victim is left unable to tell her story. The court only knows the realities of victimization allowed to filter through the process. In brief, the victim becomes an object (Umbreit, 1985), and the human need for closure is not met (Zehr & Umbreit, 1982).

PURPOSE OF RESTORATIVE JUSTICE

Restorative justice presents an alternative to the exclusive nature of the criminal justice system, as it has been passed down through the years. Critics such as Braithwaite (1989) and Walgrave (2008) talk about "displacing"—though certainly not eliminating—criminal justice professionals to bring about more personally meaningful and appropriate resolutions to essentially human conflicts. The more participation by those with a direct stake in the crime, the better will be the resolution (outcome), and the benefits that accrue from citizens directly resolving their own disputes (process). Therefore, to the degree possible given the circumstances, the court's role would be "facilitator" rather than "decider." Professionals would serve as catalysts for providing the means necessary to facilitate resolutions by stakeholders in the offense, and would oversee the process. Those most closely involved in the dispute would be the active participants (Christie, 1977).

In addition to arriving at better, more satisfactory and meaningful decisions at the individual level, advocates see this shift as affording greater teaching/ pedagogical benefits, by which societal values can be reaffirmed. Although there are laws against stealing, virtually all societies share the moral conviction that stealing is wrong. Historically, the legal system is directed to address both the legal and moral violation. The moral violation which led to the creation of the law may not be given due consideration in the rationally based, dispassionate atmosphere of the criminal court. Offenders face the power of the court, though not the full impact of the wrongfulness of their behavior that only the direct expression of the victim can provide. The offender is directed toward self-defense, rather than self-reflection.

To Christie, this usurping of conflicts between people by lawyers and criminal justice professionals has deprived societies of the ability to develop norm consensus beyond narrow legal definitions. In focusing on the legal violation, we lose out on the opportunity to fully explore the "wrongness" of the act and to give serious attention to the victim's loss. Our traditional justice system conveys the wrongness of the act in a one-dimensional manner through the amount of punishment imposed. However, in emphasizing punishment, we may miss opportunities to more fully and directly stress the moral violation, and thus reaffirm the values of society (Christie, 1977).

According to Umbreit and Armour (2011), "Only the victim can really confront the offender at this level of violation with the profound meaning and impact of what he or she did. Likewise, only the offender can address the injury at the level it was experienced by the victim by accepting that what he or she did was wrong, that it came from him or her, and that he or she repudiates that aspect of self—weakness or failing—that caused the harm to occur" (p. 91). Victims often feel that their sense of security has been shattered by the harm done to them and have a vested interest, not in seeing accountability "imposed" on the offender, but in having the offender's own personal assurances that he has learned his lesson and he will take remedial steps. Restorative justice advocates believe that the meeting itself is therapeutic, allowing both victim and offender to "tell their stories,"[1] beyond simply the facts of what occurred.

Today, restorative justice policies and programs are developing in nearly every state, with many states (including Minnesota, Vermont, Wisconsin, and Oregon) invoking systemic changes around restorative principles. Nineteen states have introduced or passed legislation to solidify the use of restorative practices in their jurisdictions. In 1994, the American Bar Association endorsed Victim Offender Mediation and provided guidelines for its use in U.S. courts. These guidelines stipulate that participation by both victims and offenders must be totally voluntary, and that offenders would not be negatively impacted by statements made during mediation sessions (Umbreit & Armour, 2011).

OUTCOME AND PROCESS COMPONENTS OF RESTORATIVE JUSTICE

As discussed, the Western practice of restorative justice has a fairly brief history and to this point, despite its continuing growth, is not widely known, even by those in the criminal justice field. Even those with some familiarity with this view tend to misunderstand its essential purpose. Zehr (2002), recognizing the misunderstandings regarding its meaning and intent, specifies what restorative justice IS NOT; namely, that it is not primarily about forgiveness, nor is it a program designed to reduce recidivism, nor is it an alternative to prison intended only for first or minor-level offenders, and it is certainly not intended as a replacement for prison. Nor is it a panacea or replacement for the justice system. Furthermore, restorative justice is not necessarily the opposite of retribution, as it shares with retribution the need to respond to the harm done and to hold the offender accountable, though in ways that are constructive to the community.

Restorative justice is then a philosophy of responding to crime that emphasizes the harm done to others as the essential problem and offender accountability for satisfying legitimate needs, as mutually defined by all involved parties, arising from the offense, as the best approach to resolving the crime. It reminds us that crimes evoke emotions and that emotions are not adequately defined by the legal violation itself and are not best dealt with in legal settings. It also reminds us that crime is a concern central to life and that it should not simply be turned over to criminal justice professionals, no matter how well intended and competent they are. However, the term "legitimate" in the above definition also reminds us that any system of sanctioning must be under the review of such professionals, lest we run the risk of violating due process traditions enshrined in our notions of justice.

Outcome

The Office of Juvenile Justice and Delinquency Prevention defines three main goals in the sanctioning of juvenile offenders that are incorporated in its Balanced and Restorative Justice (BARJ) approach (U.S. Dept. of Justice, 1998):

Accountability: "When an individual commits an offense, this offender incurs an obligation to individual victims and the community." (p.6)

Competency Development: "Offenders who enter the juvenile justice system should be more capable when they leave than when they entered." (p. 6)

Community Safety: "Juvenile justice has a responsibility to protect the public from juveniles in the system." (p. 6)

The above goals must be appropriately balanced in a given case. Though accountability may seem to imply punishment, it is intended in a fuller sense:

+ "Understanding how that behavior affected other human beings (not just the courts or officials).
+ Acknowledging that the behavior resulted from a choice that could have been made differently.
+ Acknowledging to all affected that the behavior was harmful to others.
+ Taking action to repair the harm where possible
+ Making changes necessary to avoid such behavior in the future." (U.S. Dept. of Justice, 1998, p. 9)

This focus on accountability can help to resolve the conflict often seen in the "rehabilitation versus punishment" decision frequently faced by the courts, since it essentially involves elements of each. Accountability serves as a means of rehabilitation, and rehabilitation is a necessary component of accountability.

Process

The process should involve all stakeholders, including the victim, the offender, and the community, as well as the government. This would augment the current sanctioning system, which typically includes only the offender and his or her legal representative and the state judiciary. The role of the judiciary would shift toward overseeing and managing the system, allowing for those involved to have more direct involvement and decision-making ability, based on the belief that the best outcomes will result when those most directly involved are making the decisions.

Howard Zehr (2002) describes the following "signposts" of restorative justice, or what the process should involve, which include a focus more on the harms than on the legal violation, showing equal concern for victims and offenders, working toward the restoration of victims and supporting offenders in taking responsibility for the offense in a way that is manageable and socially useful, providing opportunities for dialogue between victim and offender, and, above all, showing respect for all involved parties. Van Ness and Strong (2015) point to four "cornerposts for restorative justice: (1) inclusion, providing the opportunity for the direct and full participation for all parties involved in the offense, (2) Encounter, where the often powerful emotions of those involved can be expressed, for the purpose of healing both victims and offenders, Amends, the opportunity for the offender to do what can be done to make things right, and Reintegration, "to help both victims and offenders reenter their communities as whole, productive, contributing members" (p. 114).

These points from both Howard Zehr (2002) and Van Ness and Strong (2015) reflect process concerns, or the actual operations of a given program or system. To the degree that the above values are incorporated in practices, the approach would be aligned with the restorative vision. Keeping these underlying values in mind is important, given that often, original goals are displaced for the sake of bureaucratic expediency (Austin & Krisberg, 1981). For instance, mediation could be used as a means of disposing of cases, with little concern for the healing process needed by the participants. Cases could be unnecessarily referred to restorative programs simply to satisfy a need for numbers, with little regard for the actual process and the degree to which it serves the needs of the victim, offender, and community. A commitment to restorative justice must also include a commitment to devoting the time and resources necessary for the preparation, the meeting, and necessary follow-up (Umbreit & Armour, 2011).

Those concerned about restorative justice providing an easy way out for the offender need to keep in mind that actually having to face the person one victimized and hear the details of the harm one caused can in itself be a form of punishment. However, it is an active form of punishment, as opposed to simply sitting in a jail cell, reporting to a probation officer, or paying a fine. In all of those cases, the offender must simply comply with the punishment and never really has to take direct responsibility for his offense. In fact, while the punishment is being decided, the offender is in the spotlight and is the main focus of the judge, prosecutor, and defense attorney. In fact, defendants get a lot of attention—maybe not the sort we ourselves would like to have—but attention nonetheless. Restorative justice alternatives require that offenders give their attention to victim needs, something they are never required to do when the typical court sanctions mentioned above are imposed. Alternative options currently in use as discussed below may provide a more active form of accountability, and even more importantly, may serve to better meet the needs of victims.

RESTORATIVE JUSTICE PRACTICES

System Implementation

Restorative justice cases can enter from various points in the criminal justice system. Cases can be (1) referred as diversion from prosecution, with referrals usually made by prosecutors, but also by police, in lieu of arrest; (2) referred by the court after a finding of guilt, but prior to sentencing, to determine an appropriate sentence, including conditions of probation; (3) referred as part of a sentencing requirement; and (4) referred while an incarcerative sentence is being served (Nicholl, 1999). The point at which the case is referred is of great significance. There are legitimate concerns about assuring that the program not be used to simply get off on the charge. Those involved in the process always need to be sure that the defendant's willingness to make good on the offense by meeting with the victim is not *solely* due to a desire to avoid stricter sanctions. Further, it would have to be concluded that the ends of justice are better met through such a referral than by proceeding in the normal fashion.[2]

The questions that arise as to whether and when a case should be referred to as a restorative justice program include:

1. Does the defendant appear to be one who would respond positively to the victim's emotional and/or material needs and follow through on any agreement made?
2. Is it likely that the program is being used *only* as a means to escape further sanctioning?
3. Are the ends of justice sufficiently met in allowing for this alternative path, as opposed to other, more formal processes?

If the above concerns are adequately addressed, restorative programs should be considered a means of better meeting the needs of the victim, offender, and community as a whole.

Types of Programs

We will describe four different types of victim-offender meetings in use today: (1) victim-offender mediation; (2) family group conferences; (3) circle sentencing; and (4) victim-offender dialogue in serious cases. Each will be discussed in turn.

1. VICTIM-OFFENDER MEDIATION (VOM)

A trained mediator, most often a volunteer rather than a justice employee, would contact both the victim and offender to determine their interest in participation. The mediator may wish to meet individually with one or both in order to gain more information, to assure voluntariness and understanding of the process, or to determine suitability for proceeding on this path. If willingness on both parts is clear and it is felt by the mediator that the chances of gain, especially for the victim (but also for the offender) substantially outweigh the possibility of an adverse outcome, a meeting between the two parties is arranged. The meeting typically occurs at a neutral site such as a community center or church office, which is acceptable to both victim and offender (Umbreit & Armour, 2011).

The session begins with the mediator explaining the ground rules for the meeting, including the need for respectful communication. After the structure is established, the mediator then remains as invisible in the process as possible, thus allowing for direct communication between victim and offender. Mediators intervene in those relatively rare circumstances when either party verges on abusiveness. Much more often, any initial anger on the part of the victim is soon dispelled, and offenders welcome the opportunity to show themselves as people who are better than the offense they committed (Umbreit & Armour, 2011).

The victim is the first to speak after the mediator. The victim discusses the facts of the offense from her or his perspective, including its personal impact. The offender then responds, explaining how the offense came about and how he now views it, especially in light of what the victim just stated. The hope is that in this response, the offender takes responsibility for the harm he has done and offers an apology, which is then met by expressions of forgiveness by the victim. If all goes well, a resolution is then discussed that often includes material compensation, though as Umbreit and Armour state, "Actions taken by offenders to repair the harm caused can take as many forms as creative minds can devise and agree upon" (2015, p.126). The synergy of the interaction could lead the search for resolution in ways that neither party may have imagined ahead of time. Instead of focusing on monetary restitution, alcohol education/treatment, community service, continued education, etc., could be part of the agreement as well.

When an agreement is reached, it is written out and signed by victim, offender, and mediator. Some form of monitoring follows to assure that the points agreed to are actually carried out by the offender. Typically, the agreement becomes part of the conditions of probation, in which case probation officers are responsible for assuring its completion. Mediators may remain in phone contact with the victim to assure satisfaction with the offender's compliance (Umbreit & Armour, 2011).

2. FAMILY GROUP CONFERENCES (FGCs)

Family Group Conferences are mainly used with juveniles as a means of diversion from the regular court process and in this sense tend to take on a more formal role. Cases that are successfully mediated, therefore, never appear in court. As described by Umbreit and Armour, "Family group conferences (FGCs) are an approach to planning and decision making about youth crime and youth care that involves the wider family network in partnership with representatives of governmental institutions and other community agencies" (2011, p.143).

FGCs include more participants, in addition to the victim and offender, as do VOM sessions. Supporters for both the victim and offender are encouraged to participate. Supporters are family members, close friends, teachers, coaches, religious leaders, probation officers, youth workers, etc. The victim's supporters often serve to verify victim accounts regarding the impact of the offense. The offender's supporters serve as a reminder that the offender is better than his offense, and also assist the offender in making good on resolving the offense and assuring that the offender will fulfill any commitments he makes. The coordinator of the session may be a member of the justice system (i.e., police officer or probation officer) or a youth services worker. The preparation for the session would be similar to VOM cases, with the added responsibility to coordinate the time and place for the session with multiple participants (Umbreit & Armour, 2011).

Though the desired outcomes of accepting responsibility, apology, and forgiveness are similar to VOM, the dynamics involved in a Family Group Conference are changed, due to the added participants and its more public nature. This offers the opportunity for the offender to respond to the victim, but also to the larger community in regard to his personal recognition of wrongdoing and resolve to change. Also, the offender's supporters and other participants can place the wrongdoing in a broader context to assure that the root of the problem is addressed (Umbreit & Armour, 2011).

To John Braithwaite (1989), the purpose of the FGC is neither to punish nor to rehabilitate, but instead to educate the offender, mainly through the process of "reintegrative shaming." The offender should experience shame when confronted by the victim's expressions about the impact of the offense. Shame is viewed in a positive sense, as affirmation that the offender shares a value system similar to that of the rest of society. Shame can serve to awaken resolve to regain a role as a productive member of society, as opposed to guilt, which instead implies isolation and exclusion. Hopefully, shame is the natural response as the offender is confronted with the pain expressed by the victim. However, this shame should be quickly dispelled as part of the restorative process as soon as an agreement or understanding is reached. Then, efforts should be directed toward inclusion of the offender in the human community. The person's "offender" status is dispelled with his or her commitment to make good on the offense (Braithwaite & Mugford, 1994).

Powerful emotions may arise in FGCs, making it important to have appropriate management of the process. First, steps need to be taken to separate the offender from the offense, in a sense. The act—not the person—is defined as "bad." This allows for communication among all parties on an equal footing and for an exploration of the event with a minimum of defensiveness. It also helps to retain the appropriate power balance and to prevent what otherwise might result in a "degradation ceremony" (Braithwaite & Mugford, 1994), where the stigma placed on the offender exceeds that which the offender can do anything about or exert any control over. Preparation and appropriate screening prior to the full session help to prevent this from occurring, as well as clear representation by the coordinator of the purpose of the session at the outset (Umbreit & Armour, 2011).

Once an agreement is reached, it is written up and signed by the multiple parties concerned with its completion. Importantly, refreshments are often served at the conclusion of the session. This helps to reinforce the informal nature of the session. More importantly, it serves the significant function of minimizing negative stigmatizing, affirming that the offender is a member of the community, willing and capable to work toward undoing the harm done by the offense.

3. CIRCLE SENTENCING

Sentencing Circles derive from practices of First Nation groups in Canada and the United States. In addition to participants in Family Group Conferences, any member of the community with an interest in the particular case may attend and participate (Umbreit & Armour, 2011). There is an emphasis on the interdependence and interconnectedness of participants, and everyone has an equal voice in the proceedings (Nicholl, 1999). Sentencing Circles are more expansive and open than are either Family Group Conferences and may include those who typically work in the regular criminal court, including judges, prosecutors, defense attorneys, and probation officers and also treatment personnel. Any type of offense can be referred for a circle; though the offender must be willing to accept responsibility for the offense, there must be a desire for rehabilitation, and there must be support for the offender within the community (Stuart, 1996).

The circle is coordinated and overseen by the "Circle Keeper," who is a known and trusted member of the community. The preparation for sentencing circles is more involved than in either of the other two models discussed above. Suitability of the candidate can involve much deliberation. Offenders may be given significant tasks to perform in order to gain entry to this process, usually involving taking steps to make good on the offense (Umbreit & Armour, 2011).

The session begins and ends with a ceremony relevant to the community and which sets the tone for moving participants from an individual to a communally based perspective. In more formal circles, the prosecutor reads the facts of the case, the offender accepts fault, and a guilty plea is formally entered. The prosecutor and defense attorney may be asked to make brief opening statements. The circle is then open to statements from the victim, offender, and others. If the preparation has been done well, the circle serves to recognize what the offender is already doing to move past the offense, and the victim and offender are allowed to tell their stories (Umbreit & Armour, 2011).

The circle moves to establish a consensus about what happened, to identify the harm caused, and to devise a suitable sentencing plan. Plans are often lengthy and involved and may include components such as treatment, restitution, or involvement in community projects. A subsequent circle may be scheduled after a period of time to review progress (Umbreit & Armour, 2011).

Circles can number anywhere from 10 to 70 people, making management a critical issue. Circle Keepers must be familiar with the process and must assure that all are given the opportunity to speak, with no one person allowed to dominate the session. A "talking piece" is used for this purpose, which may simply be a feather or a pipe. Its significance rests in the role that it plays in the ensuing dialogue. Only the person who is given the talking piece is allowed to speak, assuring that all who wish to speak will be heard and that no one participant is more important than another (Umbreit & Armour, 2011).

Though sentencing circles are most prominent in Native American and other aboriginal communities, there is some interest in adopting these practices elsewhere in and outside the United States. Also, the use of circles outside the justice system such as school settings has shown positive results. Among the restorative justice models discussed earlier, circles provide the most impressive demonstration that lay community members are equal to the task of capably handling the complex problems that communities face (Umbreit & Armour, 2011).

4. VICTIM-OFFENDER DIALOGUE IN SERIOUS CASES

You might well ask why a close relative of one who was murdered would ever want to consider meeting with the person responsible. In a sense, whenever an offense is committed, a relationship is necessarily established between the victim and offender; the more serious the offense, the more intense the relationship. Restorative justice may provide victims a better means of managing this relationship. In this writer's experience as a probation officer, some homicide victims, even a long time after the offense, had intense feelings of anger and hatred that were by all appearances debilitating. Parents who lost their daughter to a drunk driver come to mind. Their profound sorrow over their daughter's tragic death, hit while she was crossing the street, was compounded by their subsequent impressions of the defendant during court appearances, as reflected in their statement, "He wouldn't even so much as look at us, let alone offer us any sort of apology." The defendant had, in fact, been correctly advised by his attorney to avoid any contact with the parents, as anything he might say in an environment not appropriately set up for dialogue would likely be viewed negatively or suspiciously. In this very real way, the pain of the victims was compounded by the limitations of the legal process. Many victims seek a form of resolution that will offer a better means of alleviating their painful emotions of anger and hate that is not possible through the legal process alone.

The use of victim-offender dialogue in serious cases must be initiated by the victim after a sentence has been imposed.[3] The decision on the part of the justice system is whether or not to offer such a program and to assist victims should they want to meet with the offender. Texas began such a program in 1993, and by 1996, there were 200 mediation requests from victims on file. Often, victims have gone to great lengths to arrange for this sort of meeting. After all, the offender is the only one who can provide answers to their questions regarding motivations, degree of remorse, details of the offense, and many others.

Should this meeting occur, it would typically be in a prison setting, where safety for all participants is well provided for. The mediator must have special skills and experience, given the intensity of emotions involved. The preparation for such a session is lengthy, often a year or longer, and involves numerous sessions with each party. During these individual sessions, the mediator must be sure that both parties are prepared for this meeting and are realistic in their expectations as to what they will hear from the other (Umbreit & Armour, 2011).

Victims who go through this process most often report that they are glad they did and report less anger and hostility, more trust toward others, less fear, and the ability to come to terms with the offender in ways that are helpful for their own healing. Offenders express that they gain an increased recognition of the consequences of their acts and feel good about having the opportunity to help the victim, whom they were now more likely to see as a person (Umbreit & Armour, 2011).

RESTORATIVE JUSTICE AND THE ISSUE OF EFFECTIVENESS

Before we briefly discuss the effectiveness of restorative justice, we need to keep in mind that it would actually be erroneous to ask, "Does restorative justice work?" because it is a vision or perspective, and not in itself a program. The four types of programs described above have demonstrated increased satisfaction with the process on the part of both victims and offenders and their supporters, when compared with traditional justice practices. Additionally, there is data to show that such programs can significantly reduce the use of incarceration and formal court processes, without unduly influencing public safety. Results are mixed regarding the influence of restorative justice programs on recidivism, though few recidivism studies have been done to date (Umbreit & Armour, 2011).

An extensive study of restorative justice programs worldwide by Sherman and Strang (2007) concludes that restorative justice programs of various sorts

+ "substantially reduced repeat offending for some offenders, but not all;
+ doubled (or more) the offences brought to justice as diversion from CJ;
+ reduced crime victims' post-traumatic stress symptoms and related costs;
+ provided both victims and offenders with more satisfaction with justice than CJ;
+ reduced crime victims' desire for violent revenge against their offenders;
+ reduced the costs of criminal justice, when used as diversion from CJ;
+ reduced recidivism *more than* prison (adults) or *as well as* prison (youths)." (p. 4)

Interestingly, Sherman and Strang (2007) found a greater impact on recidivism reduction in the more serious types of cases, as compared with less serious cases. Overall, the writers conclude that restorative justice showed results as favorable as any other effort used to reduce recidivism and that their study would support a continued growth of restorative justice programs, "especially if that is done on a continue-to-learn-as-you-go basis (p. 8)." However, it may be unrealistic to expect that accountability alone will be sufficient to bring about positive of-fender change in all cases. The offender who sincerely apologizes to the victim and who has it in mind to meet the obligations to which he has agreed may yet become involved in crime again, due to factors that are beyond the reach of mediation alone.

Rehabilitation advocates Cullen and Jonson (2012) remind us that problems underlying crime are typically long-standing and require treatment services that are proven effective (evidence based) in order to presume that desistance from crime will occur. Restorative justice advocates might counter that personal ac-countability should be a component of any type of rehabilitation program, while recognizing that demonstrating accountability may be insufficient in meeting rehabilitation needs and safety needs as well.

FUTURE CONSIDERATIONS

Should we proceed in incorporating a restorative justice vision within our sanc-tioning system, many questions will have to be addressed, including:

1. *Can restorative justice become part of the way of doing business in the criminal courts without becoming swept up or co-opted by bureaucratic concerns?*

Restorative justice *is* idealistic, given the value it places on the importance of ideas over expediency. Efficiency is best gained by a closed system of tightly controlled processes under the management of experts with insider information.

The question becomes whether the system will serve vision needs, or will the vision be compromised to serve the needs of the system? More to the point, can the criminal courts change sufficiently to allow for restorative justice processes to unfold as intended?

Restorative justice critics point to the amount of time required to adopt this new way of doing business. Possibly they have not experienced the amount of time that is often consumed in criminal cases, with the countless continuances that frequently occur, as well as the lengthy plea negotiations between prosecutor and defense attorney.[4] Processing restorative justice resolutions does—and should—take much time, though it would be a mistake to assume that it would be more costly or necessarily less efficient than current practices. The main task would be to constantly monitor the process to assure that the goals of restorative justice are still evident in whatever processes are adopted by a sanctioning court. Additional time investment would need to be considered in relation to added benefits, not only to the victim and offender, but also relative to the opportunity for norm clarification.

2.   *Will a restorative justice movement result in "net widening?"*

Net widening refers to a tendency to extend a given program beyond what it was originally intended for. Restorative justice is an attempt to substitute formal social control with more informal social control. However, there is always the need to guard against unintended consequences (Austin & Krisberg, 1981). We see similar concerns relating to the use of treatment programs. Drug treatment programs intended to keep people out of jail can result in a net increase in the number of people going to jail, given that program failures often result in incarceration, due to a technical violation of probation or parole. It is important that all diversion programs do not inappropriately extend the reach of the state.

3.   *How should power be shared between the state and important stakeholders?*

Restorative justice "purists" advocate for a minimum of state involvement in restorative programs. These critics (see Sullivan & Tifft, 2001; Christie, 1977) believe that its ideals will only be kept alive by avoiding the contamination of state authority. They resist reliance on the coercive powers of the criminal court system to effect restorative justice, given its need for free expression and authenticity. For instance, an apology from the offender to the victim will always be suspect if the offender has the clear idea that a perceived successful mediation will help assure favorable treatment in court (Walgrave, 2008).

The concerns of the "purists" are certainly valid, given the strong currents of and pressures found in the criminal courts. But is their recommendation realistic, when considering the use of restorative justice in criminal processes? Would we ever want to turn over criminal disputes to nonprofessionals, with absolutely no oversight? Where would we draw the line as to the seriousness of cases that should be referred? Who would make those decisions? How would we deal with situations where offenders are noncompliant, or possibly even those very rare times when she or he is abusive to the victim or mediator? What mechanism would we use to ensure that the agreement is fulfilled? Can we always count on the offender to meet such obligations if there is no threat of further court action if he fails to do so? If the process goes on independently from the formal court and there is no relationship between mediation and the formal court system, we might be more confident that expressions in the mediation session are truly from the heart, but that poses another problem. Should the offender be given no credit at all in court for operating in good faith and meeting the needs of the victim? If so, are we losing out on incentives that could make restorative processes more likely?

Given questions such as those raised above, most advocates of restorative justice support a system that essentially involves power sharing between the state and community. This system would allow credit for the offender in the formal court based on performance in the informal restorative process, notwithstanding the concerns about sincerity that arise. The system would require a good working relationship between those particularly entrusted with the "vision" and those who have more far-reaching sanctioning responsibilities. There is nothing unusual about this, given that the courts are constantly interacting with substance abuse, mental health, and countless other treatment personnel, where such shared understandings are essential. Treatment professionals often welcome the oversight and especially the leverage that the court holds over the offender in attaining treatment goals. The important issue is respect between the two sides, and the ability and willingness to understand different points of view.

4. *Can we preserve the vision of restorative justice when participants are lacking?*

The many victims who do not wish to have any form of personal contact with the offender may still find it helpful to tell their story in a small group setting (Walker, 2013). A form of shuttle dialogue can be arranged, whereby the victim may utilize mediation services to get answers to their questions indirectly from the offender. Victims should also have access to information about their case and the ability to be included in important decisions, the right to assistance and advocacy for the duration of the case, and also a hearing by the sentencing court concerning the impact of the offense (Van Ness & Strong, 2015).

Should offenders who are willing to accept responsibility for their offense be denied the opportunity of a restorative justice option due to an unwilling victim? The restorative vision can still be utilized in ways that do not require direct victim involvement. In addition to cooperating with the shuttle dialogue referred to above, offenders can meet with Victim Impact Panels, comprised of individuals who have been victimized by similar offenses and who can therefore represent the harmful impact of the offense to the community. Various other programs such as Reentry Courts for those newly released from prison, Drug

Courts for those who are facing criminal charges due to drug arrests, and Community Reparative Boards share the restorative vision of a collaborative, community-based approach that allows for the offender to publicly demonstrate willingness to get beyond the offense.

One of the more innovative approaches in this regard are Circles of Support and Accountability (COSA), which have sprung up in Canada and the United Kingdom and are also being tried in the United States. Sex offenders, probably the most stigmatized of offenders leaving prison, are matched with four to seven volunteers, who agree to provide support for the offender, but also take on the responsibility of ensuring that the offender is complying with release conditions (Hannem & Petrunik, 2004). Roberts (2006) describes the volunteer role as "both supporter and watchdog," and adds that the main goal is to do whatever is needed to prevent further victimization. Recidivism results for COSAs have been very encouraging to date (Hannem & Petrunik, 2004; Wilson, Picheca, & Prinzo 2007; Duwe, 2012).

5. *Can we preserve the voluntariness of all participants?*

Van Ness and Strong (2015) believe that voluntariness is not an either/or proposition, but instead is correctly thought of as points on a continuum. Should we presume that an offender who agrees to meet with a victim because it will yield favorable treatment in court is not participating voluntarily? While some may question the voluntariness of a defendant who complies with more favorable treatment by the criminal court as an inducement, we need to remember that ulterior motives are common to all of us. The fact that we might study for an exam in order to get good grades does not mean we are not interested also in the broader goal of education. External incentives do not rule out the possibility of internal motivations. The problem drinker ordered by the court for alcohol treatment does not necessarily lack an interest in treatment. Possibly this person would not operate on this interest if not for court pressure, just as the student may not be inclined to pick up that textbook if not for the exam. In both cases, the goal lies beyond mere compliance.

6. *When in the justice process is restorative justice intervention best initiated?*

Generally speaking, the more serious the case, the later in the process restorative initiatives should be considered. Courts interested in restorative options are also responsible for the multiple considerations referred to at the beginning of the chapter. The perceived need for incapacitation may outweigh any benefits that might accrue from mediation as part of a sentencing option. However, this does not preclude the use of a restorative option as part of an incarcerative sentence. Also, the court may conclude that the use of a restorative justice option in the pretrial stage might send out the wrong message regarding respect for the law (deterrence), either on the part of the public or the defendant himself.

7. Will restorative justice compromise the integrity of the justice system?

Restorative justice programs will introduce more discretion into the sanctioning system, and as a result, will reduce the level of consistency from one case to the next. Would the potential benefits of stakeholder involvement in decision making make up for the potential loss in retribution and deterrence that can be attained in a more specified, guidelines-type of sentencing process? Hopefully, the ends of retribution and deterrence are also served, possibly in a fuller way, when the harmfulness of the act is at the forefront and the offender takes personal responsibility for the act. Restorative justice programs do have the potential to enhance the collective consciousness regarding law-abiding behavior and increase the possibility that people will be deterred from crime because of their own internal misgivings about being responsible for such a violation. Also, deterrence advocates need to keep in mind that only a very small fraction of criminal cases result in incarceration, given (1) the small percentage of cases reported to police; (2) the small percentage of cases reported that result in arrest; (3) the small percentage of cases of arrest that are convicted; and (4) the small percentage of convicted cases that result in jail or prison time.

The need for balancing these various demands still exists in a restorative system, though possibly a restorative vision provides greater clarity as to how to attain this balance. Ideally, justice could erase the offense for the victim—clearly an impossibility. Neither mediation nor vengeance will bring about this outcome. Victims can be helped by the justice system only to a degree. Certainly, in our attention to their anguish and pain, we should refrain from facile and routine responses and the presumption that they will benefit at all.

Should we adopt restorative justice? If we do, it will no longer go by that term, but instead will simply be what comes to mind when we think of the word justice. The paradigm will have shifted in this direction, and the roles of all involved in the justice process will evolve to accommodate that change. Since this vision firmly incorporates the need for offender accountability to victim and community, incarceration will continue to be essential for those whose lack of control over their behavior renders them incapable of demonstrating this accountability as free citizens in the community. The "new lenses" (Zehr) will necessarily provide a fuller, clearer vision of criminal sanctioning, an outcome that would be poorly served by instead putting on blinders. Restorative justice advocates look to use programs compatible with this vision to the extent possible, given the unique circumstances of each case.

REFERENCES

Austin, James, and Barry Krisberg (1981). Wider, stronger, and different nets: The dialectics of criminal justice reform. *Journal of Research in Crime and Delinquency*, 18 (1), 165–196.

Braithwaite, J. (1989). *Crime, Shame and Reintegration*. Cambridge, UK: Cambridge University Press.

Braithwaite, John, and S. Mugford (1994). Conditions of successful reintegration ceremonies. *British Journal of Criminology*, 34(2), 139–171.

Christie, Nils (1977). Conflicts as property. *British Journal of Criminology*. 17 (1), 1–15.

Cullen, Francis T., and Cheryl L. Jonson (2012). *Correctional Theory: Context and Consequences*. Washington, DC: Sage Publications.

Duwe, Grant (2012). Can Circles of Support and Accountability (COSA) work in the United States? Preliminary results from a randomized experiment in Minnesota. *Sexual Abuse: A Journal of Research and Treatment*, 25 (2), 143–165.

Haley, J. O. (1989). Confession, repentance and absolution. In M. Wright and B. Galaway, eds. *Mediation and Criminal Justice*. London: Sage Publications, 1999.

Hannem, Stacey, and Michael Petrunik (2004). Canada's circles of support and accountability: A community justice initiative for high-risk sex offenders. *Corrections Today*, Dec. 98–101.

Maruna, Shadd (2011). Judicial Rehabilitation and the "Clean Bill of Health" in Criminal Justice. *European Journal of Probation*, 3(1), 97–117.

Moore, D. B. (1993). Shame, forgiveness, and juvenile justice. *Criminal Justice Ethics*, winter/spring: 3–23.

Nicholl, Caroline G. (1999). *Community Policing, Community Justice, and Restorative Justice: Exploring the Links for the Delivery of a Balanced Approach to Public Safety*. Washington, DC: U.S. Department of Justice, Office of Community Oriented Policing Services.

Packer, Herbert (1968). *The Limits of the Criminal Sanction*. Stanford, CA: Stanford University Press.

Roberts, Yvonne (2006). They're not monsters. *Guardian*, July 11. Retrieved Jul. 28, 2014, from http://www.theguardian.com/news/2006/jul/11/crime

Sherman, Lawrence W., and Heather Strang (2007). *Restorative Justice: The Evidence*. London: Smith Institute.

Stuart, Barry (1996). Circle Sentencing: Turning Swords into Ploughshares. In Burt Galaway and Joe Hudson, eds., *Restorative Justice: International Perspectives* (pp. 193–206). Monsey, NY: Criminal Justice Press.

Sullivan, Dennis, and Larry Tifft (2001). *Restorative Justice: Healing the Foundations of Our Everyday Lives*. Monsey, NY: Willow Tree Press.

U.S. Dept. of Justice, Office of Juvenile Justice and Delinquency Prevention (1998). *Guide for Implementing the Balanced and Restorative Justice Model*, Washington, DC.

U.S. Dept. of Justice. (n.d.). Crime in the United States, 2012. Retrieved Nov. 2, 2014, from http://www.fbi.gov/about-us/cjis/ucr/crime-in-the-u.s/2012/crime-in-the-u.s.-2012/tables/29tabledatadecpdf

Umbreit, Mark (1985). *Crime and Reconciliation*. Nashville: Abingdon Press.

Umbreit, Mark, and R. B. Coates (1993). Cross-site analysis of victim-offender mediation in four states. *Crime and Delinquency*, 39(4): 565–585.

Umbreit, Mark, and Marilyn Peterson Armour (2011). *Restorative Justice Dialogue: An Essential Guide for Research and Practice*. New York: Springer.

Van Ness, Daniel, and Karen Heetderks Strong (2015). *Restoring Justice* (5th ed.). Boston: Elsevier.

Van Wormer, Katherine S., and Loreen Walker, eds. (2013). *Restorative Justice: Practical Applications*. Los Angeles: Sage.

Walgrave, Lode (2008). *Restorative Justice, Self-Interest and Responsible Citizenship*. Portland, OR: Willan Publishing.

Walker, Loreen (2013). Restorative justice for victims without offender participation. In Katherine Van Wormer and Loreen Walker, eds. *Restorative Justice: Practical Applications*. Los Angeles: Sage.

Wilson, Robin J., Janice E. Picheca, and Michelle Prinzo (2007). Evaluating the effectiveness of professionally facilitated volunteerism in the community-based management of high-risk sexual offenders: Part two: A comparison of recidivism rates. *Howard Journal* 46 (4), 327–337.

Wright, M. (1991). *Justice for Victims and Offenders*. Philadelphia: Open University Press.

Zehr, H., and M. Umbreit (1982). Victim offender reconciliation. An incarceration substitute? *Federal Probation* 46 (4): 63–68.

Zehr, Howard (1990). *Changing Lenses: A New Focus for Crime and Justice*. Scottsdale, PA: Herald Press.

Zehr, Howard (2002). *The Little Book of Restorative Justice*. Intercourse, PA: Good Books.

END NOTES

1. See Umbreit and Armour (2011) for the significance of storytelling in the mediation process.

2. According to Umbreit and Armour (2011), 45 percent of programs surveyed serviced juvenile offenders only, while 46 percent serviced both juveniles and adults. Most cases are referred either as diversion or prior to sentencing, and two-thirds of these are misdemeanors and one-third felonies. The most common referred offenses are vandalism, minor assaults, theft, and burglary; the primary sources for referrals to restorative justice programs are probation officers, judges, and prosecutors.

3. Imagine how insulting it would be to the victims were I to suggest such a meeting on my own.

4. This writer often spent hours waiting around in court while a single case was being discussed that neither this writer nor many of the other court professionals who were also waiting had anything to do with!

15. Religious Violence

By William J. Cook Jr.

OVERVIEW

In this chapter, we'll examine some of the explanations for religious violence, especially when it manifests itself as terrorism. What is so troubling about religious violence is that most people associate religion with bringing *peace*, and fortunately, that is often the case. In fact, most religious people do not engage in religious violence. But when religion is used to justify violence, it frequently results in death and destruction that is sometimes nearly incomprehensible in its scope. During the past 30 years, there has been a change in the commonly used justification for terrorism: prior to the 1980s, most terrorists were politically motivated; since that time, their typical justification is now religious.

MOTIVATION

What causes someone to become religiously violent? There are two possible factors that seem to surface consistently: alienation and humiliation. Alienation is a sociological term derived from the Latin word *alieno*, which can mean to estrange or to avoid. It refers to the disappointment that someone might feel in his or her life in society, especially if there is "the perception that large organizations of many kinds (including the government, political parties, labor unions, and businesses) were unresponsive, detached, and untrustworthy in meeting the public's needs."[1] There are persons in our society today who find themselves feeling threatened by changes in conditions—especially socio-economic conditions. For some men, especially white males from mainstream religious denominations, there was an expectation that *they*, by virtue of what they saw as their birthright, should have certain prerogatives, especially in the workplace and in social status. But that has not been the case: women and minorities progressively have been taking more prominent roles in society during the past 50 years, while good jobs in factories and trades diminished. Some people felt very threatened by those changes. Others felt threatened by the rapid changes in society, especially in an increasingly secularized society. Finally, some felt undermined by modern changes in gender and sexuality, as well as in the redefinition of roles, especially as the role of the patriarchal male waned.

Thus, persons who felt alienated by such changes could begin to attempt to find ways to return to "old times" when they imagine or believe that things would have been better for them. One way to do this might be to join a new religious group—one that promises to be a source of strength in times of uncertainty. Such a religious group can offer: (1) community; (2) a general belief system; and (3) a clear set of behavioral guidelines.[2] None of this should be a problem unless that religious group which has been joined has a perception of already being under attack, so there is "a coalescence of a peculiar set of circumstances—political, social, and ideological—when religion becomes fused with violent expressions of social aspirations, personal pride, and movements for political change."[3] In other words, from their perspective, their world is already "at war." Such a theme has been present in the Christian Identity Movement (Christian Identity members are right-wing fundamentalists and conspiracy-minded survivalists, millennialists, and neo-Nazi groups like Aryan Nations, the Order, and some factions of the Ku Klux Klan),[4] whose "preachers cite the biblical accounts of Michael the Archangel destroying the offspring of evil to point to an albeit 'cosmic' war between the forces of darkness and the forces of light."[5]

The other factor that has surfaced repeatedly is humiliation. When one feels humiliated, there follows a sense of shame; this is the opposite of pride and self-respect. The psychiatrist James Gilligan has argued that shame is a primary cause of all violence and that the purpose of the violence is to diminish the sense of shame and replace it with its opposite, this pride.[6] In his book, *Violence: Reflections on a National Epidemic*, Gilligan was writing specifically about inmates in American prisons, but the principle he discusses can be applied more widely and can also explain terrorist violence as it arises in other parts of the world.

"When we are hurt, we want to hurt back," observes the psychiatrist Aaron Beck, who says that "we feel helpless when others control us." In this case, he was writing about interactions on a more personal scale, but the principles can be extended to explain terrorism, too. How do we protect ourselves? Beck answers: "the most obvious defense is to become angry at the offender and counterattack ...

we communicate the message, 'Don't mess with me.'" He concludes by saying, "Fighting can ward off not only present but future transgression and can help restore a sense of power and efficacy, crucial components of self-esteem."[7]

An illustration of the kind of situation described by Beck can be seen in the results of a psychological study that was done in Northern Ireland, a scene of much religiously motivated terrorism in the past. Previous victimization in such an environment may be a factor in drawing an individual into violence, too. Children in Northern Ireland who had experienced the burning down of their homes or the torture or imprisonment of persons in their families were tested using a projective instrument known as the Thematic Apperception Test (a test using pictures to elicit stories so as to probe an individual's emotional concerns or conflicts). The children who were tested showed that they saw themselves as having little or no control over their fate, and they had marked drives for destruction, which they felt helpless to control.

A compounding factor when one experiences humiliation and shame is that there is the possibility of a person feeling so much psychological pain from this situation, especially in the presence of believing that one is ineffective or unacceptable, that he or she can no longer bear the burden of individuality. The result can be *depersonalization*, which occurs when she abandons her individuality and merges with a group; the person then becomes the instrument of the group.

When one feels humiliated, there can be an attraction to religion because involvement in religious practice can itself bring honor, and if one is seen as a defender of his faith, then there is the prestige, in a sense, of being heroic. As Juergensmeyer observes: "(i)n the cultures of violence that have led to religious terrorism, the anxieties of all young men—concerns over careers, social locations and sexual relationships have been exacerbated. Experiences of humiliation in these matters have made them vulnerable to the voices of powerful leaders and images of glory in a cosmic war." One can see then that being drawn into religious violence has been "in part a counterbalance to their marginality, a way of empowering them within their own religious communities. The marginality often preceded their acts of violence and became more extreme afterward."[8]

There are countries in the Middle East, in Africa, and in some parts of Asia where perceived humiliation is an important part of the way that persons have defined their experience of the global community. For example, Sayyid Qutb (1906–1966) was Egypt's "most influential writer in the radical Muslim tradition," and he believed that the government of Egypt had allowed the country to be culturally, politically, and economically dominated by the West. Qutb rejected this situation, which he perceived as a humiliation, and "he maintained that humanity is fundamentally defined by religion rather than race or nationality and that religious war is the only morally acceptable form of killing." Qutb argued that the "ultimate war is between truth and falsehood," and he believed that "the satanic agents of falsehood" were to be found "entrenched in the Egyptian government."[9]

One last comment about motivation: it is rarely singular. In other words, the motivation to commit a terrorist act may be religious in conjunction with another motive, such as to gain money or material resources for one's family; this has certainly been the case with some suicide bombers in the Middle East.

Theoretical Explanations

There are several ways that attempt to explain how religious violence occurs. In this section, we'll examine three of those theories: Terror Management Theory (TMT), the staircase model of terrorism, and the sacralization (i.e., making sacred) of violence.

Terror Management Theory is the work of Hirschberger and Pyszczynski, and it looks at how existential concerns can underlie the tendency to choose violent solutions to ethno-political conflicts.[10] TMT argues that the "instinctive animal desire" for continued life, placed side by side with the human awareness of the inevitability of death, creates a potential for paralyzing terror (terror is intense, overpowering fear). But this terror needs to be managed, in order to continue with life's ordinary business. This terror can be managed in three ways: (1) having a cultural worldview that provides a basis for existence and standards through which one can attain a sense of personal value and the promise of a literal or symbolic immortality to those who live up to these standards; (2) having self-esteem, which is acquired by believing in the cultural worldview and living up to its standards; and (3) having close personal relationships.

The problem occurs when there are threats to this worldview. Threats to the symbolic constructions (i.e., the worldview) undermine the security that it provides and motivates people to protect their death-denying mechanisms to ward off the threats. The threats come when another group holds beliefs that conflict with one's own basic conceptions and proclaim their culture's superiority or moral righteousness over one's own.

These threats to the person's worldview and self-esteem can strip away his defensive shield; this will likely result in the person expressing anger and derogating the source of the threats. And sometimes, the threatened persons may choose to demonstrate their own group's superiority by subduing, defeating, or even annihilating a group that challenges their worldview.

The theory (TMT) has been tested by priming subjects with thoughts of death (called mortality salience, or MS) and examining cultural worldview defenses. Over 400 studies in 21 countries have shown that mortality salience (thoughts of death) increased a person's motivation to invest in one's worldview and to avoid, derogate, or aggress against those who threatened that worldview. Studies also show that mortality salience increases the tendency of people to view their own group in a positive light and other groups in a more negative light.

An interesting application of TMT was to study the influence of mortality salience on support for suicide bombers. In 2006, Pyszczynski et al. conducted a study of Iranian college students examining attitudes toward suicidal terrorism. Participants were assigned to either a mortality salience (MS) or control condition and then read a description of a student's political positions. Half of the subjects read a description supporting suicide terrorism, while half read a description disapproving it. Results indicated that subjects in the MS condition tended to support suicide terrorism or would even consider it themselves, if they were exposed to a description that approved of it. In the same study, American college students were asked if they would support extreme military interventions that could kill thousands of civilians. Students who were under the MS condition who were also politically conservative tended to support such interventions, whereas politically liberal students did not.[11]

The second theory to examine is the staircase model of terrorism. This model, described by Moghaddam, was designed to examine the psychological processes involved in the radicalization of young Muslims; but this model is adaptable for use with extremists of any religious background. Figure 15.1 illustrates the five levels or steps which a person can take as he or she advances to violence. One the

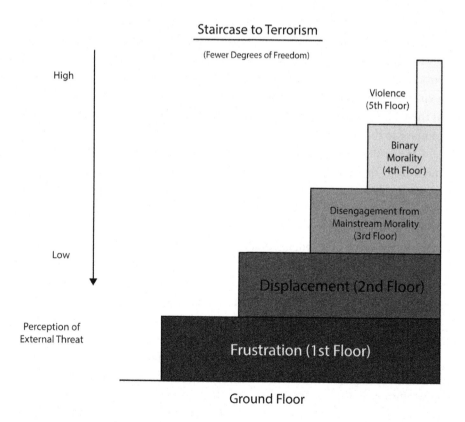

Figure 15.1: Staircase to Terrorism.

left side of the diagram, is an indicator of the perception of an external threat; each step is labeled with its dominant characteristic: Frustration (first step), Displacement (second step), Disengagement from Mainstream Morality (third step), Binary Morality (fourth step), and Violence (fifth step). The staircase is envisioned as an increasingly narrowing structure of five steps, which signifies that as a person moves up the stairs, she has a correspondingly decreasing set of alternatives for action; finally, at the last step, terrorism is seen as the only solution. It then can be seen as a rational choice, given the decreasing number of options as one "ascends the staircase."[12]

Most people are imagined to be on the ground floor and never begin to ascend the staircase; in other words, they do not consider terrorism. The people who have moved up to the first step are "concerned about mobility"—they want to improve their lives and advance within the system. But they find that their paths are blocked because of limited opportunities, as well as the need for family connections to open doors and the presence of corruption. Thus, they experience injustice. They become frustrated because of their inability to get ahead and angry about the situation in their home countries and the "threat that globalization poses for Muslim identity."

Those who climb to the second floor find ways to vent their frustration. This is done through a process of displacement of negative sentiments onto "outgroup targets"; this enhances the cohesion of the group. In addition, leaders can secure greater support by focusing the group's attention on external threats. Thus, instead of criticizing the governments of their own countries, those on the second step will direct their displaced negative sentiments toward other countries such as the United States. If this displacement of frustration occurs, it leads a person to move to the third step.

On the third step, there is a shift in moral thinking, implying a disengagement from the morality of mainstream society, which holds that terrorism is unacceptable and immoral. The moral thinking at this stage supports terrorism, as it is consistent with a utilitarian calculation: the end justifies the means. It is at the third step that a person is drawn into the terrorist group because of the identity and sense of belonging that it offers. Those who will eventually take the next step to the fourth level now have taken on the moral viewpoint that "Our enemy is evil and against God, and every means available to us must be used to win the war of good against evil"; and that "if innocent people are killed as a result of this war, they will go to heaven, and if they are guilty, they will go to hell."[13] Thus, there is now a devaluation of members of the outgroup.

At the fourth level, the person takes on even more rigid thinking that is characterized by "splitting," or a "binary morality." This means that the individual now categorizes the world into "us" and "them," good and bad, the godly and the godless; there is no gray area or in-between in this way of moral thinking. At this point, the person believes that the terrorist organization is legitimate and begins to be trained for a particular role, which results "in a sidestepping of the inhibitory mechanisms, behavioral signals that make it difficult for one human being (or animal) to kill another." The would-be terrorists now can circumvent the inhibitions against killing by learning to see the potential victims as "against God" or "deserving to die," or even "in league with Satan."[14]

Once having moved to the top of the staircase, the fifth floor, the person can only see one option: violence. The person at this level of the staircase has mastered the ability to neutralize inhibitions against killing and distance themselves psychologically from the persons they would kill. They kill because "at the top of the stair case there is no room for complexity. Dichotomous categorical thinking predominates: 'us' versus 'them,' 'Islam versus the West,' 'heaven versus hell.'" Moghaddam, Warren, and Love conclude by saying that: "Terrorism is not the result of a handful of psychopaths … . Rather, it is the result of a series of psychological processes driven by an unprecedented globalization and catastrophic evolution." They believe that terrorism will develop "in other communities where collective ingroup identity is perceived to be threatened, and experiences of humiliation and fear arise in association with global trends." The authors predict that there will continue to be "an association between religious extremism and terrorism, because of the important role that religion plays in the group life of 21st century humans—but not because religion per se causes terrorism."[15]

The staircase to terrorism theory was tested by Lygre, Eid, Larsson, and Ranstorp by conducting a literature search of 2564 publications on terrorism and further evaluating 38 studies. The authors concluded that "most of the theories and processes linked to Moghaddam's model are supported by empirical evidence"; yet, the researchers did question whether there is the exact linear progression through the steps or stages that the model proposes. The methodology used by the evaluators of the staircase to terrorism theory is subject to question, so the best that can be said now is that it appears that some significant parts of this theory are supported by empirical research, but that a more probative study remains to be done.[16]

The third approach to explaining religiously motivated terrorism involves the sacralization (i.e., making sacred) of violence. This theory of the "violent sacred" was developed by René Girard, in his book *Violence and the Sacred* (1979), and though in that work, the general topic of criminal violence was discussed, his understanding also can be applied to religious terrorism, which is simply a specific kind of criminal violence.

Girard begins by talking about sacrifice (derived from the Latin *sacrificium*, an offering to a deity); the two Latin root words for this term are *sacer* (holy) and *facio* (to make). Thus, to sacrifice means to make holy. Girard notes that in "many rituals the sacrificial act assumes two opposing aspects, appearing at times as a sacred obligation to be neglected at grave peril, and other times as a sort of criminal activity entailing perils of equal activity."[17] Thus, one can see that a sacrifice can have a nuanced, dual meaning. Further, Girard says that, "(i)f a sacrifice resembles criminal violence, we may say that there is, inversely, hardly any form of violence that cannot be described in terms of sacrifice as Greek tragedy clearly reveals."[18]

Girard says this about the sacred and violence:

> *The sacred consists of all those forces whose dominance over man increases or seems to increase in proportion to man's efforts to master them. Tempests, forest fires, and plagues, among other phenomena, may be classified as sacred. Far outranking these, however, though in a far less obvious manner, stands human violence—violence seen as something exterior to man and henceforth as part of all the other outside forces [that] threaten mankind. Violence is the heart and soul of the sacred.*[19]

What is this all about? To understand what Girard means, it is important to know what his assumptions about human nature are. First, he believes that human beings are *mimetic* by nature (*mimetes* in ancient Greek means an imitator); that is to say, "we learn everything from others" and we also "want what they have." And it is the *desire* to have what others have that leads to acts of violence.[20] Additionally, Girard examines "the metaphors and archetypes of violence in the Master Stories of the great religions." He analyzed the manner in which they shape human culture.[21] In other words, Girard thinks that everyone in a given culture has been steeped in the religious myths that permeate that culture, and that people can be unconsciously influenced in their behavior as they "imitate" the heroes of these stories. As people begin to imitate the heroes or generations of the past, they compete with one another as to "who gets it right"—that is, who is acting most like the hero or in accordance with the tradition. Eventually, according to J. Harold Ellens, a religious studies scholar who explains Girard's theory, the "mimetic and competitive process eventually becomes institutionalized in the structure of dogmas, orthodoxies, codes of social control and rituals."[22] Then, all of this will lead to judgments and condemnation of those who do not try to conform to the expected behaviors, or perhaps have tried too hard and excelled in performing as expected, when the majority has not. Finally, it happens that both those who did not conform to the expected model or were "overachievers" must then be removed (i.e., killed); hence, they are sacrificed.

What does the sacrifice or elimination of those who were underperformers or overachievers accomplish? According to Girard, "society is seeking to deflect upon a relatively indifferent victim, a 'sacrificeable' victim, the violence that would otherwise be vented on its own members, the people that it most desires to protect."[23] He also says that the "sacrifice serves to protect the entire community from its *own* violence; it prompts the entire community to choose victims outside itself …. the purpose of the sacrifice is to restore harmony to the community, to reinforce the social fabric."[24] After the sacrifice and the rejected person or group has been eliminated, then society justifies what happened.

This justification can "take the form of remembering the eliminated figure (or group) as a victim of his own evil, thus a symbol of the purification of society."

Interestingly, Girard mentions that, if our own system (of justice) seems more rational (than the system of sacrifice just described), it is "because it conforms more strictly to the principle of vengeance. Its insistence on the punishment of the guilty underlines this fact."[25]

To apply Girard's theory to religious terrorism, think of the events of recent years; for example, the attacks on 9/11. First, jihadists pronounced a litany of the many ways in which, in their view, the West had failed to measure up to the religious standards the Islamists held; then, there followed the negative judgments and the pronouncements of a "holy war" to destroy those in the West who had been lost to recalcitrance or ignorance. The horrific attacks occurred, followed next by the justifications that "the Great Satan" had gotten what it deserved. Evidence of this justification was seen months after the attacks, when some individuals in the Persian Gulf region commemorated and celebrated the 9/11 attacks by wearing T-shirts bearing images of the blazing, toppling World Trade Towers.

In summary, we can see that there are three parts to the mimetic process of using violence to reduce conflict in a society that René Girard described: (1) the codification of control structures or prohibitions; (2) the creation of rituals for enacting both the event of redemptive violence and the patterns of required conformity in society; and (3) the killing of the scapegoat(s).[26] Next, we'll focus on the second of these elements, "the rituals for enacting the event of redemptive violence."

As this chapter is being written, probably no more shocking ritual of redemptive violence (i.e., the type described by Girard) can be seen than the beheading of individuals by jihadists. There is a ritual that is followed: a statement is read by the victim, then a statement by the jihadists justifying their actions (the beheading), followed by the graphic display of the mutilated body. How can such brutality be explained? Arthur Saniotis argues that such jihadists should not be dismissed as simply "crazy," but instead be seen as *liminal beings* "because radical Islamist violence is diversifying and becoming increasingly creative and unpredictable."[27]

Perhaps you will recall our discussion in Chapter Four on the work of Victor Turner, who wrote about ritual behavior and his idea of the *limen* (e.g., threshold), where there is a blurring of the boundaries. So, when a person leaves the ordinary social structures, they enter a "liminal state," which Turner maintains is a kind of "magical state in which individuals are allowed to create new kinds of symbolism, unencumbered by the constrictions of status, privilege, and class, often via ludic [playful] or highly symbolic performance."[28] Jihadists have entered a liminal state by entering lawless zones—that is, committing unconventional and lethal acts against their victims.

We also must remember the symbolic nature of such terrorist events. A symbol is something that represents something else, and it can also be a vehicle for the expression of an emotion. Thus, in writing about religious terrorism, Juergensmeyer says that "such explosive scenarios are not tactics, directed toward an immediate, earthly, or strategic goal, but dramatic events intended to impress for their symbolic significance. As such, they can be analyzed as would any other symbol, ritual, or sacred drama."[29] These terrorist acts, according to Juergensmeyer, are like rituals that invoke the imagery of a cosmic war. Juergensmeyer notes that a confrontation is likely to be characterized as a "cosmic war" when three conditions occur: (1) the struggle is perceived as a defense of a basic identity and dignity; (2) losing the struggle would be unthinkable; and (3) the struggle is blocked and cannot be won in real time or real terms. The idea of a cosmic war gives a "sense of destiny and importance to men who find the modern world to be stifling, chaotic, and dangerously out of control."[30]

And it can be said that the "savage nature of religious violence derives from its perpetrators transposing 'images of divine struggle' ... [that are used] in the service of worldly political battles." The world is split into a dualistic view: there is the good, and there is the bad. This cosmic war of the terrorists is portrayed by them as an unending conflict between the opposing forces of good and evil. In such a battle, the jihadists believe that one cannot compromise with the enemy—because he is seen as evil—but rather, he must be destroyed.

The ritualized beheadings are a way for the jihadists to symbolically restore their "existential autonomy"—to show that the West is powerless to stop them. Saniotis describes this in the following way:

> the performative feature of these killings positions the internet as a crucible for new ritualized forms for restoring existential autonomy to Jihadists. Consider the sacrificial nature of these killings, the conflation of religious and profane discourse in the statements, the manner in which the hostages' heads were severed and displayed on their bodies; these are similar to sacrificial rites in various religions that may incite both performers and audience "awesome fascination" ... that the apparent fascination with such "spectacle killings" is because "the symbolic sacrifice of life is unthinkable ... in our contemporary times."[31]

There is a "magical" power to such destructive acts as the beheadings because of the fear they can cause among the Internet or television audience. Saniotis says this about the jihadists: "their actions seek to re-enchant the world with sacred meaning." What he means is that, by using violence, they have evoked the sacred, and it (e.g., violence) becomes "a means for restoring the power of the sacred cosmos in an otherwise 'disenchanted world' characterized by rationalization and secularization." Additionally, the jihadists may feel that such rituals have given them magico-religious powers that enable them to achieve their goals.

This phenomenon is called "symbolic empowerment" by Juergensmeyer, who observes that "(i)n all cases, the act of being involved in violence provided a sense of empowerment disproportionately greater than what the violence actually achieved."[32]

In concluding this section on theoretical explanations for religious violence, it is important to keep in mind that there are many similarities among the different types of religious groups that employ violence. One sees the common factors of alienation and humiliation, as well as a sense that things would be better if things returned to the "old ways." In speaking about the similarities among violent religious groups, Juergensmeyer declares the following:

> The radical religious movements that emerged from these cultures of violence throughout the world are remarkably similar, be they Christian, Jewish, Muslim, Buddhist, or Sikh. What they have in common are three things. First, they have rejected compromises with liberal values and secular institutions that were made by most mainstream religious leaders and organizations. Second, they refuse to observe the boundaries that secular society has imposed on religion—keeping it private rather than allowing it to intrude into public spaces. And third, they have replaced what they regard as weak modern substitutes with the more vibrant and demanding forms of religion that they imagine to be part of their tradition's beginnings.[33]

CHAPTER SUMMARY

In this chapter, we have explored both the basic motivations for religious terrorism, as well as three of the theories that can be used to understand the phenomenon. The two commonly found motivations are alienation and humiliation. A person who feels alienated is one who believes that society has failed her—so, she no longer trusts the institutions in society and looks for a substitute. Those who feel humiliated may have suffered economic hardships or may have been living in an occupied area that is controlled by another government, either directly or indirectly, through economic and political meddling. Individuals can be drawn to radical religious beliefs in response to feeling alienated or humiliated, or both. They may imagine themselves to be representing and defending ancient faiths, but the reality is that they have often created a traditional religion that is not really the ancient faith, but something that is more reflective of their own fears, needs, and desires.

Terror Management Theory (TMT) examines how an individual's existential concerns can lead a person to choose violent solutions to ethno-political conflicts. When an individual has heightened concerns about mortality (death), he tends to grasp more closely to his worldview. And when that worldview is threatened and the individual has heightened concerns about mortality, the person may be drawn into a violent response. The staircase to terrorism is a model that suggests that most people never consider terrorism, but when a person has a desire to be upwardly mobile—and those desires are thwarted—he can begin to climb a staircase that takes him along a series of steps that ultimately lead to no other choice than violence. Both of these models are used to explain terrorism generally, but can be applied in the explanation of religious terrorism as well.

The third theory looks at violence and the sacred. The theory suggests that human beings tend to be mimetic and imitate the heroes in religious stories and compete with one another. The competition leads to negative judgments about nonconformists or those who do not measure up, and there is a drive to eliminate them. Killing becomes sacred—a sacrifice—and serves as a way of bringing unity to a group and dissipating internal tensions. Thus, this theory examines the interaction between terrorism and religiously symbolic activity.

END NOTES

1. "Alienation." In *World of Sociology* (Farmington, MI: Gale, 2001). http://scroll.lib.westfield.ma.edu:4826/content/entry/worldsocs/alienation/0 (accessed Nov. 18, 2014.)

2. Levi, Ken. "Jonestown and Religious Commitment in the 1970s." In *Violence and Religious Commitment: Implications of Jim Jones's Peoples Temple Movement*, ed. Ken Levi (University Park: Pennsylvania State University Press, 1982), 4.

3. Juergensmeyer, Mark. *Terror in the Mind of God: The Global Rise of Religious Violence* (Berkeley: University of California Press, 2000), 10.

4. Insko, Jeffrey. "Christian Identity." In *Conspiracy Theories in American History* (Santa Barbara, CA: ABC-CLIO, 2003). http://scroll.lib.westfield.ma.edu:4826/content/entry/abcconspir/christian_identity/0 (accessed Nov. 18, 2014.)

5. Juergensmeyer, 35.

6. Gilligan, James. *Violence: Reflections on a National Epidemic* (New York: Putnam, 1996).

7. Beck, Aaron T. *Prisoners of Hate: The Cognitive Basis of Anger, Hostility, and Violence* (New York: HarperCollins, 1999), 69.

8. Juergensmeyer, 191, 218.

9. Juergensmeyer, Mark. *Global Rebellion: Religious Challenges to the Secular State, from Christian Militias to Al Qaeda* (Berkeley: University of California Press, 2009), 44.

10. Hirschberger, Gilad, and Tom Pyszczynski. "An existential perspective on violent solutions to ethno-political conflict." In *Human Aggression and Violence: Causes, Manifestations, and Consequences* (Washington, DC: American Psychological Association, 2011), 297–314.

11. Pyszczynski, T., A. Abdollahi, S. Solomon, J. Greenberg, F. Cohen, and D. Weise. (2006). "Mortality Salience, Martyrdom, and Military Might: The Great Satan Versus the Axis of Evil." *Personality and Social Psychology Bulletin* 32, 525–537.

12. Moghaddam, Fathali M., Zachary Warren, and Karen Love. "Religion and the Staircase to Terrorism." In *Handbook of the Psychology of Religion and Spirituality*, 2nd ed. Raymond F. Paloutizian and Crystal L. Park, eds. (New York: Guilford Press, 2013), 632–648.

13. Moghaddam, et al., 643.

14. Moghaddam, et al., 644.

15. Moghaddam, et al., 645.

16. Lygre, Ragnhild B., et al. "Terrorism as a process: A critical review of Moghaddam's 'Staircase to Terrorism.'" *Scandinavian Journal of Psychology* 52, no. 6 (Dec. 2011): 609–616.

17. Girard, René. *Violence and the Sacred*, trans. Patrick Gregory (Baltimore: Johns Hopkins Press, 1979), 1.

18. Girard, 1.

19. Girard, 31.

20. McGuire, Cheryl. "Judaism, Christianity, and Girard: The Violent Messiahs." In *The Destructive Power of Religion: Violence in Judaism, Christianity, and Islam*, vol. 2, ed. J. Harold Ellens (Westport: Praeger, 2004), 57.

21. Ellens, J. Harold. "Religious Metaphors Can Kill." In *The Destructive Power of Religion: Violence in Judaism, Christianity, and Islam*, vol. 1, ed. J. Harold Ellens (Westport: Praeger, 2004), 264.

22. Ellens, 265.

23. Girard, 4.

24. Girard, 8.

25. Girard, 22.

26. Ellens, 266.

27. Saniotis, Arthur. "Re-Enchanting Terrorism: Jihadists as Liminal Beings." *Studies in Conflict and Terrorism* (2005) 28: 533–545.

28. Saniotis, 534.

29. Juergensmeyer, *Terror in the Mind of God*, 122.

30. Juergensmeyer, *Terror in the Mind of God*, 159, 190.

31. Saniotis, 537.

32. Juergensmeyer, *Terror in the Mind of God*, 188.

33. Juergensmeyer, *Terror in the Mind of God*, 221.

16. Religion and Virtues in the Lives of Police Officers

Thoughts on *My Father and His Partner*

By James F. Keenan, SJ

As I approach this topic, I realize that there is very little material published on it. When one turns to religion and the police, one finds research that highlights when police are co-opted into political face-offs about religion. For instance, in *Lethal Allies: British Collusion in Ireland*, Anne Cadwallader describes the collusion between the police and the Protestant loyalists in the killing of Catholics during the "troubles" in Northern Ireland.[1] But similar stories are found elsewhere as well.

The few scholarly articles on virtue and the police are, for the most part, about particular situations in which the researcher is concerned with the character dispositions of the police. For instance, in "Police Officer Attitudes and Use of Discretion in Situations Involving the Mentally Ill: The Need to Narrow the Focus," the authors recognize that many scholars argue that often enough the police are the first civil servants who encounter persons suffering from mental illness and that this forces the police into a precarious position of being "primary gatekeepers." Often, they determine whether the mental health system or the criminal justice system can best meet the needs of a psychologically disordered individual, and the authors argue what further research they need to do to apprise the situation, including the question of the relationship of police officers to the community they patrol.[2]

The only work that deals with the question of virtue and its impact on a police officer's character is Edwin Delattre's very laudable

Character and Cops: Ethics in Policing. This very impressive and sizable work (over 550 pages), first published in 1989, is in its sixth edition.[3] Its foundational character development material is based on the insights of some of the best philosophers known, both classical and contemporary. While conceptually well developed, it is very accessible, in part because Delattre has a natural capacity to relate the concepts to ordinary, familiar occurrences.

For the most part, it serves to train police officers to be moral so as to perform well their duties for the good of the community and the nation. It specifically focuses on integrity and trustworthiness as the cardinal virtues of police life. Behind the integrity issue is the topic of corruption, and behind the trustworthiness is the reliance of the citizen on the police officer. Throughout, there are common, ordinary occasions described in which we see by a police officer's detail opportunities for moral excellence. It is instructive in a compelling way, especially highlighting the critical claim of personal integrity as foundational for service.

Its strongest trait is that throughout the book, Delattre enters into a police officer's "head"; that is, into her or his own particular professional moral logic as a police officer. In that moral logic, a police officer realizes that in many instances, her own need to think critically and quickly in urgent situations deserves further reflection. Delattre provides that further reflection. His work is sympathetic to a police officer's way of thinking and acting, and Delattre assumes the role of a moral dialogue partner with the thinking, but unspeaking, police reader. Whether a police officer is faced with the mistaken judgment of an individual or of a community, the betrayal of trust by a "bad cop," or the impact of injury or death to one's partner, the author has a deeply compassionate stance, capable of appreciating the sentiments of his readers, in particular that sometimes the more adversarial stance between police officer and others comes not from the police, but from the other.

VIRTUE

In my view, Delattre provides a significant invitation to police officers to consider their vocational character development. I want to take a different tack. I would rather not write as an ethicist another instructive essay for police officers; I would rather write about what a future ethicist learned from a police officer—his father—about character formation and virtue.

My father, Francis A. Keenan, was a police officer in New York City from 1951 to 1971. He rose through the ranks of the department, working in several locations, among them Williamsburg, the Youth Squad, and finally, Manhattan South Homicide, where he was a sergeant-detective.

He was a very fine story-teller, and I remember many of his stories; he had a life that was fairly exciting in my book. As a boy growing up, I knew that he was. Besides, after hearing these stories as a little boy , I developed an appreciation for his vocabulary—after all, what six-year-old knows what a "perp" (or perpetrator) is?

I would like to share what I learned from him because they became lessons that affected my interests in ethics. As I relate these insights, you will see that in many ways, police officers, in order to be police officers, actually define themselves by ethics, or at least an ethical logic that guides them.

Let me add that, although the stories I tell here are nameless, I can remember every name, even though these stories are from when I was a boy living in Brooklyn until the age of 13 and then from 13 to 17 years of age on Long Island. The stories made vivid imprints in my memory, unforgettable impressions.

In Brooklyn, my father was deeply involved in the neighborhood. Even though we lived in Flatbush and Flatlands and he never had an assignment in the neighborhood, still he was the man to whom everyone in our neighborhood went. One day, I remember a knock on the back door. Our babysitter, a young woman who lived only two houses down, came in crying and beseeching my father to see her mother, who had collapsed. She had called the ambulance, but after she made that call she came to get my father next. My dad rushed over, but our neighbor was already, unfortunately, dying.

Another day, my dad saw a police car go surging down our street in pursuit of someone. My father took off after him, with all sorts of neighbors directing my father to find the suspect, who was hiding behind a garage at the end of the street. The neighbors were very proud of him when he caught the suspect. Effectively, my father worked two beats: his precinct and our neighborhood.

As neighbors depended on him, he cared for them. I remember one day that the daughter of one of our neighbors had been arrested in a drug ring sting. She was only about seven years older than I, and photos of her arrest were in the newspapers. Neither my family nor I knew her well, though we lived on the same block in Brooklyn, but in that context, everyone knew one another.

What I did not know, but later learned from my mom, was that my dad knew ahead of her arrest that she was in trouble and had warned her parents that their daughter was hanging around with drug dealers and that they should try to get her out of the network before she was arrested. When he told them this, they told him to leave their home. Later, a few weeks after her arrest, the family moved away from the neighborhood.

I often think of what ethical prudence he had that prompted him to warn a neighbor about their child. I know that he was not on the investigation, but obviously he had heard about it. Had a fellow officer told him? I do not know. Moreover, though we were not friends with the family, my father was clearly more concerned with the family's well-being than with some more remote notion of the law-and-order demands that the daughter be punished and arrested.

His prudence was something I admired. I am not sure if other police officers would have done the same thing, but I am sure his friends would have, and most certainly his partner, Frank Tornabene. Frank, my father, and our families did everything together.

My father was proud of the discretionary prudence that he occasionally exercised. It was a prudence that was at once apart from the law, yet in keeping with the law. I learned from my father that the law does not tell us everything about a matter. As in informing the family about their daughter, my father taught me that the law's spirit had to be understood and interpreted. In this case, he felt that if he could get the daughter to trust the parents, maybe they could get their daughter out of bad company. That was, after all, what the law was seeking in this instance.

What I did not understand then, but what I would learn later, was that the virtue for interpreting the law was *epikeia*.[4] Epikeia is the word the Greeks used to say that someone knew how to interpret the law. Think here of the Supreme Court Justices. What makes them qualified to interpret the law? Epikeia! I think that good police officers have the same virtue. My father was teaching me that the application of the law requires the same humanity that articulated and promulgated the law in the first place.

Relationality was really what animated my father's discretionary judgments. After all, this is what the law wants, for the law exists for the common good, as Thomas Aquinas tells us in the famous definition of law in the *Summa Theologiae*: "an ordinance of reason for the common good, made by him who has care of the community, and promulgated."[5] Law instructs us to build through human reason toward the common good; that is, the well-being of all in the community to which we belong.

My colleague, Cathleen Kaveny, provides an updated view of that definition in her book, *Law's Virtues: Fostering Autonomy and Solidarity in American Society*.[6] There, she argues that the law protects both our autonomy and our relatedness toward our solidarity with one another by promoting the common good. The three goods are intimately linked. This is how I saw my father act with the law.

Another instance of my father understanding the law as something that must be prudently applied—that is, with compassionate discretion—is when he dispensed discretionary justice. In the 1950s and the 1960s, drunk driving had different sanctions than it does today, but if my father encountered a drunk driver who had no previous citations, who had a family, and who seemed to have become inebriated at some sort of social function, he would take pity on the driver (at that time, almost always a man). He would take the car keys of the driver and toss them in the sewer.

My father thought there was something redemptive in this action. The driver would not have been arrested, nor earned a police record, thus jeopardizing his ability to remain his family's breadwinner. By the same token, the loss of his car keys and the humiliation of his having to sleep it off on the streets or to wander home in an alcoholic fog to his wife without his car was enough of a shaming lesson to keep the driver from another drunk-driving episode.

Along with his prudential judgments and insights, my father had sayings or aphorisms that he would share. In order to stress to my siblings and me that we should think before we speak, he would say, "a spoken word can never be retracted; a written word can always be erased."

Along with prudence, my father taught me about moral integrity. When I was in high school, living on Long Island, we went into the city one day. We were in the car and we saw some women standing on the corner soliciting customers. By this point in my boyhood I realized that they were prostitutes. After we parked the car and were now walking, my father told me he thought that prostitutes were the most honest people he ever met. He talked about their backgrounds, their needs, and their honesty. He felt that other police officers like him thought the same way. If he asked a sex worker to identify someone or to assess what had occurred in a criminal situation, he felt that whatever the sex worker said would be closer to the truth than anyone else's account would be.

He was obviously teaching me that integrity was deeper than appearances and that credible people were often people in very limited situations. Later in my life, I would realize that a person's goodness was different from the rightness of the life they lived. A person's goodness is like their moral effort; that is, a person's goodness is about whether one strives for right as best as one can, about whether they bother to love. I think my dad was able to recognize that in their horrible profession, the sex workers were able to be true and loving of their families, neighbors, and friends in ways that others, with many greater social goods, were not.

Conversely, he thought their pimps were the lowest of people. Way before we had a concept like human trafficking, my father recognized the pimp as a predatory man who kept others in slavery. He felt that they were people who brutalized others and who managed to lose their humanity in the process.

These two ends of the moral spectrum, the sex worker and the pimp, gave me an underlying ruler with which I would be able to train my own moral intuitions.

RELIGION

Behind all this moral instruction was grace. My dad had a strong faith; like many of his colleagues, he was a practicing Catholic. He went to Sunday mass, taught us the rosary that we prayed on Sunday nights, and was a member of the Holy Name Society.

He believed in prayer. I remember telling him that I prayed to St. Joseph for him, especially for a promotion that he was hoping for. One day, he learned he got the promotion and was convinced that his promotion was such a long shot that it could only be by the prayer and not his record that he was promoted, though he was very proud of his record.

Grace for him was tangible. Like the answer to my prayer, my father thought that where he was in life, hard as he worked to be there, was, after all, a blessing. Not surprisingly, "Amazing Grace" was his favorite religious song. He often told us that when he died, there was only one thing we were to attend to: make sure "Amazing Grace" was played at his funeral. And we did.

Another time, while we were walking in the city, my father suddenly took out his wallet and gave a man down on his luck a dollar. "Why did you do that?" I asked. "It could have been me." I don't know why at that moment the insight had come to him. We had passed men begging before, but this time, unsolicited, my father gave the man this dollar. Why then?

My father had these redeeming qualities about him in which, I think, he felt he was always close to the life of the beggar, the drunk driver, or the sex worker. We were, after all, working class, and bad fortune was just around the corner, but he believed as precarious as our condition was, we should not be fearful, but rather grateful. That is why he gave the man the money: it was an act of compassion that was also an act of gratitude.

I think my father specifically appreciated the vulnerability of his and our situation. If there was one sense of the police officer's identity then that was different from what it is today, it is this sense of vulnerability. He lived with the vulnerability daily; he never abandoned or suppressed it.

For instance, wherever my father went, he went with his gun. Everywhere. Whenever we went to friends' or family's homes, he would ask the host to come with him into their kitchen and he would usually look for the cupboard above a refrigerator, something high enough that no child could access. He would ask the host if he could put it up there. Strangely enough, there was never any expression of unease. On the contrary, they knew my father was a police officer and that he kept a gun.

But the gun inevitably became a topic of conversation. If there was one phrase my father repeated most often about his job, it was the answer to the question about what it felt like to use his gun. "I have never used my gun." It was a remarkable utterance that he made because he was very proud of his 20-year record. It was like his not arresting that drunk driver; my father liked not having to harm anyone. He liked that he could stay away from the use of the gun. It was a line he was glad to never have crossed. Inevitably, people would look to my father as a fairly simple man with very clear values about his humanity.

The precariousness of our lives was always on his mind, I believe. One time, he took me to see a friend of his. We drove to the "projects," as subsidized housing was called at the time. His friend, another police officer, had moved into the projects, and my father wanted to see how he was. The friend acknowledged that there were challenges, but it wasn't half bad. I remember my father saying good-bye, and while walking away saying to me, "Could you imagine living here?" He wasn't waiting for an answer; he was counting his blessings.

The precariousness of our lives was, nonetheless, evident even in our neighborhood. Our car, for instance, would get stolen from time to time, taken on a joyride by some kids, my father would say. Whenever the car was stolen, he would eventually find it, probably through his fellow police officers. In time, he learned to leave only a little gas in the car so that if anyone stole it, they couldn't get too far.

Once, a good neighbor of ours saw the car go by his house and the neighbor waved and shouted, "Hey, Frank." Later, he asked my father why he didn't wave back. "Because that wasn't me; it was someone driving my car away and instead of stopping them, you were waving to them!" The two of them laughed and laughed.

The precariousness of our lives always came out, like this story, in my father's sense of humor. My father loved telling very funny stories. Often, they were cop stories, but there were stories about our frailties, our vulnerabilities, our good luck (or grace) of not having to pay for occasional, predictable, stupidities. It was like a scene from *Barney Miller*, the television show he thought was the closest approximation to his office.

Whenever he was with his partner, Frank Tornabene, the stories were the funniest because each would interject into the other's stories, always riddling the narratives with irony and insight, prompting even stronger laughter and longer tales. They were always about the police force, and Frank and my father couldn't keep themselves from telling the stories. They loved these stories that included at times the folly of a criminal's actions or their own stupidity. They laughed at themselves as much as they laughed at others. We were all in the comedy together, a very Catholic disposition.

Because my father was a police officer, we had great relationships with other people. He was attuned to these relationships, each and every one. As a boy, I sometimes could never figure out why we were friends with some people. Once, during a Christmas season, I was leaving someone's home with my brother and sister and my parents. "How do we know these people?" I asked. "Frank and I got a call one night to take a woman who was going to have a baby to the hospital. She was later than we realized, and I delivered her firstborn in the back seat of the car." We were invited to her home every year about the time of his birth.

That ability to make, sustain, and develop relationships was a very moral capacity my father had. It made him, I think, a very good police officer. In turn, it explains why so many others put in him the trust they did. I have since thought that making and keeping relationships is the sign of an ethical person.

I have now become a moral theologian who teaches many, many people what moral reasoning is, what the virtues are, and what conscience is. My initial instruction came mostly from my father, at least the intuitive insights that guided his own moral logic. That moral logic was guided by his conscience, a part of him that was always quite apparent. It was, after all, the conscience of a cop that guided him who taught me.

END NOTES

1. Cadwallader, Anne. *Lethal Allies: British Collusion in Ireland* (London: Mercer Press, 2013).

2. Patch, Peter C., and Bruce A. Arrigo. "Police Officer Attitudes and Use of Discretion in Situations Involving the Mentally Ill: The Need to Narrow the Focus." *International Journal of Law and Psychiatry* 22.1 (1999) 23–35, at 23.

3. Delattre, Edwin. *Character and Cops: Ethics in Policing* (Washington, DC: AEI Press, 2011).

4. Aristotle's *Nicomachean Ethics* V. 10. 8, 1137a17ff.

5. Thomas Aquinas. *Summa Theologiae* (London: Burns Oates and Washbourne, Ltd., 1927), I. II. 90.4c.

6. Kaveny, Cathleen. *Law's Virtues: Fostering Autonomy and Solidarity in American Society* (Washington, DC: Georgetown University, 2012).

17. An Institution in Search of Meaning

By Andrew Skotnicki

I t is now commonplace for organizations to create and publicize mission statements. Meant to inspire a sense of identity and devotion among both employees and the public at large, one generally need not look far in the lobby of an institution's headquarters, on its website, or perhaps even on the facade of a building or, as in the case of the police, emblazoned on each squad car (e.g., "To Serve and Protect") to learn the highest articulated aspirations of a given firm or association. One study revealed that the Boston-based Bain & Company recently reported "that of the 400 firms it surveyed, nine out of ten had used a mission statement some time in the last five years—thus making it the most popular management tool deployed in recent decades."[1]

There is good reason for this strategy. Whether from the viewpoint of religious organizations or Fortune 500 companies, an institution that has lost touch with its history and the qualitative principles and objectives that inspired its inception—its raison d'être—is one that will lack the capacity to successfully process new information and especially to withstand and adapt to the new challenges that inevitably confront its day-to-day operation and the morale and cohesiveness of its members. As Jurgen Habermas writes: "[A] social system has lost its identity as soon as later generations no longer recognize themselves within the once constitutive tradition."[2]

Despite the necessity on both a theoretical and practical level for an organization to attend to its founding ideals, however, the reality of institutional life does not easily lend itself to mission-oriented reflection on both its short- and long-term goals. Gregory Baum remarks that each organization exhibits an inevitable tension between mission and maintenance, between the vision of its founders and the day-to-day needs of managing and integrating the various components of the corporate or institutional structure. He asks the reader to imagine a typical board meeting, wherein a particularly energetic colleague proposes a bold initiative to "shake up" the stolid and once successful strategies beginning to show signs of entrenchment in the midst of shifting social and cultural dynamics. The proposal, Baum suggests, will inevitably be challenged by someone whose focus is fixed upon the logic of maintenance, who "will explain the difficulties the proposed activities will create: there is not enough money; the staff is already overburdened; the supporters of the organization will be offended; many people, possibly the most influential in society, will not like it."[3] Baum's contention is that social scientific studies and monographs by scholars in the field of management repeatedly reveal "that in all large organizations the logic of maintenance tends to become dominant and overshadow the logic of mission."[4]

The thesis to be presented here is that the contemporary prison in the United States and in many other countries of the world is an institution that has lost virtually all contact with its original mission. Lacking an ongoing conversation between its initial motivation and strategy, located in the Catholic sacramental and monastic systems, and its current manifestation, it has not only failed to confront adequately significant political, economic, racial, and social challenges that call its very existence into question, it has also—in the best of cases—become virtually aimless due to a cacophony of competing voices, interests, and theoretical perspectives; in the worst of cases, it has become a system for sale to profit-seeking private management firms and business concerns intent on exploiting the massive human energy housed within its sprawling network of facilities.[5]

The chapter will first reveal the role that religion in general, and the Catholic Church in particular, have played in the development of modern institutions of confinement. It will then explore the spiritual and psychological dynamics that led to the development of the prison and the integrated intra-institutional network that reinforced the purpose of incarceration. Finally, it will argue that the present emphasis in modern penology, either on retribution and social control or on therapeutic, medical, and cost/benefit models of treatment has, if anything, underscored the continued relevance of the motives and practices of the early Church as rates of recidivism continue to rise, demonstrating with vivid clarity the regrettable consequences that ensue when an institution has forgotten the very reason why it came into existence.

THE MISSION OF THE PRISON

It would probably come as a surprise to many that the prison is a very late innovation in the history of criminal justice. If we assume the prison to be an institutionalized expression of social disapproval in which detention is meted out in segments of time upon those convicted in a court of law for purposes such as rehabilitation, retribution, deterrence, or incapacitation, then the prison did not appear until the end of the 18th century in England, and in the United States, not until the early 19th century.[6]

Prior to that time, no society developed a penal system per se. Prisons were, first of all, uneconomical. It is costly to build and maintain a facility, particularly one wherein the most dangerous or disreputable persons are housed. By far, the most ancient, commonly employed and efficient means of punishment has been the fine.[7] The other frequently used practices have been exile and physical violence. The former was a benefit generally provided for the rich. In ancient Greece, for example, Socrates was given the opportunity to leave Athens and only suffered death by poison when he refused the offer.[8] For the indigent, the outcast, the predatory, and the despised, societies have devised any number of violent ways to abuse, maim, or destroy them.[9]

Detention, when employed, was a pragmatic, ad hoc affair. Most frequently, suspects, enemies, hostages, or the condemned were housed in makeshift quarters within a castle or placed in a gatehouse or town wall. This approach is verified in the etymology of the word jail, which derives from the Latin word, caveola, meaning a hollow cavity or a cage.[10]

The very idea that a culprit would be housed in a separate dwelling or "cell" for the idea of reformation or doing penance (penitentiary) would have been just as unthinkable in the ancient world as it was for the most part in the West until the turn of the 19th century. It was in the unique sociology of the early Christian communities and prototypical monasteries, with an equally unique theology and code of ethics, that the practice of "excommunication" for a determinate or indeterminate amount of time, depending on the given ecclesiastical authority, was instituted.

The early Christians already possessed a correctional methodology from the gospels. In one passage, Jesus tells his disciples that if an infraction occurs between two persons, the offended party must first seek redress from the offender privately; failure to win accord should be followed by an intervention by several communal members; if this too fails, then the matter should be brought before the church community; and if the offender does not abide by the church, then he or she should be treated "as a Gentile or a tax collector" (Mt 18:15–17; Lk 17:3–4).[11] This normally implied a temporary exile from the fellowship until the guilty party made amends for the sin and sought reinstatement.

The history of penance in the Catholic Church is both long and complex, but its origin and structure—despite variations in time and place—are reducible to several key ideas that would lay the template for the development of criminal justice in the West.

First, the Christians had to develop their own system of internal correction, as they were wary of any use of Roman courts due to injunctions against this in the New Testament (Lk 12:57–59; Mt 5:25–26; I Cor 6:1–8) and due also to their frequently brutal mistreatment at the hands of the Roman authorities.[12] Catalogs of sins enumerated in the gospels and writings of St. Paul normally provided the content of proscribed behavior.[13] For most offenses, exomologesis (the discipline required to address the fault) required a private and humble acknowledgement of sinful conduct, accompanied by prayer, almsgiving, and works of self-denial. Serious sins, however, required that the penitent come before the bishop or presbyter, or later, a church council, and receive the required penitential discipline.

Second, the leaders of the early Christian community not only had received a mandate from Christ to forgive sin (Mt 16:18–20; Jn 20:23), but also understood that the example left to them by Christ meant that all sin was capable of earning forgiveness and reconciliation of the offender within the community.[14]

Third, the actual development of the practice of penance, again with variations (particularly between the Eastern and Western Christian churches), involved several key elements. Upon confession of the offense before the leader of the assembly, hands were laid upon the guilty; they were enrolled in what was termed the ordo paenitentium (the order of penitents); and a "binding" penance was imposed. The term binding refers to the power given to St. Peter and his descendants by Christ to "bind" those seeking forgiveness and to "loose" them from disciplinary bonds once the necessary acts of mortification had been completed and the period of prescribed excommunication had come to an end (Mt 18:18). A garment known as the cilicium, or sackcloth, was placed upon the penitent to denote their status and motivate them to turn away from their sins. Also, members of the community were given the obligation to oversee the comportment of penitents and encourage them during the period of contrition.[15] Finally, after completion of the sentence, the offenders were brought back before the leader of the assembly, the cilicium was removed, and they were restored to their place within the community.[16]

What the penal historian finds here, in effect, are the basic rudiments of a correctional system: a legal code; a method of intervention in the lives of the delinquent; a hearing before a judge or leader of the community; a sentence given in which the offender is "excommunicated," often in segments of time; a procedure for overseeing the penitent during the time of exclusion; and a ritual of "loosing," in which the offender is reconciled to the community after the exculpatory demands have been met.

This basic structure derived from the practice of penance was given its enduring penal justification and architectural shape with the growth of monasticism. Beginning with the first extant monastic rule, that of Pachomius in the fourth century and especially in the rule of St. Benedict in the sixth century, the rudiments of monastic life created the idea of the prison as we know it today. The most fundamental of these rudiments is that monks take a vow of permanent stability. Once they entered the enclosure, they were literally prisoners for life, or to put it another way, the first formal prison in the West was the monastery. Of course, monks enter voluntarily and for the purpose of spiritual perfection, but there is abundant evidence that those who sought to flee their confinement were forced to return and endure penitential discipline.[17] There were also many instances of both ecclesiastical and royal officials confining unruly clerics or family members in local monasteries.[18] All of this was given official sanction in what appears to be the oldest surviving papal decree, that of Pope Siricius in the fourth century. Commenting on the unruly behavior of clerics who had violated both local and ecclesiastical norms, the pope ordered them to be sent to monasteries, confined in a room in which they would be given work (ergastulum), and in so doing, melt away their sins in penitential fire.[19]

Within the monasteries, each rule stipulates a formula for confronting the disruptive and/or destructive behavior of errant monks. In the case of Benedict, whose monasteries numbered in the thousands by the end of the first millennium, a penal system was developed that was based on the example from the gospel stated above: the wayward monk was to be spoken to privately after the first and second offenses and then brought before the entire community. It the third intervention also failed to inspire a change in conduct, the offender would be separated from the community, where he would eat alone and undergo fasting, although Benedict, ever solicitous of a lifelong member of the community, assigned a wise older monk to be a spiritual guide, lest the isolated individual be overcome by anger or self-pity.[20]

The other monastic rules had similar provisions for detaining malefactors.[21] There was thus an extensive prison complex throughout Christendom by the time of Gregory VII, who, in the 11th century, after a series of heated exchanges with secular princes who had been appointing bishops friendly to their parochial interests, declared the independence of the Catholic Church from all external influence. The resulting "revolution" not only instituted the first universal legal code, Canon Law, it also led Pope Boniface VIII in 1298 to normalize the prison throughout the Catholic world by inscribing its justification within the law of the church. His decree and others that followed by local bishops led to the building of prisons in each diocese for the confinement of clerics who had broken civil and ecclesiastical statutes. It was only a matter of time before secular authorities and secular legal codes, virtually all of which were patterned on Canon Law, began to imitate the Church and erect prisons of their own.[22]

THE SPIRITUAL AND PSYCHOLOGICAL ELEMENTS OF CONFINEMENT

It is the contention of this chapter that the penal system has lost touch with its mission: the set of assumptions that led to the idea that locking people up for a specific period of time is somehow beneficial to them and to the communities from which they come. While the justification for the practice can indeed be traced to specific elements of the sacrament of penance and the monastic life, the person seeking to place the various ideologies portraying the contemporary meaning of confinement in conversation with those motivating its original architects need not embrace the set of theological principles that animated the early Christian community. What I am suggesting is necessary, however, is to attend to the set of moral—and, for lack of a better word, psychological—assumptions, without which the prison would never have become such a ubiquitous institution in the Catholic Church. It was precisely these assumptions that inspired early secular attempts to introduce penal detention as an alternative to sanguinary punishments and most certainly provided the template for the two penitentiary models in the United States—Philadelphia and Auburn—that became the prototypes for most of the prisons throughout the world.[23]

What was the particular anthropology or theory of the human person that Benedict and the other founders of the monastic movement held as truthful? The entire Catholic ethical system, including penance, the contemplative life, and the institution of the prison, is based on a belief in the fundamental goodness of the human person. Being created in the image of God is more than a theological belief; it is the foundational starting point for moral action and reflection upon that action. While it would have been heretical to think that any human person could achieve moral perfection, there was clearly a belief among Benedict and other architects of the prison in a level of human perfectibility that enabled one to live in harmony with oneself, one's fellows, nature, and the divine. It was arguably this very belief and longing that prompted "normal" human beings to undergo a lifelong incarceration.[24] Moreover—this is particularly relevant for the history of the prison—there was a belief that, barring the distractions and self-preoccupation that due to socialization inevitably create and sustain a given person's parochial or dualistic worldview, the "true self" in every person is relational by nature, and thus meant to live in harmony with itself, its Creator, and all of creation.[25] It is precisely the insistent and insatiable hunger for this expansive harmony that generates human restlessness in its relentless pursuit of a sense of fullness and peace that is so often misdirected because of attachment to transient and finite ends. This error, called idolatry in theological terminology, leads inevitably to a narrow (and thus distorted) worldview, a divided consciousness marked by division, judgment, and suspicion of those outside one's cultural circle and, ultimately, violence.[26]

In other words, sin in theological terminology is nothing more than alienation from one's true self, from God, from nature, and from the human community; and alienation produces pain. Given this anthropological view, there would be little need in the monastic model of confinement to inflict punishment for its own sake, since the exclusion of the monk (or penitent) from the common life adds additional anguish to what the offense proves is already an anguished heart.[27] Hence, Benedict likens the abbot's role in regard to the offender as similar to that of Christ's image of the shepherd who went out looking for the lost sheep and who, upon finding it, "placed it on his own shoulders and carried it back to the flock."[28] The founders of the first prisons insisted that what was needed was a set of practices that enable the heart to reconnect to its deepest self and prepare it to reenter the social world. The acquisition, or reacquisition, of "prosocial" virtues is by nature painful, as it demands that some part of the person die and something new be born. So, Benedict saw to it that those in isolation would be visited by senpectae—"wise elderly brothers who know how to comfort the wavering brother as if in secret. By this means, they can urge him to make humble satisfaction and also console him so that he be not devoured by too much sorrow. But, as the apostle likewise says, let love for him be reaffirmed and let everyone pray for him."[29] A contemporary criminologist, Graham Newman, is among the few in his discipline who affirm the need for the penal system to reappropriate the original Christian approach. He states that the early penal experiments understood guilt in a fully moral way, "which is to say that the offender has a guilty mind, and that only by a series of ritually purgative functions can this guilt be assuaged." He then adds: "Unfortunately, penologists have lost sight of this important function of retribution, so that they have allowed punishments to destroy souls rather than save them."[30]

How the prison might once again save rather than destroy souls will be discussed in the final section.

THE FUTURE OF THE PRISON

There are several things we know about the state of criminal justice in the United States in this second decade of the 21st century. We know that we as a nation continue to rely on the prison as the dominant expression and symbol of social and legal recrimination against unlawful citizens. We also know that as a result of dissatisfaction with the rehabilitative, "penal welfare" model of systemic organization, new strategies based on retribution, deterrence, and incapacitation have led to an unprecedented increase in the number of confined persons, to the extent that America now imprisons more of its citizens and a higher percentage of its citizens than any nation on Earth.[31] We know that most of the approximately 675,000 men and women released from custody in any given year will not only be rearrested, but that the rates of recidivism continue to rise.[32] Finally, we know that for the first time in 40 years, there is not only a serious national conversation on the future of imprisonment, but also a host of initiatives in both state and national government as well as the academy to reform the correctional system.[33]

We began this chapter with the well-documented conviction that an institution out of touch with its founding vision and ethos is one that faces what Habermas calls a "legitimation crisis."[34] The material proof of this crisis is objectively apparent in recent statistical analysis, but the root cause of the crisis is the result of a formal or even meta-ethical error: the lack of any consensus among academics, policy makers, and penal officials about what exactly they are doing when they force persons to spend a period of their lives, or all of their lives, behind bars. Since the answer to that question is so much in dispute at present, two default principles have risen to the fore: order and law. Zygmunt Bauman states: "'Order' and 'norm' are sharp knives pressed against the society as it is. They are first and foremost about separation, amputation, excision, expurgation, exclusion … . they single out, circumscribe and stigmatize parts of reality denied the right to exist—destined for isolation, exile or extinction."[35]

Sociologists and legal philosophers remind us that law is by its nature a set of behavioral requirements made compelling by the violent means at the disposal of the state to ensure compliance.[36] Legal scholar Robert Cover corroborates this relation between law and violence. He states that, if convicted in a court of law, "the defendant customarily walks—escorted—to prolonged confinement … . most prisoners walk into prison because they know they will be dragged or beaten into prison if they don't walk. They do not organize force against being dragged because they know that if they wage this kind of battle they will lose— very possibly lose their lives."[37]

In an institution that is no longer challenged by or in conversation with its inherited past, the implicit violence of the court is often made explicit, if not by direct consent, then by a penal culture characterized often by judgment, indifference, and a belief in the justly deserved punishment of those whose deviation from the norm has rendered them "abnormal." From this perspective, "[i]t is the fault of the excluded that they did nothing, or not enough, to escape exclusion. … Excluding them is an act of good sense and justice; those who do the exclusion might feel sensible and righteous, as they become the defenders of law and order and guardians of values and standards of decency."[38]

This default institutional language of the self-righteous constraining the reprobate forms the "symbolic universe" of the system of confinement, reinforced continually in conversation, official documents, and internal memoranda; a language that is self-protective and defensive of alternate portrayals of the meaning of the "correctional experience."[39] And it is precisely within this universe that the vast array of well-intentioned educational, vocational, medical, and recovery programs are introduced. The common result is that even when offenders attempt to reform their lives, these programmatic spaces, what Erving

Goffman calls "islands of vivid, encapturing activity" within the "total institution" are repeatedly inundated beneath the "dead sea" of the penal environment that tends to compromise or deconstruct whatever positive motivations have been constructed.[40]

Within this environment, psychologists such as Craig Haney, who, like many social scientists, maintains that the experiential context is the most salient factor in predicting behavior, argues that in the contemporary prison, one must often assume an exterior persona to maintain one's safety, a demeanor characterized by "hyper vigilance, projecting a tough veneer, suppressing outward signs of emotion, and becoming generally distrustful of others." Such an exterior persona cannot help but colonize to varying degrees the moral center of all but the most resolute or self-determined persons: "[M]any people come to prison already having begun to think of themselves as marginal, as outlaw, as 'other.' In any event, prison tends to foist such an identity on new arrivals and then 'fix' or harden it by virtue of the way prisoners subsequently are treated, referred to, and looked at by many staff members … . Thus the experience of imprisonment instills its own sense of stigma, an often internalized version that compounds the effects of social stigma."[41]

The need for innovative experiments that are cognizant of the determinative role of the context of the penal environment in stimulating character formation is being addressed with greater frequency and emphasis in the academy, the legislative arena, and specific correctional institutions.[42] One such example is what are termed "faith-based prisons." They are patterned on the unique transformation of a detention facility by several Brazilian reformers in a way reminiscent of the original monastic prisons. When the newly sentenced offenders are delivered, chained hand and foot, their first experience is to be met by fellow prisoners, who remove the chains and say to them: "In this place you are chained, not by steel, but by the love of Christ."[43] The institutional atmosphere is then patterned on the inculcation of virtue, the development of practical life skills, and spiritual reformation. Currently, there are facilities in numerous countries around the world attempting to imitate the success of the Brazilian model.[44] What is ironic in this admirable, and in the current state of affairs, novel, development is that the information on how prisons ought to be constructed and organized has been part of the historical record for over 1500 years.

CONCLUSION

It is certainly not the intent of this essay to suggest that one must replicate the theological beliefs that animated the first penal experiments within the early Christian congregations and within the first monastic communities, but it is essential, in my opinion, that whatever prosocial effects are intended by the criminologists, politicians, and administrators who determine the ethos of contemporary corrections will only be attained consistently by studious attention to the anthropological, moral, and structural commitments of the Christians who laid the foundations for the prison as we know it today. These reasons include the belief that human beings are fundamentally good and capable of genuine contrition, character growth, and a harmonious existence in the world, despite whatever errors they may have made. Consequently, the practice of imprisonment would lose a core principle in its justification if a ritual of absolution or forgiveness, followed by active social reintegration, were not extended to the offender after the necessary time for repentance. Additionally, to be faithful to its mission, the prison must be understood as a place where reform and conversion are actively sought due to a belief that both are eminently achievable if the proper environment is created and if proper care is shown to those in custody.

Stated negatively, and not without some degree of sarcasm, it would be a betrayal of the very meaning of penal confinement to structure it solely in terms of punishment, or put differently, for the purpose of inflicting suffering upon the guilty. The early tradition tells us that one's alienation from one's own self, from God, and from the human community is the punishment. Time, solitude, compassionate companionship, and a deprivation of the easy substitutes that inoculate us from our inherent oneness with all are the necessary and only requirements for coming to one's true self.

The monastic model was the initial and truest template for incarceration. Despite whatever anomalies necessarily exist in institutions run by fallible people, it teaches us that anything less than a careful and sympathetic response to human destructiveness says more about the misplaced aggression of humans against their own waywardness than against any purported malevolence on the part of those who are made to pay the added price in suffering for the guilt of others. Stated simply, there were no prisons until there were monasteries. There will be no true reform of the prisons until they once again recover their monastic roots.

END NOTES

1. Bart, Christopher K. "Sex, Lies, and Mission Statements." *Business Horizons* 40 (1997), 9–18 at 9.

2. Habermas, Jurgen. *Legitimation Crisis*, trans. Thomas McCarthy (Boston: Beacon Press, 1975), 4. Concerning religious organizations, see Patricia Wittberg, *The Rise and Fall of Catholic Religious Orders* (Albany: State University of New York Press, 1994). From a business perspective, see Bowen H. McCoy, "The Parable of the Sadhu," *Harvard Business Review* (1983), 103–108; Jeffrey T. Polzer, "How Subgroup Interests and Reputations Moderate the Effect of Organizational Identification on Cooperation," *Journal of Management* 30 (2004), 71–96.

3. Baum, Gregory. *Compassion and Solidarity: The Church for Others* (Concord, Ontario: House of Anansi, 1987), 42.

4. Ibid 42–43. Both institutional language and role understandings are the result of "intersubjective sedimentation." A phenomenon wherein a "symbolic universe" is created, legitimated, and reproduced within a given social setting, to the exclusion of competing conceptions of reality. See Peter L. Berger and Thomas Luckmann, *The Social Construction of Reality* (New York: Anchor, 1966), 67–79, 92–104.

5. Shichor, David. *Punishment for Profit* (Thousand Oaks, CA: Sage Publications, 1995); Donna Selman and Pau Leighton, *Punishment for Sale* (Lanham, MD: Rowman & Littlefield, 2010); Andrew Skotnicki, "The Ethics of Prison Labor," *Journal of Catholic Social Thought* 9 (2012), 117–128.

6. Ignatieff, Michael. *A Just Measure of Pain* (New York: Pantheon, 1978); David Rothman, *The Discovery of the Asylum* (Boston: Little Brown, 1974), 1971; Andrew Skotnicki, *Religion and the Development of the American Penal System* (Lanham, MD: University Press of America, 2000).

7. Drapkin, Israel. *Crime and Punishment in the Ancient World* (Lexington, MA: Lexington Books, 1989); Julius Goebel, *Felony and Misdemeanor* (Philadelphia: University of Pennsylvania Press, 1976); John T. McNeill and Helena Gamer, *Medieval Handbooks of Penance* (New York: Columbia University Press, 1938).

8. Garnsey, Peter. *Social Status and Legal Privilege in the Roman Empire* (Oxford: Clarendon, 1970); Plato, "The Crito" in *Plato: Six Great Dialogues*, trans. Benjamin Jowett (Mineola, NY: Dover, 2007), 23–33.

9. Drapkin, *Crime and Punishment*; George Ives, *A History of Penal Methods* (Montclair, NJ: Patterson Smith, 1970); Edward Peters, "Prison Before the Prison." In Norval Morris and David J. Rothman, eds. *The Oxford History of the Prison* (New York: Oxford University Press, 1995), 3–47.

10. Dunbabin, Jean. *Captivity and Imprisonment in Medieval Europe, 1000–1300* (Houndmills, UK: Palgrave Macmillan, 2002), 23.

11. The irony of this final sanction is that it was precisely the Gentiles and tax collectors who were most amenable to Jesus' message and the ones most often pointed out as heirs of the Reign of God.

12. A decree from a Roman legal manual in the early fourth century describes the punishments experienced by many Christians during periods of persecution: "Those who commit capital crimes ... from the lower classes are crucified, burnt alive, or thrown to 'beasts.'" See Richard A. Bauman, *Crime and Punishment in Ancient Rome* (London and New York: Routledge, 1996), 1.

13. Meeks, Wayne A. *The Origins of Christian Morality* (New Haven and London: Yale University Press, 1993), 66–71.

14. Although the practice of penance as we know it now, a private interchange between priest and penitent, did not emerge until the sixth century; and although access to the sacrament was restricted, particularly in the West, also until the sixth century; the early Christian community was largely unanimous in its assertion that all sin was forgivable and offenders to be reconciled to the fellowship after suitable penance had been performed. See

Joseph Favazza, *The Order of Penitents* (Collegeville, MN: Liturgical Press, 1988); Cyril Vogel, "Sin and Penance." In Philippe Delhaye et al., *Pastoral Treatment of Sin* (New York: Desclee, 1968), 177–282.

15. Favazza, *Order of Penitents*, 24–47; Bernhard Poschmann, *Penance and the Anointing of the Sick*, trans. Francis Courtney, SJ (New York: Herder and Herder, 1964), 87–88; Vogel, "Sin and Penance," 228–232.

16. Particularly in the early centuries, there were at times more lifelong consequences to serious sins, such as sexual abstinence. See Favazza, *Order of Penitents*, 247–248; Vogel, "Sin and Penance," 239.

17. Gregory the Great. "Epistles." In *A Select Library of Nicene and Post-Nicene Fathers of the Christian Church*, vol. 12, trans. Rev. James Barmby (Grand Rapids: Wm. B. Eerdmans, 1956) Bk I, xlii. See also, Donald F. Logan, *Runaway Religious in Medieval England* (Cambridge: Cambridge University Press, 1996).

18. Skotnicki, Andrew. *Criminal Justice and the Catholic Church* (Lanham, MD: Rowman & Littlefield, 2008), 84–85.

19. Peters, "Prison Before the Prison," 28; Skotnicki, *Criminal Justice*, 83.

20. St. Benedict, *St. Benedict's Rule*, trans. Terrence G. Kardong (Collegeville, MN: Liturgical Press, 1996), 23–28.

21. The rule of Pachomius (d. 346) follows a similar pattern: "If someone is prone to slander, he is to be separated from the assembly of the brothers for seven days and only receive bread and water until he firmly proposes to convert from that sin." St. Pachomius, "Precepts and Judgments." In *Pachomian Koinonia*, vol. 2, trans. Armand Veilleux (Kalamazoo, MI: Cistercian Publications, 1981), 1, 4, 5.

22. Berman, Harold. *Law and Revolution* (Cambridge, MA: Harvard University Press, 1983); Gabriel LeBras, "Canon Law." In C. G. Crump and E. F. Jacobs, eds. *The Legacy of the Middle Ages* (Oxford: Clarendon Press, 1926), 321–361; Peters, "Prison Before the Prison."

23. On medieval secular prisons and their relation to Catholic culture, see Guy Geltner, *The Medieval Prison* (Princeton, NJ: Princeton University Press, 2008). On the influence of Catholic prison models on the development of the penitentiary, see Gustave de Beaumont and Alexis de Tocqueville, *On the Penitentiary System in the United States and Its Application in France*, trans. Francis Lieber (Philadelphia: Carey, Lea, and Blanchard, 1833); Luigi Cajani, "Surveillance and Redemption: The Case di Correzione of San Michele a Ripa in Rome." In Norbert Finzsch and Robert Jutte, eds. *Institutions of Confinement* (Washington, DC: German Historical Institute, 1996), 301–324; John Howard, *Prisons and Lazarettos* (Montclair, NJ: Patterson Smith, 1973) [originally published 1789]; Thorsten Sellin, "Dom Jean Mabillon: A Prison Reformer of the Seventeenth Century," *Journal of the American Institute of Criminal Law and Criminology* 17 (1927), 581–602.

24. The penal metaphor is not accidental for reasons already discussed. It was also used by contemplative monks and nuns to describe their lives. For example, St. Teresa of Avila writes about the convent in Toledo and its "inmates," while, in her autobiography, St. Therese of Lisieux states that she made herself "a prisoner at the age of fifteen." St. Teresa of Avila, *The Letters of St Teresa of Jesus*, 2 vols., trans. E. Allison Peers (London: Burns,

Oates, and Washbourne, 1966), I, 26; St. Therese of Lisieux, *Story of a Soul*, trans. John Clarke, OCD (Washington, DC: ICS Publications, 1975), 175.

25. Catholic mystical theology is a vast subject. Among the classical sources that speak of the need to overcome a dualist worldview, see Francisco De Osuna, *The Third Spiritual Alphabet*, trans. by a Benedictine of Stanbrook, New York (New York: Benziger, 1931), I, 2.; St. John of the Cross, "The Ascent of Mount Carmel." In *The Collected Works of St. John of the Cross*, eds., Kieran Cavanaugh, OCD, and Otilio Rodriguez, OCD (Washington, DC: ICS, 1979), II, 12, 8; Pseudo-Dionysius, "The Divine Names." In *The Complete Works*, trans. Colm Luibheid (New York and Mahwah: Paulist, 1987), 1 , 2; 4, 11; *The Cloud of Unknowing*, ed. William Johnston (New York: Image Books, 1973), Chs. 3, 6.

26. This theme of sin as alienation requiring some form of penance and solitude as its remedy is ubiquitous in Catholic thought. St. Augustine's autobiography is replete with memorable passages of a soul surreptitiously and self-destructively seeking God until recognizing the true source of its quest. See *Saint Augustine: Confessions*, trans. R. S. Pine-Coffin (Harmondsworth: Penguin, 1961), I, X.

27. The reader need not think that this positive portrait of the ideology behind the prison necessarily means that monastic prisons adhered to the ideology in practice. Thorsten Sellin relates in his presentation of the penal theory of the 17th-century Benedictine monk and historian, Dom Jean Mabillon, abundant evidence of abusive and violent treatment of incarcerated monks. See Sellin, "Dom Jean Mabillon."

28. Benedict's Rule, 27.

29. Ibid.

30. Newman, Graeme. *Just and Painful* (New York: Harrow and Heston, 1995), 82.

31. Allen, Francis. *Decline of the Rehabilitative Ideal* (New Haven: Yale University Press, 1981); David Garland, *The Culture of Control* (Chicago: University of Chicago Press, 2001); Andrew Von Hirsch, *Past or Future Crimes* (New Brunswick, NJ: Rutgers University Press, 1985); James Q. Wilson, *Thinking About Crime* (New York: Vintage, 1985); Pew Center, *One in One Hundred* (Washington, DC: Pew Center, 2008).

32. A recent report on recidivism revealed that in a 30-state study for prisoners released in 2005, "two-thirds (67.8%) of released prisoners were arrested for a new crime within 3 years, and three-quarters (76.6%) were arrested within 5 years." Alexia D. Cooper, Matthew R. Durose, and Howard N. Snyder, "Recidivism of Prisoners Released in 30 States in 2005" (Washington, DC: Bureau of Justice Statistics, 2014). Available online: http://www.bjs.gov/index.cfm?ty=pbdetail&iid=4986

33. Cullen, Francis T., Cheryl Lero Jonson, and Mary K. Stohr. *American Prisons: Imagining a Different Future*; The Sentencing Project, "Fewer Prisoners, Less Crime," http://sentencingproject.org/doc/publications/inc_Fewer_Prisoners_Less_Crime.pdf

34. Habermas, *Legitimation Crisis*.

35. Bauman, Zygmunt. "Social Issues of Law and Order." *British Journal of Criminology* 40 (2000), 205–221 at 206.

36. Cover, Robert. "Violence and the Word." Ronald Dworkin, *Taking Rights Seriously*; Max Weber, *Economy and Society*.

37. Cover, "Violence and the Word," *Yale Law Journal* 95 (1986) 1601–1629 at 1607–1608.

38. Bauman, "Social Issues of Law and Order," 207.

39. This "symbolic universe" erects a "sheltering canopy" over the institutional order. It not only fosters and reinforces identity, it also gives meaning to history: "It locates all collective events in a cohesive unity that includes past, present, and future. With regard to the past it establishes a 'memory.' ... With regard to the future, it establishes a common frame of reference for the projection of individual actions. Thus the symbolic universe links [people] with their predecessors and their successors in a meaningful totality." Berger and Luckmann, *Social Construction of Reality*, 102–103.

40. Goffman, Erving. "On the Characteristics of Total Institutions." In *Asylums* (New York: Anchor Books, 1961), 1–124 at 69–70.

41. Haney, Craig. *Reforming Punishment* (Washington DC: American Psychological Association, 2006), 174, 178.

42. See, e.g., Cullen et al. *The American Prison*; Byron R. Jonson, *More God, Less Crime*; Andrew Skotnicki, "Religion, Conversion, and Rehabilitation." *Criminal Justice Ethics* 33 (2014), 104–128.

43. Colson, Charles. "Forward." In Mario Ottobani, *Kill the Criminal, Save the Person* (Washington, DC: Prison Fellowship International), 1–3 at 2.

44. Ibid, 3.

18. Stress and Yoga

By Allison Drude Cook

Stress in the lives of criminal justice professionals is a well-documented and serious health threat, both emotionally and physically. In a time when our society is plagued by terrorism, school violence, civil disorder, and prison overcrowding—just to name a few of the issues confronting those who serve and protect our society—there is no doubt the stresses will increase.

Even criminal justice students have some difficult moments. How often have you heard comments like these: "*I forgot to file my FAFSA on time so I'm no longer eligible for financial aid. How can I afford school?*" or "*I studied for the test in my required science class, but I'm worried that I'll fail it because I missed the last two labs.*" or "*I'm stuck in traffic, now I'll be late for work at my part-time job!*"

Sound familiar? Stress is a part of our everyday lives and can come from even the smallest of missteps. Whatever your particular narrative is, even if it doesn't match any of the scenarios above, chances are you can point to some aspect of your life that creates difficulty or anxiety. We're all susceptible to the hassles of everyday life. But what is stress? How much stress is too much, and what can be done to handle it in a healthy way?

You can do something about the stress you encounter: yoga is a powerful tool that can be used to control stress and build resilience. In this article, we'll discuss information about stress and yoga, then cover some simple yoga techniques that you can use to begin to limit the effects of stress on your well-being. Studying yoga can even be

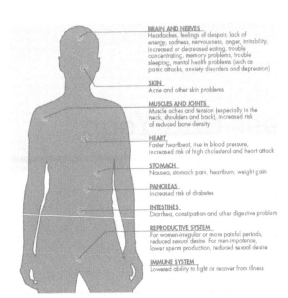

BRAIN AND NERVES
Headaches, feelings of despair, lack of
energy, sadness, nervousness, anger, irritability,
increased or decreased eating, trouble
concentrating, memory problems, trouble
sleeping, mental health problems (such as
panic attacks, anxiety disorders and depression)

SKIN
Acne and other skin problems

MUSCLES AND JOINTS
Muscle aches and tension (especially in the
neck, shoulders and back), increased risk
of reduced bone density

HEART
Faster heartbeat, rise in blood pressure,
increased risk of high cholesterol and heart attack

STOMACH
Nausea, stomach pain, heartburn, weight gain

PANCREAS
Increased risk of diabetes

INTESTINES
Diarrhea, constipation and other digestive problem

REPRODUCTIVE SYSTEM
For women-irregular or more painful periods,
reduced sexual desire. For men-impotence,
lower sperm production, reduced sexual desire

IMMUNE SYSTEM
Lowered ability to fight or recover from illness

Figure 18.1: The Stress Diagram shows the effects of stress on different parts of the body.

the first step on the path to developing a deeper spirituality, an important factor in coping with stress.

The word stress comes from the Latin word *stringere*, meaning to be drawn tight, but the correct term is actually strain, which is derived from engineering (it is a reference to load-bearing structures). These definitions provide images of how we feel when we're on overload, but it isn't just the mind that responds to stressful situations—the body does, too.[1] The *fight-or-flight response* is the physical reaction to a threat, be it real or imagined. People cannot differentiate between a real or perceived threat. This means that a math test can be stressful to the body in the same way that falling off a bicycle could be. So, identifying the actual stressor is extremely important in understanding and managing one's response to it.

When the body is stressed and goes into the fight-or-flight response, there is an immediate (and familiar) reaction—it ranges from shallow, fast breathing to sweating and a pounding heart and clenched muscles. This is a disruption to *homeostasis*, your body's natural equilibrium. Beyond the sensations you experience, there is also a hormonal response that causes the internal organs to slow as a person's body shuts down nonessential functions. In addition, the body's immunity becomes inhibited, and the perception of sensations like pain is also affected. The classic example of this diminished sense of pain is that of a soldier in the midst of battle who has been injured, but feels a numbing sensation instead of acute distress when he is hurt.

The stress response, then, is actually what your body does to return to equilibrium in the wake of the fight-or-flight response. When the stressor subsides, things begin to return to normal. But if the threat continues, so does the disruption of homeostasis. Overloaded by stress, the body tires. Stress begins to take its toll, creating fatigue and by-products like illness and diminished memory.[2] When stress becomes chronic, the body's ability to heal itself is impaired, and the fatigue caused by stress becomes something more threatening: it can bring about high blood pressure, ulcers, back pain, immune dysfunction, and depression. Other health problems begin to emerge.[3]

In spite of all these realities, stress in moderation can be a good thing. Too little stress can lead to lack of engagement and boredom. But with the right amount of pressure, performance is actually optimized. The sense of urgency can bring about adrenaline and focus.[4] Some scientists even hypothesize that if we view stress as the vehicle of improvement, we can leverage it to our advantage.[5] Recently, Kelly McGonigal gave a TED Talk[6], in which she explored the idea of "making stress our friend." McGonigal demonstrates through her research that if stress could be viewed as our body's natural response to a challenge, it could be harnessed as a tool to improve performance. If stress is viewed in the opposite way or as an impediment, it creates barriers to success.[7]

It is estimated that stress costs the U.S. economy $50–$90 billion annually, but some less conservative economists place the number closer to $150 billion. These figures include the expense of stress-related health treatments, as well as decreased productivity and time spent out of office.[8] Although these numbers are staggering, they don't factor in the human costs. Too much stress can impact many intangible factors that determine a person's quality of life. As we experience greater impatience, fatigue, upset digestion, and other problems as a consequence of stress, our everyday lives become more complicated, leaving a lessened capacity to enjoy the things that are otherwise taken for granted.

For criminal justice professionals who deal with elevated levels of stress, there are higher rates of suicide, depression, and reported feelings of isolation, as they bring the trauma from their work home with them.[9] This means that it is doubly important for individuals working in this field to have strong defenses to limit the toll of stress. To that, this question needs to be answered: How do we begin to change our relationship with stress and optimize our response? Stress management techniques range from pursuing counseling therapy or pharmaceutical intervention to massage or the development of an exercise regimen.

Mind-body techniques have proven to be especially helpful in managing stress. Meditation and yoga offer many different exercises that can provide relief in stressful moments and assist in the recovery from stress-related trauma. Mind-body techniques also offer a method to change the patterns of engagement with stressors, providing the means to transition, as McGonigal suggests, from viewing stress as an impediment to an asset.

Research demonstrates that yoga assists in the reduction of muscle tension and also improves circulation, two important components of relaxing after being stressed.[10] It also helps to combat the two emotional by-products of stress: anxiety and depression. But perhaps most importantly, yoga also raises our tolerance for *being* stressed. Scientists have performed experiments that demonstrate the ability of a yoga practice to improve concentration and focus, thus allowing participants to shift attention away from stressors. In comparison to other methods of stress management, yoga is proven to be as effective. A study was conducted, in which participants were placed into either a cognitive-based therapy program or a yoga program to deal with stress. At the end of the study, it was determined that the programs were equally successful.[11]

So, what exactly is yoga? It's an omnipresent craze in fitness, but often hard to pin down. In America, it is estimated that some 16 million people have a regular practice.[12] But what is it exactly that they're practicing? American yoga is a modern interpretation of an ancient discipline. It has inspired diverse spin-offs ranging from Yollet, a dance-infused exercise class, to mindfulness-based festivals like Wanderlust that happen annually and attract thousands of visitors. Yoga is also big business: in November 2014, it was estimated that in total, U.S. yoga studios generated some $7 billion in revenue.[13]

DEVELOPMENT OF YOGA

Yoga is much more complex than a series of exercises. Although it has undertaken a secular application often linked to health-and-wellness initiatives, yoga is a practice that is derived from one of the six orthodox systems of Indian philosophy. Codified in texts like the *Yoga Sutras* of Patañjāli and the *Bhagavad Gītā*, it is a system that provides principles for holistic living and historically, a path to spiritual development. The word yoga is derived from Sanskrit and has a complex meaning that encompasses several English words, including to yoke, join, and bind. In the most basic (and modern) sense, yoga can be seen as the aligning of mind and body to achieve a harmonious or unified state of being.

Yoga has been explained by Hindu philosophers as "the yoking of all the powers of the body, mind and soul to God; it means the disciplining of the intellect, the mind, the emotions, the will, which that Yoga presupposes; it means a poise of the soul which enables one to look at life in all its aspects evenly".[14] This "poise of the soul" is achieved through what Patañjāli called the "Eight Limbs," or stages, of yoga. The limbs are directed toward the practitioner (or yogi) and also toward the outside world. The limbs range from defining a moral code for the yogi to meditation to directing *asana*, the poses typically associated with modern yoga. Thus, they provide a road map for living a life in pursuit of spiritual development.

But the aim of asana was never fitness or health, although today's research confirms the benefits of practice. The poses were physical preparation for seated meditation. The sequences yogis practiced served a distinct purpose: to encourage discipline and the requisite strength to sit for extended periods of time in meditation. It was through meditation that the most important spiritual development was achieved. This facet of yoga's purpose plays an important role in the expansion of yoga in the 19th century.

When yoga arrived in the United States in the 19th century, it was not a physical practice of asana. In fact, it would be hardly recognizable in comparison to the exercises we know today. Yoga first came to America as a result of an interest in the Far East and an Orientalist vogue that emerged in popular culture.

The East has served as both a foil and a parent for European Western society. As explained by Edward Said in his seminal work, *Orientalism*, the Orient was a land of biblical promise and historical significance. But the East was also considered savage and wild; the Orient inspired works of art, marketing campaigns, and many travel writings. It was omnipresent and accessible to a diverse range of audiences.[15]

For America, the Orient was especially alluring. Manifest Destiny linked America's heritage to the East as well, conceiving of the young nation as a "New Jerusalem," binding itself to the European fascination with the Orient.[16] In times of war, American culture looked to the East to provide models for idealized rebellion. During the American fight for independence, wives of Revolutionary fighters dressed themselves in Oriental costume in portraits to show that they were different from royal supporters.[17] This costume carried great significance and communicated that the rebels were paragons, like the heroes of the East fighting for great causes.

In the years following the devastation of the Civil War, a recovering United States looked to the East for inspiration. It became a "construct that enabled people to both revisit the past and envision the future. It allowed people to affirm their convictions and affirm their values."[18] Although the Orient served as the ideal, it also served as the "other." It was thought to be home to uncivilized and uneducated heathens. This dual tendency made it a space that was at once admired and admonished, the Orient both mainstream and different from popular culture.

But in spite of this, audiences wanted to know more about the exotic cultures of the East. An important part of this Orientalist movement was the availability and circulation of written information about the religions and philosophies of the East. As the Orient was opened through increased trade and colonial expansion in the 18th and 19th centuries, texts that had been previously unavailable to Western audiences were translated and disseminated through Europe. One of the most important translations to circulate was the *Bhagavad Gītā*, published by the East India Trading Company.[19] The *Gītā* is an important Hindu scripture that follows the form of an epic poem. It is comprised of over 700 verses and is part of a larger work called the Mahabharata, which has been likened in significance to the Greek *Iliad*.

The *Gītā* is considered the first book to describe yoga in depth; it is the vehicle through which the West first gained widespread familiarity with the ancient system. The *Bhagavad Gītā* reached America in the 19th century, and scholarship confirms that important figures like Ralph Waldo Emerson, Henry James Thoreau, and Walt Whitman were all influenced by this work within the context of the larger Orientalist school. Some went so far as to characterize Thoreau, author of *Walden*, as the first American yogi.[20]

In his attempts to "live deliberately" after encountering the *Bhagavad Gītā*, Thoreau reflects in a letter: "Rude and careless as I am, I would practice the yoga faithfully … . To some extent, and at rare intervals, even I am, a yogin."[21] Thoreau is thought to have understood yoga as it was defined by the *Gītā* and other encyclopedic texts like H. H. Wilson's *Religious Texts of the Hindus*. Wilson explains yoga thusly:

> *The practices consist chiefly of long continued suppressions of respiration; of inhaling and exhaling the breath in a particular manner; of sitting in eighty-four different attitudes; of fixing the eyes on the top of the nose, and endeavoring, by the force of mental abstraction, to effect a union between the portion of vital spirit residing in the body and that which pervades all nature. … When this mystic union is effected, the Yogi is liberated in his living body from the clog of material encumbrance, and acquires an entire command over all worldly substance.*[22]

In Wilson's view, yoga was a means of spiritual transcendence that was achieved through breath and meditative inquiry—but it was something that was not suitable for Western or modern practitioners.

This belief in the suitability of yoga for contemporary audiences was challenged as awareness of yoga began to grow at the end of the 19th century. This interest was fueled by the first swami to visit America. Swami Vivekananda came to the Unites States to offer insight into the Hindu faith, but as a by-product brought greater awareness to the practice of yoga. He is credited as being the first teacher of yoga in America.

Vivekananda was a dynamic personality who had a unique background: he was a Western-educated monk with progressive political beliefs. He came to the United States with the aim of raising money for his impoverished countrymen after traveling extensively through India, but this goal was not realized.[23] But, when Vivekananda arrived in America, he was confronted with the impact of the Orientalist discourse that had pervaded public opinion through the circulation of texts and imagery.

Vivekananda's message was clear: Hinduism was a universal spiritual path. This truth is underscored in his book, *Raja Yoga*, which provides a scientific approach to the practice of yoga. The swami's approach, as suggested by David Gordon White, was extremely important because it seized "upon the symbolic power of

Figure 18.2: BKS Iyengar (1918–2014) was a famous teacher who helped introduce hatha yoga to the West and made the practice accessible for many.

yoga as a genuinely Indian, yet non-sectarian, type of applied philosophy."[24] This philosophy also served as a "unifying sign of the Indian nation ... not only for national consumption but for consumption by the entire world."[25]

Vivekananda began to develop a following. His teachings, in addition to being scientific, began to introduce a new element to the meditative practices of yoga that had been previously known. He began to delve into the "subtle body," which emphasizes body awareness and energy. This was an interesting departure, as the subtle body is more closely associated with hatha yoga or the asana poses that arrived the following century with B. K. S. Iyengar, K. Pattabhi Jois, and T. K .V. Desikachar.[26]

Iyengar, Jois, and Desikachar were the famous disciples of the same revered teacher, Krishnamacharya, but each interpreted his teachings differently and infused their own influence into his style of hatha yoga. These three teachers brought hatha yoga to the West. In America, Jois and Iyengar were most influential. Jois developed the rigid and demanding Ashtangha style of yoga that consists of a series of poses that change rapidly from one to the next.[27] Iyengar, in contrast, developed a style of yoga that is slower and focuses on precise execution of postures. But his work and name have become synonymous with yoga.

RESTORATIVE YOGA

Iyengar suffered many illnesses as a child: malaria, typhoid, influenza, and tuberculosis. At age 16, he began studying yoga with Krishnamacharya, but his body still bore the hallmarks of illness. It took six years before he reclaimed his health and could complete his yoga training. He dedicated himself fully to the practice, eventually beginning to teach and publish on the subject of yoga. His most important book, *Light on Yoga*, has become the cornerstone of American yoga and has an influence that spans the globe; it has been published in 17 languages.[28]

Iyengar traveled first to Europe in the 1950s and arrived in America in 1956. He gained distinction for his methods of teaching yoga and the creative use of props. This creativity is perhaps Iyengar's most important legacy. By utilizing objects that had never been incorporated into a physical practice before, Iyengar democratized yoga. Poses that were difficult were made accessible, even to beginners. This made the practice of yoga accessible in ways that it never was previously.

The renowned student of Iyengar yoga, teacher Carrie Orwenko, describes the impact of Iyengar's use of props by explaining the origins of the best known yoga prop:

> Take the yoga block. Everybody knows a yoga block. It's something you can
> get at Bed Bath & Beyond. The prototype of the yoga block was actually a
> rock or cinder block from B. K. S. Iyengar's garden. When he was teaching
> students, he would sometimes place students over his knee for a supported

back arch if they couldn't support themselves. The story goes that he asked his daughter to go in the yard and bring this cinder block to help. That was the beginning of the yoga block. He would use whatever was in the environment—tables, chairs, ropes. The more common props—belts, straps, blocks and chairs, this is the type of equipment that was not really used in the practice of yoga. Now everybody is using them. There are never enough props to go around.[29]

A block sounds like a simple modification, but this inclusion of objects in a yoga practice was unprecedented. It allowed students to begin practicing yoga in spite of injuries that might restrict their movement. Props also constituted a starting point from which improvements in flexibility and strength could be developed.

Props also played an important development in the role of new and revitalizing practices such as restorative yoga. This type of yoga originates from the Iyengar method of hatha yoga; it is paced very slowly and utilizes techniques of mindfulness to bring about deep rest and renewal. Iyengar developed this practice as a result of teaching yoga and encountering many students who were injured as a result of straining, or "over-muscling," in a yoga pose. So, he began to intervene, and through the use of props came restorative yoga, in which targeted support is brought to the body so that relaxation and release can happen without effort. Poses are held for as little as three minutes or as many as 20. This type of yoga can be referred to as "slowga" because the goal is to take time in specific poses to relax and heal from injury, illness, or stress.

Restorative yoga works, not just by creating the requisite support needed to relax, but because of the order in which poses are practiced. Although there is not a single uniform restorative sequence, the poses are typically linked together in such a way that the spine is moved in all directions. This adheres to the yogic philosophy that spinal movement is essential to good health, but also promotes flexibility and greater joint mobility.

Restorative sequences also include inversions or poses that reverse the flow of gravity. This is important because daily activities like sitting at a desk cause blood and lymphatic fluid to gather in the lower half of the body. By "going upside down," this process is reversed: fluid comes back to the upper body and the function of the heart is improved. In addition to reversing the flow of fluids, inversions also help balance hormone levels associated with the stress response. Research shows that brain arousal, blood pressure, and fluid retention decrease as a by-product.[30]

Restorative yoga offers tools that criminal justice professionals can draw on to recover from the stressors they encounter every day at work. Poses can be practiced at home at any time of day. In order to prepare, wear comfortable, loose clothing and find a quiet space.

Although there are bolsters, blankets, and yoga blocks that are helpful to use in a restorative practice, channel Iyengar and get creative. Swap out books for blocks, and try using towels to replace yoga blankets. Bolsters can be made by folding towels lengthwise into thirds and rolling them up like cinnamon buns. If you have pillows, those also make great substitute bolsters.

Begin your restorative practice with a few moments of seated breathing to focus your attention. Be patient with yourself—you might find it challenging to be still and harness your thoughts. It's natural to struggle with being quiet, but it becomes easier with repetition. The poses below have instructions for setup and some directions to help you begin to explore the pose. Consider these helpful guidelines; skim them once or twice before you try a pose, and use them to frame your experience.

Simple Restorative Yoga Practice

Seated Meditation

Setup:

Come to a comfortable seated position with your ankles crossed. If you are uncomfortable, sit on one of your towels or bolster rolls. Stack your shoulders over your hips so that your spine is long. Bring your hands to rest on your knees and close your eyes.

In the Pose:

Begin to notice your breath and allow thoughts to pass. Anchor your focus to the cycle of inhaling and exhaling; allow this rhythm to fascinate you. Each time a distraction arises, return to your breath. Don't force your attention; instead, as ideas arise, choose to stay committed to your experience. Use your breath as a tool to stay grounded and detach from your thoughts. If thoughts persist, try counting your breaths: inhale one, exhale one, inhale two, exhale two, etc.

Stay for three to five minutes to start, working up to longer sessions of about 15–20 minutes.

Relaxation Pose

Setup:

Lie down on the floor. Come to a neutral position with your hands along your hips, with the palms facing toward the ceiling. You might be comfortable like this. If not, take a rolled blanket and place it underneath your knees if your lower back is sensitive. If your neck is uncomfortable, place a folded towel underneath your head. Be careful to not elevate your head; keep your chin level to your chest.

In the Pose:

Bring your right hand to your heart and your left hand to your lower belly. Start to breathe into your hands. Feel the movement of your palms. Notice if one hand is moving more than the other and try to balance out the movement. Start to focus on the expansion of the chest, lungs and abdomen. Bring your attention to the front body and observe as your inhale deepens. Notice your in-breath; start to observe your body's response. Is the breath moving in any particular way? Now, do the same with the back body. Feel the extension as you breathe in through the shoulders and side ribs. Attune yourself to sensation, but this time focus on your exhale. What do you notice about the out-breath? If you are distracted by thoughts, come back to the rhythm of your breath. Bring a quality of expansion to the inhale, creating space and ease with every breath in that you take. With every breath out, begin to feel yourself relax, releasing a little more into the ground beneath you.

Stay for three to five minutes to start, working up to longer sessions of about 10–15 minutes.

Legs Up the Wall

Setup:

Sit facing a wall with your knees bent. Touch your toes to the surface of the wall, then lie back and swing your legs up. Shift your hips forward so the backs of your legs are as close to the wall as they can be and your body is (almost) a right angle. If your lower back is tight, fold a towel or blanket, and place it underneath your hip bones. Let your eyes close, and bring your hands out alongside your body so they rest alongside your hips, palms facing upward. Begin to notice your breath.

If your hamstrings are too tight to allow you to comfortably keep your legs resting along the wall, try this alternative variation. Sit facing your desk chair, and move your hips as close to the front legs as you can. Lift your legs up and place your calves on the seat. Lie back toward the floor, allowing your arms to fall out, with palms facing the ceiling.

In the Pose:

Begin to notice your breath, perceiving the support of the ground beneath you. When you inhale and the back body expands, feel the floor create resistance. As you exhale, let that resistance brace you and relax into the ground. Each time you breathe in, focus on the back expanding. Each time you breathe out, focus on releasing down into the floor. Notice sensation in your back and shoulders, using your breath to soften areas of pain or tightness.

Stay for three to five minutes to start, working up to longer sessions of about eight to ten minutes.

Supported Forward Fold

Setup:

Sit cross-legged in front of a chair and face toward the seat. If this isn't comfortable, sit on one of your bolster rolls or pillows. Placing your arms one on top of the other, bring your head to rest on the forearms.

In the Pose:

Breathe deeply into the base of your abdomen, settling the weight of your body down toward the floor. Try to soften your hips and let your knees fall out toward the floor. Let your inhale broaden the back of your chest. Notice if muscle tightness across the top of the back is preventing you from inhaling fully. Keep focusing on inhaling more deeply and creating space across the top of the back, softening muscle tightness. Each time you breathe out, relax your head toward your hands, and drop closer toward the floor beneath you.

Stay for three to five minutes to start, working up to longer sessions of about eight to ten minutes. Change the cross of your legs and arms halfway through.

Restorative Child's Pose

Setup:

Bring your big toes to touch, and spread your knees wide. Sink the hips back toward your heels. Let your torso come between your knees, and reach your arms forward. Bring your forehead toward the ground. If your forehead doesn't reach the ground comfortably, place a pillow or towel underneath your head.

If your hips are tight and this pose is uncomfortable, create more support. You can take a towel or blanket and place it behind your knees to release pressure in the lower back as you move the hips toward the heels. An alternative variation of the child's pose involves using a bolster (or two rolled towels) underneath the chest and head. Placing this support underneath your torso, come to the child's pose with one arm to either side of the bolster. With eyes closed, face looks toward one side. Halfway through, look to the other side.

In the Pose:

Breathe into the muscles of the core. Notice the engagement of the abdomen as it presses into the prop with each inhale. As you exhale, focus on releasing your torso down toward the bolster and letting the hips move toward the floor. Follow the path of

Figure 18.3 Child's Pose is a basic restorative posture that is calming.

your breath. Notice if you are clenching your hands and try to relax your fingers; let that sensation of release travel up the arms, imaging that the shoulders also relax in response. Let this rhythm of rest build as you stay in the pose.

Stay for two to four minutes to start, working up to longer sessions of about five to ten minutes.

CONCLUSION

If you want to learn more about these exercises or others that might be helpful to you, there are many resources and tutorials online that are easily accessible. Working with a teacher at a studio or gym might be the next step if you are struggling with these poses. For those who are newer to yoga, a gym can be the best place to start learning it. Classes are typically paced for beginners and non-yogis.

Restorative yoga and meditation are subtle, but powerful. They offer strong tools to combat the vast array of stressors that criminal justice professionals face daily in their work life. Through the development of a mind-body practice, stress management becomes more than a stopgap because the methods have the potential to transform our response to stressors. As the tolerance to stress is raised, so too is our quality of life through the consistent practice of yoga.

END NOTES

1. Parker, Henry. *Stress Management* (Chandni Chowk, Delhi: Global Media, 2007). Internet resource, pp. 4–10.

2. Sapolsky, Robert M. *Why Zebras Don't Get Ulcers: Guide to Stress, Stress-Related Diseases, and Coping* (New York: Henry Holt and Company), 1–15.

3. Lasater, Judith Hanson. *Relax and Renew: Yoga for Stressful Times* (Berkeley, CA: Rodmell Press), 4.

4. Cunningham, J. B. *The Stress Management Sourcebook* (Los Angeles: Lowell House, 2000). Internet resource, p. 22.

5. Keller, Robert M., et al. "Does the perception that stress affects health matter? The association with health and mortality." *Health Psychology*, September 2012.

6. TED is a nonprofit that offers short videos on new ideas available at www.TED.com.

7. McGonigal, Kelly (June 2013); *Kelly McGonigal: How to Make Stress Your Friend* [Video File]. Retrieved from: http://www.ted.com/talks/kelly_mcgonigal_how_to_make_stress_your_friend/citations

8. Cunningham, 19.

9. This is discussed at length by W. J. Cook in Chapter 20 of this text. Additional information from Kevin M. Gilmartin. *Emotional Survival for Law Enforcement* (Tucson: E-S Press, 2002).

10. Lasater, p. 5.

11. Simpkins, Annellen M., and C. A. Simpkins. *Meditation and Yoga in Psychotherapy: Techniques for Clinical Practice* (Hoboken, NJ: John Wiley, 2011). Internet resource, pp. 1–20.

12. White, David Gordon. Yoga in Practice (Princeton, NJ: Princeton University Press, 2012), 1.

13. Turk, Sarah. IBISWorld Industry Report OD4185 Pilates and Yoga Studios in the US. Retrieved Nov. 26, 2014, from IBISWorld Database.

14. Iyengar, B. K. S. *Light on Yoga* (New York: Schocken, 1966), 1.

15. Said, Edward. *Orientalism* (New York: Random House, 1978).

16. Edwards, Holly. *Noble Dreams, Wicked Pleasures: Orientalism in America, 1870–1930* (Trenton, NJ: Princeton University Press, 2000), 193.

17. Breskin, Isabel. *Winterthur Portfolio*, vol. 36, no. 2/3 (summer-autumn 2001), 97–123.

18. Edwards, 120.

19. Wilkins, Charles, trans. *Bhagavad Gita or Dialogues of Krishna and Arjun, Translated from Sanskrit* (Bombay: Bombay Theosophical Publication Fund Society, 1887).

20. Syman, Stephanie. *The Subtle Body: The Story of Yoga in America* (New York: Farrar, Straus and Giroux, 2010), 18–22.

21. Ibid, 11–12.

22. Ibid, 206–207.

23. Sen, Amiya P. *Swami Vivekananda* (New Delhi: Oxford University Press), 28–37.

24. White, 20.

25. Van der Veer, Peter. *Imperial Encounters: Religion and Modernity in India and Britain* (Princeton, NJ: Princeton University Press, 2001), 73–74.

26. Syman, 55.

27. Bajaj, Vikas. "Krishna Pattabhi Jois, Leading Expert in Yoga, Dies at 93." *New York Times.* N.p., May 20, 2009. Web. Nov. 27, 2014.

28. Waldman, Amy. "For Yoga Guru, Reaching Perfection Is a Stretch." *New York Times.* N.p., Dec. 14, 2002. Web. Nov. 27, 2014.

29. Parker-Pope, Tara. "What Is So Special About Iyengar Yoga?" *New York Times.* N.p., Aug. 20, 2014. Web. Nov. 27, 2014.

30. Lasater, 4–5.

19. Understanding Apocalyptic Writings

By William J. Cook Jr.

Then I saw the Lamb open one of the seven seals, and I heard one of the four living creatures call out, as with a voice of thunder, "Come!" I looked, and there was a white horse! Its rider had a bow; a crown was given to him, and he came out conquering and to conquer. When he opened the second seal, I heard the second living creature call out, "Come!" And out came another horse, bright red; its rider was permitted to take peace from the earth so that people would slaughter one another; and he was given a great sword. When he opened the third seal, I heard the third living creature call out, "Come!" I looked, and there was a black horse! Its rider held a pair of scales in his hand, and I heard what seemed to be a voice in the midst of the four living creatures saying, "A quart of wheat for a day's pay, And three quarts of barley for a day's pay, but do not damage the olive oil and the wine!" When he opened the fourth seal, I heard the voice of the fourth living creature call out, "Come!" I looked, and there was a pale green horse! Its rider's name was Death, and Hades followed with him; they were given authority over a fourth of the earth, to kill with a sword, famine, and pestilence, and by the wild animals of the Earth.

The Revelation to John, 6:1–8.[1]

OVERVIEW

The Revelation to John, also known as the Book of Revelation or the Apocalypse, is the last book of the New Testament of the Christian Bible; Apocalypse (ἀποκάλυψις) is an ancient Greek word meaning revelation or disclosure. It is a genre of writing that was popular in the ancient world and also appears in two other biblical books, Daniel and II Esdras. Apocalyptic writings present revelations about future events that are given to special persons such as Daniel or John in visions; there are symbols and unusual images used in these writings. Apocalyptic writings really were not meant to give readers clues about actual future events so much as to give them hope and strength during difficult times.

It is not known exactly when *The Revelation to John* was written, nor is the identity of its author known with certainty. There are two plausible times when it might have been written: the first is during the reign of the Roman emperor Domitian (81–96 CE); the second is possibly during the Emperor Nero's rule (54–68 CE). In any case, it is clear that the book was written during a persecution of early Christians.[2]

Revelation is of interest to those studying criminal justice because it was part of the story of the siege at Waco, as well as some other very dramatic events. Today, those who study terrorism know that apocalyptic thinking is quite often an issue among violent extremists; obviously, for those extremists who are in some way related to the Christian tradition, imagery or ideas from Revelation will probably be present in a group's communications or rationale.

If one were to ask the average person about what comes to mind when he or she hears of the Book of Revelation, the image frequently described is that of the Four Horsemen. In fact, one might even argue that the Four Horsemen are truly emblematic to the ordinary person's mind of the Apocalypse. Though many people may not even be sure exactly why the Four Horsemen are to be feared, they do seem to know they are the harbingers of trouble or evil.

We will examine the images of the Four Horsemen of the Apocalypse from three perspectives. First, there will be a presentation of an exegetical (i.e., an analysis of a text) view of the images; this view will be represented primarily by the work of Gonzalez and Gonzalez, who are scripture scholars. Then, an Evangelical interpretation will be discussed; this is to show how a mainstream religious leader might interpret Revelation. One exponent of this view to be studied in this chapter will be the evangelist Billy Graham; in contrast, another interpretive perspective, that of Tim LaHaye and Jerry Jenkins, will be discussed as well. Finally, we will examine contemporary secular uses of the images of the Horsemen; sources for this contemporary view will be primarily drawn from recently printed media (i.e., since the year 2000) such as newspapers, magazines, and journals. We will conclude with a comparison of the three perspectives, with an emphasis on the growing significance of the secular use of the images.

Traditional Exegetical View of the Four Horsemen

From the exegetical perspective, Revelation can be understood by examining it with reference to its historical and social background, as well as its scriptural antecedents and context.

According to Gonzalez and Gonzalez as they discuss the opening of the Seven Seals in their book, *Revelation*, one sees that "the first four seals form a unit and parallel each other. Together, they tell of what has come to be known as the 'Four Horsemen of the Apocalypse.'"[3] Speaking of the same passage from Revelation, Bruce M. Metzger, another scripture scholar, notes that "this vision has features borrowed from Zechariah 6:1–5, which also involves horses of various colors—red, black, white, and dappled grey ... and instead of yoking horses to chariots, he sets on each of them a rider in whom the interest of the vision is centered."[4]

Describing the appearance of the first horse (a white one) and its rider, Gonzalez and Gonzalez note that, though some have thought the white color of the horse indicates goodness, they reject this interpretation because of the circumstances of its arrival. They also note that the text does not use the typical word for rider, but instead uses the unusual expression "the one sitting on it" to refer to him. They observe that "these are exactly the same words used to refer to God as 'sitting on the throne,'" and conclude that such a horse is a "false seat of power," which may seem to be powerful, but is actually not.[5] This is a reminder that God is the ruler of the universe, regardless of how things may sometimes appear.

The rider of this white horse is discussed next. Gonzalez and Gonzalez explain that the model for this rider is most likely a Parthian warrior. The Parthians, feared enemies of Rome in the area of Asia Minor, "were noted for their mounted archers" because archers in the ancient world typically operated as foot soldiers. Therefore, the authors suggest that the effect on a person reading or hearing this passage at the time it was written would "immediately have brought to mind thoughts of a Parthian invasion." Further, because the horse was white (the color of victory in that time) and the rider was given a "crown," this passage would suggest to its original audience that "God had given victory to the Parthians, Rome's hated enemy, and that foreign invasion, destructive though it might be, was not beyond God's control."[6]

The second horse is bright red and has been given a "great sword" to take peace from the Earth. This sword was known in Greek as a *machaira* (μάχαιρα). According to Gonzalez and Gonzalez, it is "the heavy sword that is used for swinging and cutting rather than stabbing. It was also a symbol of the emperor's authority—in particular, the emperor's authority to decree the death penalty, which was called the 'right of the sword' and which could also be exercised by provincial governors."

Therefore, this sword carried by the second rider would have evoked the image of the Roman Empire in the minds of those who heard Revelation in the ancient world. Rome took great pride in its policy of a *Pax Romana*, by which it had supposedly pacified the lands it had conquered. There was a peace that Rome did bring; for example, this peace was evident in the flourishing trade associated with the presence of the Roman Empire. But rebellions simmered among the conquered. There was a dark underside to this peace: "But, it is also true that many of the conquered people were recruited as Roman auxiliaries to fight against their former neighbors. … For many of the conquered peoples, the much-vaunted Roman peace was the peace of death."[7] It was this irony of the Roman peace that John depicted in the image of the second rider.

The third rider, borne by a black horse, bears a pair of scales in his hand. The scales are an image of trade. Rome had facilitated trade among its territories through effective control of the sea lanes.

But this trade brought hardship to the conquered peoples of Asia. Roman and local landowners found that it was more profitable to use their lands to develop vineyards and olive groves rather than raise grains; this brought them wealth. But the effect of this policy upon others was "food scarcity for the lower echelons of the population."[8] The third rider, then, is the image of starvation caused by the unbridled greed of the landowners.

The fourth horseman rides a "pale" horse or, as described by the scripture scholar Metzger, a horse that is "the color of decaying flesh."[9] This rider, named "Death," is followed by Hades, the abode of the dead. Thus, death follows "foreign invasion, domestic injustice and turmoil, and unjust trade."[10]

The meaning of the Four Horsemen of the Apocalypse might be considered, from the perspective of such authors as Gonzalez and Gonzalez as well as Metzger, to be a symbolic casting of the problem of humankind's penchant for doing evil. Metzger states the following concerning the horrors brought by the Four Horsemen: "Notice that these disasters are the results of the working out of God's righteous laws for the universe. God does not approve of famine and death and hell, but they are what must follow if people persist in opposing God's rule. … Neglect moral laws and disaster ensues just as surely."[11] In a similar fashion, Gonzalez and Gonzalez sum up the meaning of the images of the Four Horsemen by quoting this statement from a sermon by Burr: "Thus is this text relevant for today, not as a book of secret prophecies that can only be decoded by a select group of alarmist paranoids, but as a constant reminder that the Divine is attentive to what we do and how we are with one another."[12]

EVANGELICAL PERSPECTIVE

The Evangelical view of the Book of Revelation, according to Billy Graham, is that it is not—as some theologians and bible scholars believe—a "description of past events." Concerning the scenes described in the Apocalypse, Graham says that "most Evangelical scholars interpret them as having to do with the future—as I do. In my view, the shadows of all four horsemen can already be seen galloping through the world at this moment ... "[13] Thus, the Four Horsemen are perceived as symbols of events that will happen in the future; they are also, to Graham's mind, "an almost exact repeat of the first four signs of the end of the age that Jesus gave in Matthew 24."[14] (Note: In Chapter 24 of the Gospel of Matthew, there is Christ's prediction of the destruction of the Temple in Jerusalem, persecutions, an "awful horror," and the coming of the Son of Man). Consequently, Graham is inclined to look at current events and listen, so to speak, for the coming of the horsemen.

Graham acknowledges that John, the author of Revelation, uses images of the Four Horsemen in the Book of Revelation because he "had perhaps watched the invading armies of Rome enter Jerusalem with the conquering Centurion riding a prancing white steed ... " He continues by suggesting that the image "may be a subtle historic flashback to an event in the Roman Empire ... Romans feared their Parthian neighbors ... (who) rode swift white horses and were deadly accurate with their bows and arrows."[15] Hence, though there may be an actual historical referent for the horsemen, he thinks this should not be where the analysis of the meaning of these images stops. Graham would now look to contemporary life to apply his interpretation of the images of the horses and riders. He also believes that the images of the Four Horsemen are meant to be warnings that call all people to repentance.

Beginning with the first rider on the white horse, Graham argues that this first horseman is a "deceiver who seeks to capture the hearts and souls of men and women. He is the one who seeks to have people acknowledge him as Lord instead of the true Christ."[16] This deceiver will offer people two alternatives to a "true faith in God." He suggests that "(T)he first alternative is to ignore religion altogether. The second alternative is to plunge into a synthetic, false religion ... "[17] In the modern world, Graham notes that many have dropped any belief in God; he believes that the second alternative, which involves choosing a false religion, can be seen in the popularity of Eastern religions in our society.

The second horseman is representative of war—he warns especially of the dangers presented by war in an age of nuclear weapons. Graham believes that another world war is inevitable and states that " ... John's vision (of the rider on the red horse) was sent as a harbinger of that final holocaust when the Messiah himself will intervene and crush the allies of evil at Armageddon."[18] Nevertheless, he also thinks that people must still work for peace, all the while recognizing the human capacity for destructiveness. He says that "(T)he second horseman of the Apocalypse will have to help teach man his responsibility to the Creator through the pain of war."[19] Graham would hold that, though Christians must work for peace, it is only Christ who can ultimately bring peace to the world.

The third rider sits on the black horse. Graham says that the "Black horse and its rider bear yet a third warning to the peoples of our planet—a warning of massive hunger and starvation."[20] It is "a symbol of the desperate plight of the world after the first two horsemen have ridden. ... With the advent of the this third rider, Jesus is indicating that deception and false religion lead to war, and this war in turn leads to famine and pestilence."[21] As he considers the modern world, Graham points to the multiple wars in so many different parts of the globe; as so much money is spent on armaments, there are so many people, especially children, who are starving. Worse, he observes, is that the situation is "a picture of famine coexisting with luxury."[22]

In summarizing the message of the rider on the black horse, Graham points to the presence of extreme poverty in the presence of extraordinary wealth. From this, he says, one can see that "(T)here is always something radically wrong with a situation in which those who have too much are indifferent to those who have too little ... the society in which it occurs is hastening to its ruin."[23]

The fourth rider sits upon a pale horse. Graham observes that the word translated as pale is actually *chloros* (χλωρος), which suggests "the yellow green color of sickly grass. Goodspeed translates <u>chloros</u> as the color of ashes."[24] The warning of this rider is that everyone will face death—the issue is whether one will also face eternal damnation, too. This can only be avoided by acknowledging one's sinfulness and seeking forgiveness from God.

Yet, according to Graham, there is more to be said about the symbolism of this rider. He suggests that the passage "concerning the pale horse probably has a double interpretation. One is literal, the other spiritual. The bible teaches that in the last days there will be a famine of the Word of God (Amos 8:11). Spiritual death follows spiritual starvation."[25]

In contrast to Graham's conservative interpretation of the imagery of the Four Horsemen, there is that of LaHaye and Lindsey, who wrote the *Left Behind* series of books. Their view, as reported by Rossing, is that they "interpret the four horses of Revelation's Chapter 6 symbolically."[26] But in their books, they suggest that these symbolic images are predictive of actual events that will happen in the future. Thus, for their readers, these books bring the Bible to life, as they seemingly give them the tools to use scripture in order to make sense of what they see happening about them. The readers, it would seem, can learn to apply scripture to current events from the characters in the novels. Rossing gives an example of such a character, a protagonist known as Rayford, modeling such a way of using scripture when he hears of the Antichrist's order for the destruction of San Francisco and Chicago. She says: "While he is disgusted by the violence, he nonetheless sees it all as the fulfillment of scripture, and that comforts him: 'On television he saw live reports from the world. *Scripture has come to life. This was the Red Horse of the Apocalypse. Next would come more death by famine and plagues.*"[27]

In summary, the message of the Evangelical view of the Four Horsemen is that they are symbolic images that are predictive of the end times, or final days. For a more conservative Evangelical advocate, this leads to a call for repentance; for an evangelical holding a more interactive view, it is a road map to the Rapture.

SECULAR VIEW

The images of the fearsome riders of the Apocalypse have come into popular culture; generally, they are used to discuss economic or business issues and quartets (of persons).

The first use of the images to describe a quartet in a sports context appears to have been by the sports writer Grantland Rice in 1924, while writing for the *New York Herald Tribune*. It is found in his story about a football game in which Notre Dame beat Army with a score of 13–7; the "Four Horsemen of Notre Dame" were the backfield players.[28] The name has also been used to describe four football players at Fordham University.[29] In another, also a recent use, a reporter humorously applies the image of the Four Horsemen to the women's basketball team at Notre Dame. In the article, the reporter observes: "The Four Horsemen never wore nail polish, it is safe to say. At Notre Dame now, the women's basketball team is stirring more than an echo."[30]

At other times, the image of the Four Horsemen is used to refer to groups of four important, powerful, or influential persons, or as a referent in comparisons. For example, Silver uses the image to refer to the four influential American philosophers—Holmes, James, Pierce, and Dewey—as "Pragmatism's Four Horsemen."[31] In a newspaper article discussing the notoriety of the singing group the Beatles, an author employs an image referring to the Four Horsemen to facilitate a comparison. He asserts that the Beatles were the "second most famous four-human collective within any context whatsoever" because they were less famous than the four Evangelists; however, they are more famous than the "Four Horsemen of Notre Dame."[32] Finally, in an article considering the appointment of Judge Sonia Sotomayor to the U.S. Supreme Court, an author wonders how she might fit in among the current sitting judges, especially when "Chief Justice Roberts is riot singing solo. His backups include the Four Horsemen: namely, Anthony Kennedy, Antonin Scalia, Clarence Thomas and Samuel Alito, Jr."[33]

Usage of the image of the Four Horsemen in an economic or business context sometimes facilitates expression of fiscal dangers or problems, but it can be used as a way of describing other salient aspects of an economic or business issue, or even to describe powerful companies. An example of how the image of the Four Horsemen can be used to describe threatening economic circumstances could be found in an article by Waggoner and Shell. In their article, which was published in 2003, they assert that the "Four Horsemen of the Depression aren't here yet, but you can hear the faint hoofbeats of three of them." The authors describe the "Four Horsemen of the Depression" as these factors (Shell 2003): unemployment, falling prices for many goods, deflationary recession, and financial collapse.[34]

In another article, Hasset contends that the markets were predicting the coming of an "apocalypse" because of the then anticipated (i.e., in 2008) changes to be made under the Obama administration; he calls them the "Four

Horsemen of Obamanomics." The first horseman is "the Fair Currency Act," which allows the United States to impose duties; the second is called "card check," which benefits union organizers; the third horseman is tax policy; the fourth horseman is regulation—that is, attacking deregulation.[35] The author concludes that if implemented by Obama, these policies would bring about an economic collapse in the United States. In a different article by a British author, who was reflecting on the state of the Western world, but especially then current circumstances in Europe, it is asserted that "chaos caused by decreased social spending, mind-numbingly dumb politics, computer viruses, spam, reality TV programmes … the situation is so bad that some feel the Four Horsemen of the Apocalypse are saddling up for what Christian evangelist cowboys might call 'The Big Ride.'"[36]

But the image of the Four Horsemen can also be used to refer to quartets of businesses or corporations. In an article by Safire about "media giantism," the author asserts that President George W. Bush's policy of encouraging the expansion of media leaders was such that it would "allow the Four Horsemen of Big Media—Viacom (CBS, UPN), Disney (ABC), Murdoch's News Corporation (Fox), and G.E. (NBC)—to gobble up every independent station in sight."[37] In a similar fashion, in an article entitled, "Four Horsemen of the Internet See Tough Times," Krantz uses the image to describe four powerful corporations. He notes that Cisco, EMC, Sun Microsystems, and Oracle had "prosperous records, real products and soaring profits earned them the nickname, 'the Four Horsemen of the Internet.'"[38]

In summary, one of the secular uses of the image of the Four Horsemen seems to focus on either quartets of persons who are influential or powerful as individuals or athletes. In a different secular usage, the image is used to describe successful and powerful corporations; it can also be used to characterize threats to business or the economy, however. Frequently, when the term Four Horsemen is applied, it has pejorative connotations, but this does not always seem to be the case. Sometimes it is almost adulatory instead. The images remain powerful in a secular usage, but there seems to be a blurring in their meaning as there are various uses, both negative and positive, of the images.

CONCLUSIONS

Three views of the Four Horsemen have been discussed. First, there was a discussion of an exegetical understanding of the images; this understanding is rooted in historical and linguistic, as well as contextual, studies. From this perspective, one might assert that a key to understanding the images is to attempt to see how they might have functioned in communicating with an audience living in the first century of the Common Era. With the second perspective, a more Evangelical view, there generally is a recognition of the symbolic nature of the images of the Four Horsemen, but there is also an emphasis on their semiotic function as "signs of the End Times"; therefore, as a person recognizes these signs in current events, she or he should also recognize that, in them there is an implicit call for repentance, or a change in how one conducts one's life. Finally, there is the secular view, which has uncoupled the images of the horsemen from their biblical context, but which allows them to maintain some sense of a negative—that is, pernicious—meaning. Nevertheless, there is something manageable about the image of the horsemen in their secular usage; they are fearsome, but hardly so compared to their original, biblical function. Now, they can be applied to sports figures, important persons, or companies with power (good or bad) and to threatening economic conditions. In the secular view, the reader understands that there are actions that can be taken to stop the horsemen in their paths; for example, a person can simply reject a given economic policy and select another to turn away the "hoofbeats."

But though there are concerns about the more extreme religious applications of the images of the horsemen, it is the secular interpretation that may now actually need more attention from scholars because its effects may ultimately be more pernicious. In an interesting book review entitled, "Fuel for Fantasy," it was noted that in this "age of mass media, The Book of Revelation is reaching far beyond the church pulpit. ... for the visions and violence that drive this final book of the Bible are tailored for a culture in which the line between reality and fantasy has blurred." The problem, according to the author, seems to be that the images of the Apocalypse have slipped, through depiction in modern media such as movies, more powerfully into the secular consciousness, but have done so in such a way that they are disconnected from their original context; they thus have a kind of unconscious power. The author then notes the following:

> Consider the big screen incarnation of J. R. R. Tolkien's
> Lord of the Rings fantasy series, which depicts an apocalyptic
> battle between the forces of good and evil. A "terrifying
> number" of people in a recent British poll thought that
> Hitler was imaginary and that the orcs' defeat at Helm's
> Deep in the movie version of Tolkien's The Two Towers
> actually occurred.[39]

And so, what may seem to be a harmless secular use of the images of the Four Horsemen may be exactly that—harmless. But one must also wonder about how such images, disconnected from their original biblical and religious context, can influence the thinking and behavior of a secular audience that has received only part of the message of the images of the Four Horsemen, albeit the wrong part.

SUMMARY

In this chapter, we have looked at three ways that imagery from the Book of Revelation can be interpreted. It is important to bear in mind that a writing such as that is two thousand years old and is difficult for a modern reader to understand because the world in which it first appeared is so different from ours. However, as one draws upon the works of scholars who have studied ancient languages, culture, theology, and history, a much clearer and more penetrating understanding of such a text is possible.

Additionally, it is essential to keep in mind the difference between *mythos* and *logos*, which was a distinction made by the ancient Greeks. Myths (i.e., mythos) are a way of telling a truth through stories and imagery that are "true," but not literally so; such stories can convey moral or religious truths. On the other hand, logos is logical and literally true; it tells us how to make things or pursue activities and is accurate and literally true. In our modern world, we expect the facts and that a story will be historically accurate; we expect literal truth because we use logos pretty much exclusively. Thus, the problems start when modern persons, steeped in logos, assume that a writing like the Book of Revelation (which, of course, was written in a mythic way) will conform to our cultural expectations and be literally true.

Finally, it is necessary for students of criminal justice to study such texts as the Book of Revelation in order to be familiar with the imagery used in them so that they can understand what is being said or written by modern religious persons who may be using or referring to them. History has shown that law enforcement officials' ignorance of the meaning and usage of such texts and imagery can have tragic results. This was certainly one the reasons that the Waco tragedy occurred.

END NOTES

1. Attridge, Harold W., ed. *The Harper Collins Study Bible* (San Francisco: HarperOne, 2006), 2095.
2. Gilmour, S. MacLean. "The Revelation of John." *The Interpreter's One-Volume Commentary on the Bible*, ed. Charles M. Laymon (Nashville: Abingdon Press, 1971), 945–948.
3. Gonzalez, Catherine G., and Justo L. Gonzalez. *Revelation* (Louisville: Westminster John Knox Press, 1997), 46.
4. Metzger, Bruce M. *Breaking the Code* (Nashville: Abingdon Press 1993), 56.
5. Gonzalez and Gonzalez, 46.
6. Gonzalez and Gonzalez, 47.
7. Gonzalez and Gonzalez, 48.
8. Gonzalez and Gonzalez, 49.
9. Metzger, 58.

10. Gonzalez and Gonzalez, 49.

11. Metzger, 58.

12. Gonzalez and Gonzalez, 50.

13. Graham, Billy. *Approaching Hoofbeats: The Four Horsemen of the Apocalypse* (Waco: Word Books, 1983), 9.

14. Graham, 10.

15. Graham, 77.

16. Graham, 78.

17. Graham, 87.

18. Graham, 122.

19. Graham, 130.

20. Graham, 149.

21. Graham, 151

22. Graham, 151.

23. Graham, 151.

24. Graham, 179.

25. Graham, 184.

26. Rossing, Barbara R. *The Rapture Exposed* (New York: Basic Books, 2004), 94.

27. Rossing, 99.

28. Ellington, Coke. "Puffed Rice: It's Time to Re-evaluate a Sportswriting Classic." *American Journalism Review*, October/November 2004, 22.

29. Harris, Jaime C. "The Four Horsemen Riding Fordham Back to Glory." *New York Amsterdam News*, Oct. 31, 2002 (Harris 2002) 50.

30. Robbins, Liz. "Irish Women Establish Tradition." *New York Times*, Apr. 3, 2001, sec. D, p. 5 (Robbins 2001).

31. Silver, Thomas B. "Pragmatism's Four Horsemen." *Human Events*, Aug. 27, 2001, vol. 57, issue 32, 4.

32. Klosterman, Chuck. "The 10th Beatle." *New York Times Magazine*, 25 Dec. 25, 2005, 51(Klosterman 2001)

33. Maddox Jr., Alton H. "Can Sotomayor Stop Roberts and the Four Horsemen?" *New York Amsterdam News*, Jun. 11, 2009, vol. 100, issue 24, 12–40.

34. Waggoner, John, and Adam Shell. "You Might Recall Your Parents or Grandparents Talking About It." *USA Today*, May 27, 2003, sec. (Money) 1.

35. Hasset, Kevin A. "The Four Horsemen of Barack Obama." *National Review*, Dec. 1, 2008, vol. 60, issue 22, 37–38.

36. Unknown Author. "The Profits of Doom." *New Internationalist*, October 2004, issue 372, 8 (Unknown 2004).

37. Safire, William. "Bush's Four Horsemen." *New York Times*, Jul. 24, 2003, 19 (Saffire 2003). (Safire 2003)

38. Krantz, Matt. "Four Horsemen of the Internet See Tough Times." *USA Today*, Oct. 12, 2003, sec. (Money) 8b. (Krantz 2003).

39. Unknown Author. "Fuel of Fantasy." *Wilson Quarterly*, vol. 30, issue 2, 87.

20. Living and Working Together

By William J. Cook Jr.

OVERVIEW

In this last chapter, we will address three topics that should help round out our discussion of criminal justice and religion. The first area we'll examine is that of the prejudice and ethnicity as it relates to frictions between different groups; the second is about the utilization of religious studies in the field of criminal justice; and, the third is the current interest in religion and spirituality in the lives of criminal justice practitioners.

Prejudice

As one looks back at the history of the United States, it is clear that there have been recurrent episodes of religious prejudice: the typical scenario is that a religious majority attempts to impose its will on a minority (that is, a *religious* minority) or categorically rejects it. In the Puritan Colony in the 1600s, there was active rejection of groups of people who did not conform to the thinking and lifestyle of the Puritan majority. For example, the Quakers were driven out of the colony, and if anyone who had been banished then were to return, he or she would be executed. Puritans also did not respect the religious beliefs of the Native Americans, whom they saw as pagans and sometimes even as diabolical.

Roger Williams (1603–1683), who settled in Salem, Massachusetts, had studied the languages of Native Americans, as well as befriending the Native Americans around him. Williams advocated a kind of laissez-faire approach and argued for their property rights. Williams, who was a minister, also believed that the church in Salem was still too connected to the Church of England. Opposition to his views grew. Eventually, an arrest warrant for Williams was issued by authorities in the colony, and he, knowing what was about to happen, had to escape in the middle of a February blizzard, leaving behind his possessions. He found safety among Native Americans living in what would later be known as Rhode Island.

Another famous example of religious prejudice (in the sense of a majority rejecting those who don't conform to expectations), but also of fear, can be seen in the events that occurred later in 1692–1693 also in Salem, when various persons were accused of witchcraft by some young girls. By the time the episode was settled, 20 people had died by hanging or being "pressed" with a stone, and many others had been accused and imprisoned. Ordinary rules of evidence were changed to allow "spectral evidence"—meaning that things only the accusers claimed to see (and thus were unverifiable empirically) could still be allowed as evidence to be used against the accused. Most of the accused were marginal people, elderly or odd in some way; one accused woman was a nonwhite slave.

During the 1800s and 1900s, there were different groups that suffered persecution that was somehow related to the victims' religion. Many immigrants during the 1800s were from Catholic countries and were subjected to being maligned and harassed by some of those belonging to the Protestant majority in America; in the early 1900s, other immigrant groups such as Jews, Italians, and Germans were subjected to the same treatment. By 1925, the Ku Klux Klan (KKK), a supposedly Christian organization known for its "religious ritual" of cross burning, had achieved preeminence as a patriotic organization, with millions of members and the ability to organize a march through Washington, D.C., with tens of thousands of participants. Known for its lynchings of African Americans, the KKK was also fiercely anti-Catholic and anti-Semitic. During the 20th century in America, other groups subjected to religious prejudice included Pentecostals, Seventh-Day Adventists, Jehovah's Witnesses, Mormons, Sikhs, and Muslims, as well as New Religious Movements such as the Unification Church of Sun Myung Moon (whose pejorative nickname is "the Moonies") and others. This is an incomplete listing of all the groups that have either suffered discrimination or discriminated against others, but the conclusion is still obvious: religious prejudice has remained an obdurate problem.

How does one explain such behavior by religious people toward others, especially other religious people (though they may be members of another denomination or religious tradition)? About 60 years ago, the prominent psychologist Gordon W. Allport (1897–1962) published a book, *The Nature of Prejudice*, in which he explored the nature of prejudice among humankind. More generally, he argues that the "core of this matter seems to be that every living being is trying to complete his own nature." In doing this, one can take one of two paths. The first path "calls for safety through exclusion, through a *rejective equilibrium*." When a person chooses this path, he "clings to a narrow island, restricts his circle, sharply selects what assures him and rejects what threatens him."[1] This is the path of the prejudiced person.

The other path, according to Allport, is "one of relation, self-trust, and therefore, trust of others. There is no need to exclude strangers ... self-love is compatible with love of others." A person who takes the second path "does not perceive the world as a jungle where men are basically evil and dangerous."[2] This is the way of the tolerant person.

Religion can have paradoxical effects: it can either cause or prevent prejudice. And while the great religions are "universalistic," and all emphasize the importance of brotherly (and sisterly) love, "the practice of these creeds is frequently divisive and brutal."[3] The reason that religion becomes the focus of prejudice, sometimes encouraging a practice of these creeds that is "divisive and brutal," is that "it [i.e., religion] usually stands for more than faith—it is the pivot of the cultural tradition of a group." Thus, piety (e.g., religious devotion or reverence) may "be a convenient mask for prejudices which intrinsically have nothing to do with religion."[4]

So, religion becomes problematic when it is used to justify and facilitate an individual's or group's efforts to become powerful, gain economic advantage and prestige, or to promote ethnic self-interest at the expense of another group. Allport writes that "it is then that religion and prejudice merge. Often one can detect their fusion in ethnographic slogans: 'Cross and Flag,' [or] 'white, Protestant, gentile, American,' [or] 'the chosen people,' [or] 'Gott mit uns' [i.e., God is on *our* side], [and] 'God's Country.'" For he observes that "nothing is easier than to twist one's conception of the teachings of religion to fit one's prejudice."[5]

Allport's explanation helps us to understand how frictions develop among different religious groups. Next, let's look at how violence can happen among religious groups or by a religious group against outsiders. In order to do this, it is important to examine more closely the link between religion and ethnicity. Of course, no one is surprised by the observation that there is a relationship between religion and ethnicity; for example, we can easily associate Buddhism with the Japanese, Catholicism with Italians or Irish people, orthodoxy with Greeks, and so on; this is the obvious aspect of the relationship. But there is the more subtle and more significant side to the relationship: it is what Karpov, Lisovskaya, and Barry refer to as the *subjective* side, which involves "how people themselves perceive, imagine, and articulate the interconnectedness of their ethnicity and faith." They note, for example, that not only is it true that Poles are Catholics, but it is also true that "many of them deem Catholicism crucial and indispensable for their ethnonational belonging." And herein lies a problem because "such beliefs are far from 'natural' or unproblematic" because, in fact, they are "socially constructed, collectively held as popular ideologies and acted upon as bases for inclusion into or exclusion from ethnoreligious groups and for conflict or coexistence with other faiths and ethnicities." This is to say that these subjective beliefs that are tied to religion serve as "popular ideologies of ethnoreligious unity and difference." The term that Karpov et al. use for this ideological phenomenon is *ethnodoxy*. Ethnodoxy can be defined as "an ideology that rigidly links a group's ethnic identity to its dominant faith."[6]

The power of ethnodoxy can be observed in a situation where the civil government collapses in an area that has more than one ethnoreligious group. Prior to such a collapse, unity (to whatever degree it existed) in society among various groups was facilitated by the secular government. When that civil structure falls, there can be a nearly immediate reversion to ethnoreligious factions. An example of this kind of situation occurred in Yugoslavia when the Communist government there dissolved. There was an "almost immediate ethnoreligious mobilization" that occurred, and it resulted "in violence along the fault lines that are ethnic and religious at once." Karpov et al. note that "(w)hen groups [such as the Bosnians and Serbs before the breakup] that are not particularly pious see their faiths as crucial for ethnic belonging, such views reflect their social imagination, or in Durkheimian terms, collective representations, rather than the reality of their religious belief and behavior."[7]

It is possible that secular society has contributed to the acceleration of a fusion between religious and ethnic identities, though obviously religion and ethnicity have been connected for millennia; in other words, it may be that secular society has introduced a factor that has transformed this relationship for the worse. Karpov et al. discuss the work of the French religion sociologist Danièle Hervieu-Léger, who observes that, "as secularization has undermined traditional religions, sacred symbols and identities are increasingly detached from the faith traditions in which they were formed." The result is that these same symbols can be used as "mere religious emblems in essentially secular contexts to reconstitute declining or threatened ethnonational identities." Ultimately, the significance of such a change is that it "leads to the proliferation of 'ethnic religions' to which people may 'belong without believing'"; the result is that the moral power of religion is lost. The practical effect of a person being immersed in ethnodoxy is prejudice: this is to say that the stronger a person's "adherence to the ideology of ethnodoxy," the more prejudiced and rejecting (i.e., intolerant) he or she is likely to be of members belonging to ethnic and religious outgroups.[8]

The important conclusion to draw from this discussion of ethnodoxy is that one should be cautious about formulating a simple causal relationship between religion and violence—that is, that religion causes violence. Obviously, there are religious scriptures that can be used to justify aggression toward others; nevertheless, within the same books such as the Bible and Qur'an, there are other writings calling for peaceful responses. But there is a popular assumption in society today that religion, in itself, is dangerous because of its absolutism, divisiveness, and irrationality. William T. Cavanaugh argues ably against this view in his book, *The Myth of Religious Violence*.[9]

Hood, Hill, and Spilka note that "it is often claimed that violence in the expression of one's faith (as in Islamic fundamentalist protest movements that utilize force) is necessarily fanatical and fueled by negative characteristics like paranoia and authoritarianism." However, "empirical studies of actual violent protesters while still alive or in prison fail to support such claims."[10]

Thus, one must keep in mind there are other social or political reasons, including both prejudice and the ideology of ethnodoxy, which can be advanced as possible and effective alternative explanations for social tensions and violence linked to religion. It usually cannot be argued that religion, by itself, causes violence.

Criminal Justice and Religion

Some years ago, an earnest criminal justice undergraduate student made an appointment to see the department chair in order to file a complaint against a senior faculty member. The chair was perplexed by the student's request, since he knew that the student was a responsible and talented young man, while he also knew that the professor in question was an intelligent and personable faculty member, one liked and respected by all; he just could not imagine what the problem could be that warranted a special meeting. As it happened, when the student did meet with the chair, he was able to articulate his complaint succinctly: "Professor X is teaching us about theory in my criminal justice class. What *does* theory have to do with criminal justice? He is wasting our time!" Needless to say, the chair then relaxed into his seat and smiled.

This story is true, and in the author's experience, reflects a common misperception among some criminal justice students which is that all one needs are the "facts"—forget the theory! But in order to make sense of the facts, one obviously needs to have a theory, or theories, to try to explain why things are as they have been observed to be; and then, one can predict what will likely happen under similar circumstances in the future.

A similar situation seems to be happening when it comes to utilizing the work of religious studies scholars in applications related to criminal justice matters. This is not to say that the door is entirely closed, for it is not; but it does not seem to have been opened enough. To understand this situation, it is best to see what scholars from other disciplines (other than those related to criminal justice) have to say about it.

In 2013, religious studies scholar Steven P. Weitzman wrote an article about the use of information by law enforcement officials that could be provided by academicians specializing in religious studies. Commenting on the events that occurred between federal law enforcement agents and the religious group known as the Branch Davidians (this was a stand-off between a New Religious Movement and federal agents after an initial raid in which four federal agents were killed that concluded after 51 days in a second raid, which resulted in the deaths of 76 members of the religious group, including 24 children, that ended in a terrible fire) in 1993, Weitzman notes that the Federal Bureau of Investigation "was drawn into the conflict, a role which brought it into confrontation with religious leaders and communities that seemed resistant to conventional tactics of deterrence and negotiation and spoke in ways that were hard to understand or interact with." But Weitzman maintains that the problem was that "the FBI sometimes approached these encounters with misinformation or deeply rooted misconceptions about the nature of religion."[11] Catherine Wessinger, another religious studies scholar, is critical of what occurred at Waco and argues that agents knowingly ignored information about the apocalyptic beliefs of the Branch Davidians and thus bore responsibility for what happened.[12] After Waco, the Department of Justice commissioned a study to understand what had gone wrong. The two sociologists who conducted the study, Lawrence Sullivan of Harvard University and Nancy Ammerman of Emory University, conclude that "law enforcement needed to learn more about religion." Ammerman observes, according to Weitzman, that "the FBI had been unable to take religion seriously as part of the social world with which its agents had to engage."

In his review of what happened at Waco, Sullivan notes that the Justice and Treasury departments had not included the topic of religion in official training conducted by the departments for more than 70 law enforcement agencies. It was also reported that "many agents saw religion as a mere cover for criminal behavior"(and they " believed that their own study of the subject was sufficient"; it was also found that agents had trouble "understanding religious orientations different from their own." Another problem emerging from the analyses conducted in the days after Waco was that the FBI had been unable to distinguish between "reliable and unreliable expertise" (i.e., advice given to law enforcement by individuals who were really just self-styled experts offering recommendations that conflicted with views of the American Psychological Association and religious studies scholars).[13]

In the late 1990s, it seemed that some of these problems would be corrected by efforts by federal law enforcement agencies to encourage dialogues with religious studies scholars and to utilize their expertise as the nation began to deal with an increasing number of potential threats for violence that were associated with religious extremists. However, in the past few years, there have been news reports describing federal law enforcement training that has reflected an anti-Muslim bias, with such statements as "Muslims are prone to be terrorist sympathizers," or "that adherence to the Qur'an is causally linked to committing terrorism."[14]

In her book, *The New Religious Intolerance* (2012), Martha C. Nussbaum, a professor of law and ethics at the University of Chicago Law School, notes that the FBI had assigned for recommended reading a questionable book about Islam that was written by an author who is associated with the group "Stop the Islamicization of America," which "has been termed a 'hate group' by the distinguished Southern Poverty Law Center." The book is called *The Truth about Mohammed: Founder of the World's Most Intolerant Religion.* Nussbaum categorizes the work as "paranoid and deeply unreliable."[15]

Nussbaum also reports on a PowerPoint presentation that was prepared by the FBI's Law Enforcement Communications Unit, which trains new recruits. She states the following about the PowerPoint presentation:

> *These slides missed a golden opportunity to provide recruits with a histori-cally informed and nuanced understanding of the varieties of Islam, the different origins of U.S. Muslims, and the different world cultures in which Muslims live today. Since most Americans think of Islam as existing mainly in the Middle East, in predominantly Arab societies, despite the fact that Indonesia and India have the two largest Muslim populations in the world, both with democratic institutions, … it is quite disturbing to find that the PowerPoint presentation itself refers to Islam as a religion of the "M.E." (Middle East) and tells recruits that to interrogate Muslims they need to know that the "Arabic Mind" is "swayed more by words than ideas and more by ideas than facts" (whatever that means!).[16]*

This misinformation, by itself, would be a concern, but the situation worsens, as the presentation then gives the following information about circumcision, something widely practiced in modern Western nations as a healthful practice (e.g., it can prevent the transmission of diseases and reduces the risk of cancer), as well as a comment about supposed antimodernism:

> *It [the PowerPoint] also tells recruits that Muslims "engage in a circumci-sion ritual"—as if this were some primitive custom, in a nation in which more than half of male newborns are circumcised, and in which ritual circumcision is a familiar Jewish custom. Recruits also "learn" that "Islam transforms countries' culture into 7th century Arabian ways.[17]*

Nussbaum later notes that a former FBI agent stated that training should be "useful, factual, and unbiased" and rejected this PowerPoint presentation as missing the mark on all three criteria. Fortunately, the FBI no longer uses either the book or the PowerPoint presentation in its current training practices. Nussbaum concludes by saying that "(o)ne depressing conclusion that emerges from this story is that the suspicion and mistrust of academic scholarship that began during the McCarthy era have never really ended."[18]

In concluding this section, one might say that the point is, as the expres-sion goes, that knowledge is power. And the corollary is that ignorance about religion can be disastrous. Thus, drawing upon the knowledge of a discipline like religious studies is a necessity for criminal justice practitioners in the modern era to be effective when they are called upon to deal with problematic situations involving religious groups of one stripe or another in the future.

Religion and Spirituality among
Criminal Justice Practitioners

Being a first responder, a police officer, or a corrections officer is unquestionably stressful. The factors causing stress can be various: seeing or being the victim of violence, attending to victims of violence or other crimes, attending to accident victims or dealing with death, post-traumatic stress disorder (PTSD), being insulted or harassed at work, dealing with administrative pettiness or caprice, having an erratic schedule and working night shifts, poor diet (e.g., donuts and coffee), and drinking after work. These are just some of the stressors discussed by Ellison (2004) in her book, *Stress and the Police Officer*.[19] Other problems that exacerbate stress for a police officer include: looking at the world differently and not trusting others (e.g., cynical ideas such as "all scout leaders must be pedophiles."), isolation, depression, suicide, and being, in a sense, addicted to the "cop role," so that civilian life pales by comparison. These are challenges described by Gilmartin (2002) in his book, *Emotional Survival for Law Enforcement*.[20] The effects of the stress, when not managed effectively, include burnout, discord, alcohol abuse, domestic abuse, and other dysfunctional behaviors.[21]

Typical recommendations as to how one should handle such stresses are the use of psychological techniques to restore emotional balance, or after trauma, to utilize counseling, and then there are suggestions about employing physical exercise as a method for coping with stress. Each of these methods has merits and can be effective. What is new, however, is the additional interest in the benefit of cultivating spirituality in keeping stress under control and effectively managing one's life.

Spirituality is a difficult term to define because it can have several meanings, depending on the context in which it is used. One definition might be that "spirituality is a fundamental human drive for transcendent meaning and purpose that involves connectedness with oneself, others, and ultimate reality." It can be a connectedness to what one considers sacred. Spirituality may or may not be expressed in religious forms, and while "spirituality is commonly manifested in an individual's relationship with God, a person's connection with the transcendent may be displayed in many forms, including those that might be considered secular in nature."[22]

Spirituality can refer to a person's internal life; it depends on one's willingness to look inward to become aware of the inner life or spirit, the inspirations and the intuitions that one can notice as they well up inside as one begins to attend to them; these are sometimes answers to "questions of the heart." Among the questions of the heart are: "Who am I really?" "Why was I born?" "What is the meaning of life?" "What is important in living one's life?" Samuel L. Feemster, a federal agent who holds law and divinity degrees, points out that finding answers to these questions is the work of a person's spiritual intelligence. He suggests that spiritual intelligence "is the deepest inner capacity (beyond the hardware of the brain, emotions, and psychological states) human beings possess that directs their perceptions or interpretations of the meaning of life and reality. ... the disciplines employed nurturing their spiritual intelligence throughout the discovery and perpetuation of meaning and value in what people do and experience is spirituality."[23]

The importance of finding meaning in life was powerfully developed by the Viennese psychiatrist, Viktor E. Frankl (1905–1997), in his book, *Man's Search for Meaning*, which describes his experiences in surviving a Nazi concentration camp during World War II. Frankl, who lost everything, including his family, during that time, came to understand that everyone has some unavoidable suffering in life, and some suffer more, some less. But none of us can change the reality that each will have some unavoidable suffering; what one can change is how he or she will strive to find meaning in suffering, for the meaning one finds will become the key to surviving, both spiritually and physically. Frankl quotes the German philosopher Friedrich Nietzsche to give an illustration of what the power of meaning could be when he said: "He who has a *why* to live can bear almost any *how*."[24]

So how does one develop such a spirituality? The culture of criminal justice agencies does not encourage—for the most part, does not generally recognize— the need for spirituality and for training individuals to attend to it. But that is changing, and authors such as Feemster argue that it should become part of the basic training that a recruit receives.[25] Lynn A. Tovar, a retired police commander, has argued for "spirituality in the workplace"—which she says "recognizes that people have an inner life that nourishes and is nourished by meaningful work in the context of a community." Further, she suggests that there are four cultural characteristics of what she terms to be a "spiritual organization": a strong sense of purpose; trust and respect among coworkers; humanistic work practices; and the toleration of employee expression in the workplace.[26]

Ginger Charles, who has both police and academic experience, conducted a small interview study (n = 10) of how police officers incorporated spirituality in their work. She describes her results using three categories: Spiritual Practices, Human Relationships, and Spiritual Responses. Under the category of Spiritual Practices, Charles found that all of her subjects report that prayer is their main form of spiritual practice, and most also go to church services. Two of the participants mentioned being in nature as an important spiritual practice for them, while a third individual referred to his practice of running. Under the category of Human Relationships, the subjects state that "the primary purpose of relationships ... included the necessity of being connected with other human beings, recognizing the humanness in all individuals, and realizing the opportunities for finding meaning in their work through compassion and integrity." Under the category of Spiritual Responses, subjects report that they are "maintaining a discipline of prayer as a way of connecting with God," and that this provided each with a "moral compass to lead them beyond the pain and destructiveness encountered in police work."[27] Because of the limited number of subjects in this study, one is restricted in how much the findings can be generalized, but the study does provide an interesting view of the spirituality of the officers who were studied.

A different approach to spirituality is described by Cheri Maples, who is a retired police captain and is now an ordained Buddhist Dharma teacher. She teaches workshops on a type of Buddhist meditation known as "mindfulness" to police officers. She says that "the workshops give cops the tools to examine their own intentions and biases—to approach their job not with anger and cynicism, but love and fierce compassion." Maples notes that often police officers are resistant to the training she offers, so she draws on her own experiences when she started meditating. She says that, "At my first-ever retreat, I had a chip on my shoulder. I said, 'I can't do mindfulness training—I'm a cop. I carry a gun!' But, then the teacher asked me, 'Who better to carry a gun than someone who does so mindfully?'" Maples also observes that "Police are peacemakers. And, you can't bring peace anywhere unless you have it inside your own heart."[28]

The importance of this new trend in developing spirituality among police officers is best described by Smith and Charles, who say: "(e)very day in America one police officer reaches the point where he feels his life no longer has meaning, and he tragically kills himself ... (i)n a recent survey of 500 police officers in the United States, 98 percent reported that they had considered suicide sometime during their career."[29] It is in developing spirituality—that is, spiritual well-being—that an officer certainly may find the resilience to survive the many and various challenges of a career in policing, corrections, or other criminal justice–related occupation.

CHAPTER SUMMARY

In this chapter, three significant practical issues were examined. First, we had a discussion about prejudice in relation to religion. Beginning with the work of the psychologist Gordon Allport, religious prejudice was seen to be a problem that occurred when a person came to look for safety through a *rejective* equilibrium. On a larger scale, the issue of prejudice and the ideology of *ethnodoxy* were discussed as factors in conflicts between different ethnoreligious groups. The second topic explored was the issue of the application of knowledge derived from the discipline of religious studies to the problems faced by practitioners in criminal justice fields. Over the past 20 years, there have been attempts to utilize this knowledge, but the trend has not been consistent, and there have been some serious problems that have occurred (such as at the siege at Waco, Texas, and the more recent revelations of the use of anti-Muslim training materials). Finally, in the third section of this chapter, our focus shifted to the importance of developing individual spirituality in the lives of police officers and others employed in criminal justice.

END NOTES

1. Allport, Gordon W. *The Nature of Prejudice* (Reading, MA: Addison-Wesley Publishing Company, 1982), 441.

2. Allport, 441.

3. Allport, 441.

4. Allport, 446, 447.

5. Allport, 447.

6. Karpov, Vyacheslav, Elena Lisovskaya, and David Barry. "Ethnodoxy: How Popular Ideologies Fuse Religious and Ethnic Identities." *Journal for the Scientific Study of Religion* (2012) 51(4): 638–655.

7. Karpov, et al., 639.

8. Karpov, et al., 641, 652.

9. Cavanaugh, William T. *The Myth of Religious Violence: Secular Ideology and the Roots of Modern Conflict* (New York: Oxford University Press, 2009).

10. Hood Jr., Ralph W., Peter C. Hill, and Bernard Spilka. *The Psychology of Religion: An Empirical Approach* (New York: Guilford Press, 2009).

11. Weitzman, Steven P. "Religious Studies and the FBI: Adventures in Academic Interventionism." *Journal of the American Academy of Religion* (Dec. 2013) 81(4): 962.

12. Wessinger, Catherine. "Deaths in the Fire at the Branch Davidians' Mount Carmel: Who Bears Responsibility?" *Nova Religio* (2009) 13: 25–60.

13. Weitzman, 968, 988.

14. Weitzman, 975.

15. Nussbaum, Martha C. *The New Religious Intolerance: Overcoming the Politics of Fear in an Anxious Age.* (Cambridge, MA: Belknap Press of Harvard University Press, 2012), 52–53.

16. Nussbaum, 53.

17. Nussbaum, 53.

18. Nussbaum, 54.

19. Ellison, Katherine W. *Stress and the Police Officer* (Springfield, IL: Charles C. Thomas, Publisher, 2004).

20. Gilmartin, Kevin M. *Emotional Survival for Law Enforcement* (Tucson, AZ: E-S Press, 2002).

21. Feemster, Samuel L. "Addressing the Urgent Need for Multi-dimensional Training in Law Enforcement. *Forensic Examiner* (fall 2010), 44–49.

22. Hodge, David R. "Implicit Spiritual Assessment: An Alternative Approach for Assessing Client Spirituality." *Social Work* (July 2013) 58(3): 223–230.

23. Feemster, Samuel L. "Spirituality: An Invisible Weapon for Wounded Warriors." *FBI Law Enforcement Bulletin* (January 2009), 2.

24. Frankl, Viktor E. *Man's Search for Meaning.* (Boston: Beacon Press, 2006).

25. Feemster. "Addressing the Urgent Need for Multi-dimensional Training in Law Enforcement," 44–49.

26. Tovar, Lynn A. "Vicarious Traumatization and Spirituality in Law Enforcement." *FBI Law Enforcement Bulletin* (July 2011), 19.

27. Charles, Ginger. "How Spirituality Is Incorporated in Police Work." *FBI Law Enforcement Bulletin* (May 2009), 22–25.

28. Hauser, Susan. "Career Changer: From Stressed-Out Cop to Buddhist Teacher." *O The Oprah Magazine* (February 2011), http://www.oprah.com/money/Career-Changer-Cheri-Maples-Cop-Turned-Buddhist-Teacher. Retrieved Nov. 13, 2013.

29. Smith, Jonathan, and Ginger Charles. "The Relevance of Spirituality in Policing: A Dual Analysis." *International Journal of Police* Science and Management (2010) 12(3) 320–338.

Appendix

Case Studies

In studying about religions, by now you have seen that, generally speaking, religion can be a force for much good in the world. Religious groups actively work for human rights, feed the hungry, assist the sick and dying, and work to bring peace to the world. Unfortunately, sometimes religious groups have become embroiled in conflicts or disruptive activities. In the following cases, we'll examine what happens when "religion becomes evil."

Here is a list of the religious traditions we have studied in this book and examples of members of those traditions who have gotten into trouble of one sort or another, so that these situations can be examined through a case study approach:

A. Christianity: David Koresh/Branch Davidians
B. Islam: Osama bin Laden/Al Qaeda
C. Judaism: Baruch Goldstein/Kahane Chai
D. Hinduism: Kirtanananda/New Vrindaban
E. Buddhism: Zen Master Rama/American Buddhism
F. New Age: Shoko Asahara/Aum Shinrikyo

A. CHRISTIANITY: DAVID KORESH/BRANCH DAVIDIANS

In 1981, a young man named Vernon Howell (1959–1993) came to Mount Carmel, Texas, to join a group known as the Branch Davidians, a sect that had become separated from the Seventh-Day

Adventists because of new beliefs held by the sect's members. (Note: The Seventh-Day Adventists are a Christian group that keeps the Sabbath on Saturdays and believes that the Second Coming of Jesus Christ is imminent.) Howell had also run up against the Seventh-Day Adventist Church: he believed it had become corrupt and compromised its original prophetic mission. Howell had two passions in life: playing the guitar and reading and memorizing passages of the Bible. He spent many hours in prayer asking God to send a living prophet to his people to lead them.

By 1983, Howell had been recognized by Lois Roden, the Branch Davidians' leader, as her successor. He entered a relationship with Roden, but in 1984, he also legally married a 14-year-old girl who was the daughter of a member of the group. (Later, he married several other girls who were between the ages of 12–20.) Howell was able to convince the members of the Branch Davidians that he had received further "light" regarding the meaning of prophecy and its application in their lives.

In 1985, Howell traveled to Israel and claimed to have had a profound experience while there; he began to assert that he had received the "seventh angel's message" that was mentioned in the Book of Revelation (Ch. 10:7). This became the basis for his claim to be the messiah (which means the anointed one, the one who was expected by the Jewish people to be in the line of King David and be a great political leader who would save them from oppression and restore God's kingdom). He called the new teaching the "Cyrus Message"; Koresh is the Hebrew word for Cyrus, and that is also the new name that he takes.

Koresh began to read into the Book of Revelation the story of the Branch Davidians. For example, in Revelation, there are seven angels mentioned. Koresh identified the Seven Angels of Revelation with the founder and five later leaders of the Seventh-Day Adventists; he said that he was the Seventh Angel and the final prophet. He believed that his mission was to "save" as many as he could reach with his message. His ideas rested on the Adventists' belief that people were living in the last days and that God's people would be guided by the voice of the living prophet.

In the Book of Revelation, there is reference to a scroll that has seven seals that can only be opened by the Lamb. Traditionally, Christians see the Lamb as an image of Christ, who has the authority to open the scroll. Koresh began to interpret this image in a new way: he said that the whole Bible was represented by the scroll and that "to open it" meant to explain it, but also bring about the events it describes. He said that a second messiah was the "lamb," and that he was that messiah, or Christ (Christ means anointed in Greek). His argument was that more than one messiah is mentioned in the Bible (for example, in the Psalms and in Isaiah), so God sent Jesus as the first messiah and now was sending Koresh as the second messiah of the final days.

What Koresh was doing is known as biblical apocalypticism. This involves three elements: (1) the use of a sacred text that is fixed and can't change;

(2) offering a supposedly inspired interpretation, which means that the interpreter gives a new meaning to the text; and (3) there is a fluid context: the text now serves as a "map" of things to come (the end times).

In late 1992, the Bureau of Alcohol, Tobacco, and Firearms (BATF) planned a search-and-arrest raid based on allegations that Koresh and the Davidians possessed illegal firearm materials, possibly converting AR-15s into machine guns. (Note: The Davidians were involved in arms sales as licensed vendors.) On February 28, 1993, the raid took place. There was a firefight, and no one knows who fired the first shot, though each side claims the other was to blame. Four BATF agents were killed, and there were 20 wounded. A standoff began.

When the raid occurred, Koresh perceived it in terms of the Book of Revelation. He said, "We are now in the Fifth Seal." The Fifth Seal talks about those who have been slaughtered for the word of God and the testimony they have given. He believed that his people had been wantonly attacked by those who were opposed to God and his prophet (i.e., Koresh). So, the Book of Revelation was the lens through which he saw those days unfold.

A cease-fire was called and negotiations begun. When negotiations did not resolve the crisis, stress and harassment techniques were then used. Finally, on April 19, 1993, two specially outfitted M-60 tanks injected CS gas (e.g., tear gas) through the walls of the Davidians' compound. At noon that day, smoke coming from the second floor was spotted. How the fire started is still disputed; only nine persons escaped. The final death toll from the fire was 76 persons belonging to the Davidian group.

QUESTIONS

1. Check news stories about David Koresh, the Branch Davidians, and the Waco siege. What do you find?
2. How did the Branch Davidians differ from mainline Seventh-Day Adventists?
3. What do you identify as being unusual in the teachings of Koresh?
4. In examining news stories about the event, what was the reaction in society to the events at Waco?
5. What went wrong for the Branch Davidians? Why?

B. ISLAM: OSAMA BIN LADEN/AL QAEDA

The history of Al Qaeda (which means "the base") begins in 1988 or 1989, the year when the Soviets, who had invaded Afghanistan in support of Afghan Marxists, finally withdrew from that country. Opposing the Soviets were the Afghan mujahideen, or holy warriors. Among those who battled the Soviets were volunteers called "Afghan Arabs" from other Muslim countries such as Saudi Arabia, Egypt, Jordan, and Syria. The originators of Al Qaeda, Osama bin Laden, a Saudi Arabian, and Ayman Al-Zawahiri, an Egyptian, were among this second group. The purpose of Al Qaeda was to wage global jihad against the enemies of Islam—they believed there was an unending conflict between Muslims and non-Muslims who were corrupt and opposed to their way of life.

The basic assertion of Al Qaeda was that it represented a group that followed a purer form of Islam, one that reflected the original ways, and maintained strict Sharia (the moral and religious code of Islam). Further, Al Qaeda would wage war against any group or country that it perceived as corrupting Islam. It spread its ideology through training camps, the media, and the Internet.

In 1991, when Saudi Arabia was facing the threat of invasion by Iraq, Osama bin Laden offered the services of his group to defend his country. The Saudi government rejected his offer and chose to have the United States military defend Saudi Arabia. To bin Laden, this was a great humiliation of the Arab people, and he set his sights on the United States as "crusaders" who had brought non-believing soldiers into Islam's holiest land and supported Israel, as well as repressive governments in the Middle East.

In November 1995, Al Qaeda attacked the American base at Riyadh, followed by the bombing of the Khobar Towers (a residence for American military personnel), both in Saudi Arabia. Attacks on American embassies in several African nations followed. There was also the attack on the ship *USS Cole* in 2000, in Aden Harbor. Then, of course, there were the September 11th, 2001, attacks on the World Trade Center in New York and the Pentagon in Washington, D.C.

When Osama bin Laden was young, he studied in a school with the brother of Sayyid Qutb, an Egyptian famous for his extremist jihadist ideology, which included avoiding the West because of its "evil and corruption." This is a kind of fundamentalist view that sees Western societies and lax Muslim societies as being in a state of ignorance, or *jahiliyya*. Those who are faithful Muslims must remove themselves from that kind of society so that they can perform an inner *jihad* (a struggle) and become strong in their practice of their faith. Then, they must direct the jihad toward society to transform it, forcefully if necessary (in Qutb's view). Sometimes, this perspective of changing society to make it more "Islamic" is known as Islamism.

Bin Laden was a follower of Wahhabism, a puritanical reform movement in Islam that had been very much a part of the history of Saudi Arabia, but which has been less influential with the modernization of Saudi Arabia. Bin Laden saw himself as a pious Muslim, who was working to restore the true faith of the founding generation of Islam (the *salaf*).

QUESTIONS

1. Check news stories about Osama bin Laden, Al Qaeda, and Islamism. What do you find?
2. How did those in Al Qaeda differ from moderate Muslims?
3. What do you identify as being unusual teachings of bin Laden?
4. In examining news stories about the event, what were the reactions of people in different parts of the world to the actions of Al Qaeda? How do you explain the different responses?
5. Bin Laden advocated violence in pursuit of his goals. What do other Muslims think about that? Look at groups like ISIS and Boko Haram; how do they compare?

C. JUDAISM: BARUCH GOLDSTEIN/KAHANE CHAI

Rabbi Meir Kahane (1932–1990) was born in Brooklyn, New York. In the 1960s, he formed the Jewish Defense League (JDL). This group claimed that its goal was to protect Jews from anti-Semitism. However, it was a vigilante group and soon also was accused of terrorist activities through bombing attacks on Arab and Soviet properties, as well as the murder of an Arab American activist and possibly others. He was convicted of conspiracy to manufacture explosives in 1971.

Kahane moved to Israel in 1971 and founded the Kach Party there. This was a right-wing fundamentalist group that advocated the replacement of Israel's democracy with a nation ruled through religious law. He was anti-Arab, wanting to deport them from Israeli-held land. Eventually, Kahane was assassinated in New York in 1990. After his death, his followers formed the Kahane Chai, or "Kahane Lives," movement that had as one of its goals the restoring of the biblical state of Israel.

Baruch (Benjamin Carl) Goldstein (1957–1994) was born in Brooklyn, New York, knew Meir Kahane, and was a member of the JDL. He attended medical school and later immigrated to Israel in 1983. He believed in the restoration of the biblical state of Israel and was a strong supporter of Kahane Chai. He accepted Kahane's belief that the secular state of Israel must pass away and that the messiah would return in a great conflict in which Jews will triumph. When Jews were raised up by their conquests over their enemies, then it was more likely that the messiah would return. And contrariwise, when Jews were humbled, then this could not happen.

In 1993, Goldstein complained that the Israeli government was not doing enough to protect Jewish settlers on the Israeli-occupied West Bank, where he lived in Kiryat Arba. Later, at the beginning of the Jewish holiday of Purim, he was upset during prayer services by disturbances by Arab youths, who were shouting offensive remarks such as "Slaughter the Jews!" outside and were not stopped by Israeli police. To Goldstein, this was very upsetting and humiliating. As a follower of Kahane, such humiliation of the Jewish people would be especially repulsive.

The next morning before dawn on Purim, Goldstein, who was dressed in his army uniform and carrying an assault rifle, entered the Cave of the Patriarchs (believed to be the burial place of Abraham). The Cave of the Patriarchs is sacred to both Jews and Muslims and is separated into two areas: the Hebron Shrine for the Jews and the Ibrahimi Mosque for Muslims. At the mosque, there were Muslim worshippers gathered for morning prayers. Goldstein fired into the group of worshippers.

When the event was over, there were 29 people who had been killed, with another 125 wounded in the hail of bullets. After the group of worshippers recovered from the immediate shock of the attack, they rushed Goldstein and beat him to death.

Goldstein was hailed as a hero by some in Israel for his actions. His grave has been treated as a shrine to which pilgrims come; his headstone refers to him as a martyr, one who has a "clean heart."

After the attack by Goldstein, the Israeli government outlawed Kahane Chai.

QUESTIONS

1. Check news stories about Rabbi Meir Kahane and Baruch Goldstein. What do you find?
2. How did the members of Kahane Chai differ from moderate Israelis?
3. What do you identify as being unusual in the teachings of Rabbi Meir Kahane?
4. In examining news stories about the event, what were the reactions of people in different parts of the world to the actions of Baruch Goldstein? How do you explain the different responses?
5. Rabbi Meir Kahane advocated violence in pursuit of his goals. What do other Jewish groups think about that? Look at a group like the Oasis of Peace; how does it compare?

D. HINDUISM: KIRTANANANDA SWAMI/NEW VRINDABAN

In 1966, a businessman from India, A. C. Bhaktivedanta Swami Prabhupada, came to New York to spread his movement, which would come to be known popularly as the Hare Krishnas. Rooted in Hinduism, the Hare Krishnas believe that Lord Krishna is the supreme god, with all other gods minor manifestations of him. Though it caught on slowly at first, soon the movement would grow to 30 temples in the United States, with about 500 adherents in a relatively short time. The largest Hare Krishna community was New Vrindaban, which opened in West Virginia in 1979.

There, one could find the Palace of Gold, a structure with large gilded spires that was compared to the Taj Mahal. The community was first founded in 1968, and the Palace of Gold was originally intended to be a residence for Prabhupada (who had returned to India, but it was hoped he would come again to America) and was built through the efforts of volunteers. It was finished in 1979.

The teachings of Prabhupada were that his followers should renounce material possessions and focus on simplicity, truth, and the spiritual; they must follow four rules: no intoxicants; no sex without marriage; no eating meat; no gambling. Members of the group would chant for 90 minutes a day; the chant involved the repetition of the name of God. Also, members must devote themselves to the service of God, Lord Krishna.

One of Prabhupada's early disciples was a young New Yorker named Keith Ham (1937–2011), who was the son of a minister. He finished college and entered graduate school, but left after some problems occurred. Ham eventually went to India, finally returning to New York, where he met Swami Prabhupada. After studying with him, he accepted Prabhupada as his spiritual guru and took the name Kirtanananda, began wearing the saffron robes, and shaved his head. Later, he became a *sanyassi* and took a lifelong vow of celibacy, with the title of swami.

In 1968, Kirtanananda was able to lease land in West Virginia and began building a Hare Krishna community, or ashram (a place of retreat for Hindus), that would be based on farming. The name given to the community was Vrindaban, a holy city in India that is associated with Krishna's birthplace. Residents of the community lived a kind of monastic existence, rising early, chanting, and depending on the temple for all of their needs. Within a decade, there would be about 500 Hare Krishna devotees living at New Vrindaban; the ashram spread over 4000 acres.

To finance the building of the Palace of Gold, Kirtanananda had his followers sell ball caps and bumper stickers that had counterfeit logos for sports teams or cartoon characters such as Snoopy on them. Selling these counterfeit items in shopping malls and at sports facilities, the group raised over $10 million.

By the 1980s, members of the ashram at New Vrindaban began to complain that Kirtanananda was not adhering to the teachings of Prabhupada. For example, the lifestyle of the Hare Krishna community was supposed to be nonmaterialistic, but under the leadership of Kirtanananda, that changed. He sent his followers to collect donations under false pretenses at public locations. He became more controlling of life at the community—watching closely who came and went, or what they were doing. Soon, men became more dominant, while women were placed in subservient roles and required to leave their children for long periods in nurseries at the ashram. Kirtanananda also introduced changes to prayer services by adding interfaith features. The leaders of the overall Hare Krishna movement excommunicated Kirtanananda in 1987, but he refused to abdicate; the whole community was excommunicated in 1988.

Fear began to spread through the community that it would be attacked by outsiders, so it soon armed itself with guns.

Allegations emerged that children were being sexually abused by Kirtanananda and some of the teachers at the school at New Vrindaban. Stories of the murders of two followers who had challenged Kirtanananda surfaced, one having been killed brutally in 1982, and the other killed in 1986. The first individual was said to have been murdered in retaliation for raping the wife of a New Vrindaban resident; the other victim had criticized Kirtanananda and accused him of sexually abusing boys. The Hare Krishna follower who actually murdered the two claimed later that he did it under the orders of Kirtanananda.

In 1990, Kirtanananda was indicted by a federal grand jury of mail fraud and racketeering; included under the racketeering were the murders of the two followers. He was convicted on most of the charges, but appealed his convictions on the basis of prejudice. During a second trial, in a plea bargain, he pleaded guilty to one count of racketeering and was sentenced to 20 years in prison.

QUESTIONS

1. Check news stories about Kirtanananda Swami and New Vrindaban. What do you find?
2. How did New Vrindaban differ from mainstream Hare Krishna communities?
3. What do you identify as unusual teachings of Kirtanananda Swami?
4. In examining news stories about the event, what were the reactions of people to the actions of Kirtanananda Swami? How do you explain the different responses?
5. Though he denied it, Kirtanananda encouraged violence in pursuit of his goals. What do other Hindu groups think about violence? Look at the community of New Vrindaban today. How does it compare to the ashram of the 1980s under Kirtanananda?

E. BUDDHISM: ZEN MASTER RAMA/AMERICAN BUDDHISM

Frederick Lenz (1950–1998) was born in California and raised in Connecticut. After high school, he moved to San Francisco and became a hippie, but was convicted of selling marijuana and sentenced to a work camp for one year. He returned to Connecticut and finished college, then completed a doctorate in English in New York.

While in San Francisco, Lenz become a follower of Sri Chimnoy, who combined Buddhism and Hinduism with physical fitness. Eventually, he had a falling out with Chimnoy and separated from his group. Then, Lenz began to gravitate toward Zen, a Japanese form of Buddhist practice. Renaming himself Zen Master Rama, Lenz began attracting people to his teachings, which were a modified form of Buddhism. Lenz's teachings, which he called "American Buddhism," encouraged materialism (while traditional Buddhism does not). Consistent with Buddhist principles, he also taught his followers to meditate and to accept the concept of reincarnation. He said that he had been a Tibetan lama and a Japanese Zen master in earlier lives.

As Zen Master Rama, Lenz asserted that he could offer his followers a quick route to Nirvana through techniques that he alone knew; he claimed that spending just one hour with him was like a century of meditating. He said that once someone was enlightened, he or she could do whatever she or he wanted, without "fear or sorrow."

According to Lenz, the measure of success in following his version of Buddhism was material success; the more wealth one acquired, the more spiritually developed a follower was said to be. Lenz rejected the traditional Buddhist approach, which he referred to as the "begging-bowl mentality," as when Buddhist monks beg for their meals. Instead, he asserted that the material world was as spiritual as anything else and that it was not noble to be poor. Lenz also became a software developer and wrote several books, one of which was listed as a *New York Times* best seller. But some criticized his lavish lifestyle, which included a mansion on Long Island, New York, and a private jet.

Zen Master Rama offered his initial courses in meditation to potential students for free or for a nominal fee. Of those who progressed further with him, he offered them computer courses for which he would charge thousands of dollars. He advertised in newspapers and magazines to attract followers who were wealthy; some still claim that they attribute their success in life to his teachings.

But other followers complained that, as they become more involved with Zen Master Rama, he started to take control over their lives. One individual decided to leave the group, but Lenz convinced him to stay, but now he had to take antipsychotic medication because the usual methods of enlightenment were not working for him. Another follower, a woman, stated that Lenz told her which clothing to wear and what movies to see. She described being summoned to his mansion to have sex with Zen Master Rama; she said that he claimed that it was a "speedway to enlightenment" and that his sperm was "liquid enlightenment." Women were told that, after having sex with Zen Master Rama, they would be assured of reincarnation in their next lifetimes as more enlightened beings. Other followers claimed that Lenz told them to stay away from their families, as the families were trying to stop them from evolving spiritually and would drain away their energy. But other devotees of Zen Master Rama negate the claim of being separated from their families.

The media began to refer to Lenz as the "yuppie guru" and the "cosmic seducer," especially after three women came forward with allegations of sexual abuse by Lenz. His response was that the relationships were consensual and that his accusers were mentally unbalanced. Some of his followers committed suicide because they felt they had not measured up to his standards.

There were also reports of LSD use at Rama's house. It was reported that Lenz used it and encouraged his followers to take the drug as well. Eventually, the drug use changed Lenz's personality, and he was said to have become delusional and suspicious. Followers began to leave the group.

Finally, in 1998, Lenz took an overdose of Valium, as did a female companion (though she survived), in a plan to commit suicide. His body was found in the bay behind his home.

QUESTIONS

1. Check news stories about Frederick Lenz and American Buddhism. What do you find?
2. How did American Buddhism differ from mainstream Buddhist communities?
3. What do you identify as being unusual in the teachings of Zen Master Rama?
4. In examining news stories about the event, what were the reactions of people to the actions of Zen Master Rama? How do you explain the different responses?
5. Zen Master Rama committed suicide, as did some of his followers. What do you think led him and some of his followers to direct violence against themselves? How would this be viewed from a Buddhist perspective?

F. NEW AGE: SHOKO ASAHARA/AUM SHINRIKYO

Shoko Asahara, born in 1955 in Yatsushiro, Japan, was originally named Chiuzo Matsumoto. He was only partly sighted and was sent to a school for the blind, where he proceeded to bully his classmates who were unable to see. Later, when he was a young man, he was arrested for fighting.

As an adult, Asahara set up an acupuncture clinic. Though not a physician, he wore a white lab coat, carried a stethoscope, and charged his "patients" about $7000 for a three-month treatment. His "treatment" was a special concoction he made using a tangerine peel in an alcohol solution.

In 1982, Asahara was arrested, charged with fraud, and fined $1000 (though he had collected around $200,000 at his "clinic." He became interested in religion and was attracted to a new sect known as Agonshu. Agonshu was a group that claimed a Buddhist heritage and promised its followers psychic powers. Asahara did not get the promised results, so he headed off to the Himalayas to seek enlightenment.

In the Himalayas, Asahara traveled the path of the Buddha and claimed that he received enlightenment. With his enlightenment, he asserted that he also received special powers such as the ability to perceive past lives, read other people's minds, pass through walls, meditate underwater for hours, and levitate.

In 1986, Asahara advertised in a magazine called the *Twilight Zone*, using photographs of himself as he supposedly levitated (in reality, he was using his thigh muscles to propel himself into the air). He claimed to have received a message from God that "I (God) have chosen you to lead God's army." Asahara also published a book, *Secrets of Developing Your Supernatural Powers.*

As a guru (spiritual teacher), Asahara would place his hands on his disciples' heads and inject his "master's energy" into them for $350. Students claimed that this led them to out-of-body experiences, miracle recoveries, and high winning rates at mah-jongg (a Chinese game).

Asahara created a sect called "Aum Supreme Truth" in 1987, and it became a huge financial success. The chief deity of his religion was Lord Shiva, the Hindu god (the four-armed Shiva ranks with Brahma the Creator and Vishnu the Preserver). Shiva lays waste to the world in a cosmic dance only to re-create it: the imagery is of a violent cycle of death and rebirth. The group attracted many professionals (e.g., scientists and physicians and college graduates), and teenagers as well. There was a "blood initiation," where a follower would pay thousands of dollars to drink Asahara's blood. He also sold his followers "Perfect Salvation Initiation" (PSI) brain hats that disciples wore. They received electric shocks that were supposed to synchronize their brain waves with the guru's; these were rented at the rate of $7000 per month. Initiates also paid to drink his bathwater and urine. Those who did not toe the line were punished by confinement and being forced to listen to audiotapes of Asahara played at a loud volume.

Problems started to develop when parents began to try to get their children away from Aum Shinrikyo. The lawyer who represented them, as well as his wife and infant child, were murdered by members of the Aum inner circle. Later, Asahara and his followers ran for office in the Japanese Parliament, but were defeated. He began to speak of Armageddon (the name of the place of the final great battle between good and evil described in the Book of Revelation, Ch. 16:16). He said that only Aum followers would be saved after Armageddon.

Aum scientists began cultivating a deadly substance: a form of anaerobic bacteria called *Clostridium botulinum*—the most poisonous substance available in the natural world. It attacks the nervous system, eventually stopping the heart and lungs. Because Armageddon was coming, Aum needed weapons to fight, so the group went to Russia and bought a military helicopter.

In April 1990, Aum technicians drove around the Japanese Parliament spraying the botulism toxin, expecting to kill officials and plunge the nation into crisis. Asahara had predicted there would be a terrible event, and this would prove him to be powerful. But the toxin did not work (the scientists had made a mistake). But in 1995, Aum members placed six packages of sarin gas on the Tokyo subway, killing 12 people and injuring more than 5000.

In May 1995, Asahara was arrested and later tried in court for the attacks. He was convicted and sentenced to death. Other members of Aum were convicted and sentenced as well.

The group changed its name to Aleph in 2000. It operates in Germany, Russia, Sri Lanka, and the United States. In Japan, it is estimated to still have over a thousand members. Some of the doctrines have been changed, with the death imagery removed from the group's writings.

QUESTIONS

1. Check news stories about Shoko Asahara and Aum Shinrikyo. What do you find?
2. How did Aum Shinrikyo differ from mainstream religious communities?
3. What do you identify as unusual teachings of Shoko Asahara?
4. In examining news stories about the event, what were the reactions of people to the actions of Shoko Asahara?
5. Asahara encouraged the use of violence in pursuit of his goals. What religious traditions did he draw upon to justify his strategy? Were his interpretations drawn from those traditions unusual? How does Aleph compare to the original Aum group?

Author Biographies

Gordon S. Bates graduated from Trinity College in Hartford, Connecticut, in 1956 with a BS in geology. He graduated from Western Theological Seminary in 1959 with a BD degree and was ordained by the United Presbyterian Church in 1959. He earned a Master of Divinity degree from Pittsburgh Theological Seminary in 1959 and a Master of Sacred Theology degree from Hartford Seminary in 1964. After several short pastorates, in 1969 the Rev. Bates joined the staff of the Connecticut Prison Association (Community Partners in Action, 1997) as Director of Volunteer Services from 1969 to 1980. He served as the executive director from 1980 to 1997. For the next seven years, 1997–2004, he served as the Associate Conference Minister for Justice Ministries for the 250 churches of the Connecticut Conference, United Church of Christ. Rev. Bates is the coauthor of the scholarly article 'Founding the Connecticut Delinquency Court, 1903–1941,' which appeared in the *Connecticut Law Journal*.

Steven Blackburn is the Director of the Library (where fully one-fourth of the library's holdings are in Arabic) at Hartford Seminary, Hartford, Connecticut, as well as a faculty associate in Semitic scriptures. He holds a BSFS and an MSc from Georgetown University, Washington, D.C. Additionally, Dr. Blackburn holds a BD (Hons) and PhD from the University of St Andrews (Scotland), with his doctoral thesis, "The Early Arabic Versions of the Book of Job," treating the interplay of linguistics and theology among Arab-speaking Jews, Christians, and Muslims. He also studied at the

Bourguiba Institute in Tunis, Tunisia, as well as the American University, Cairo, Egypt. Dr. Blackburn's interest in Arabic and Islam is due to the influence of his maternal grandparents, who were born in Algiers. An ordained Congregational-Christian minister, he has served as a parish pastor and denominational executive, as well as pro-tem chair of Middle Eastern Studies at Trinity College, Hartford, where he lectured in Islam, International Studies, and Arabic. Dr. Blackburn's Middle Eastern experiences include work with Saudi Bedouins in the field of literacy. Closer to home, he has served on the Board of the National Council of Churches Office for Christian-Muslim relations.

Allison Drude Cook is a life-long studio artist with a graduate degree in art history from the University of Massachusetts, Amherst, Massachusetts, and an undergraduate degree in economics from Smith College, Northampton, Massachusetts, with study abroad at Oxford University. After graduating from Smith, Ms. Cook continued on to a postbaccalaureate year at the Massachusetts College of Art and Design, concentrating in jewelry fabrication. Looking to delve more deeply into the business of art, she also completed a certificate in Appraisal Studies of Fine and Decorative Arts at New York University in 2013. A long-time student of yoga, she also holds professional certification as a yoga teacher (RTY 200 certification through Back Bay Yoga in Boston in 2011), and has since been teaching at colleges, studios, and gyms in the Pioneer Valley. In 2012, she was a finalist in the Entrepreneurship Initiative Business Plan competition at the University of Massachusetts, gaining recognition for a start-up business offering therapeutic yoga programs.

James F. Keenan, SJ, is the Canisius Chair, Director of the Jesuit Institute, and Director of the Gabelli Presidential Scholars Program at Boston College. A Jesuit priest since 1982, he received a licentiate and a doctorate from the Pontifical Gregorian University in Rome. He has edited or written 16 books and published over 300 essays, articles, and reviews in over 25 international journals. He has been a fellow at the Institute of Advanced Studies at the University of Edinburgh, the Center of Theological Inquiry, Princeton, and the Instituto Trentino di Cultura. Fr. Keenan is the founder of Catholic Theological Ethics in the World Church (CTEWC) and chaired the First International Cross-cultural Conference for Catholic Theological Ethicists in Padua, Italy. Following that experience, he hosted another international conference of theological ethicists in Trento, Italy. Today, CTEWC is a live network of over 1000 Catholic ethicists (www.catholicethics.com). Fr. Keenan is presently working on two manuscripts, *University Ethics: Why Colleges Need a Culture of Ethics* (Rowman & Littlefield, 2015) and *A Brief History of Catholic Ethics* (Paulist Press).

Timothy Oslovich is the pastor of Trinity Evangelical Lutheran Church, a congregation of the Evangelical Lutheran Church in America, in Vernon, Connecticut. He has served there for 11 years. Prior to serving at Trinity, he was the pastor of Shishmaref Lutheran Church in the Inupiaq village of Shishmaref, Alaska, for six years. Pastor Oslovich attended Deep Springs College and graduated from Swarthmore College with a Bachelor of Arts in political science. He received a Master of Theological Studies degree from Harvard Divinity School and a Master of Divinity from the Lutheran Theological Seminary at Philadelphia. He has been active in the Amahoro Africa conversation and traveled to Uganda, Kenya, Rwanda, and Burundi to participate in gatherings with African pastors and other church leaders. Pastor Oslovich has also been active in advocacy against genocide and poverty. He served as the chairperson of the Connecticut Coalition to Save Darfur from 2007 until 2013. He currently serves as the vice-chairperson of the Collaborative Center for Justice, an organization that advocates for systemic change to aid poor and marginalized people in Connecticut.

Wayne G. Rollins is Professor Emeritus of Biblical Studies at Assumption College, Worcester, Massachusetts, and Adjunct Professor of Scripture at Hartford Seminary, Hartford, Connecticut. Additionally, he has taught religion, biblical history, and biblical studies at Princeton, Wellesley, and the Hartford Seminary Foundation. Dr. Rollins served as Coordinator of the Graduate Program and Director of the Ecumenical Institute at Assumption College. His writings include *The Gospels: Portraits of Christ* (1964), *Jung and the Bible* (1983), and *Soul and Psyche: The Bible in Psychological Perspective* (1999), in addition to scholarly articles. He received his BD from Yale Divinity School and received a Master's and PhD in New Testament studies from Yale University. Dr. Rollins is the founder and former chairman (1990–2000) of the Society of Biblical Literature's Section on Psychology and Biblical Studies.

Thomas Roscoe is an associate professor in the Department of Criminal Justice, Westfield State University, Westfield, Massachusetts. He is a retired Chief Probation Officer (State of Connecticut), with a PhD in criminal justice from the State University of New York at Albany. He also has a bachelor's degree from Villanova University, an MS in psychology from the University of Hartford, and an MA in psychology from the University of New Haven. As a probation officer, Dr. Roscoe was intimately involved in the criminal sanctioning process. He conducted hundreds of presentence investigations, which involved an examination of social and criminal background information, with the objective of making sentencing recommendations. Dr. Roscoe's expertise encompasses both theory and the real-life challenges of sentencing criminal offenders. His academic and professional experience affords him keen insight into the potential benefits to be gained from the "new vision" of restorative justice.

Andrew Skotnicki is Professor of Christian Ethics at Manhattan College in New York City. He received his BA from Marquette University, his MA from the Washington Theological Union, and his PhD from the Graduate Theological Union in Berkeley, California. He is the author of *Religion and the Development of the American Penal System* (2000), *Criminal Justice and the Catholic Church* (2008), *The Last Judgment: Christian Ethics in a Legal Culture* (2012), and numerous articles, essays, and book chapters on the intersection of theology, ethics, and criminal justice. He is also founder and director of the program "Engaging, Educating, and Empowering Means Change" (E3MC), a partnership between Manhattan College and the New York City jail complex on Rikers Island, in which an equal number of students from the main campus and incarcerated men or women take an accredited college course together. Upon successful completion of the course, the incarcerated students are given the opportunity to continue their education free of charge at the main campus upon release from confinement.

About the Editor

William J. Cook Jr. is a professor in the Department of Criminal Justice, Westfield State University, Westfield, Massachusetts. He holds an AB in psychology from the College of the Holy Cross, Worcester, Massachusetts, a graduate certificate in religious studies from Hartford Seminary, Hartford, Connecticut, an MA in forensic psychology from John Jay College of Criminal Justice in New York City, and a PhD in criminal justice from the Graduate School and University Center, the City University of New York. Dr. Cook's doctoral research focused on the psychological effects of terrorism on business executives and on executive safety. Before completing his graduate studies, he served as an investigator in an Inspector General's office, as well as in the office of the Deputy Commissioner of Investigation of the City of New York. There, as a peace officer, he was assigned to work with the Special Prosecutor in the Kings County (Brooklyn) District Attorney's Office investigating corruption in the New York City School system. He also has worked as a security consultant and has written a variety of academic articles and a book, *Security Systems: Considerations, Layout, and Performance* (1982), related to electronic security systems. Dr. Cook was a naval reservist who was recalled to active duty after 9/11, serving both domestically and overseas as an intelligence officer and credentialed agent assigned to the Naval Criminal Investigative Service, achieving the rank of commander and was awarded two Navy Commendation medals. His current areas of interest include terrorism, political corruption, and exploring the nexus between religious studies and criminal justice.

Image Credits

Index

CPSIA information can be obtained
at www.ICGtesting.com
Printed in the USA
LVOW05s2139240717
542466LV00001B/1/P